MEL BAY PRESENTS

HANDBOOK
of Guitar and Lute Composers

BY HANNU ANNALA & HEIKI MÄTLIK

TRANSLATION BY KATARINA BACKMAN

MW00804239

1 2 3 4 5 6 7 8 9 0

© 2007 HANNU ANNALA AND HEIKI MÄTLIK. ALL RIGHTS RESERVED.
EXCLUSIVE SALES AGENT FOR THE ENGLISH VERSION, MEL BAY PUBLICATIONS, INC. PACIFIC, MO 63069
INTERNATIONAL COPYRIGHT SECURED. MADE AND PRINTED IN U.S.A.
No part of this publication may be reproduced in whole or in part, or stored in a retrieval system, or transmitted in any form
or by any means, electronic, mechanical, photocopy, recording, or otherwise, without written permission of the publisher.

Visit us on the Web at www.melbay.com — E-mail us at email@melbay.com

Contents

Preface 3

The Authors 4

Introduction to the Musical Instruments 5

Renaissance and Baroque Guitar Composers 12

Vihuela Composers 19

Renaissance Lute Composers 23

Baroque Lute Composers 31

Composers for Other Plucked Instruments: (Chittern/The English Guitar, Colascione, Theorbo) 39

Guitar Composers Since 1750 41

Composers Whose Music Has Been Arranged for the Guitar 150

A Catalog of 430 Guitar or Lute Concertos 156

Complementary List of Composers who have Composed Music for the Guitar 165

Many books on the classical guitar and the lute were published in the 20th century. However, it came to our attention that books on guitar and lute composers and their works are very rare. Most of the books now available are general history which present performing artists or guitar builders, but have little information about composers. In our profession as teachers we constantly longed for a book in which the pupils could find the most important biographies and composition lists of both traditional and modern guitar and lute composers. We were also aware of the performing guitarists' need for information when they write composer introductions to the programs of their concerts. In our opinion there was a great need for a book that would present these composers.

We have used more than 70 music books as sources as well as dozens of composer leaflets acquired from the musical information centers of several countries. During the writing process, which lasted for more than three years, we received extra information from many modern composers, Leo Brouwer and Reginald Smith Brindle among others. In addition, several internationally renowned performing guitarists gave us valuable information; we are indebted to the following: Magnus Andersson (Sweden), Rémi Boucher (Canada), Margarita Escarpa (Spain), Aleksander Frauchi (Russia) and David Tanenbaum (USA) among others.

Our aim was to write a book with a clear structure and therefore there are separate chapters for each instrument, such as the Renaissance and the Baroque guitar, the Renaissance and the Baroque lute, and the vihuela. We have not seen such division in any other books. This kind of structure enables the reader to easily discover which composers have composed for a certain instrument during a certain era. In the beginning of the book there are short introductions about guitar and lute instruments as well as basic facts about their history.

In addition to traditional composers, the book presents several modern composers, on whom there has been little information available. The section with composer introductions also contains a list of each composer's solo and chamber music works, in which one can find many interesting pieces of music. The list of concertos is a new invention; it contains information on more than 400 guitar and lute concertos dating from the Baroque until the present day. Previously there have only been brief lists made by individual publishers. The book contains a handy complementary list as well (including composers that are not presented in the actual section on composers), which lists over 600 guitar composers; the years when they lived, and their nationalities – information that is often surprisingly difficult to obtain. The most important composers, whose music has been arranged for the guitar also, have a section in the book.

We hope that the Handbook of Guitar and Lute Composers serves as a practical guide for both amateurs and professionals, encouraging them to study the history of these instruments and the situation today. We are convinced that writing short composer and composition presentations in concert programs or sharing about them in concerts will increase the interest in guitar culture. We hope that this book will make the great compositions of hundreds of composers known to performing musicians and the public.

We wish to convey our warmest gratitude to all those who helped us in various ways during our writing process.

Hannu Annala & Heiki Mätlik

The Authors

Hannu ANNALA began his guitar studies in 1971 at the Music Institute of Central Ostrobothnia (Kokkola, Finland). He continued his music studies in 1974 at the Sibelius Academy with Ivan Putilin and Jukka Savijoki and received his guitar diploma in 1982 with excellent grades. Annala furthered his studies in master classes with Oscar Ghiglia, John W. Duarte, Göran Söllscher, Konrad Ragossnig and Vladimir Mikulka.

Mr. Annala is a guitar lecturer at the Conservatory of Central Ostrobothnia and also teaches at the Department of Arts in Central Ostrobothnia University of Applied Sciences in Kokkola, Finland. He also teaches regularly in guitar workshops and classes at the Helsinki Summer University and at the Ostrobothnian Summer University. As a guitarist, Hannu Annala has performed in Finland, Estonia, Italy and Sweden. He has made recordings for Finnish Radio and appeared on television in Finland and Sweden. He has also lectured on guitar subjects in Finland, Sweden and Denmark.

Heiki MÄTLIK is a guitar lecturer at the Estonian Academy of Music and Theatre from 1990. As a soloist and chamber musician Mätlik has performed in all of the Baltic states as well as in Nordic, Russia and other European countries and made tour in Australia, USA and Canada. Heiki Mätlik has recorded over 30 CDs and 5 DVDs which include lute music of J. S. Bach, music by Astor Piazzolla, Joaquín Rodrigo, Julian Arcas, Sello Suites by Max Reger. His recordings has been released for Warner Music Company, Harmonia Mundi (USA) & Alba Records (Finland) etc. Heiki Mätlik is also the author of five practical guitar tutors, such as *The ABC of Guitar Playing, The School of Classical Guitar I-III, Exercises for Guitar and Acoustic Guitar Book.*
www.er.ee/klassik/rost/matlik_eng.htm

Photo © Mico Wikstrom

Hannu Annala (right) and Heiki Mätlik.

4

Introduction to the Musical Instruments

The structure of the guitar

The guitar (Spanish *guitarra*, Italian *chitarra*, French *guitare*, German *gitarre*) is a plucked instrument (or *cordophone*), with a wooden figure-eight body, to which a neck with a fingerboard is attached. The slotted headstock of a modern classic guitar has tuning machines which replace the wooden tuning pegs that formerly pierced the headstock as in string family instruments. The back of the body and the sides of the guitar are usually made of either Indian or Brazilian rosewood, the top of spruce or cedarwood, the neck of mahogany and the fingerboard of ebony. Of the six strings, the three treble strings are made of nylon and the three bass strings of either nylon or silk braiding, which is wound with either silver or bronze alloy. The fingerboard of the guitar usually has 19-20 fixed metal frets. The total range of the guitar covers three and a half octaves (E-b2). The guitar is a transposing instrument; i.e., its notes are written in the treble clef an octave higher than they actually sound (E-b3). The normal tuning of a classical guitar is (low to high) E A d g b e1.

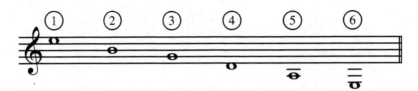

Each string has its own natural sound. The length of the strings between the bridge and the nut, the so-called "scale length", is usually 65 cm (25½ inches), but several manufacturers also make guitars with a scale length of 64 or 66 cm (ca. 25 - 26 inches). Today even smaller guitars of high quality are available, and in order to learn to play and maintain motivation it is very important that the player has a suitable instrument.

The history of the guitar

According to etymology, the word 'guitar' is derived from the Greek word *kithara*; the Romans also used the word *cythara*, although they both are lyres. It is thought that the word kithara derives from the two Persian words *char* - "four" and *tar* – "string." The char-tar was a four-string instrument, the name of which was loaned to different languages in various forms, such as the Greek kithara. The origin of the guitar is largely a mystery, and different sources provide contrasting information. It is possible that the guitar descends from the ancient Greek kithara or from the ancient Egyptian (Mesopotamian) *chitarrone*. In addition, the Arabian *al-ud* is often referred to as the forefather of guitars. According to recent research the al-ud is regarded as an early predecessor of the lute.

In the 7th and the 8th centuries AD Arab conquerors brought to Spain a plucked instrument which resembled the guitar, and over the course of a thousand years it developed into the classical guitar we now know.

Names of different guitars are mentioned in literature from the 13th century onwards. The most famous of these texts was written by a Spanish priest Juan Ruíz de Hitan (circa 1330); names of early guitars appeared in *El libro de buen amor*. These texts mention the Moorish guitar (*guitarra morisca*) and the Latin guitar (*guitarra latina*), and the Duke of Normandy's list of musicians, one of whom played the *guiterre latine* and another the *guiterre moresche*. The Moorish guitar was oval, the back of its body was rounded and its top had several soundholes. The sides of the Latin guitar were curved, the frets were on the fingerboard and it had four strings. The headstock was carved so that it resembled the head of an animal. The author Adenet le Roi used the name *quinterne* and *guitare* in his poem "Li roumans di Cléomades"; M. Praetorius used the name *quinterne* when referring to a Renaissance guitar.

The four-course Renaissance guitar

The four-course guitar, the so-called *chitarra da sette corde*, from 1552. Note the single first string. Altogether this guitar has seven strings, including the paired strings, from which it has gotten its nickname 'seven-string guitar'. This guitar has eight frets, a rosette in the soundhole and, as was common at the time, wooden tuning pegs which pierce the headstock.

The Spanish called the Renaissance guitar *la guitarra*, the Italians *chitarra da sette corde*, the French *guiterre* or *guiterne* and the English *gittern*. (The 16th century gittern must not be confused with the older *tremble lute*, which has the same name). The 16th century guitar was considerably smaller than the modern guitar. For example, the scale length of the guitar that Belchior Dias made in 1581 was only 55,4 cm (21.8 inches). As in most of the plucked instruments of that time, there was a beautiful rosette in the soundhole. The Renaissance guitar had four pairs of strings, i.e. four "courses", with the first string sometimes being single. The intervals between the strings were at first, counting from the bass, a fifth – a major third – a fourth (*a los viejos* - the old tuning) and later a fourth – a major third – a fourth (*a los nuevos* - the new tuning). The three upper pairs in both tunings were tuned in unison, and the pair of the fourth course is an octave apart.

The Renaissance guitar was adequate for satisfying more modest demands in music because of its simplicity. It was mainly used in Spain, Italy and France. As it had only four courses, chords had to be played without a bass tone.

The four-course guitar was mostly used by troubadours for accompanying songs and dances (M. Summerfield p. 10). It was also used by the upper class for accompanying the popular dances *pavana* or *galliarda* without having to compete with professional lute players (OTIM). In the 16th century the Spaniards predominantly played an instrument called the *vihuela*. As Juan Bermudo wrote in 1555:

"Between a guitar and a vihuela there is only a difference in the size of the instrument and the number of strings. The vihuela has six pairs of strings, which, excluding the highest and the lowest strings, are the same as the four-course guitar." Bermudo continues to explain that together with the vihuela and other plucked instruments, the guitar forms an excellent ensemble. Ensembles of this kind were common. Unlike the guitar, which was mainly favored by common people, the vihuela flourished among the upper classes in Spain for half of the 16th century.

In addition to playing chords, Renaissance guitar music also included the technique of plucking the strings with the right-hand p-i-m-fingers (thumb, index- and middle finger) in the so-called *punteado* style, as in lute or vihuela music. Right-hand technique included "posting" on the bridge or top with the little finger. Guitar music was written in tablature that resembled the modern way of writing pop or flamenco music. Tablature was written in three different ways: the Spanish and the Italian systems using numbers and the French using letters.

The earliest pieces of four-course guitar music were published in *Tres libros de música en cifra* by Alonso de Mudarra in 1546. The volume contains four fantasies, a pavana and a suite of variations on the theme *"O guardáme las vacas."* An Italian lutist, Melchiore de Barberis, and a Spanish vihuela player, Miguel de Fuenllana also wrote guitar music. The four-course guitar flourished most rigorously in France, where it nearly displaced the lute. The great music publishers Adrian Le Roy, Guillaume Morlay and Simon Gorlier published nine guitar tablature books in 1551–55. These books contained, among other items, fantasies and songs to be accompanied with the guitar. An English expert in Baroque guitars, James Tyler, gives a tip to guitar players today: The fantasies of Morlay, Brayssing and da Ripa (in the fourth book by Morlay) are of high quality and deserve the attention of guitarists who are planning concert programs (*The Early Guitar* p. 28). In the Netherlands the publisher of four-course guitar music was Pierre Phalèse, who used a great deal of Adrian Le Roy's material. The last published method for the small four-course guitar was *A Booke of New Lessons for the Chittern and Gittern* by Englishman John Playford. At this time the four-course guitar was common in Europe.

The five-course guitar, the Baroque guitar

The changeover to the five-course guitar started in the 16th century when it still had pairs of gut strings. Bermudo cites evidence that the Spaniards already used five-course guitars in the first half of the 16th century. At the beginning of the 17th century the five-course guitar was already widely known. There were two different types of guitars in use: the *chitarra battente*, with a bowl back and metal strings that were mostly played with *rasgueado* technique with fingers or a plectrum, and the *guitarra española* with a flat back and gut strings. The Baroque guitar differs from a modern classical guitar in that the fretboard is level with the top and it has wooden tuning pegs that pierce the headstock; in addition the bridge is placed further away from the soundhole. The scale length of the instrument had already increased and varied between 61 and 66 cm (24 – 26 inches). There were three different tunings for the Baroque guitar, of which the first one shown here was the most commonly used.

Amat, Colonna,
Millioni, Ribayaz

Corbetta, Foscarini,
Granata, Roncalli, Visée

Asioli, Carré,
Sanz

As can be seen in the above illustration, the Baroque guitar was largely incapable of producing modern bass sounds. It can therefore be regarded as an alto instrument. The five-course guitarra española, which was played with a combined rasgueado-punteado (chord-plucking) technique, became famous in almost all European countries as a solo instrument. Thanks to a famous Italian guitar teacher, Françesco Corbetta (1615–1681), the instrument became very popular in France in the palace of Louis XIV, the "*Sun King.*" Not only Corbetta, but also Robert de Visée (ca.1660–ca.1724) and François Campion (ca.1680–1748) were famous French Baroque guitar players. Giovanni Paolo Foscarini (1621–1649), Giovanni Battista Granata (1622–1687) and Ludovico Roncalli (17th century) were the most famous guitar virtuosos in Italy in the 17th century. Gaspar Sanz (1640–1710), Lucas Ruiz Ribayaz (ca.1650–?) and Francisco Guerau (1659–?) were representatives of the punteado technique, which was more common in Spain. Jan Antonin Losy [Logy] (1650–1721) was another famous Baroque guitarist whose music - arranged for the modern classical guitar - has remained popular to the present day. The music for the Baroque guitar was typically written in dance suites which included the most popular European dances of the day, e.g. allemande, courante, sarabande, and gigue and the gavotte, bourrée, minuet and passacalle. The Spaniards also used many of their national dances, such as *canarios, jacaras, paradetas*, and so on. Baroque music typically contains a variety of ornaments.

Tablature writing

Until the end of the 18th century music was written in tablature while chords were indicated with letters and numbers. There were three different ways of writing tablature. The most popular was the French system, whereby the uppermost line represents the first string and the lowest line the fifth string. The spaces between the frets are marked so that *a* indicates an open string, *b* the first space, *c* the second space and so on. Duration is marked above the staff. In addition to French tablature, there were also Spanish and Italian tablature systems, in which the music was written by means of numbers. In Spanish tablature the first string is represented by the lowest line. Nowadays Baroque music is played in arrangements for the six-string guitar. Due to these tuning and structural differences, it is not easy to play Baroque music with a modern guitar. Most modern arrangements ignore the differences in tuning and are quite different from the original works.

The six-stringed guitar

The six-string guitar with the tuning E A d g b e1, came into use in Spain in the 18th century. At this time the guitar still had paired strings. Most guitar historians believe that the addition of the sixth pair string as the bass string took place around 1780, almost simultaneously in Italy and Germany (M. Summerfield p. 11). The first published collection for a six-course double-string guitar is, according to Robert Spencer, a song accompaniment *Guitarre portant une corde de plus* published by an unknown composer in France in 1785 (Tyler p. 57). Instruction on the early six-course guitar was also available in *Obra para guitarra de seis órdenes* (1780), a guitar composition by Antonio Ballestro, and in *Principios para tocar la guitarra de seis órdenes* (1799) by Federico Morretti. Moretti's guitar method established the technique of playing the classical guitar and created the basis for future development. The changeover took place in the 18th century.

In the middle of the 19th century a certain practice concerning the size of the guitar was established: the scale length was defined as 65 cm (25½ inches) and the width of the fingerboard at the point where it meets the side at least 5 cm (2 inches). The shift from pair to single strings started in the last decades of the 18th century. In 1825 a guitar school for the six (single) string guitar by Dionisio Aguado (1784–1849), *Escuela de guitarra,* was published in Madrid. There the modern notation system as well as the modern playing technique were present. Reforms in the playing included the development and establishing of the posture, the more frequent use of the right-hand ring finger and not leaning to the lid with the right-hand little finger. The players also started to use special effects such as flageolet-notes, the use of left hand only and imitating different instruments such as the drums, the harp and the trumpet. The guitar again became a popular instrument in the major musical centers in Europe, i.e. in Paris and Vienna. The Spaniards Dionisio Aguado and the Fernando Sor (1778–1739) were famous guitar players then. Other virtuosos in Paris at that time were the Italians Ferdinando Carulli (1770–1841), Matteo Carcassi (1792–1853) and Francesco Molino (1768–1847). The guitar was also favored by violin virtuoso Niccolò Paganini (1782–1840) and composer Hector Berlioz (1803–69). Berlioz added the guitar to his work about instruments, *Grand traité d'instrumentation et d'orchestration modernes* op. 10 (1843). The most important Italian guitarist was Mauro Giuliani (1781–1829), who worked in Vienna in 1806–19. Also the composer Anton Diabelli (1781–1858) worked in Vienna. He was a productive guitar composer and a remarkable musical publisher, who published among others Giuliani's works. In the middle of the 19th century, guitar music was so popular that in 1856 a Russian manor owner, Nikolai Makaroff, arranged a guitar contest, which also included a contest for guitar composers. A Hungarian composer-guitarist, Johann Kaspar Mertz (1806–56) won the contest and Napoléon Coste (1805–83) came second. They both were the most productive composers in the Classical-Romantic era. There were also other guitar composers, for instance Franz Schubert (1797–1828), Carl Maria von Weber (1786–1826) and a concertina and guitar virtuoso Giulio Regondi (1822–1872). The works in the 19th century were typical of the Classical period: sonatas, rondos, variations, fantasies (often from the popular operas) as well as little songs and etudes. In addition to the solo guitar, some composers (M. Giuliani, F. Carulli, etc.) composed concertos for the guitar and an orchestra. Various works of chamber music were composed by Luigi Boccherini, Anton Diabelli, Mauro Giuliani, Niccolò Paganini, Franz Schubert, Fernando Sor, Carl Maria von Weber, etc.

The modern classical guitar

The Spanish guitar maker Antonio Torres (1817–92) had a noticeable effect on the development of the classical guitar in the second half of the 19th century. Torres developed the bracing of the guitar and he invented the fan-shaped placement of the braces. He also enlarged the body, and thus developed the sound qualities of the guitar.

The promoter of the new technique was the Spanish composer and guitarist Francisco Tárrega (1852–1909). When playing the classical guitar he used the apoyando-technique, which has its origin in flamenco music. Tárrega's pupil Miguel Llobet (1878–1938) adopted Aguado's example of using the nails when playing the guitar. Tárrega's methods are well presented in a four-volume guitar school, *Escuela razonada de la guitarra*, written by his pupil Emilio Pujol (1886–1980) and in a seven-volume guitar school, *Lecciones de guitarra…* written by the Argentinean guitar teacher Julio Sagreras (1879–1942). In South America the Paraguyan guitarist and composer Agustin Barrios Mangoré (1885–1944) played a major role in developing the guitar culture. The Spanish guitarist Andrés Segovia (1893–1987) has contributed considerably to the establishment of the guitar as a concert instrument. Segovia worked in cooperation with most of the remarkable composers of the 20th century, such as Mario Castelnuovo-Tedesco, Federico Moreno Torroba, Joaquín Turina, Manuel Ponce, Joaquín Rodrigo and Heitor Villa-Lobos.

Among the first modern guitar works of the 20th century is the *Homenaje* composed by Manuel de Falla (1876–1946) in 1920. Many famous composers of the 20th century have composed works for the guitar, for instance Pierre Boulez, Luciano Berio, Benjamin Britten, Elliot Carter, Peter Maxwell Davies, Franco Donatoni, Alberto Ginastera, Hans Werner Henze, Jacques Ibert, Frank Martin, Darius Milhaud, Francis Poulenc, Toru Takemitsu, William Walton, Anton Webern, Arnold Schönberg, etc. Among the most famous composers from the second half of the 20th century is the Cuban Leo Brouwer (born 1939), whose works have reached a stable position in the programs of a huge amount of guitarists around the world from the 1960s onwards. Many famous guitarists have worked in cooperation with composers, who again have dedicated their works to the artists.

Vihuela

The vihuela (Italian vihuela, Spanish vihuela) is a cordophone, which in the 15th century has developed from the string family into an instrument that resembles the guitar. In the early stage, there were three different types of vihuelas: the vihuela de arco, which was played with a bow; the *vihuela de peñola*, which was played with a plectrum; and the *vihuela de mano*, which was plucked with fingers. In the middle of the 16th century 'vihuela' referred to the vihuela de mano, the other types had already disappeared from use. The vihuela is thought of as the developed form of the folk music instrument at that time. They differ from each other in measures, number of strings, and the tuning. The vihuela has 6-7 pairs of strings in unison, (courses), which in a six course vihuela were tuned similarly to the lute (a quarter – a quarter – a major third – a quarter – a quarter) and fixed to the bridge as in the guitar and the lute. In the fingerboard there are usually 10 moveable frets. The lute and the vihuela are different in shape but similar in sound, number of strings and tuning. The vihuela had the same status in the Spanish court as the lute later in other European courts. The four and later five-course guitar was a popular instrument among the common folk, but it got its own music only in the 17th century. The vihuela reached a higher position as an instrument in the musical elite during the era of Charles V and the popularity continued in the court of Philip II. Towards the end of the 16th century the popularity of the vihuela diminished whereas the popularity of the guitar grew.

The playing technique of the vihuela

Not much has been written about how to use the left hand when playing the vihuela, but it does not differ much from the way of playing the lute. With regards to right hand technique, there is more detailed information. The fast melodies (*redobles*) can be played in three alternative ways: 1) by only moving the index finger up and down (*dedillo*), 2) by plucking with the thumb and the index finger in turn (*dos dedos*) and 3) by plucking with the index and middle finger in turn. The vihuela players marked the tempos very carefully, and they also wrote down other marks concerning the performance, such as *trills*, *vibratos* and *appoggiaturas*.

Vihuela music

Most vihuela players used Italian tablature when writing down their works, but there was also a Spanish clavere tablature in use. In vocal music the leading voice was often written in mensure writing and the vihuela accompaniment in tablature. In some tablatures the numbers indicating the solo voice are red or marked with a comma. The most common types of 16th century music using vihuela accompaniment are *romance* and *villancico*. They are usually accompanied by improvisation and played in a virtuoso manner. Because of Charles V's great appreciation of Flemish music intavolatures were made, for instance Josquin de Prez's or Gomberti's masses were arranged for the vihuela. In the programs there were also *ricercares and fantasies, variations (differencias) based on romances and dances such as pavanas and galliardas.*

The most famous vihuela composers are Luys de Milán, Luys de Narváez, Alonso Mudarra, Enríquez de Valderrábano, Diego Pisador, Miguel Fuenllana and Esteban Daza. Most of the "old music" performed today on guitars date back to the Spanish 'Golden Century', *Siglo de oro*.

Orfeus playing the vihuela
In the cover of the vihuela book *El Maestro*
by Luis Milán (1536)

Vihuela books published in Spain during the Siglo de oro, 'the Golden Century':

1536   Luis de Milán: *El Maestro*. Valencia.
1538   Luys de Narváez: *Los seys libros del Delphin de música*. Valladolid.
1546   Alonso de Mudarra: *Tres libros de música en cifra para vihuela*. Seville.
1547   Enríquez de Valderrábano: *Silva de Sirenas*. Valladolid.
1552   Diego Pisador: *Libro de música de vihuela*. Salamanca.
1553   Diego Ortiz: *Tratado de glosas sobre clausulas y otros genero de puntos en la música de violones*. Rome.
1554   Miguel de Fuenllana: *Orphénica lyra*. Seville.
1557   Luis Venegas de Henestrosa: *Libro de cifra nueva para tecla, harpa y vihuela*. Alca de Hanare.
1565   Tomás de Santa Maria: *Libro llamado Arte de tañer Fantasía para tecla, vihuela y todo instrumento…* Valladolid.
1576   Esteban Daza: *El Parnasso*. Valladolid.
1578   Antonio de Cabezón / Herman de Cabezón: *Obras de música para tecla, Arpa y vihuela*. Madrid.

The History of the Lute

The lute (German *laute*, Italian *liuto* or *leuto*, Spanish *laud*, French *luth*) is a plucked instrument of Arabian origin (Arabian al'ud = made of wood)., which was used in Europe from circa 11th century until the beginning of the 19th century. The European lute has a rounded or convex body and a straight, almond shaped top, to which the relatively wide and short neck is fixed. In the middle of the top there is a decorated soundhole and in the lower part there is a bridge, which also acts as the point where the strings are fastened. Since the 15th century the lute has had frets that are made of removable gut braiding. The pair strings are also made of gut, but the highest string is usually single. In the 16th and 17th centuries string makers were highly respected. The best strings were available in Italy and Germany and they were very expensive. Now there are also lute strings made of nylon.

Most sources dating from the 16th and 17th century mention three different kinds of lutes: the treble, tenor and bass lute. The most frequently used lute is the tenor lute and its tuning is Gg, cc1, ff1, aa, d1d1, g1. The level was approximate; it depended on how tight the player could get the highest string. In the middle of the 17th century an extra metal bass string was introduced, and in a typical 17th century lute there were several (7-10) bass strings. In the 17th century the French invented different tunings and the most common was the so-called French D minor tuning Aa, dd1, ff1, aa, d1d1, f1. In the 17th century a need for louder lutes arose, as it became a continuo instrument. The Italians invented the chitarrone or the *theorbo* to be the bass continuo in an orchestra. It was as large as a bass lute, but it was tuned as the tenor lute. This could not be done with the two highest strings, but they were left an octave lower. The bass strings were made louder by making them longer with the help of a special longer neck. According to Caccini, the chitarrone was the best instrument to accompany a song. There is also excellent solo music composed for this instrument. In 1594, the lute player Piccinini invented the chitarrone (Italian *archiliuto*) with a longer neck. It was mainly used as a solo instrument, but gradually it became more popular as a continuo instrument. Another special type of the lute is a small treble lute, *mandora*, with 4-6 pairs of strings. It is considered as the forefather of the mandolin. The mandora was used in Italy by Vivaldi, among others.

In the Middle Ages the lute was played with a feather as was the al'ud. In the 16th century the players started to pluck the strings in order to be able to play polyphonic music. The right-hand little finger leaned to the top and fast melodies were played by plucking with the thumb and index finger in turns. The lute player Piccinini also mentions a technique where the bass string is played with the thumb (apoyando). The lutist used the barrée, legato and vibrato techniques when playing with the left hand. The legato technique was used in playing ornaments in the 17th and 18th century.

Lute music was written in tablatures where there is a line for each string and the rhythm was written on top of the staff and the notes were marked on the lines with different symbols. The most famous tablatures are the French, the Italian and the Spanish tablatures. The French tablature used letters to indicate notes whereas the Italian used numbers. In the German tablature there was a special symbol for each note so there was no need for a staff at all.

Lute music

A lot of lute music from the 16th – 18th centuries has been preserved in museums and libraries all around the world. Pohlmann mentions over 1,200 different works in his bibliography (1972). In addition to solo music, the lute has also been in use in accompanying singers and widely in chamber music.

The most remarkable lute composers from the 16th century are the Italian Francesco Canova da Milano (*Il Divino, 'the Divine'*) and the English John Dowland. The 17th century French lute technique, *style brisé* was developed by the members of the Gaultier lute family. The most famous lute virtuoso and composer of the German 18th century (*the Golden Autumn of the Lute*) was Silvius Leopold Weiss. He worked in Dresden and met there the master of Baroque, Johann Sebastian Bach. There are seven preserved lute works left from Bach's productions, BWV 995–1000, BWV 1006a, three of which are manuscripts.

In the 18th century the popularity of the lute diminished as new music styles were invented – louder instruments were needed for the growing ensembles. In the 20th century the music researchers became again interested in the lute, and today's musicians have added lute music to their programs. Usually it is composed by some of the 20th century lute composers, i.e. Benjamin Britten, Peter Maxwell Davies, Hans Werner Henze or Toru Takemitsu.

Renaissance and Baroque Guitar Composers

AMAT, Juan Carlos (ca. 1572–1642), a Spanish guitarist, mathematician, astrologer, poet, doctor of medicine. Amat wrote the first printed school and a chord chart for five-course guitars, *Guitarra española y vandola*, which appeared in Barcelona in 1596. The popularity of the work is seen in the numerous reprints all the way to the end of the 18th century.

In the chord chart the 12 major and 12 minor chords are marked with numbers, which Amat calls *puntos*. He thus tried to make the tablature system clearer. This system quickly spread to Italy, where Francisco Palunbi created a similar system, in which numbers were replaced by letters. This system was called *Alfabeto* and it was in use until ca. 1630. Amat's chord chart also contains pictures that show how to hold chords on the fingerboard. The guitar school contains directions of how to use chords, how to accompany songs and how to play solo works. With the help of these schools even an amateur could play simple accompaniments or variations. The chord chart may be the predecessor of the modern chord finders. Harvey Hope has published an article presenting Amat's guitar school, *"An Early Guitar Tutor, Juan Carlos Amat"* (Classical Guitar May/June 1983).

ASIOLI, Francesco (1645–50 –ca. 1676), an Italian composer, guitarist. Asioli worked as a guitar teacher in Parma. He is known by two collections of guitar music: *Primi scherzi di chitarra...* (Bologna 1674) and *Concerti armonici per la chitarra spagnuola op. 3* (Bologna 1676). Both collections are typical of conventional guitar music of the period.

BACH, Johann Christian (1735–1782), see "Composers of Other Plucked Instruments."

BANFI, Giulio (ca. 1630–1670), an Italian guitar composer born in Milan. His tablature book, *Il maestro della chitarra*, was published in Milan in 1653. There he, as Giovanni Foscarini, used the combined rasgueado-punteado technique. Banfi also worked in Spain.

BARTOLOTTI, Antonio Michele (ca. 1669), an Italian guitarist, theorbist and composer. Worked later as a theorbist in Paris. Bartolotti published two tablature books for the guitar: *Libro primo di chitarra spagnola* (Florence 1640) and *Secondo libro di chitarra* (Rome ca. 1655).

BOTTAZZARI, Giovanni (17th century), an Italian guitarist and composer. Published a guitar music collection *Sonate nuove per la chitarra spagnola...* in Venice in 1663. This collection used the combined rasgueado-punteado technique.

BRICEÑO, Luis de (early 17th century), a Spanish composer and guitarist. Briçeño was born in Galicia and worked in Paris from 1614 onwards. His guitar book, *Método mui facilissimo para aprender a tañer la guitara a lo espagñol*, was published in Paris in 1626, and it was the first Baroque guitar school published in France. Local word forms in Briçeño's guitar school suggest that he may have been of Galician origin. Also his scheme to designate chords with a number or a special sign differs from that of Amat's, which is called the Catalonian system. The book, as also other contemporary alfabeto books, contains song accompaniments and chords to dances. Briçeño also gives detailed instructions of the tuning and suggests that the first string should be tuned as e1.

CALVI, Carlo (early 17th century), an Italian guitarist and composer. He edited a collection of pieces for the five-course Baroque guitar entitled, *Intavolatura di chitarra, e chitarriglia* (Bologna 1646). The book contains brief instructions on how to read tablature and how to tune the instrument, followed by 65 battute (strummed) and 24 pizzicate (plucked) pieces comprising such typical mid-17th century Italian forms as the *passacaglia, ciaccona, folia, spagnoletto and ruggerio*.

CAMPION, François (ca. 1680–1748), a French guitarist, theorbist and composer of English extraction. He was a theorbist and guitarist at the Académie Royale de Musique from 1703 to 1719 and acted as a theorbo and guitar teacher at the Royal Music Academy. Campion's tablature book, *Nouvelles Découvertes sur la guitare*, was published in Paris in 1705. It contains nine dance suites for the guitar and a few sonatinas and fugues. Campion also published two collections, which contain instructions for a theorbo player on how to play the bass continuo (Paris 1716, 1730).

CARBONCHI, Antonio (early 17th century), an Italian guitarist and composer. He was in the service of Prince Mattias of Tuscany in 1640 and of Marquis Bartolomeo Corsini in 1643. He published two books of pieces for the five-course Baroque guitar: the first, *Sonate di chitarra con intavolatura franzese* (Florence 1640) was written in the French tablature and the second, *Le dodici chitarre spostaten* (Florence 1643) in the Italian tablature. The latter contains 40 pieces for the solo guitar and 32 pieces for an ensemble of 12 guitars. All of these are rasgueado pieces.

CARRÉ, Antonio (17th century), a French Baroque guitarist and lutist. His guitar book, *Livre de pièces guitarre...* was published in Paris in 1671, and it is dedicated to Princess Palatine. Minkoff Reprint printed a facsimile of that book in Genoa in 1977. A collection, *Livre de guitare et de musique*, was also published in Paris, but the year of the first edition is unknown. The influence of Francesco Corbetta can clearly be seen in both his books.

COLISTA, Lelio (1629–1680), an Italian lutist, Baroque guitarist and composer. Except for a visit to Paris in 1664, Colista lived all his life in Rome. Most of the younger members of the Colista family also worked as professional musicians. Lelio Colista taught Gaspar Sanz to play the guitar when he made an excursion to Rome. Colista was a highly appreciated contrapuntist and he is thought of as the most important model for Henry Purcell when he developed the structure of his trio-sonatas. The only surviving piece of Colista's Baroque compositions is the *Pasacaille* and it is kept in the Brussels Academy of Music.

COLONNA, Giovanni Ambrosio (early 17th century), an Italian Baroque guitarist and master printer. In 1620 two of his guitar music collections were published in Milan: *Intavolatura di chitarra alla spagnuola…* and *Il secundo libro d'intavolatura di chitarra alla spagnuola*. In 1623 a third book was published in Milan, *Il terzo libro*. Yet another tablature book by Colonna was published in Milan in 1627, *Intavolatura di chitarra spagnuola del primo, segondo, terzo, quatro libro*, its second edition was printed in 1637.

CORBETTA, Francesco (1615–1681), an Italian Baroque guitar virtuoso and composer. His contemporaries regarded him as the greatest guitar player of that time. Corbetta worked as a guitar teacher from 1639 in Bologna, he taught such virtuosos as the Italian Baroque guitarist Giovanni Granata. After being in the service of the Duke of Mantova since 1643, Corbetta went to Austria in 1648, after which Cardinal Mazarin invited him to Paris. In the beginning of the 1660s the King of England Charles II, who was an enthusiastic guitarist, invited Corbetta to London, where he taught the king and got a high position in the court. Because of this, the popularity of the guitar was greater than that of the lute.

The favorite guitarist of Louis XIV, Francesco Corbetta, enchanted his audience in Paris and London.

In 1671, Corbetta returned to Paris to work for the Sun King, and he shifted from the use of the Italian tablature to the French. In Paris, he taught such French guitarists as François Campion and Robert de Visée.

The three first tablature books by Corbetta are: *Scherzi armonici* (Bologna 1639), *Varii capriccii* (Milan 1643) and *Varii scherzi di sonate*. (Brussels 1648). The first book contains dances, where the rasgueado (battute) technique is in use. The second and the third contain compositions, where a combination of rasgueado and punteado are used. The most important guitar tablatures by Corbetta were published in Paris in 1671 and 1674 under the heading *La Guitarre Royalle* ("the Royal Guitar"). The first of these is dedicated to the King of England and it contains 14 dance series. The second is dedicated to the King of France. The tablatures contain pieces, which use the rasgueado-punteado technique and because of the Sun King's preference the music is modern and chromatic. Corbetta's fancy style did not please everyone and so he wrote in the foreword of *La Gitarre Royale*: "As there have always been envious people, who claim that my way of playing is far too complicated and resembles the style of the lute, I want to say that I do not know lute music and I have never wanted to play any other instrument than the guitar." (M. Giertz p. 63). There is also a reference to Corbetta's nails written by his German contemporary: "Lately a world famous guitarist Corbetta visited the Turin festival. He has taught several European sovereigns. Unfortunately his nail was broken and thus he could not perform with his group although he would have wanted to." (M. Giertz p. 64). Corbetta, who died in England in 1681, is described shortly by the Spanish guitarist Gaspar Sanz: "El mejor de todos (the best of all)."

CORRETTE, Michel (1709-1795), a French organist, teacher, composer-arranger and author. He published at least 17 schools for strings, horns and clavers. Corrette's guitar school *Les Dons d'Apollon, méthode pour apprendre la guitare*. was published in Paris in 1763. He was a widely known teacher, but his reputation was not always a high one, and his schools were criticized roughly. Nowadays his works are valuable sources when studying the performance policy of that period.

CORIANDOLI, Francesco (?–1670) an Italian amateur composer and guitarist from Ferrara. He is only known for his collection, *Diverse sonate ricercate sopra la chitarra spagnuola op. 1* (Bologna 1670). In it he explains that he has written the music 'during hours free from the exercise of my profession', but it is not known what his profession was. The volume is a conventional collection of guitar pieces; there are 35, nearly all of them the usual dances, allemands and sarabands.

DEROSIER, Nicolas (late 17th century), a Baroque guitarist and composer. He lived in the Netherlands and in France. He published four guitar tablature books: *Douze overtures pour la guitare op. 5* (1688), *Les principes de la guitare.* (Amsterdam 1690), *Les principes de la guitare* (1696) and *Noveaux principes pour la guitarre…* (Paris 1699). His schools contain instructions about the interpretation of the tablature, tuning, ornamentation, arpeggiation of chords and continuo accompaniment.

DOIZI de VELASCO, Nicolás (ca. 1590–ca. 1659), a Portugese guitarist. He lived in Spain and Italy and was the chamber musician of the King of Spain, Philip IV. In 1640 he published a guitar school called *Nuevo modo de cifra para tañer la guitarra* in Naples. It was the method of playing the guitar diversely and most perfectly and showing it to be an excellent and most versatile instrument. Besides guitar music it contains information on tuning, playing and the chromatic chords.

FOSCARINI, Giovanni Paolo (1621-1649), an Italian Baroque guitarist, lutist, theorbist and composer. He bore the nickname *Il Furioso ("Passionate")*, which appears on the first page of several publications. Foscarini served in several courts, such as Brussels (1640), Paris (1647) and Venice (1649).

The Italian Giovanni Paolo Foscarini was a famous Baroque guitar composer and he was called "Il Furioso."

In Brussels Foscarini served Archduke Albert, who gathered artists around himself, the most famous of whom was the painter Rubens. Foscarini's guitar tablatures were published in Italy, among others *Il primo, secondo, e terzo libro della chitarra spagnuola* (Macerata 1629), which later expanded to five parts, *Li 5 libri della chitarra alla spagnuola.* (Rome 1640). A second edition was published that same year, *Inventions di toccate sopra la chitarra spagnuola.* After 1630, Foscarini started to use both rasgueado and punteado thus being a developer of guitar technique. Foscarini's style has been described as courageous and personal. Gaspar Sanz called him the *"Master of Rome."*

FUENLLANA, Miguel de (ca. 1525– after 1585), see 'Vihuela composers'.

GATAYES, **Giullaume-Antoine** (1774–1846), see 'Guitar composers'.

GEMINIANI, Francesco (1687–1762), see 'Composers of Other Plucked Instruments'

GRANATA, Giovanni Battista (1622– 1687), an Italian composer and guitarist, Francesco Corbetta's pupil, one of the greatest Baroque guitar virtuosos of his time in Italy. His production was published in 7 volumes in Bologna in 1646–84. The first collection, *Capricci armonici sopra la chitarriglia spagnuola* was published in 1646, the second, *Nuove suonate di chitarriglia spagnuola* circa 1650, the third, *Nuova scielta di capricci armonici e suonate musicali in vari tuoni for the guitar and bass continuo op. 3* in 1651, the fourth, *Soavi concenti di sonate musicali for the guitar, violin and bass continuo op. 4* in 1659, the fifth, *Novi capricci armonici musicali in vari toni b for the guitar, violin and bass continuo… et altre sonate per la chitarra sola op. 5* in 1674, the sixth, *Nuovi soavi cocenti di sonate musicali, for the guitar* in 1680 and the seventh, *Armoniosi toni de varie suonate musicali for the guitar… op. 7* in 1684.

GRÉNERIN, Henri (mid- 17th century), a French guitarist, a chamber musician of the French court since 1641. Grénerin played the theorbo in the ballet of Lully. He published a guitar book in Paris in 1680, *Livre de guitare… avec une instruction pour jouer la basse continue*, which contains 16 dance suites for the guitar and other instruments and lessons for the guitar of the bass continuo.

GUERAU, Francisco (1659–?), a Spanish Baroque guitarist. He got his musical education as a member of the Royal Chapel Choir in Madrid. After the breaking of the voice Guerau became the chamber music composer of the king. Guerau's guitar tablature book *Poema harmonico, compuesto de varias cifras por el temple de la guitarra española* was published in Madrid in 1694 and is dedicated to King Charles II. Guerau's music is influenced by the polyphonic music of the Catholic Church. He often used the variation form in his works.

HÄNDEL, **Georg Friedrich** (1685–1759), a German-British Baroque composer. He got a thorough musical education from the organist of the Lutheran Church of Halle. In his youth he worked as an organist in Halle and as an opera violinist and cembalist in Hamburg. In 1708–09 Händel made an excursion to Italy, where he met many of the great composers of the period, such as Alessandro Scarlatti. He got the position of the chamber conductor in Hannover in 1710. In 1712 Händel moved to England, where he spent the rest of his life as a British citizen and where he became a famous opera composer. His influence on British composers was tremendous.

Händel's production includes 40 operas, 12 concerto grossos, 20 organ concertos and chamber and claver music. Compared to the chromatic style of Bach, Händel's works represent a diatonic mood. There is monumentality and impression in his works. During his visit to Italy Händel composed in 1708–09 a vocal piece to be accompanied with the guitar, a Spanish cantata, *No se emenderá jamás*, for a soprano, a Baroque guitar and viola da gamba, from which there is a modern print by Edition Sikorski. The repertoires of today's guitarists contain Händel's flute and violin sonatas whose bass continuo parts have been arranged for the guitar.

For a soprano and a guitar: Spanish Cantata, No se emenderá jamás.

LE ROY, **Adrian** (ca. 1520–1598), see 'Renaissance Lute Composers'.

LOSY, Jan Antonin (ca. 1650–1721), see 'Baroque Lute Composers'.

MARELLA, **Juan Baptista [Giovanni Battista]** (ca. 1700), a Spanish composer, who mostly lived in Italy. In 1760 Marella went to England and in 1762

Giovanni Battista Granata

he published a collection, which contains dance suites for two guitars.

MARTIN, François (the mid- 17th century), a French guitarist and composer. In 1663 he published a guitar tablature book, *Pièces de guitairre à battre et á pinser* in Paris.

MERCHI, Giacomo (1730–1789), an Italian guitarist, player and composer of the colascione, who mainly lived in Paris. In 1752 he and his guitarist brother Josephin Bernard made a concert tour to Germany. Giacomo Merchi acted later as a guitar teacher in England. He published several guitar books: *Le guide des écoliers de guitare op. 7, XVIe Livre de guitarre... op. 20, Les soirées de Paris... op. 22b, XXe Livre de guitare op. 24, XXVIe Livre de guitarre op. 30* and *XXXIVe Livre de guitarre op. 36*. The books are for both the five-course and the six-course guitars. The music meant for those instruments was written using the modern notation system already in 1777. Some of Merchi's publications are for an English guitar.

For a solo guitar: *op. 3; op. 4; op. 25; Sonata op. 26*. For two guitars or for a violin and a guitar: *Duo op. 12; 12 Divertissements op. 21. 6 duo op. 33*. For two guitars: *Quatro duo op 3; op. 4*. For a voice and a guitar: *op. 15*.

MILLIONI, Pietro (early 17th century), an Italian guitarist and composer. In 1627 he published six guitar schools in Rome: *Il primo, secondo et terzo libro d'intavolatura di chitarra spagnola, quatro libro... quinto libro and Prima scielta di villanelle accomondate con l' intavolatura per cantare sopra la chitarra spagnola* (Rome1627). Millioni's guitar school, *Vero e facili modo*, was written in cooperation with a guitarist Lodovico Monte and it was published in eleven editions during 1637–1737. The school presents the right hand's rasgueado technique and the accompaniment of the 17th century dances ciacona, passacaglia, gagliarda and romanesca.

MONTESARDO, Girolamo (early 17th century), an Italian guitarist, composer and singer born in Naples. He worked as a singer in the choir of the St. Petronio church in Bologna in 1607, became the choir master (maestro di cappella) in Fano in 1608. Since 1611 he lived in Naples. Montesardo's guitar tablature book, *Nuova inventione de intavolatura per sonare li balletti sopra la chitarra spagnuola* was published in Florence in 1606 and his other tablature book, *I lieti giorni di Napoli... op. 11* in Naples in 1612.

MORLAYE, Guillaume (ca. 1510–1558), see 'Renaissance Lute Composers'.

MUDARRA, Alonso de (1508–1580), see 'Vihuela Composers'.

MURCIA, Santiago de (late 17th century–early 18th century), belongs to the most remarkable Spanish guitarists of the early 18th century. Murcia is one of the last guitar composers using the tablature writing. He taught piano playing to Queen Gabriela, the first wife of King Philip V. Murcia's *Resumen de acompañar la parte con la guitarra* was published in Madrid in 1714.

Domenico Pellergini, a representative of the 17th century Bolognese guitar school.

PELLEGRINI, Domenico (? - ca. 1662), an Italian guitarist and composer, a member of the Bolognese music academy Accademia dei Filomusi. Pellegrini, together with Corbetta, Bartolotti and Granata, was a representative of the 17th century Bolognese guitar school. Pellegrini's guitar tablature, *Armoniosi concerti sopra la chitarra spagnuola* was published in Bologna in 1650 and it contains 38 pieces for the guitar. The book gives advice on interpretation, arpeggiation of chords and execution of ornaments such as the strascio (slur) or tremolo (both trill and left-hand vibrato). The book contains a noteworthy *Passacaglia*, which during its 208 variations modulates through 22 different keys before ending in its original key!

PESORI, Stefano (ca. 1650), an Italian guitarist and composer. He served in the courts of Marquise M. A. Sagramos and B. Gherdini. His four guitar tablature books, *Galeria musicale di Ghitarriglia* (Verona 1648), *Lo scrigno armonice opera seconda* (Mantova ca. 1648), *Toccate di chitarriglia Parte terza* (Verona ca. 1650) and *I concerti armonici di chitarriglia* (Verona ca. 1650) were published in 1648-1650. They contain dances where the rasgueado technique is used, and where Foscarini's punteado technique is also present. Pesori's *Ricreationi armoniche overo toccate di chitarriglia* (Verona ca. 1650) is a new edition from the tablature. *Toccate di chitarriglia*. All books excluding *Galeri* also contain villanella songs with words and chords.

PICO, Foriano (the shift of the 16th and the 17th century), an Italian guitarist and composer. His guitar tablature book *Nuova scelta di sonate per la chitarra spagnola* was published in Naples in 1608 and in Rome in 1609. Pico was the first to use a different rasgueado technique (two strikes down with the m- and p-fingers and two strikes up with the p- and i-fingers), which later was known as the so-called repicco technique.

RICCI, Giovanni Pietro (late 17th century), an Italian guitarist. Published in Rome in 1677 a guitar school, *Scuola d'intavolatura... la chitarriglia spagnuola* for the Baroque guitar, this book contains alfabeto tablatures. In his guitar school Ricci presented dissonance chords, the so-called lettere tagliate and transposing on the fingerboard etc.

RONCALLI, Conte Ludovico (17th century), an Italian Baroque guitarist and composer, whose name is often spelled incorrectly "Roncelli" or "Rancalli." Roncalli composed dance suites typical of the Baroque period, which were often based on the same parts: preludio, alemanda, corrente, sarabanda and giga. Though these names are Italian, Roncalli's music has French influences. Roncalli's tablature book, *Capricci armonici sopra la chitarra spagnola op. 1* for a Baroque guitar was published in 1692 in Bergamo. It contains nine dance suites, where the combined punteado-battente ("plucking-strumming") technique is present. Although in Roncalli's works there is no mention about the tuning used, he apparently used a similar tuning as e.g. Corbetta, de Visée, Foscarini and Granata, where the fourth course is a pair where the other string is an octave lower. The German A. Stingl has arranged Roncalli's dance suites for a six-course guitar. (Ed. Musikwerlag, Leipzig 1968).

RUIZ de RIBAYAZ, Lucas (ca. 1650–?), a Spanish guitarist, harpist, composer and priest. He was in the service of Counts Lemos and Andrade. Ribayaz's guitar book shows that he also visited the Spanish colonies in the New World (the America). His guitar book, *Luz y norte músical para caminar por las cifras de la guitarra española* was published in Madrid in 1677. It contains important information on how to play the five-course Baroque guitar, ornaments and the 17th century Spanish Baroque dances such as folia, jácaras, canario, passacaglia etc.

SANSEVERINO, Benedetto (early 17th century), an Italian guitarist, musician and composer. Worked as a musician in Milan, where he published a tablature book for a five-course guitar, *Intavolatura facile delli passacalli op. 3* (1620), whose second edition was published two years later with the name. *Il primo libro d'intavolatura per la chitarra alla spagnuola*.

The book contains detailed information on battute, i.e. chord playing and also on accompanying the popular compositions of that time, such as passacaglia, ciacconne, romanesca and saltarello. The 1622 edition also contains six canzonas, which are only marked with words and chords.

SANZ, Gaspar (1640–1710), a Spanish guitarist and priest. He was born in the town of Galienta near Saragosa to an old and wealthy family. Sanz studied theology at the University of Salamanca and later music in Italy under Cristoforo Caresana and Lelio Colista. Sanz also knew the works of other Baroque guitarists such as Foscarini, Granata and Corbetta. Sanz respected Corbetta most, and he mentioned in his book that Corbetta was the greatest of all. Sanz took part in a diplomatic delegation to visit Paris, where he played a piece for the Sun King, who also was a guitar player.

Sanz's guitar tablature book *Instrucción de música sobre la guitarra española* was first published in Saragosa in 1674. This tablature was the most thorough guitar school at that time and it contains almost 90 Spanish Baroque pieces for the five-course guitar in three volumes. The work contains instructions on both rasgueado and punteado styles and accompaniment. It also contains a long essay on figured bass accompaniment for the guitar and gives advice on the use of different ornaments, such as trino, mordent, tremblor and arpeado (trill, mordent, vibrato and arpeggio). Sanz was influenced by the French polyphonic lute music, he uses ornaments and his style is very Spanish. Sanz's guitar works have been arranged for the modern guitar and published with the name *Transcripcion de la Obra completa para guitarra de seis cuerdas por Rafael Balaguer* (Ed. Union Musical Española). As the tuning that Sanz uses differs much from the modern tuning, it

The Baroque guitar tablature published in 1674 by Gaspar Sanz contains popular dances and folk music of that time. Here written in the French tablature.

is not easy to play his music with a modern guitar. The tuning that Sanz used (one of the three different tunings of the Baroque guitar) made it possible to use the campanella effects that take advantage of the free strings. The Spanish composer Joaquín Rodrigo used Sanz's themes in his composition *"Fantasía para un Gentilhombre"* for the guitar and orchestra.

STRAUBE, Rudolf (1717–1785), see 'Composers of other Plucked Instruments'.

VISÉE, Robert de (ca. 1660–ca. 1724), a French Baroque guitarist and theorbist, composer and singer. A pupil of Francesco Corbetta. De Visée was as a chamber musician in the court of Louis XIV since 1680. The diary of the Count of Dangeau tells how Visée often entertained the king by playing the guitar beside his bed. Since 1719 he was the guitar teacher of the king. Visée published two tablature books for the Baroque guitar: *Livre de Guitarre dédié au Roy* (Paris 1682), which is dedicated to the Sun King, and *Livré de Pièces pour la Guitarre* (Paris 1686). The first book contains eight dance suites, the last of which uses a scordatura tuning, and a chaconne in F major. The other book contains four dance suites and five single parts of a suite. Visée's lute music collection *Pièces de théorbe et de luth* was published in Paris in 1716. The music has been written on two lines in a treble and a bass clave. Visée's music for a solo theorbo was gathered in a manuscript by his pupil Vaudry de Saizenay. Visée's style has been described as more sensitive than that of his teacher Corbetta, it contains less rasgueado chords. Visée himself tells in his preface that he tried to reach the nuances of monsieur Lully, although he could not imitate him. The whole production of Visée has been printed as a modern publication in *Oeuvres complétes pour guitare* (Robert Strizich Ed. Heugel & Cie, Paris 1969).

The chamber musician of the Sun King Louis XIV, Robert de Visée was a guitarist, theorbist and singer. His suites for the Baroque guitar are often played as arrangements for the modern guitar.

CABEZÓN, Antonio de (1510–1566), the most famous composer of the *"Spanish 'golden Century'"*, *"Siglo de Oro"* (the 16th century), organist and vihuela player, blind from early childhood. Cabezón studied music under the organist of the Valencian cathedral, García de Baeza. Since 1525 Cabezón served Charles V in Toledo, and since 1548 King Philip II, with whom he visited the most important countries of Europe. Cabezón composed a lot of clavere and vocal music. In his compositions he often used the variation form (diferencias) or tiento, where one theme makes a fantasy. Cabezón's compositions have been described as resembling bass continuo and fresh in chords. His son Hernando de Cabezón edited his father's composition collection *Obras de música para tecla, arpa y vihuela* in Madrid in 1578. A Mexican Manuel Ponce has composed a variation for the guitar from a theme by Cabezón.

DAZA [DAÇA], Esteban (mid-16th century), Spanish composer and vihuela player. Daza's vihuela book *Libro de música en cifras para vihuela*, with the heading *El Parnasso*, was published in 1576 in Valladolid. The book is the only vihuela tablature which was published during the reign of King Philip II and it also is the last vihuela tablature published in Spain. The book contains over 60 works, of which 25 are solo fantasies for the vihuela. Some of them were composed so that the players could develop their playing skills to an advanced level.

FUENLLANA, Miguel de (ca. 1525–after 1585), a Spanish vihuela virtuoso and composer, blind from his early childhood. Served under Marquise Tarifa. During 1562–68 he served as a chamber musician for King Philip II's wife Elisabeth da Valois. Fuenllana's vihuela music collection *Libro música para vihuela, intitulado Orphénica lyra* appeared in 1554 in Seville. As most vihuela players, Fuenllana probably paid to get his book printed. This explains why he was granted the royal licence to print his books for a period of 15 years. Orphénica lyra contains 52 fantasies, eight tientos (for a five or six course vihuela) and a few song accompaniments, such as the famous *"Tant que vivray."* In addition to vihuela music, the collection contains nine pieces for a four-course Renaissance guitar: six *Fantasías; Romance; Villancico; Intavolatur* (an arrangement from a vocal piece). Unlike other vihuela players, Fuenllana did not give advice as regards the tempo, but allowed the performer to choose the tempo his abilities dictated.

HENESTROSA, Luis Venegas de see VENEGAS de…

MILÁN, Luys de (1502–1561), the best-known vihuelist in Spain, a remarkable composer and author. Milán, who was of aristocratic origin, was not a professional musician. Milán lived most of his life in Valencia and he has told that music was not taught to him, but music taught him. Milán's vihuela book *Libro de música de vihuela de mano intitulado El Maestro* was published in Valencia in 1536 and it is dedicated to John III of Portugal. The book is the first vihuela book ever published and it contains Milán's own compositions only. El Maestro is the first book with verbal indications of tempo, e.g. *algo apriessa* (somewhat quickly) or *apressurado* (agitated measure…rushed). The book contains a wide repertoire of original vihuela music, e.g. 40 fantasies, six pavanas, four tientos and different types of vocal music to be accompanied with the vihuela.

Milán's fantasies are more like improvisations than compositions, and he himself thinks that they are all fantasies, because they are products of his imagination. He divides his fantasies into two categories: the simple ones, that have no additional name, and the *'tañer de gala'* fantasies that are to be played elegantly in rubato. These fantasies are divided into two groups, the chord fantasies and the scale fantasies, *'fantasías de conconancias y redobles'* and the wider fantasies, the tientos. Miláni's compositions are characteristically formally free with a typical blend of homophony and polyphony. He advises to play the chords slowly and the scales quickly so that the performer has a possibility to show his skills. Milán's fantasies and pavanas have also established their place in the programmes of guitarists. In 1561 Milán published a book, *El Cortesano*, which describes the culture and court life in Valencia.

MUDARRA, Alonso de (1508–1580), a Spanish vihuelist and composer. He was brought up in Guadalajara in the

Mudarra's best known vihuela composition "Fantasía que contrahaze la harpa en la manera de Ludovico" imitates the playing of the harpist of King Ferdinand V, Ludovico.

households of the third and fourth dukes of Infantando. Later he worked in that court and since 1546 in the cathedral of Seville. In 1568 he became the canon of the cathedral of Seville and he was elected Major Domo of the cathedral. Mudarra's vihuela tablature *Tres libros de música en cifra para vihuela* was published in Seville in 1546. The book contains more than 70 compositions for the vihuela, pieces for song and vihuela and four fantasies, a pavana and a galliard and variations from theme *Guárdame las vacas* for a four-course Renaissance guitar. Mudarra's vihuela music is also played with the modern classical guitar. The most famous one is *"Fantasía que contrahaze la harpa en la manera de Ludovico"*, which imitates the echo of the harp of the harpist of King Ferdinand V, Ludovico. The work contains very daring dissonances and it is the first printed work, which contains the descending Phrygian tetrachord, which is now considered a hallmark of the Andalusian style.

NARVÁEZ, Luys de (ca. 1500–1555), a Spanish vihuelist and composer. He may have been in the service of Charles V's secretary, Francisco de los Cobos, in Valladolid. In the 1540s Narváez, as music teacher to the children in the chapel of Prince Philip (later Philip II), traveled to Italy and to the northern Europe. Since 1548 Narváez worked as the conductor of the court chapel's boy's choir.

In 1538 Narváez published six books of vihuela music in Valladolid, titled *Los seys libros del Delphin de música*. The music is notated in tablature similar to that used in Italian lute sources. In addition to instrumental music, the books contain many vocal pieces arranged for the vihuela, such as Josquin de Prez's and Gombert's works. The most famous of these is an arrangement of a song by de Prez, Mille regretz, it is known by the name *"La canción del Emperador"*, because it was the favorite song of King Charles V. Narváez's book is the first to contain instrumental music in variation form (diferencias) and symbols indicating tempo.

The most famous variation for vihuela by Narváez is *"Diferencias sobre Guárdame las vacas"*, which has remained popular until our days. The work contains seven variations, which are based on ostinato harmonies, three of the variations are romanescas and the three remaining are passamezo anticos. Other variations by Narváez are *"O gloriosa Domina"* and *"Conde Claros."* The latter contains 22 bergamasca variations with bravura scale passages, unusual arpeggio patterns, sudden changes of register and one variation which 'imitates the guitar'. In "O gloriosa Domina", the hymn tune appears in each of the six variations. The variety of texture, rhythm, tempo and placing of the cantus firmus provides contrast between the six differencias. The source of inspiration in Narváez's fantasies has been the Dutch vocal polyphony. His creative and instrumentally fluent style has been described as the most lyrical of the vihuela composers. Narváez's excellent skills in improvisation can be deduced from the words of a contemporary, Luis de Zapa: "In my youth in Valladolid there was a vihuelist called Narváez, who was so skillful in music that he could improvise his own tetrachord music based on some other tetrachord music without having seen the piece before. This seemed amazing to those who did not know music, but even more amazing to those who did." Zapata, who was born in 1526 and was in the service of Empress Isabella (the wife of Charles V), really had a chance to hear Narváez's music at the time that he published his *Los seis libros.*

ORTIZ, Diego (1525–after 1570), a Spanish composer. Worked in the court of Duke of Naples. He published a gamba school, *Tratado de glosas sobre clausulas y otros genero de puntos en la música de violones*, in Rome in 1553. It is the most remarkable source of the Renaissance instrumental music. It contains such pieces as four ricercares for the viola da gamba and the vihuela, and they belong to the repertoires of today's guitar and cello duos.

PISADOR, Diego (1509–1577), a Spanish vihuelist and composer, a chamber musician of King Philip II. Pisador's vihuela music collection *Libro de música de vihuela*, was published in Salamanca in 1552. In the preface he says that he admires the music of Josquin de Prez. Pisador's vihuela collection contains the vihuela arrangements of eight masses by de Prez. It also contains 22 Spanish songs and other vocal music and original compositions for the vihuela, i.e. fantasies, variations and dances. The best known compositions by Pisador are the variations from theme *"Conde claros"* and a romanesca *"Guárdame las vacas."*

SANTA MARIA, Tomás de (? –1570), a Spanish theorist and composer. In 1536 he became a Dominican monk and after that he served as an organist in a Dominican monastery in Castilia. In 1565 he published a collection, *Libro llamado Arte de tañer fantasía para tecla*, in Valladolid. It is a performance and diminution school. It also contains instructions on performing vihuela music.

VALDERRÁBANO, Enríquez de (ca. 1500–1557), a Spanish composer and vihuelist, worked for Count Miranda. A collection of Valderrábano's vihuela music was published in 1547 under the heading *Libro de música de vihuela, intitulado Silva de Sirenas*. In addition to polyphonic vihuela music it also contains variations, folk songs and dances and music for two vihuelas.

VENEGAS DE HENESTROSA, Luis (ca. 1510–n. 1557), a Spanish composer. Worked for the cardinal of Toledo, Juan Tavera, in 1534–1545 and in 1543 he worked as a priest in Hontova in the county of Toledo. In 1557 in Alcalá he published a collection, *Libre de cifra nueva para tecla, harpa y vihuela*, which contains 138 compositions, of which 20 are for the vihuela. Venegas de Henestrosa's vihuela pieces are also present in other vihuela and lute tablature books dating from that period.

20. Mille regretz. Canción I, del Emperador

Cuarto tono

Josquin-Narváez

Mille regres

Mille regrès

f. 40ᵛ (=44ᵛ) En la quinta en el tercer traste está la clave de fe fa ut.
En la tercera en el primer traste está la clave de ce sol fa ut.¹⁾

An arrangement by Luys de Narváez from Josquin des Prez's song
Mille regretz was the favorite song of the Emperor of Spain Charles V.

22

ABONDANTE, Giulio (mid-16th century), an Italian lutist and composer. He also used the names *"Abundante"* and *"dal Pestrino."* He published at least five collections of lute music, of which three have survived to our days. They contain the typical lute music of that time: the first contains only dances, such as galliardas and pavanas, the second fantasies and arrangements from vocal music and the third fantasies, paduanos, passamezzos and a bergamesca. The collections were published during the years 1546–1587.

ALISON, Richard (late 16th century–early 17th century), an English composer. Alison lived in London and his consort compositions were published by Thomas Morley in 1599 in his collection *First Booke of Consort Lessons*. Alison's lute song collection *The Psalmes of David* was published in London in 1599. His production also contains solo lute music and works for two lutes (a facsimile Leeds, 1975).

ANDRIAENSSEN, Emanuel (? –1604), a Dutch lutist and composer. His two lute books, *Pratum musicum* and *Novum pratum musicum,* appeared in Antwerpen, the first in 1584 and the second in 1592.

ATTAINGNANT, Pierre (ca. 1494–ca. 1552), a Parisian music publisher. He published the works of French composers, e.g. two lute collections: *Tres brève et familiére Introduction* (Paris 1529) and *Dixhuit basses dances* (Paris 1530). They contain 66 pieces for the lute, e.g. Wolf's, Bruger's and Attaingnant's own works. The first collection also contains 35 French songs. There are also versions of these songs for the solo lute

BAKFARK, Valentin (1507–1576), a Hungarian lutist and composer. He also used the last name Greff. His brother Michael was also a lutist. Bakfark studied in Italy and worked later, in 1549–1566, in the court of the Polish King, Sigismund Augustus, in Krakov. In the late 1540s Bakfark visited Paris. He published two lute books, *Intavolatura Valentini*

Bakfark (Lyon 1553) and *Valentini Greffi Bakfarci Pannonii Harmoniarum Musicarum.* (Krakov 1565). They contain Orlando di Lasso's and Josquin des Prez's arrangements from vocal pieces and fantasies for the lute, etc.

BARBERIIS, Melchiore de (early 16th century), an Italian lutist and priest (Padua). In 1546 and 1549 he published two of his lute tablature books in Venice, both with the name *Intabulatura di liuto.* The latter contains four fantasies, which are more like dances, for the four-course guitar (printed in Gitarrenmusik der 16. –18. Jahrhunderts I Ed. VEB Deutscher Verlag Für Musik, Leipzig).

BARTOLOTTI (early 17th century- ca. 1669), see 'Baroque Guitar composers'.

BESARD, Jean-Baptiste (ca. 1567–1625), a French lutist and medical doctor. His first tablature book, *Thesaurus harmonicus,* appeared in 1603 in Cologne and the second, *Novus Partus,* in 1617 in Venice. A collection published in England in 1610 by Robert Dowland, son of John Dowland, called *Varietie of Lute lessons*, contains parts of Besard's tablature books translated into English, *Necessaire observations belonging to the playing.*

BORRONO, Pietro Paolo (early 16th century), an Italian lutist and composer. Worked in 1531–34 for Francois I, and after that for the county governor of Milan. Borrono's works have been published in three collections in 1536, 1546 and 1548. The last of these was his tablature book. It appeared in Venice and it also contained pieces for two lutes.

BOSSINENSIS, Franciscus (late 15th century – early 16th century), an Italian arranger and lute composer. His collections, *Frottolas for Song and Lute,* were published by Petrucci in 1509 and 1511. The collections contain 126 frottolas from different composers, such as M. Cara and B. Trombonico, whose tenor and bass notes Bossinensis arranged for the lute. The collections also contain 46 ricercares.

The French lutist, composer, and medical doctor Jean-Baptiste Besard.

CAMPION, François (ca. 1680–1748), see 'Renaissance and Baroque Guitar Composers'.

CAMPION, Thomas (1567–1620), an English composer, lutist and physician, who lived in London. Campion studied law and medicine and he was also a poet. Campion was a very productive composer of lute songs, who also wrote the texts to his songs. Campion published in 1613 a harmony school, *A New Way of Making Houre Parts in Counterpoint,* where the bass provided the foundation for the music. The book anticipates a book by Rameau, which appeared a hundred years later. Campion's four lute song books *Bookes of Ayres* were published in London in 1601–17.

CAPIROLA, Vincenzo (1474–after 1548) an Italian nobleman, lutist and composer. He is thought to be the phenomenal Brescian lutist, who visited the court of Henry VIII in 1515. One of Capirola's pupils prepared in 1515–20 a so-called *Capriola lute book* which is illustrated, and which contains music by e.g. F. Spinacino and J.A. Dalza. The book is an important document on Italian lute music between Petrucci's publications and Francesco da Milano's first works. The book contains practical information on technical aspects of lute playing, ornaments, strings, frets etc.

CARA, Marchetto (ca. 1470–1525), an Italian composer, singer and lutist. Worked in the court of Gonzaga and was known as a singing lutist in the whole of northern Italy as he performed in places like Mantova, Venice, Milan, Parma and Padova. Cara composed more than 100 frottolas, and some of them are accessible in lute versions. The lute frottolas were published in a co-collection by Cara and another frottola composer, Bartolomeo Tromboncino (ca. 1470–1535), in Rome in 1520. Some of Cara's frottolas were published in collections of Franciscus Bossinensis in 1509 and 1511.

CAROSO, Marco Fabrizio (1530–1605), an Italian dance teacher from Venice. Caroso used lute music in his dance school books, which were published in Venice: *Il Ballerino* 1581 (facsimile Broude-Brothers 1967 New York) and *Nobilita di dame,* 1600 (facsimile Forni Editore Bologna 1970).

CATO, Diomedes [Venetus] (ca. 1570–after ca. 1607), a lutist who was born in Venice, but lived in Poland since 1589. His works were published in many of the tablature books which appeared in the 17th century. Cato, who was often known by his first name only, worked in the court of the King of Poland, Sigismund III in 1588–93. In 1593–4 he, together with the king, traveled to Sweden. Diomedes Cato also composed vocal, claver and string music, but he is best known for his lute music. Cato's lute fantasies, which are extremely interesting, represent the ricercare style. Edition WDMP (Wydawnictwo dawnej myzyki Polskiej) has published Diomedes Cato's lute tablatures in the form of a modern notation book (1953, 1973).

CUTTING, Francis (late 16th century–early 17th century), an English lutist and composer. Cutting is one of the most remarkable lute composers in the 16th century. His works are accessible in at least Barley's and Pickering's lute books. Cutting's lute compositions have been published in a modern style in *Music for lute F. Cutting - Selected Works*, Oxford University Press, London 1968.

CUTTING, Thomas (late 16th century–early 17th century), an English lutist, probably was a member of the same family as Francis Cutting. Thomas Cutting acted for three years as a lutist for Christian IV in Denmark and since 1611 for Prince Henry in England.

DALZA, Joan Ambrosio (late 15th century–early 16th century), an Italian lutist and composer, probably born in Milan. He is the composer and arranger of a lute collection published by Ottavino Petrucci, *Intabolatura de Lauto libro quatro* (Venice 1508). The collection contains lute arrangements from vocal works by Flemish composers, Dalza's original music and three dances for two lutes.

DENSS, Adrian (late 16th century), a Dutch lutist and composer. Lived in Antwerpen and moved in ca.1590 to Cologne, where his lute collection *Florilegium omnis* was published in 1594. Denss used the French tablature in his collection, which contains vocal arrangements for over 80 pieces, 11 fantasies, eight passamezzos and other dances.

DLUGORAI, [Wojciech] Albertus (1557–1619), a Polish lutist and composer. Worked for magnate Samuel Zborowskiov and later in the courts of Hetman Zamojski and King Stefan Batory. Dlugorai's works were published in J-B. Besard's collections. Dlugorai's lute works have been published by the Polish Edition PWM.

DOWLAND, John (1562–1626), an English composer and lutist. He composed almost 100 solos for the lute and over 80 lute songs, which were printed and played all around Europe. In 1580 Dowland went to France with the English ambassador Sir Henry Cobham. He returned to England ca. 1586 and in 1588 he took a Bachelor of Music degree in the Christ Church College at Oxford. After 1597 Dowland referred to himself as Bachelor of Music in both the Universities, which

The English lutist John Dowland composed over 100 solo works for the lute. His chromatic fantasies are among the best in lute music.

71. *A Fantasia*

Copyright 1967 by Faber Music Ltd, London. Reprinted by permission.

indicates that he also took the degree in Cambridge. In 1594 Dowland applied for the position of Queen Elizabeth's chamber lutist to replace John Johnson after his death. He was not accepted and he went to Italy via Germany. In Florence he got in touch with the Catholics that had escaped from England and he fled to Nürnberg. In 1596 he returned to Kassel, where he had already previously been as a guest of Count Moritz of Hessen. In December of the same year he, persuaded by a friend Henry Noel, returned to England and applied for the lutist's place in the court, but did not succeed. Since 1598 Dowland served as a lutist in the court of Kristian IV of Denmark. He did not feel comfortable in Denmark, but spent most of his time in England under various excuses. In 1606 he was dismissed either because of his journeys or his lifestyle. In 1610 he helped his son to publish a collection of lute compositions called *Varietie of Lute-Lessons*. In 1612 Dowland worked at first as the chamber lutist for Lord Teophilus of Walden until he finally got the place as a lutist in the court of James I. Dowland was called a doctor since 1621, but references to a possible university degree do not exist. On February 20, 1626 he was buried in Blackfriars to St. Anne's cemetary.

Dowland differed from his contemporaries by only composing for the lute and chamber orchestras, but not at all church music. The reason may have been conflicts with regards to religious opinions. His conversion to Catholic during his time in Paris no doubt affected his possibilities to get a position in the English court. J. Dowland's lute compositions are regarded as the best in the field and they are marked with melancholy although there are some hilarious moods in them sometimes. Still

Dowland is mostly known by his songs, they were published in London during 1597–1612 in four collections: *The Firste Booke of Songes* (1597), *The Second Booke of Songs* (1600), *The Third and Last Booke of Songs* (1603) and *A Pilgrimes Solace* (1612). These songs are accompanied by the lute and the viola da gamba. Dowland's chamber music collection *Lachrimae, or Seven Tears for four or five gambas and a lute* appeared in 1604. His lute works were published in Robert Dowland's (1610), J. Hove's (1612)

Francesco Canova da Milano

and G.L. Fuhrmann's (1615) tablature books.

Diana Poulton has published a book, *The Collected Lute Music of John Dowland* (Faber Music Ltd, London 1974), which contains Dowland's lute music. Dowland's lute music has been arranged for the guitar by many guitarists, such as Behrend, Benkö, Burley, Cáceres, Davezac, Duarte, Kilvington and Scheit.

DOWLAND, Robert (ca.1591–1641), an English lutist, son of John Dowland. Robert Dowland published in London in 1610 a tablature book *Varietie of Lute Lessons*, which contained both his father's and the French lutist J.B. Besard's lute music. In the same year Robert Dowland also published a lute song collection called, *A Musical Banquet*, which contains the best English, French, Spanish and Italian songs. In the beginning of 1626 Robert Dowland inherited the lutist's post in the court of England.

FERRABOSCO, Alfonso (ca. 1578–1628), an English composer with Italian roots, lutist and singer. It is known that his career as a lutist started in the funeral of Queen Elisabeth. Since 1604 Ferrabosco worked for Prince Henry of Wales and when Henry died in 1612 Ferrabosco became the teacher of Prince Charles. Ferrabosco published a collection, *Ayres, lute songs* in London in 1609. His songs are also accessible in other lute collections (see. E. Pohlmann).

FRANCESCO CANOVA DA MILANO (1497–1543), the most famous lutist and composer in Italy in his time. Francesco was taught by Giovanni Testagrossa, who had a post in the court of Isabella d'Este. During 1516–39 Francesco worked as the lutist of bishops Leo X, Clement VII and Pope Paul III. He was probably also the cathedral organist in Milan around 1530 for one year. In 1535 Francesco returned to Rome and worked as the lutist of Cardinal Ippolito de'Medici. Francesco published lute books *Libro I, Intavolatura de viola o vero lauto* (Naples 1536), *Libro II, Intavolatura di Lauto* (Venice 1546) and *Libro III, Intavolatura di Lauto* (Venice 1547). He used the composition techniques for vocal music of that time in the limits of idiomatic lute texture and was very skillful in editing and making use of short motives, which then formed a constantly developing structure. Francesco was the first musician of Italian Renaissance to become famous abroad. His works were published in more than 40 lute collections and they were played all over Europe. Francesco got nicknames, such as *Il Divino* - "the Divine" and "*absolutely the Prince of lutists.*" After his death Francesco was described as "a wonderful lutist." The lutist Ioanne Matelart composed another melody for another lute to one of Francesco's ricercares and it was published in Rome in 1559. Francesco da Milano's whole production, *Opere complete per liuto* has been republished by Ruggero Chiesa (Edition Suvini Zerboni, Milano 1971) and A.J. Ness *The Lute Music of Francesco Canova da Milano* (Harvard University Press, 1970).

FUHRMANN, Georg Leopold (late 16th century–early 17th century), a German publisher, bookseller, engraver and amateur lutist. Fuhrmann is known for his lute music collection *Testudo Gallo-Gèrmanica* (Nürnberg 1615), which contains 180 pages of music from Germany, France, Italy and England by the famous musicians of that time.

GALILEI, **Michelangelo** (late 16th century–early 17th century), an Italian lutist, son of Vincenzo Galilei and brother of the famous astronomer Galileo Galilei, who lived in Munich in Germany. He published a collection of lute music, *Primo Libro de Intavolatura di Liuto* in Munich in 1620.

GALILEI, Vincenzo (ca. 1520–1591) an Italian lutist, violinist, composer and theoretician. He was the father of the famous astronomer Galileo Galilei and a member of the assembly of famous artists, "*Camerata Firenze.*" Galilei brought out the ideals of the monodia style and antique. His book *Dialogo della musica antica e della moderna* was published in 1581. It is considered a manifesto of the modern style. The style was later developed by J. Peri and G. Caccini. In 1563 a lute

tablature book by V. Galilei, *Intavolatura de lauto Madrigali e Recercate*, was published in Rome and in 1568 a tablature book, *Il Fronimo* in Venice. A second edition of that book came out in 1584. V. Galilei's son Michelangelo was also a lutist (see previous entry).

GASTOLDI, Giovanni Giacomo (ca. 1550–1622), an Italian composer. Worked from the year 1581 as a singer in the court of Mantova, in 1582–1609 he was the conductor of the church of Santa Barbara in Mantova and also for some time in the cathedral of Milan. Gastoldi was one of the most important representatives of the *balletto* (dance choir music). The ballettos that were meant to be performed by dancing, were performed by imitating a certain person in the same way as in the pantomime. In 1594 a book by Gastoldi was published in Venice, *Balletti a tre voci con intavolatura del Liuto, per cantare, sonare & ballare*. The popularity can be seen in the numerous reprints.

GERLE, Hans (ca. 1500–1570), a German instrumentalist, lute builder and arranger of instrumental music. Hans was the brother of the famous lute builder, Conrad Gerle. A publisher, Hieronymus Formschneider from Nürnberg, published three of Hans Gerle's lute music collections: *Musica Teutsh auch Lautten* (1532), *Tabulatur auffdie Lautten* (1533) and *Eyn Newes sher Künstlichs Lautenbuch* (1552).

GIOVANNI, [Joan] Maria da Crema (early 17th century), an Italian lutist and composer. Giovanni was probably one of the members of the viola da gamba sextet that played in the court of Henry VIII in 1540. The two lute collections that have survived from Giovanni to our days were published in Venice in 1546. The first collection contains 17 ricercares, seven dances and 25 vocal song arrangements for the lute. The second collection contains 13 Francesco da Milano's new ricercares and 12 arrangements from the music by Seng.

GORZANIS, Giacomo (ca. 1520–

1579), an Italian composer and lutist. Spent his youth in Spain in the court of Bar. Around 1557 he visited Austria and settled in Italy, the town of Trieste, before 1567. Gorzanis' lute works were published in Venice during 1561–1579: *Intabolatura di Liuto di Jacomo Gorzanis ciego Pugliese* (1561), *Il secondo libro de Intabolatura di Liuto* (1561), *Il terzo libro de Intabolatura di Liuto* (1564) and *Opera nova de Lauto, composta da Messier Jacomo Gorzanis* (1579).

HECKEL, **Wolff** (ca. 1515–ca. 1562), a German lutist, composer and tablature arranger. He published two lute books in Strasbourg in 1556 and 1562. Heckel also plays an important role in the German music for two lutes. The first 40 pieces in his book are for two lutes.

HOLBORNE, Anthony [Antony] (? –ca. 1602), an English composer and player of chittern. He published a chittern school *Cittharn Schoole* in London in 1597. The book contains 58 solo pieces for the chittern and 24 pieces for the chittern and bass continuo. John Dowland dedicated the first song in his second song book, I saw my lady, weepe - to the most famous Anthony Holborne. His lute music has been published in several collections of European lutists. Brian Jeffery has published a doctor's thesis on A. Holborne's music, *The Lute Music of Anthony Holborne*, the University of Oxford (1966/67).

HOVE, Joachim van den (1567–1620), a Dutch lutist, composer and teacher. His family moved to Antwerpen in 1584. Joachim van den Hove is, together with Emmanuel Adriaensen and Nicolas Vallet, the most important representative of 17th century Dutch lute music. Hove's lute books were published in Utrecht, the first, *Florida, sive cantiones* in 1601 and the second, *Delitiae Musicae* in 1612.

JOHNSON, **John** (?–ca. 1598), an English lutist. Worked in Shakespeare's Theater and as a lutist in the Royal Chapel during 1581–1595. John Johnson is one of the

The front page of Hans Judenkünig's lute book "Ain schone kunstlische underweisung…" published in 1523 in Vienna.

earliest representatives of the English *"golden period of the lute."* He is the father of lutist Robert Johnson (1583–1633). John Johnson used a lot of traditional dances, such as pavana-galliarda and allemande in his lute music, and almost no fantasy style as most of his contemporaries. In addition to his lute solos, his productions contain lute duos, such as *Flat Pavan & Galliard* and chamber music for two lutes, a treble instrument and a bass instrument.

JOHNSON, Robert (1583–1633), an English composer and lutist, son of John Johnson.

Worked since 1596 for Lord Chamberlain and since 1604 for King James I. R. Johnson worked from 1628 until his death in the court of King Charles I as a Composer of lute songs with the title *"Composer for the Lute and Voices."* There are only about 20 pieces of R. Johnson's lute music that have survived, but they represent the best compositions of that time. There is a collection, which contains the survived compositions, *Complete Works for Solo Lute* (ed. A. Sundermann, London 1970).

JUDENKÜNIG, Hans (ca. 1450–1526), a German lutist and lute teacher, worked mainly in Vienna. Judenkünig's two lute books written in the German tablature, *Utilis et compendaria introductio* (Vienna ca. 1515–19) and *Ain schone kunstlische underweisung* (Vienna 1523) were important books when learning to play the lute by oneself.

L'AQUILA, Marco da (15th century–16th century), an Italian lutist and composer. In 1505 he was granted a 10-year licence to publish lute music in Venice, but unfortunately he did not use it. Many of his hand-written works are in poor condition and it has demanded a lot of editing to get them into such a condition that they can be performed. L'Aquila's style is a fascinating combination of rhapsody and improvisation of the early Venetian school and the more song-like style of da Milano and da Ripa, where again harmonies and an imitating bass continuo meet.

LAURENTINI, see **LORENZINI**.

LE ROY, Adrian (ca.1520–1598), a French music printer, lutist, guitarist

and composer, who together with his cousin Robert Ballard obtained from King Henry II the right to publish and sell different types of music books. In February 1553 Le Roy & Ballard got the title of *"Royal Music Printer,"* which had been vacant since the death of P. Attaingnant's death in 1552. Le Roy was the artistic director, while Ballard took care of the business side. During 1551–71 they printed several lute collections. According to Ernst Pohlmann four lute collections have survived from Le Roy: *Premier livre de tabulature de Luth* (Paris, 1551), *Tiers livre de tabulature de luth* (Paris, 1552) *Sixièsme livre de Luth* (Paris, 1559) and a song collection *Livre d'Airs de cour miz sur le Luth* (Paris, 1571). The English translation from Le Roy's lute tablature schools, *A Briefe and easye instruction to learne the tableture* was published in London in 1568. In addition to lute music they printed five collections of tablature books for the four-course Renaissance guitar (chitarrino) *Livre Tabulature de guiterre* in Paris in 1551, -52, -53, -54 and -56.

LORENZINI, [di Roma, Eques Romanus] (late 16th century), an Italian lutist and composer. His works are accessible in lute collections from the late 16th century. Lorenzini, *"Cavaliere del liuto"* (the Knight of Lute), worked in 1570–71 for cardinal Ippolito d'Esten and probably also as the lute teacher for J.B. Besard. He (1603) and Robert Dowland (1610) published several of Lorenzini's lute pieces in their own collections.

MATELART, Ioanne [Johannes] (ca. 1538–1607), a Flemish composer. During 1558–62 he probably was in Italy and in 1565 he received the title *"Maestro di cappella"* for the church of Sanct Lorenzo in Damaso, where he worked for more than 40 years. Matelart's lute books, which are written in the Italian tablature, contain arrangements from Francesco da Milano's and Morales' works and 15 of Matelart's own fantasies. A lute book, *Responsoria*, contains 21 of Matelart's own songs and music by Lasso and Palestrina, etc. Matelart's, *Intavolature de leuto* was published in 1599.

MERTEL, Elias (ca. 1561–1626), a German lutist and composer and intabulator (writer of tablatures). Worked until 1595 for Friedrich IV, after which he was the financial manager in the Academy of Strasbourg. The most remarkable lute collection by Mertel, *Hortus musicalis*, was published in Strasbourg in 1615. It contains 235 preludes and 120 fantasies and fugues, but the researchers are not sure whether they all are his own compositions.

MESANGEAU, René, see 'Baroque Lute Composers'.

MILANO, Francesco da see FRANCESCO da...

MORLAYE, Guillaume (ca. 1510–after 1558), a French lutist, music publisher and composer. Lived in Paris and in 1552 received from Henry II a 10-year licence to publish books. In co-operation with Michel Fezandanti he published four lute collections during the next six years, (1552, -54, -58 and -58) and six lute collections compiled by his teacher Alberto da Ripa (de Rippe). Morlaye also published three music books for the four-course Renaissance guitar in 1552–53. They contain fantasies and the favorite dances of that time, galliardas, pavanas, branles and allemands. The books also contains lute arrangements from other composers', such as Sermisy's and Certo's, works.

MORLEY, Thomas (1557–1602) an English composer, theoretician and organist. Morley was a pupil of William Byrd in the University of Oxford and received there the baccalaureate degree in 1588. Morley belongs to the most famous Elizabethan madrigal composers. He also published music, editing for example John Dowland's 2nd and 3rd song book. A tablature book with Morley's own lute songs appeared in 1600, it was called *The First Book of Ayres... Play to the Lute with the Base Viole*, and music for the chittern was published in his collection, *The First Booke of Consort Lessons*, (London, 1599).

NEGRI, Cesare [detto il Trombone] (ca. 1535–ca. 1604) an Italian dance teacher, also known by the name *"Il Trombone."* His remarkable dance school, *Le gratie d'amore*, appeared in Milan in 1602 and he dedicated it to the King of Spain, Philip III. It contains 43 dance compositions written in the lute tablature or using mensural notation. Negri's second dance school, *Nuovo inventioni di balli*, appeared in 1604.

NEUSIDLER, [Newsidler] Hans (ca. 1508–1563), a German composer, lutist and lute builder. He lived in Nürnberg from 1530 onwards. In 1536–49 he published in Nürnberg eight collections: *Ein Newgeordent Künstlich Lautenbuch...* (1536), *Der ander theil das Lautenbuchs...* (1536), *Ein newes Lauttenbüchlein...* (1540) and *Das Erst Buch...* (1544). His most famous lute piece is *"Judentanz"* (a Jude dance), where the tuning of the lute is A-d-f#-a-d´-g´. Hans Neusidler's sons Melchior and Conrad were also famous lutists. Together with Judenkünig and Gerle, H. Neusidler belongs to the most important German early lute musicians.

NEUSIDLER, [Newsidler] Melchior (1531–1591) a German lutist and composer, son of Hans Neusidler. Melchior Neusidler lived short periods in several places, such as Augsburg (1551), Stuttgart (1576) and Innsbruk (1580). In 1566 he published his two first lute tablature books, *Il primo libro intabolatura di liuto...* and *Il secondo libro Intabolatura di liuto...* in Venice. The third lute tablature by M. Neusidler, *Teütsh Lautenbuch...*, appeared in Strasbourg in 1574.

PALADINO [Paladin], Giovanni Paolo (ca. 1505–1566), a lutist and composer with Italian roots. Paladino got training in lute playing in Milan and moved in his youth to France, living in Lyon. During 1516–22 he worked as a lutist for François I and since 1544 for the Emperor of Lorraine, Charles III and in 1548–53 for Queen Mary of Scotland. Paladino published two lute collections in Lyon, *Tabulatura de lutz...*

(1549) and *Premier livre de tabulature de luth...* (1560).

PHALÈSE, Pierre (ca. 1510–ca. 1573), a Flemish music publisher. In 1545 he founded a publishing company together with Jean Bellére. They published several collections of lute music in Louvaine and Antwerpen in 1545–74, and in 1570 a large collection of music for a four-course guitar with the heading *Selectissima in Guiterna Ludenda Carmina...*, from which Le Roy already had published several works in Paris.

PICCININI, Alessandro (ca. 1566–1638), an Italian lutist and composer. His father Leonardo Maria and his brothers Girolamo and Filippo and his son Leonardo Maria were also lutists. Since 1582 Piccinini worked for the Duke of Mantua. Later he worked for Cardinal Pietro Aldobrandini. Piccinini published two books for the lute: *Intavolatura di liuto et di chitarrone, libro primo...*, which also contained chitarrone music (Bologna 1623) and *Intavolatura di liuto...* (Bologna 1639). Piccinini used the nails when playing the lute and talked in his books about the technique of playing forte/piano when playing the lute.

PILKINGTON, Francis (ca.1570–1638), an English composer and lutist. Studied in Oxford in the Lincoln College, where he took the baccalaureate degree in 1595. He sang in the Chester Cathedral Choir and also conducted the choir a few years from 1625 onwards. Pilkington's lute song collection *First Book of Songs or Ayres* was published in London in 1605. D. Lumsden published F. Pilkington's lute compositions in London in 1970.

RIPA [da Mantova], Alberto da [RIPPE, Albert de] (ca. 1500–1551), an Italian lutist and composer. Worked for the cardinal of Mantova, Ercole Gonzaga, since 1529. Later he moved to France where he was the lutist of the Royal Court until his death. According to Ernst Pohlmann his lute music was published by Parisian publishers; Fezandat published six collections in 1552–58 and Le Roy & Ballard five collections in 1553–62. Ripa's lute compositions are accessible as modern publications with the heading *A. de Rippe Oeuvres* (ed. J.-M. Vaccaro CM, Corpus des luthistes français 1972–75).

ROBINSON, Thomas (the shift of the 16th and the 17th century), an English lutist, composer and teacher. His lute tablature book *The Schoole of Musicke* appeared in London in 1603 and it was the first lute school published by an English lutist. Before this, J. Adford's translation of the French lutist Le Roy's school (Paris 1567), *A Briefe and Easye Instruction* (1568), had appeared in England. Thomas Robinson's second work, *Medulla Musicke*, appeared in 1603, but it has not survived to our days. Some of his lute duos, such as *"A Toy"*, *"A Plain Song"* and *"Fantasie"* also belong to the repertoires of guitar duos. Thomas Robinson published also a collection for the chittern, *New Chitaren Lessons* (London, 1609).

ROSSETER, Philip (1568–1623), an English chamber musician, lutist and composer, who worked in the court from 1603 until his death. Rosseter is known for his songs and lute compositions and he also composed consort music. His compositions were published in the collections *A Booke of Ayres...* (London 1601) and *Lessons for Consort...* (London 1609).

SPINACINO, Francesco (late 15th century– early 16th century), an Italian lutist and composer. The poet Philippo Oriolo da Bassano mentions in his poem Monte Parnaso that Spinacino is one of the most remarkable lutists of the 15th century. The publisher Petrucci published in 1507 two lute collections in Venice, both containing Spinacino's lute music. It is thought that these collections belong to the first printed lute tablature books.

SWEELINCK, Jan Pieterszoon (1562–1621), a leading Dutch composer of his time, organist and pedagog. Sweelinck composed mainly music for vocals and keyboards, but some of his works are also written in the lute tablature, such as *"3 Psalms"*; *"3 Voltes"*; *"Courante"* (see The New Grove Dictionary).

WAISSEL [Waisselius], Matthäus (ca. 1535–1602), a German lutist, player, arranger and composer. He graduated from the University of Frankfurt am Oder in 1553 and studied in the University of Königsberg since 1561 and stayed in Königsberg. Waissel played and composed for the six-course lute. His four lute compositions were published in Frankfurt am Oder: *Tabulatura in continens insignes* (1573); *Tabulatura Allerlei künstlischer...* (1591); *Lautenbuch, darin von der Tabulatur...* (1592); *Tabulatura Guter gemeiner Deutscher Tenze...* (1592) of which the last contained eight dances for two lutes.

VALLET [Valet], Nicolas (n. 1583–n. 1642), a Dutch lutist and composer with French roots. He moved to Amsterdam in 1614 and concentrated on composing until 1620. All of his lute books date from this time. After this period he worked as a lutist and a teacher. Vallet is one of the most remarkable lutists in the Netherlands together with E. Andriaenssen and J. van den Hove. Vallet's lute works were published in Amsterdam. Lute collections: *Secretum musarum ...* (1615), *Het tweede boeck van de (30) luyt-tablatuer... for one and four lutes* (1616) and *Regia pietas, hoc est (150) Psalmi Davidici* (1620) (see The New Grove Dictionary). Lute song collections: *21 Psalmen Davids* (1615 and 1619).

J.S Bach's lute works and arrangements of his other solo instrument suites belongs to the essential part of the repertoire of a guitarist.

BACH, Johann Sebastian (1685–1750), German Baroque composer. J.S. Bach's wide production also contains works for the lute. It is not known whether Bach himself played the lute, but he was in contact with many of contemporary lutists, such as S. L. Weiss, J. Kropfgans and J.C. Weyrauch, an amateur lutist. A. Falckenhagen was a lute teacher in Leipzig at that time. Some of Bach's pupils also played the lute, J.L. Krebs, R. Straube, H.N. Gerber etc. The researchers do not know which of Bach's works are actual Baroque lute compositions and which have only been inspired by the lute although they are meant for keyboard instruments. In Bach's collection there was an instrument that was only found after his death. This instrument (lautenwerck, lute-cembalo or lute-claver) was a mixture of the lute and the cembalo, it had gut strings but a keyboard similar to that of the cembalo. With the help of this instrument he could combine the properties of these instruments and compose without having to think about the possible restrictions that the playing technique of the lute could cause. This instrument is also mentioned in the heading of his works.

Of the seven surviving solo lute works Bach probably composed the earliest ("*1. Lute Suite*" and "*Prelude BWV 999*") in ca. 1707–1717 and the latest ("*2. and 4. Lute Suites*" and "*Prelude, Fugue and Allegro*") in Leipzig until year 1745. Bach's solo lute works are included in a list of Bach's productions (*Thematisch-systematisches Verzeichnis der musikalischen Werke von J.S. Bach*) by W. Schmieder under numbers BWV 995-1000 and BWV 1006a. The works have been composed using different tunings (each suite has its "own" tuning), not using the typical D minor tuning of the lute. Also the number of strings varies between 12 and 15. Three of Bach's lute compositions have survived as original copies: "*Prelude, Fugue and Allegro BWV 998*", "*Lute Suite nr. 3 G minor BWV 995*" and "*Lute Suite nr. 4 E major BWV 1006a.*" The "*Prelude, Fugue and Allegro*", in the script "*Prelude pour la Luth. ò Cémbal. par J. S. Bach*", is, to conclude from the tex-

ture in the Prelude, composed to the lute, but apparently it has been possible to play it with the cembalo also. *Lute Suites 3 and 4* are arrangements from Bach's own works. The third is an arrangement from "*Cello Suite nr. 5 C minor BWV 1011*" and the fourth from "*Violin Partita nr. 3 E major BWV 1006.*"

From "*Lute Suite nr. 1 E minor BWV 996*" there is no original script by Bach, but in the collection by one of his pupils, J.L. Krebs, there is a piece "Praeludio - con la Suite da Gio: Bast. Bach" under which there is in unidentified handwriting "aufs Lauten Werck." Despite the reference to the lute cembalo, the texure seems to indicate that it was written for the lute (though not as much as in other compositions, but this may be due to the fact that it was composed at an early stage). There are other scripts, e.g. one written by another pupil of Bach, H.N. Gerber, but they have disappeared. Neither is there an original script accessible of "*Prelude C minor BWV 999.*" Nevertheless in a collection by J.P. Kellner there are short preludes for the keyboard under "*Prélude in C mol Pour la Lute di Johann Sebastian Bach,*" and unlike the later lute works by Bach, the prelude is meant to be played with a 10-string lute. Originally it still is composed for the mandora, a treble lute with 4-6 pairs of strings.

Although there is no original script of "*Lute Suite nr. 2 C minor BWV 997*", there are a few of copies of it and in the lute tablature by a lutist J.C. Weyrauch there is also one copy, but it only contains parts 1, 3 and 4. Further, the technical facilitations and other changes have reduced the reliability of that copy. The texture of that suite is not likely to have been written for the cembalo and that is one reason why it is considered to be a lute composition. Of "*Fugue G minor BWV 1000*" there is no original script, but there is a lute tablature for a 13-string D minor lute by Weyrauch with the heading "*Fuga del Signore Bach.*" In addition to the copy by Weyrauch there are no other lute scripts. The work is a copy of the *First Solo Violin Sonata* fugue by Bach (BWV 1001) for which there is an original script by the composer, a reliable copy made by his wife Anna

Magdalena and a couple of other copies. Of that same fugue there is an anonymous organ version BWV 539 transposed to D minor, but it is considered very unauthentic.

Bach used the lute as a bass continuo instrument at least in "*St. John's Passion BWV 245a-c*" and "*St. Matthew's Passion BWV 244*" and the colascione in "*Trauerode*" (Funeral ode) BWV 198.

All the seven lute works by Bach belong to the repertoires of guitarists, arranged and transposed to other keys (BWV 995 a, BWV 996 e, BWV 997 a, BWV 998 D, BWV 999 d, BWV 1000 a, BWV 1006a E). Edizioni Suvini Zerboni has published the scripts of the lute works by J. S. Bach. A lot of Bach's other production has been arranged for the modern classical guitar. F. Tárrega and A. Segovia first arranged parts of *Cello Suites* and *Violin Partitas*, and later several arrangements of whole works have appeared. The second part, Chaconne, from *Violin Partita nr. 2*, is nowadays one of the works by Bach that is played most with the modern guitar. Bach's keyboard productions are also popular among guitarists. The lute works by Bach have been recorded entirely by lutists H. Smith and N. North and guitarists J. Williams and G. Söllscher.

For a solo lute: Lute Suite nr. 1 E minor BWV 996; Lute Suite nr. 2 C minor BWV 997; Lute Suite nr. 3 G minor BWV 995; Lute Suite nr. 4 E BWV 1006a; Prelude, Fugue and Allegro BWV 998; Prelude C minor BWV 999; Fugue G minor BWV 1000.

BARON, Ernst Gottlieb (1696–1760), a German lutist and composer. His father was a maker of gold lace, who expected his son to follow his footsteps. Still Ernst Gottlieb started to take lute lessons in 1710. Since 1715 he spent four years in the University of Leipzig studying philosophy and law. Baron worked in the courts of Friedrich II and Friedrich Wilhelm as a theorbist. His most important work is a book which appeared in Nürnberg in 1727, *Historisch-theoretische und Praktische Untersuchung des Instruments der Lauten*. It is a valuable, though not always so reliable source of information on the lute and lutists of the Baroque period. The book is divided into two parts: the first handles the history of the lute and contains references to the musicians of that time, the second part concentrates on the practice of the instrument. Of the few works by Baron that are accessible, his dance suites contain typical late Baroque idiomacy, but he moved in the direction of the galant style in his concertos. Works by Baron: *"Suite D major"* (1728); *"Fantasia for the lute F major"* (1757); two concertos for the lute, violin and bass continuo; six partitas for the lute; six trios for the lute, viola and cello; Sonata for two lutes.

BITTNER, Jacques [apparently the same as Jakob Büttner] (late 17th century), a Baroque lutist who lived in Nürnberg, Germany. Published two collections, *Pièces de luth...* (1682) and *Galantheste Methode die Laute zu tractieren...* (Nürnberg 1683).

BRESCIANELLO, Giuseppe (1690–1757), see 'Composers for Other Plucked Instruments'.

DAUBE, Johann Friedrich (ca. 1730–1797), a German theorist, composer and theorbist. Worked in Berlin for Fredrik the Great. In 1744 he got a vacancy as the chamber theorbist for the Prince of Württenberg in Stuttgart. Daube worked from 1770 onwards in Vienna as the secretary in the Franciscan Academy and he is considered the first to bring the French theorists' concept of the three fundamental chords (I-IV-V7) to Germany. Lute compositions: *"2 Trios for the lute, flute and bass continuo"*; *"Solo-Sonaten F major, E minor, D minor for the Baroque lute"* (in the library of Rostok).

DIX, Aureus [Aurius] (ca. 1669–1719), a Bohemian lutist and composer, apparently a pupil and friend of J.A. Losy. According to E.G. Baron, Dix

*The German
Baroque lutist
Ernst Gottlieb Baron in 1727.*

was a highly appreciated lutist. His works are mentioned in a list of music by the Breitkopf Publishing Company in 1761. Lute works: *"Two suites A major, G minor"* (a modern version Prague 1968); *"Allemanda Aurej; 6 pieces: Allemande, Courante, Gavotte, Menuet, Gigue, Ballo en Rondeau."*

DUFAUT [Du Fault, Du Foy, Dufau] (? –ca. 1682–6), a French lutist and composer, apparently a pupil of lutist Denis Gaultier. According to E.G. Baron and Le Sage de Riché, Dufaut is one of the most remarkable lutists of the late17th century. In 1670 Dufaut visited England. About 80 of his Baroque dances have survived to our days. The publisher Pierre Ballard published in 1631 13 of Dufaut's lute pieces and in 1638 11 pieces. Dufaut's lute works in modern prints: *Ouvres de Dufaut* ed. A. Souris & M. Rollin (Paris, 1965).

FALCKENHAGEN, Adam (1697–1761), one of the most important representatives of the German lute school together with S.L. Weiss and E.G. Baron. He learnt to play the cembalo and the lute in Knauthain near Leipzig and later he studied lute in Dresden under S.L. Weiss. In 1719 Falckenhagen studied at the University of Leipzig and after that he worked seven years as a lute teacher in Weissenfels. At the same time Falckenhagen worked for Count Christian together with his singer wife Johanna Aemilia. During 1729–32 he worked as a musician in Weimar, since 1734 in the court of Bayreuth and since 1746 in Brandenburg-Culmbach. Falckenhagen represents the late Baroque and his style is more towards the galant style. Lute compositions: *"(6) Sonate op. 1"* (1740); *"6 Partite op. 2"* (n.1742); *"6 Concerti for the lute, flute, oboe/violin and cello"* (ca.1743); *"Duetto in F for two lutes."* Also several *concertos* and *small lute pieces*.

FASCH, Johann Friderich (1688–1758), a German composer, pupil of the composer J. Kuhnau among others. Fasch worked since 1722 as the conductor of the orcestra in the court of Magdenburg. In addition to theater music he composed almost 60 instrumental concertos in the Italian concerto style, a few of which were for the Baroque lute. One of Fasch's preserved works is a *Lute Concerto D minor*. Its script is in the library of Dresden.

FRESCOBALDI, Girolamo (1583–1643), an Italian composer and organist. He got the position of the organist and singer in Accademia di Santa Cecilia in 1604. Later he worked as an organist in churches in Rome, Mantova and Florence. Frescobaldi has a central position both as an early Baroque composer and a developer of playing the organ. In his time he was praised as a virtuoso player and improviser.

Adam Falckenhagen - one of the most important representatives of German Baroque lute.

Frescobaldi published two song collections: *Il primo Libro delle Canzoni...* (Rome 1628), in which the accompanying instrument is marked to be the spinet or lute and violin, and *Il secondo libro d'Arie musicali ... una due e tre voci* (Florence 1630), where the accompanying instruments are cembalo and theorbo. Andrés Segovia has arranged an organ composition by Frescobaldi, *"Aria con variazioni"* for the guitar.

Girolamo Frescobaldi is known among guitarists for his organ work Aria con variazioni, which Andrés Segovia has arranged for the guitar.

GALLOT, Jacques (?–ca. 1690), a French lutist and composer, also known by the name *"vieux Gallot de Paris."* Both Jacques' brother, Antoine Gallot *"Gallot d'Angers"*, and his nephew (first name unknown) *"Gallot le jeune,"* were lutists. Jacques Gallot was a pupil of Ennemond Gaultier. J. Gallot's lute collection *Pièces de Luth composées sur differens modes* was published in Paris in 1670 (E. Pohlmann). J. Gallot's works are also accessible in other lute collections with the name *"Gallot de Paris"* or just *"Gallot."* Jacques Gallot's lute works are often musical pictures, for example *La Fontange* or *La Montespan.* J. Gallot's production contains several *tombeauxes* i.e. memorial pieces, which he usually has composed to honor the memory of a court member. The lutist Robert de Visée has in turn composed a *Tombeaux to the memory of J. Gallot.*

GAULTIER, Denis (1603–1672), a French lutist and composer, the most famous of the members of the Parisian lute family. The family was called *"Gaultier le jeune"* or *"Gaultier de Paris."* Denis was a cousin of Ennemond Gaultier and they are often confused, as they used to refer to themselves by the family name only. They also shared pupils, such as Dufaut and Gallot. In 1630 Denis Gaultier moved to Paris, where he studied composition under the organist of Notre Dame, Charles Racquet. Denis played the 11-13-string Baroque lute, giving concerts in the salons in Paris and in the French court. Published works by Denis Gaultier: *La Rhétorique des Dieux* (ca.1652), *Pièces de Luth* (1669) and *Livre de tabulature...* (1672). Denis Gaultier's works have been republished by Edition Minkoff Reprint Chene-Bourg, in Genoa in 1975. *Le Rhétorique... a modern print* (Libraire E. Droz, Paris 1932.)

GAULTIER, Ennemond (ca. 1575–1651), a French lutist, the developer of the French Baroque lute style, *"style brisé"* and the establisher of the D minor key tuning. Ennemond belongs to the famous family of lutists and he is also known by the name "Gaultier le vieux" or "Gaultier de Lyon." Other famous lutists of that family were his cousin Denis Gaultier (1603–1672), with whom he often was confused, Jacques Gaultier ("Gaultier d'Angleterre", late 16th century–before 1660) and Pierre Gaultier ("Gaultier de Orléans", late 16th century–ca. 1638). Jacques and Pierre are not related to him. Ennemond Gaultier worked in 1600–31 for the spouse of King Henry IV. He was sent to England in ca. 1630, where he performed to King Charles I, Queen Henrietta Maria and the Duke of Buckingham. Ennemon Gaultier's works were not published during his lifetime. The works have been reprinted by Edition Minkoff Reprint Chene-Bourg Genoa (1975).

JELINEK, Ivan (1683–1759), a Bohemian organist, lutist and composer. Worked as an organist in a Benedictine monaster. Of Jelinek's lute compositions a few dances have been survived and the guitarist Vladimír Mikulka has arranged for the guitar the Suite A major. In the museum of Prague there is a handwritten script of *Lautenpartie for the lute, French horn, violin and bass.*

KAPSBERGER, Johann Hieoronymus [Giovanni Girolamo] (ca. 1575–1650), a composer who was born in Germany but lived in Italy, a chitarrone virtuoso and lutist. He lived the first 20–25 years of his life in Venice and in ca. 1604 he went to Rome, where he quickly became famous as a virtuoso of the instruments in the lute family. He was called the *"Nobile Allemanno"* a German nobleman. After 1610 Kapsberger founded a so-called *Academy,* because of which he gave concerts and arranged meetings in his home. Kapsberger had excellent relations with cardinal Francesco Barberini, and his son Philipp Bonifaz worked for the cardinal. Johann Kapsberger has a major role in developing plucked instruments and in using ornaments in lute music and the battuto (rasgueado) technique in Baroque guitar music. He composed and published nearly 30 collections of vocal music with bass continuo accompaniment in 1609–33 and instrumental music for the chitarrone, lute and theorbo. A part of his music has disappeared. According to Ernst Pohlmann, these publications have survived: For the chitarrone: *Libro primo d'intavolatura de Chitarrone...* (Venice 1604, additional prints 1611,16,26); *Libro quatro d'Intavolatura di Chitarrone...* (Rome 1640). For the lute: *Libro primo d'intavolatura di Lauto...* (Rome 1611, reprint 1623). For the theorbo: *Capricci à due strumenti Tiorba e Tiorbino* (Rome 1617). A song collection with chitarrone accompaniment: *Libro primo di Villanella...et Alfabetto per la Chitarra spagnola* (Rome 1610, additional editions 1619,23,30); *Libro prima de Arie...* (Rome 1612, additional edition 1623); *Libro terzo di Villanella...et Alfabetto per la Chitarra spagnuola* (Rome 1619). The first and the third song collections mention also the battuto or rasgueado technique for the Baroque guitar.

KELLNER, David (ca. 1670–1748), a German organist, lutist and composer, a pupil of J.S. Bach. Kellner worked from 1711 as an organist in Stockholm in the Jacob Church and as a player of the chimes in a German church. Kellner is one of the late composers of virtuoso lute music. In 1747, 17 of Kellner's solo pieces for the Baroque lute were printed in Hamburg under *Auserlesene Lauten-Stücke.* Hubert Käppel arranged these fantasies and dances for the guitar and they were published by Chorus. The father of D. Kellner, Johan Peter Kellner, wrote a version for the tablature of "*Prelude for the lute C minor BWV 999*" by J.S. Bach.

KOHAUT, Karl (1726–1784), an Austrian lutist and composer. Worked in the state office of Joseph II as a secretary. Kohaut studied the lute under

Gottfried van Swiete and got familiar with J.S. Bach's cantatas and the oratories by Händel. According to Fétis, Kohaut was a highly appreciated lute virtuoso and his compositions, especially his lute concertos, are one of the best of his era.

For a solo lute: "Sonata D major." For a lute, violin and cello: "4 trietti (trios)." For a lute, viola and cello: "Trio." For a lute, violin and bass continuo: "Divertimento primo" (Leipzig 1761). For a lute and chamber orchestra: "8 Lute Concertos."

KREBS, Johann Ludwig (1713–1780) a German composer and organist, son of Johann Tobias Krebs. A handwritten version by J. Tobias Krebs of J.S. Bach's, "Suite E minor" BWV 996 has survived. Johann Ludwig Krebs studied composition under J.S. Bach in Thomasschule in Leipzig. In addition to that he studied lute and violin playing and claver, cembalo and organ playing. During his long career he had three positions as an organist: In Leipzig in 1737–43, in Zeitz in 1744–1755 and in the Altenburg castle in the court of Prince Friedrich. Most of his claver works were published during his lifetime. He composed two concertos for the lute: *"Concerto C major"*, and *"Concerto F major"*, of these both the Italian Ruggero Chiesa made guitar arrangements, which were published by Edizioni Suvini Zerboni.

KREMBERG, Jakob (ca. 1650–ca. 1718), a German composer with Polish roots, an instrumentalist and a poet. Kremberg studied at the University of Leipzig and worked as a chamber musician in the opera of Hamburg. Kremberg lived in several countries during his lifetime, e.g. in Sweden, Italy and England. As a bass continuo instrument he used the lute, angélique (a lute with two necks and single strings) and the guitar in his publication *Musichalishe Gemüths-Ergötzung...* (Dresden 1689). A few of Kremberg's lute works have survived.

KÜHNEL, August (1645–ca. 1700), a German viola player and composer. Served since 1661 in several courts e.g. in Zeitz, Frankfurt am Main (1669),

and München (1680–81) and as a conductor in Kassel (1695–99). In 1665 Kühnel made excursions to Paris and in 1684–85 he visited London. August Kühnel's son Johann Michael was a well-known player of gamba, violin and lute.

For a lute: "Konzert für die Laute" (library of Rostok); "Suite à Luthe solo" (Hague); "Allegro D minor" (Augsburg); "3 Konzerte für Laute, Gambe und Bass" (Brussels) (Ernst Pohlmann).

LAUFFENSTEINER, Wolff Jakob (1676–1754) an Austrian lutist. Settled in Graz in 1709 and in 1712 he was appointed the chamber lutist and servant for the court of Bavaria. He acted as a servant for the princes and taught them to play the lute and other instruments. In 1715 he followed Duke Ferdinand to Munich and later he traveled with the duke to Germany and France. As a lutist he used also the French style, the *"style brisé,"* but mainly his style represents the Italian cantabile style.

For a lute: "Sonata in A for one or two lutes, violin, viola da gamba and cello"; "Partitas and three preludes for the solo lute"; "Concerto G minor for the lute, two violins and a cello" and further three other concertos of which only the lute score has survived.

LE SAGE DE RICHÉE, Philipp Franz (late 17th century), a German lutist and composer with French roots. According to some sources he was the pupil of Charles Mouton. In 1695 he probably worked for Baron von Neidhart in Breslau.

The same year he published a lute collection, *Cabinet der Laute.* It contains almost a hundred lute pieces, which form 12 Suites. T. Wortmann published a doctoral thesis on Le Sage de Richée, *Ph.F. Le Sage de Richée und sein Cabinet der Lauten,* the University of Vienna 1919.

LOSY [LOGY] Jan Antonin Losinthalu [von Losinthal] (ca. 1650–1721), one of the best known Czech (Bohemian) lutists and composers. The family of Count Losy has its origins in Switzerland. During

1661–68 Losy studied philosophy at the University of Prague, after which he traveled to Italy and France, where he became familiar with the new French lute school and with the guitar art of F. Corbetta. In the European libraries there are almost 50 of Losy's compositions, but only one of those was published during his lifetime, his lute composition *"Courante Extraordinaire"* in his collection *Cabinet der Laute*. It was published by Philipp Franz Lessage de Richée in 1695. A German lutist, S. L. Weiss, composed a piece to honor his memory, *"Tombeau sur la Mort de Monsegineur Comte de Logi,"* in September 1721. Ed. Supraphon published J. A. Losy's guitar pieces in his suite *Musica Antiqua Bohemia* in 1979. Nowadays guitar teachers use a lot of Losy's guitar pieces, which apparently are arrangements from his lute compositions. Losy's lute music is accessible in the libraries of Berlin, Nürnberg, Brno, London, Prague and Vienna (Ernst Pohlmann).

MACE, Thomas (ca. 1613–1709) an English lutist, singer, composer and writer. In 1635 he was appointed a singer in the choir of Trinity College in Cambridge. He visited London in 1676 preparing the lute school *Musick's Monument*, which he published in 1671-75. The book is about church music, building of instruments (especially the lute) and ensemble playing. Mace's music has also been arranged for the guitar and it has been published by Edition Ricordi.

MESANGEAU [Mezangeau], René (late 16th century–1638), a French lutist, lute teacher and composer. Served in the court of France and in 1621 Louis XIII appointed him *"Musicien ordinaire du Roi"*, a title which he had until his death. Mesangeau was one of the most remarkable lutist-composers of that era. Pierre Ballard thinks of him as a developer of the new tuning of the lute at the time Renaissance was being replaced by Baroque. Mersenne used in 1636 one of Mesangeau's allemandes as an example of the new tuning. Mesangeau taught Ennemond Gaultier,

who later became very famous. Mesangeau's lute works have been published in modern prints in *Ouvres de René Mesangeau* ed. A.Souris & M.Rollin, Corpus des luthistes français (Paris 1971).

MOUTON, Charles (ca. 1626–after 1699), a French lutist and composer, probably a pupil of Denis Gaultier. He spent most of his youth in the court of Savoy in south-eastern France. In 1678 he moved to Paris and worked there as a lute teacher. One of his pupils was the famous lutist Le Sage de Richée. In the Louvre in Paris there is a painting of Mouton made by François de Troyes. The first lute collection by Mouton, *Pièces de luth sur différents Modes* was published in Paris in ca. 1698. It contains accurate finger charts for both hands. The second lute collection was published in 1699 (Ernst Pohlmann).

REUSNER, Esaias (1636–1679), a German composer and lutist. He worked in Poland in the court of Prince Radziwillowa. Since 1670 he worked in Vienna in the service of Emperor Leopold II and in 1672–74 he taught lute playing at the University of Leipzig. Since 1674 he worked for Prince Friedrich Wilhelm in Berlin. His father Esaias Reusner senior (died ca. 1660–80), also a lutist, arranged Martin Luther's *"98 protestant chorals for the lute."* E. Reusner Junior published lute tablatures *Delitae Testudinis* (1667) and *Neue Lautenfrüchte* (1676).

SAINT LUC, Jacques de (1616–ca. after 1684), a lutist from the southern Netherlands, guitarist, theorbist and composer. Served in the court of the Sun King. During 1673–84 he was a member of the Brussels chamber orchestra and took part in the first opera performance in the king's palace. A Dutchman, Constantijn Huygens, with whom Saint Luc was in correspondence, talked highly of his compositions.

For a solo lute: "Sonata in A." For two lutes: "Duet in A."

SAINT LUC, Laurent Alexandre de (1663–ca. 1700), a composer from the southern Netherlands, lutist, theorbist and guitarist, son of J. Saint Luc. Laurent Saint Luc was for some time a lutist in the chamber orchestra of Louis XIV. In 1700 he moved to Vienna to serve Prince Eugéne of Savoy. Laurent Saint Luc's lute music has been described as light and conventional. His lute pieces are listed in *Lacoste catalogue* (Amsterdam).

For a lute, flute/violin or oboe and bass continuo (Amsterdam): Four manuscripts of compositions. For the lute, violin and bass continuo: Two manuscripts of concertos. More than 200 solo lute works.

SCHEIDLER, Christian Gottlieb (ca. 1752–1815), see 'Guitar Composers'.

SEIDEL, Ferdinand (1705–?), an Austrian lutist, a well-known representative of the galant lute music. F. Seidel's *12 Minuets for the Baroque lute* were published in 1757 in Leipzig.

STRADELLA, Alessandro (1644–1682), an Italian composer, one of the most important Baroque composers in Italy. He studied singing and composing. His patron was the New Roman Brotherhood. As a composer Stradella created a basis for the Concerto grosso style, which influenced Corelli and Händel. Stradella composed almost 200 cantatas, 27 motetts and instrumental music, e.g. *"Concerto grosso D major"* for two violins, for the lute and the strings. Ruggero Chiesa has arranged it for the guitar (Edizioni Suvini Zerboni).

STRAUBE, Rudolf (1717–1785), see 'Composers of other Plucked Instruments'.

TELEMANN, Georg Philipp (1681–1767), see 'Composers Whose Music Has Been Arranged for the Guitar'.

For two lutes: "Partie Polonoise B-dur für 2 Lauten;" "Partie g-moll für 2 Lauten."

WEICHENBERGER, Johann Georg (1676–1740) an Austrian lutist and amateur composer, who worked as an accountant. He composed several pieces for the lute and concert pieces for the lute and the strings: *"Lauthen-Konzert, 6 Partiten für Laute, Violine und Bass"* (library of Bratislava). Weichenberger's lute works are also accessible in the libraries of Brno, Prague and Kremsmünster.

WEISS, Johann Sigismund (1690–1737), a German lutist and composer, younger brother of S.L. Weiss. J. Sigismund served together with his father Johann Jakob (?1662–1754) in Düsseldorf for Prince Johann Wilhelm. In 1727 Sigismund Weiss was appointed the conductor of the Chamber Orchestra and he had this position until his death. Edition Chanterelle has published J. Sigismund Weiss' *Lute Concerto*. Its manuscript is in the library of Dresden.

WEISS, Silvius Leopold (1686–1750), a German lutist and composer. Learned to play the lute from his father Johann Jakob (?1662–1754). Also his brother Johann Sigismund (1690–1737), his sister Margaretha (1690–?) and his son Johann Adolf Faustinus (1741–1814) played the lute. Since 1706 S.L. Weiss worked for Count Karl Filip in Breslau. In 1708 he traveled with Prince Alexander Sobiesky of Poland to Italy, where he stayed until 1714. In Rome he met Alessandro Scarlatti and due to his influence Weiss converted from a Protestant into a Catholic. After returning to Germany, Weiss worked in Düsseldorf and Hessen. In 1718 he gave concerts in London and that same year he got the position of the best-paid lutist in the court of Dresden. In 1739 Weiss met J.S. Bach in Dresden and they competed in improvising, Weiss with the lute and

Bach with the cembalo. The width of S.L. Weiss' lute productions can be seen in the fact that in 1767 there was an auction where Luise Gottshed's scripts were sold. They contained 53 solo partitas, 16 duets, 5 trios and 10 concertos for the lute, but unfortunately all of these have not been preserved. Nowadays two of Weiss's manuscripts are accessible, the first one in London (*28 Lute Suites*, a modern print by Edizioni Suvini Zerboni), and the other in Dresden (*34 Sonatas*, a facsimile by Edition Zentralantiquariat Leipzig). The number of surviving works is 48, because some of the works in London and Dresden are identical. Weiss's works have been

Silvius Leopold Weiss was one of the most important representatives of the 18th century lute music. He is told to have competed in improvising with J.S. Bach, Weiss with a lute and Bach with a cembalo.

arranged for the guitar, e.g. *"Fantasia"*; *"Passacaglia"*; *"Ciacona"*; *"Sonate E minor"* (D minor); *"Sonate London n:o 25 A minor L'infidéle"*; *"Tombeau sur la mort de M. Comte de Logy."* S.L. Weiss' lute works have been published in the collections *Intavolatura di Liuto, Vol. 1 & 2*, ed. R. Chiesa (Ed. Suvini Zerboni, Milan 1967–68), *34 Suiten für Laute solo*, facsimile

(Zentralantiquariat, Leipzig 1977) and S.L. Weiss (*Complete Works*), ed. D.A. Smith (Frankfurt 1980). Edition Zen-On has published 27 lute works, which are in the manuscripts in Moscow.

VISÉE, Robert de (ca. 1660–after 1720), see 'Baroque Guitar Composers'.

VIVALDI, Antonio (1678–1741), an Italian Baroque composer, one of the most important developers of instrumental concertos. Vivaldi was born and lived in Venice; in 1704–1740 he worked as a teacher, musical director and composer in the nursing home Ospedale della Pietà, which was an orphanage and music school for girls. Vivaldi got the nickname Il prete rosso or "the red priest", because he was a priest and had red hair. Vivaldi has a wide production: ca. 450 concertos, 23 symphonies and 90 sonatas. In addition to these he composed 46 operas, 39 cantatas and motetts and oratories. Vivaldi's works have been listed by Antonio Fanna in 1968 (marked with F) and Peter Ryom in 1973 (marked with RV). Vivaldi also composed concertos for the treble lute: *"Concerto con 2 violini, Liuto e Basso, D major F. XII nr. 15"*; *"Concerto à Viola d'amore e Liuto e con tutti gli strumenti sordini, D minor F. XII n:o 38."* In addition to these he also composed 2 lute trios: *"Trio per Liuto, violino e Basso C major F. XVI n:o 3"* and *"G minor F. XVI n:o 4."* The works have been arranged for the guitar. The most famous of them are *Concerto in D major* and "trios", which were composed in 1730 and are dedicated to the Count of Prague J. J. Vrtby. Vivaldi's *Mandoline Concerto "C major RV 425"* is also played with the guitar and the *Concerto for two Mandolines "G major RV 532"* is played with two guitars. In the library of Dresden there is a manuscript of the concerto for two theorbos, *Concerto con due Theorbe*.

The Baroque concertos by Antonio Vivaldi created a basis for the development of instrumental concertos. Vivaldi's Lute Concerto in D major also belongs to the favorite works of guitarists.

Composers for Other Plucked Instruments:

BACH, Johann Christian (1735–1782) a German composer, the youngest son of J.S. Bach, a pupil of Father Martini in Bologna. J.Ch. Bach worked from 1760 onwards as an organist in the cathedral of Milan and from 1763 onwards as the conductor in the King's Theatre in London. He was called with the nickname *"London Bach."* In London he composed a *Sonata* for the English guitar or chittern accompanied with the violin.

BRESCIANELLO, Giuseppe (1690–1757), an Italian composer. Worked in 1721–1751 as a conductor in the principality of Stuttgart. In addition to other works of chamber music, a manuscript by Brescianello has been found. It contains 18 sonatas and partitas for the colascione, *18 Piecen fürs Gallichone.* Colascione or gallichone is a bass lute with a long neck, a small body and almost the same tuning as in the guitar (D, G, c, f, a, d). Brescianello's works have been arranged for the guitar, e.g. *G. A. Brescianello- Complete Works* (Ed. Suvini Zerboni).

CORELLI, Arcangelo (1653–1713), an Italian violin virtuoso and composer. He also worked in Germany and in Sweden as the concert master in the court of Queen Christina. Corelli is one of the most skillful violin virtuosos ever and he had a tremendous impact on the development of violin music. Corelli also used the theorbo and chitarrone for accompanying the violin sonatas, e.g. *"Sonate (12) da chiesa... op.1"* (Rome 1681), *"Sonate studiose... op.2"* (Modena 1685), *"Sonate (12) da chiesa... op.3"* (Modena 1689), *"Sonate da chiesa... op.4"* (Bologna 1694) and *"XII Sonates..."* (London 1710). See Ernst Pohlmann.

GEMINIANI, Francesco (ca. 1687–1762), an Italian composer, violin virtuoso and theorist. He was a pupil of A. Corelli and A. Scarlatti in Naples. There are different alternatives for the year of his birth, they are in between 1679 and 1687. According to the *Grove Dictionary* he was baptized in 1687, so one could draw a conclusion that this year is close to his birth. In 1714 he moved to London and from 1749–1755 he lived in Paris. His music collection, *The Art of Playing the Guitar or Cittra...* for the chittern, was published in 1760 in Edinburgh, it contains 6 sonatas for the English guitar or the chittern with cembalo accompaniment.

HOLBORNE, Anthony (? –ca.1602), see 'Renaissance Lute Composers'.

STRAUBE, Rudolf (1717–1785), a German lutist, guitarist, player of the chittern and composer, a member of a Silesian lutist family. Straube studied at the University of Leipzig and was also a pupil of J.S. Bach. In 1759 he moved to London, where he lived until his death. Straube's tablature for the lute appeared in 1746 in Leipzig. In 1768 R. Straube published a collection for the English guitar (C major third tuning), of which Chanterelle has published a modern version. The collection contains *Three Sonatas* for the guitar, cembalo or cello; *Two Sonatas* for the English guitar and violin; *32 Exercises and Songs* accompanied with the English guitar.

TELEMANN, George Philipp (1681–1767), an important German Baroque composer. In the 18th century he was better known than J.S. Bach. Telemann used the colascione as an accompanying instrument in two of his concertos: *"Concert a Fl. traverse ou 2 Violons concert avec 2 violins, viola, Calchedon ou Basson e Clavecin"* and *"Concert a 2 Fl. traverse avec 2 Violins, Viole, Calchedon et Basse."* The manuscripts of these works are accessible in the library of Dresden. See also 'Composers Whose Music Has Been Arranged for the Guitar'.

VIRCHI, Paolo (ca. 1550–1610), an Italian organist, lutist, player of the chittern and composer. The first information about Virchi is available in the cover of a chittern tablature published in 1574, where he calls himself a Brescian organist. In the preface of a collection from 1580 he calls himself the organist and instrumentalist of the Prince. He taught music for the children of the Prince. In Ferrara Virchi was appointed the organist of the court of Mantova in 1598, and he had that position until his death. Virchi was a remarkable composer of madrigals, whose compositions created a basis for e.g. Luca Marenzio and Claudio Monteverdi. Virchi published a collection for the chittern, *Il primo libro di tabolatura di citthara...* (Venice 1574). It contains 10 madrigal arrangements, 7 canzona arrangements and 4 dances and 27 fantasies etc.

MUSIC FOR THE LUTE, VIHUELA AND BAROQUE GUITAR
BY 20TH CENTURY COMPOSERS.

BORUP JÖRGENSEN, Axel (born 1924). For a mezzo sopran and lute (or guitar): "3 Old Chinese Poems op. 103 No. 1" (1983).

DODGSON, Stephen (born1924). For two lutes: *Sketchbook for Two Lutes* (1983). For a sopran, bass and for a solo lute: *Music's Duel* (a cantata for the poems by Richard Crashaw,1985).

FONGAARD, Björn (1919–1980). For a vihuela/Renaissance lute/Baroque guitar (1 player), drums and a tape: "Sonata for Historical Instruments, Percussion and Tape op. 141" (1977).

For a Renaissance lute and tape: "Concerto op. 131 No. 39" (1976). For a Baroque lute, flute, oboe and tape: "Concerto op. 131 No. 31" (1976);

LUTYENS, Elisabeth (1906–1983). For a tenor and a lute: "Dialogo op. 88" (1972).

KARKOFF, Ingvar (born1958). For a lute (or alto guitar): *Fyra stycken für luta/altgitarr* (1985)

HOSOKAWA, TOSHIO (born1955). For a solo lute: "Intermezzo" (1991).

RECHBERGER, Herman (born 1947). For scene machinery, slides and lute: "Tree-O" (1975).

RODRIGO, Joaquín (1901-1999). For a sopran, piccolo flute, cornet and vihuela: "Despedida y soledad"; "Espera de Amado"; "San Juan y Pascua" (from suite Liricas Castellanas, 1980)

TAKEMITSU, Toru (1930–1996). For a flute, guitar and lute: "Ring" (1961). For a flute, guitar, vibraphone and antique cymbals (3 players): "Sakrifice" (1962).

ABLÓNIZ, Miguel (1917-2001), an Italian guitarist, pedagogue and composer, born in Cairo into a Greek-Italian family. Started to play the guitar by himself at the age of 8 by playing the guitar schools of Carulli, Carcassi, etc. Later he studied in Barcelona with Emilio Pujol. Since 1953 Ablóniz taught guitar playing in Milan in Italy and in the Ithaca College in New York. He published a noticeable amount of guitar schools, e.g. *50 Arpeggios for the Right Hand, Essential Exercises for the Left Hand, 10 Melodia Studies*. He also composed and arranged almost 350 pieces for the guitar. Most of Ablóniz's solo guitar works are small Latin American style pieces.

For a solo guitar: "Sonata del Pórtico, An Incorrigible Dreamer", bossa nova; "Arietta Medievale"; "Back from Pernambuco", bossa nova; "Blues for Rosy"; Brazilian Ragtime; "2 Capricci; Malagueña"; "Capriccio Flamenco"; "Guitar choro"; "3 Ritmos sudamericanos"; "4 Bagatelle"; "Tango andaluz"; "Tarantella Burlesca & Bossa Nova"; "You and Me", waltz and samba. For two guitars: Divertimento.

ABRAHAMSEN, Hans (born 1952), a Danish composer who first studied the French horn. He studied composing with Pelle Gudmunsen-Holmgreen, Niels Viggo Bengtson and Per Nørgård

Photo © Per Morten Abrahamsen

Hans Abrahamsen

in the Århus Academy of Music. Abrahamsen was a member in the *"Gruppen för alternativ musik"* and *"Lungby unge Tonekunstnere,"* which opposed the Darmstadtian aesthetics in the 1960s. He first adopted a simplicity typical of folk music, which opposed modern influences. Later he combined the elements of tonal traditions with newer phenomena.

For a flute and a guitar: "Double" (1975). For song, flute, guitar and cello: "Efterar" (1970–72) For a voice (soprano), flute, alto saxophone, guitar and percussion: Aria (1979). For a flute, clarinet, guitar, percussion, piano, violin and cello (part II contains a guitar 'vocal' section without text): "Winternacht" (1987).

ABRIL, Antón García (born 1933), a Spanish composer. Abril studied piano playing in the Music Academy of Valencia. He continued his studies in the Music Academy of Madrid and in Accademia Chigiana in Siena studying with Vito Frazzi and conducting with von Kempe. Since 1974 he has been the teacher of composition in the Music Academy of Madrid. As a composer, Abril has specialized in theater and film music, in which he has been productive and received several prizes. Anton Abril became interested in the guitar because of Ernesto Bitetti. Bitetti has both performed and recorded Abril's guitar compositions, which are dedicated to him.

For a solo guitar: "Fantasía Mediterránea"; "Vademecum I & II, 24 piezas"; "Plantón y Topata"; "5 Evocaciones"; "Dedicatoria." For a guitar and an orchestra: "Concierto Mudéjar" (1985); "Concierto Aguediano" (Bitetti's recording 1979).

ABSIL, Jean (1893–1974), a Belgian composer, studied in the Music Academy of Brussels and composition with Paul Gilson. Jean Absil had the position of the leader of the Etterbeck Music Academy in 1922–58 and since 1930 he was a professor in the Music Academy of Brussels. As a composer Absil was influenced by Milhaud, Hindemith, Schoenberg and Bartók. Polyphonic writing, polytonality and in parts polyrhythms are typical of his

compositions. Absil had a central position in the music life of his country as a performer of new music, etc. In 1936 he established the concert series *"La Sirène"* to help young artists in their career. Absil composed several works in the modern and new classical style.

For a solo guitar: "10 Pièces op.111" (1962); "Suite op. 114" (1963); "Pièces caractéristiques op. 123" (1964); "Sur un paravent chinois op. 147" (1970); "Quatre pièces op. 150" (1970); "Petit bestiaire op. 151" (1970); "10 Pièces op. 159" (1972). For two guitars: "3 Pièces op. 119" (1963); "Suite op. 135" (1967); "Contrastes pour deux guitares op.143" (1969); "Scherzo." For a guitar and an orchestra: "Concerto pour guitare et petit orchestre op. 155" (1971).

AGUADO [y GARCÍA], Dionisio (1784–1849), a Spanish guitar virtuoso, composer and guitar pedagogue. Aguado was born in Madrid April 8, 1784. Two days later he was baptized in the church of San Millán. He spent his childhood in Madrid. Already as an eight-year old Aguado studied Latin, philosophy and French, and in addition to that started to take guitar lessons from a monk, Padre Basilio. He (his real name was Don Miguel García) was one of the famous guitarists and a good teacher in his time. Aguado's mother's maiden name was María García, and people have wondered whether Aguado and his teacher were related. It is thought that Aguado studied humanities and worked as a paleographer in the court of Castille. This is not a reliable statement, but his writings indicate that he was highly educated. After his father died in 1803 Aguado moved with his mother to live on the farm that he inherited. It was located in the village of Fuenlabrada, about 22 kilometers (ca. 14 miles) south of Madrid. In 1808, when France attacked Spain, Aguado, unlike his colleague Fernando Sor (1778–1839), did not take part in the war, but took care of his farm and studied the techniques of playing the guitar. After the war Aguado moved back to Madrid with his mother. In 1824 Aguado was a famous guitarist, who in 1819 had composed his first collection of etudes, *Colección de Estudios* (published in ca.

1819–20). In 1825 he published a thorough guitar school, *Escuela de Guitarra*, where the new ideas about the possibilities of the guitar can be seen. In 1826 Aguado moved from Madrid to Paris and lived in Hôtel Favart, where Fernando Sor also lived (the hotel still exists). They became friends and performed together in at least three concerts, and a proof about their friendship is a guitar duet by Sor, *"Les Deux Amis"* op. 41, where the first and the second guitars are marked with names *"Sor"* and *"Aguado."* Also Sor's *"Fantaisie"* op. 30 and *"Fantaisie villageoise"* op. 52 are dedicated to Aguado. Sor had a wide musical education and was active in different fields of music also taking part in politics, whereas Aguado, despite his education and sophistication, was more a guitarist and did not compose works other than guitar solos. Aguado dedicated his whole life to guitar playing and the development of its technique. Unlike his friend Sor, Aguado was one of the first guitarists who in his right-hand plucking technique used his nails. This technique is still dominant among guitar players today. He was also one of the first guitarists to take his finger off the lid. The old habit of leaning to the lid with the little finger was still in use. It was used by Carulli, Carcassi and Molino. Aguado also invented equipment to make the playing easier, such as a new stand, which still is in use, and a tripodi, a three-legged stand. With the help of it the guitarist does not have to hold the guitar with his hands and thus does not stifle the vibration with his body. Aguado has described the use of tripodi as follows: "The guitar is as much insulated as possible…The player has a perfect control over both hands' physics… The position of the player is natural and charming, the most suitable and elegant for women…" (*Nuevo Método para Guitarra* p. 7). Nevertheless, the tripodi did not establish its position among guitarists.

A friend of Aguado, François de Fossa (1775–1849), a talented guitarist and composer, translated Aguado's school *Escuela de guitarra* into French and it was published in Paris in 1826

with the title, *Méthode Complète pour la Guitare*. "We may estimate that this French book has best made Aguado known at this time." (B. Jeffery p. xii). The next guitar school by Aguado was published in Paris in 1834 called, *Nouvelle Méthode de Guitare, op. 6* and it was meant for amateurs. Aguado describes his school as follows: "In this work I have wanted to offer an opportunity to those that love the guitar to learn pleasant pieces in a short time",

Dionisio Aguado was interested in developing the guitar playing technique and he wrote excellent guitar schools. He was among the first guitarists to use nails when playing. In the picture Aguado uses the tripodi he invented.

and he continues: "By using this book you can reach satisfactory results already in six months" (B. Jeffery p. xiii). After about eleven years in Paris Aguado returned to Madrid in 1837 and lived there teaching and preparing his guitar school *Nuevo Método para Guitarra*, which was published in 1843 and its appendix, *Apéndice al Nuevo Método*, in 1849/50.

Aguado's *Nuevo Método para Guitarra*, which was one of the most

important guitar schools in the 19th century (and later), is, because of its several editions, historically important when studying the development of the techniques. The book contains the basis of the modern technique, and it is often thought that it was invented by the guitarists that have lived after Aguado. He died in Madrid December 20, 1849. Aguado's works can be found in a publication by Chanterelle, *Aguado's Collected Guitar Works* (ECH 800).

For a solo guitar: *Collección de estudios* (Madrid, 1820); "Douze valses op. 1"; "Trois Rondo (sic) Brillants op. 2"; "Huit petites pièces op. 3"; "Six petites pièces op. 4"; "Quatre andantes et quatre valses op. 5"; "Valses faciles op. 7"; "Contredances et valses faciles op. 8"; "Contredances non difficiles op. 9"; "Exercices très faciles et morceaux agréables non difficiles op. 13"; "Dix petites pièces non difficiles op. 14"; "Le Menuet affandangado op. 15, Le Fandango Varié op. 16"; an arrangement from Sorin Gra's solo op. 14; For the solo guitar without an op. number: "Douze Walses"; "Marche militaire & Thème varié"; "Muestra de Afecto y Reconocimento (Seis valses)"; "Allegro"; "Variaciónes"; "Variaciónes Brilliantes"; "Colleción de Andantes, Valses y Minuetos"; "Valses caractéristiques." Aguado's arrangement: "Grand Solo (F. Sor op. 14.)"

AHO, Kalevi (born 1949, Finland), studied the violin in the Music Institute of Forssa, in the youth department of the Sibelius Academy in 1965–68 and also composition with Einojuhani Rautavaara and got the diploma in 1971. He continued to study composition with Boris Blacher in 1971–72 in West Berlin. Kalevi Aho worked as a lecturer in musicology at the University of Helsinki in 1974–1988 and as an acting professor at the Sibelius Academy. Aho also writes about music, and he has discussed ethical matters and questions concerning the composer's world view. He established a place among the most important composers in Finland as an exceptional young man.

Kalevi Aho is as a composer keen

on wide shapes and his music is described as massive and full of emotions, and he often combines different styles with opposite emotions. Instrumentally his works are often very demanding. His production is comprised of 11 symphonies, 3 chamber symphonies, and 4 operas: "Avain (the Key)" and "Hyönteiselämää (Insect life)." It also includes concertos for a violin, piano and cello, and also chamber music and solo works. Aho has composed a *Quartet* for a flute, alto saxophone, guitar and percussion (1982). In this three-part work the sixth string of the guitar is tuned half a degree lower and the guitar is also played with a bow. The rhythmic and melodic parts are virtuoso. The instruments try in turn to get musically closer to each other and in turn they try to show their own natural way of playing.

For a flute, alto saxophone, guitar and percussion: "Kvartetto" (1982).

ALBRIGHT, William [Hugh] (1944-1998), a composer from the United States. Studied in the Juilliard School in 1959–62 and at the University of Michigan in 1963–70, after which he studied in Paris from 1970 onwards with Oliver Messiaen. Albright worked as a professor in composition at the University of Michigan. Selective serial music is typical of him.

For a solo guitar: "Shadows" (1977).

ALMEIDA, Laurindo (1917–1995), a Brazilian guitarist, composer and arranger. In his youth he took piano lessons from his mother, who was a concert pianist. Almeida made his debut as a guitarist at the age of 13 and performed on the radio at the age of 15. He gave concerts in Brazil and Europe, where he heard jazz guitarist Django Reinhardt play and became interested in jazz. From 1947 onwards Almeida worked in Hollywood and played with several well-known jazz musicians and joined the jazz band of Stan Kenton. He left the band in 1950 and continued to play as a solo guitarist and concentrated on composition. Almeida has composed more than 200 pieces for the guitar, and as an arranger he has made guitar reper-

toire much more accessible. He has recorded for Capitol and Decca and in 1966 was the first American to record the *"Guitar Concerto"* by Villa-Lobos and *"Concerto de Copacabana"* by Gnattali. In the 60s, he was the first to bring Bossa Nova into the United States and has also been in cooperation with the Modern Jazz Quartet.

For a solo guitar: "Amazonía"; "Baa-Too-Kee"; "Berimbau Carioca"; "Brazilliance"; "Chôro e Batuque"; "Chôro Fino"; "Chôro para Olga"; "Escadoo"; "Garoto"; "Guitarriana (18 solos)"; "Insomnia"; "Obstinacy"; "Samba Chôro for Liona"; "Sueño"; "Bossa Guitarra (6 solos)"; "Amor flamenco"; "Contemporary Moods", ym. For two guitars: "A la Viana"; "6 Famous Serenades"; "Vistas de los Angeles"; "Tango Alegre"; "Malagueña Pomposa"; "Serenata Española"; "Soleares." For three guitars: "Brazilliance"; "Discantus, Divertimento"; "Rio Rhapsody." For a guitar and an orchestra: "Amazonia"; "Concerto no. 1."

AMBROSIUS, Hermann (1897–1983), a German composer, choir leader and music pedagogue. He studied composition in Berlin with H. Pfitzner. Ambrosius worked as a teacher of the theory of music in the Music Academy of Leipzig and as a reporter for the Leipzig Radio. He composed 13 symphonies, 20 concertos and chamber music. As a composer he was influenced by folk music.

For a solo guitar: "a sonata E"; "Sonatines: A, G; Suites: a, C, G; 2 inventios"; "Impressionen." For three guitars: "5 Bagatellen"; "Eggerberger Trio." For a guitar and an orchestra: "Konzerte no. 1"; "Konzerte n:o 2."

AMY, Gilbert (born 1936), a French composer and conductor. Studied since 1954 in Conservatoire National de Supérieur with Oliver Messiaen and Darius Milhaud. Getting to know Boulez became crucial in respect of Amy's esthetic attitudes. Amy worked since 1973 for French Radio and TV as a musical leader and in 1976–81 as the conductor of The New Philharmonic Orchestra of the French Radio and since 1984, as the director of the Music

Academy of Lyon. Amy's works are often performed in the festivals of modern music in Europe and in the concerts of new music. Amy has used the guitar in his vocal works. For solo quitar: Quasi une toccata (1981).

APIVOR, Denis (1916-2004), an Irish composer with Welsh roots. Got his first musical upbringing when being a singer in the choir of Christ Church College, Oxford. Apivor studied medicine at the University of London, as a composer he learned the art of composing through self-study. When he was 21 years old he took private lessons from Hadley and Rawsthorne. Since 1948 he has been interested in the 12-tone technique, which became his composition style. Apivor has published a book called *An Introduction to Serial Composition for Guitarists.*

For a solo guitar: "Variations op. 29 (1956)"; "Discanti op. 48 (1970)"; "Saeta op. 53 (1972)"; "Ten Pieces op. 72"; "Nocturne op. 78 (1984)." For a violin and a guitar: "Ten String Design op. 44 (1968)." For voice and a guitar: "Seis canciónes de F. García Lorca op. 8." For a guitar and keyboards: "Liaison op. 62 (1976)." For a flute, guitar and viola: "Cinquefoil op. 79 (1984)." For two percussions, marimba, hammond, guitar and a double bass: "Crystals op. 39 (1965)." For a guitar and an orchestra: "Concertino op. 26 (1954)." For a guitar and a chamber orchestra: "The Tremulous Silence (El silencio ondulado) op. 51 (1972)."

APOSTEL, Hans (1901–1972), an Austrian composer, a remarkable representative of the "second school in Vienna." Apostel first studied music in his home town, Karlsruhe, then studied in Baden to be a conductor and studied composition in Vienna since 1921 under Arnold Schoenberg and Alban Berg. Apostel worked in Vienna as a composer, composition teacher and a publication chief. He was granted the title of a professor in 1948 and the *"Great State Prize of Austria"* in 1957. Apostel's style varied from the tonal late Romanticism to atonal Expressionism and through free dodecaphony later ending in strict seriality. For a solo guitar: "Sechs Musiken op.

25." For four guitars: "Er waren zwei Königskinder, op. 10 n.o 3"; "Höhe des Jahres, op. 29." For a flute, viola, guitar and double bass: "Studie op. 21." For a flute, viola and guitar: "Studie op. 29"; "Kleines Kammarkonzert op. 38 (1958 rev. 1964)."

ARCAS, Julián (1832–1882), a Spanish guitarist and composer. Received lessons of classical guitar from his father who had been a pupil of D. Aguado. Arcas acted as a school mediant between Aguado and Tárrega being the teacher of the latter. Julian Arcas probably belonged to the first guitarists, who in classical guitar music started to use the *"apoyando"* technique, which already was in use in flamenco music. Arcas was also interested in the structure of the guitar and he worked in cooperation with the guitar builder Torres in 1860–70. He made concert visits to Spain and Europe in general and performed for the royal family in Brighton in England in 1862. Arcas lived in Barcelona since 1864, and visited other cities of Europe giving concerts, some of them with the pianist Celestino Patanas. In 1870 he moved to Almeria, where he worked almost 10 years as a grain merchant. After this he again became interested in the concert career, which ended in 1882 when he fell ill. Arcas's music is mainly based on traditional Spanish folk music and flamenco. Arcas composed and arranged over 50 solo pieces for the guitar.

Julian Arcas

Malcolm Arnold dedicated Serenade op. 50 to Julian Bream, here arranged for guitar and piano.

For a solo guitar: "Estudio en sol mayor"; "Estudio en la menor"; "Andante y estudio, Prudent-Arcas"; "Preludio de la opera Guillermo Tell"; "Preludio en re mayor"; "Minuetto en sol mayor"; "Minuetto en mi menor"; "Mazurca La saltarina"; "Mazurca Gaetana"; "Vals Manuelito"; "Vals El fagot"; "Vals Tanda de valses"; "Vals Il bacio Arditti Arcas"; "Polonesa en mi menor"; "Polaca Fántastica"; "Fantasía La favorita"; "Fantasía El Delirio"; "Fantasía La Batalla"; "Fantasía Fausto"; "Fantasía sobre la Traviata de Verdi"; "Fantasía sobre motivos heterogéneos"; "Fantasía sobre el paño"; "Fantasía Ballo in Maschera"; "Sinfonía Mi segunda epoca"; "Sinfonía Marta, Bellini-Arcas"; "Sinfonía Norma, Bellini Arcas"; "Variaciónes sobre un tema de Sor"; "Capricho El Incognito"; "Andante"; "Rondó"; "Sueño de Rosellen"; "Trovador"; "Lucia de Lammemor"; "Motivo Barbero de Sevilla"; "Tango-sobre 'Marina'"; "El postillón de la Rioja"; "Visperas Sicilianas"; "Marcha Fúnebre, Thalberg-Arcas." Populares: "Soleá"; "Rondeña"; "Bolero en la menor"; "Boleras"; "Los Panaderos-Bolero"; "Murcianas"; "El madrileño-Chotis"; "Jota Aragonesa." Tangos: "Collección de Tangos"; "Tango-Guayabito"; "Tango-La cubana"; "La Rubia de los lunares Habanera, Iradier-Arcas." For two guitars: "Fantasía sobre Rigoleto"; "Soleares populares"; "Populares La Rubia de los lunares Habanera, Iradier-Arcas."

ARNOLD, Malcolm (1921-2006), an English composer. In his childhood he took violin and trumpet lessons. Later he studied composition in the Royal College of Music and played the trumpet in the London Philharmonic orchestra. He also studied orchestration with G. Jacob. As a composer he was noted in 1943 because of his overture *"Beckus the Dandipratt"*; the actual breakthrough were two symphonies, which are influenced by Sibelius (1949, 1953). In 1948 he was granted a Mendelssohn Scholarship, by means of which he studied one year in Italy. Arnold was one of the most versatile composers of his generation. His production contains a lot of orchestral and chamber music, and also film music, of which the most famous is the

Malcolm Arnold

soundtrack of *"Bridge Over the River Kwai,"* which received an Academy Award, and which Arnold composed in ten days.

"Guitar Concerto op. 67" was composed in 1958–59 and it was first performed by Julian Bream and the Melos in the Aldenburgh Festival in 1959. The concerto is dedicated to Julian Bream, and as time has passed it has become a classic among guitarists and friends of guitar music. The concerto has been instrumentated for the flute, clarinet, French horn and the strings. The guitar solo lacks the typical 'Spanish' conventional features; it resembles more the English lute music from the Baroque era. The second part is the central part in the concerto. It is a kind of elegy and a homage of respect to the French gypsy guitarist Django Reinhardt, whom Bream greatly admired. It looks back on Bream's time in the army, when he played in a jazz group.

For a solo guitar: "Fantasia op. 107" (1970–71). For a guitar and an orchestra: "Concerto op. 67" (1958–59), dedicated to Julian Bream. For a guitar and a chamber orchestra: "Serenade op. 50" (1955).

ARRIGO, Girolamo (born 1930), an Italian composer. Studied in the Music Academy of Palermo with Belfiore among others and took a diploma in French horn playing and in composition. He has lived in Paris, New York and Berlin. Arrigo has been succesful in several composition contests.

For a solo guitar: "Serenata" (1962).

ASAFJEV, Boris (1884–1949), a Russian music researcher and composer, pseudonym *"Igor Glebov."* He studied harmonization in 1904–10 in the Music Conservatory of St. Petersburg with Nikolai Rimski-Korsakov and composition with Anatoli Ljadov. Asafjev also studied at the University of St. Petersburg and took in 1908 a degree in history and linguistics. He acted since 1910 as the correpetitor in the Mariinski Theater in St. Petersburg and from 1925 onwards as the professor in music history, theory and composition in the Music Academy of Leningrad. Since 1943 he was the professor in the Music Conservatory of Moscow and the head of the research institute. As a music researcher Asafjev has become famous through his intonation theory, which he presented in his works "Muzykalnaja forma kak protsess" (Musical form as a process, 1930) and "Intonatsija" (Intonation, 1947). Asafjev is regarded as the founder of Soviet music research. His compositions include operas, ballets, orchestral, chamber and solo music.

For a solo guitar: "12 Preludes"; "2 Etudes"; "6 Romance"s; "Theme & Variations"; "Prelude & Valse." For a guitar and an orchestra: "Concerto" (1939), the concerto is accessible in the library of Ivan Putilin in the Sibelius Academy.

ASENCIO, Vicente (1908–1978), a Spanish composer and music teacher, taught e.g. Narciso Yepes. His favorite composers were Maurice Ravel and Domenico Scarlatti. Asencio has stated that he is not interested in atonal music, and that each composer should find a way of expressing himself and a composing technique that pleases himself. His tonal composition style is largely based on the folk music of eastern Spain.

For a solo guitar: "Danza valenciana"; "Elegía y Sonatina"; "Suite valenciana"; "Suite Mística: Getsemani, Dipsô, Pentecostés"; "Tango de la casada infiel"; "Collectici Intim" (5 pieces, 1970).

AURIC, Georges (1899–1983), a French composer. Graduated from the Music Conservatory of Paris in 1913 and studied composition with d'Indy in Schola Cantorum in 1914–16. During these years he got to know Satie, Milhaud and Honegger.

For a solo guitar: "L'Hommage à Alonso Mudarra."

AZPIAZU, José de (1912–1986), a Spanish (Basque) composer, arranger and guitarist. Azpiazu started to play the guitar under the guidance of his uncle at the age of 13. In his youth he was a very enthusiastic painter, and in addition to that he was very active in the Basque national culture association. Azpiazu's career as a guitarist began at the age of 24 after a debute in Radio Bilbáo. Since then he concentrated on guitar playing and gave concerts frequently. In 1950 Azpiazu met the son of Andrés Segovia, painter Andrés Segovia, junior in Switzerland on a concert tour. This is how he also got to know Maestro Segovia, and due to his recommendations Azpiazu got a vacancy as a teacher at the University of Music in Genoa. In addition to his pedagogic work Azpiazu is known as an arranger and a composer of guitar music.

For a solo guitar: "Cachucha"; "Cubana"; "Fandanguillo de Huelva"; "4 Preludes chinois"; "Five Iberian Miniatures for Guitar"; "Jota on popular themes"; "Minué del Baztán Errimina-Nostalgie"; "Six Children's Stories"; "Theme with Variations-Homage to Sor"; "Tonadilla - Homage to Granados." For a flute and guitar: "Sonata Basque." Azpiazu's arrangements for the guitar: "Enrique Granados's 12 Danzas Españolas op. 37"; "Lutoslawski's 9 Melodies populaires." For guitar and ochestra Concerto Baroque.

BABBITT, **Milton Byron** (born 1916), a composer and theorist from the United States. He started to play the violin already at the age of four and played later the clarinet and the saxophone. Babbitt studied mathematics at the University of Pennsylvania and music at the University of New York with Philip James and Marion Bauer among others. He first studied composition by himself and later with Roger Session at the University of Princeton, where he later also taught. He was interested in the music of Varèse and Stravinsky and already in the early 40s he studied the production of the "New school in Vienna," Schoenberg, Berg and Webern and their composition technique based on the 12-note system. Babbitt, who had got acquainted with mathematics, reached very quickly the position as one of the most remarkable theorists in the 20th century and established new theoretic terms to music, originating from mathematics, such as 'combinatoriality' and 'set'. Babbitt also belongs to the pioneers of electronic music. From the early 1950s onwards he worked with the synthesizer of RCA and was one of the developers of its new model, Mark II, and from 1959 on he worked as the leader of the Columbia-Princeton electronic music studio. He has applied the results of his theoretic study to his compositions and had a major influence on the development of serial and electronic music in the United States.

For a solo guitar: "Composition for guitar"; "Scheer Pluck" (1984). For two guitars: "Soli e duettini." For a voice and a guitar: "4 Cavalier Settings."

BACARISSE, Salvador (1898–1963), a Spanish composer, graduated from the Music Academy of Madrid as a pianist and composer. Bacarisse was a member in the group of Spanish composers, *"Grupo de los Ocho."* After the Spanish Civil War he worked since 1939 in the French Radio producing Spanish programs. The influence of Spanish folk music can be heard in his music.

For a solo guitar: "Ballade"; "Passepied II"; "Petite suite"; "La Fille aux yeux d'or." For a solo guitar and an orchestra: "Concertino op. 72" (1953).

BADINGS, Hénk (1907–1987), born in Java, where his Dutch father worked

as a colonial officer. He had to move to the Netherlands at the age of eight, as an orphan. There he got his education. His wish to follow a musical career met with strong opposition from his guardian, who forced him to train at the Technical University in Delft. He graduated with honors in 1931. In addition to his technical studies he studied music by himself, until Willem Pijper took him as a pupil. Badings taught in the Music Academies of Rotterdam and Amsterdam and he was the head of the Conservatory of Haag in 1941–45, after which he was a free composer. Badings is one of the pioneers of electronic music in his country (since 1952), and the interest he had in technology can be seen in some of his works where he uses the 24-31 parted tunings. A romantic pathos and a diatonic writing are typical of his style.

For a solo guitar: "12 Preludes" (1961). For a flute and guitar: "Sonata" (1983). For a violin and guitar: "Introduction, Theme and Variations" (1983). For a guitar and organ: "It is Dawning in the East, Balladesque Variations on an Old Dutch Love Song" (1967). For a flute, guitar and viola: "Trio no. 9" (1962). For a clarinet, cembalo, guitar, violin and cello: "Quintet no. 6" (1986).

BALLIF, Claude (1924–2004), a French composer, studied in the Music Academy of Bordeaux (1942–48) and after that in Paris with Oliver Messiaen, Tony Aub and Noël Gallo (1948–51) and in Berlin with Boriher (1953–55). Ballif avoids conventional solutions in his music and has developed a "metatonality", which is based on an 11-tone scale. In 1971–90 he acted as a professor of composition and musical analysis in the Music Conservatory of Paris.

For a solo guitar: "Solfeggietto op. 36 no. 6" (1976).

BARRIOS FERNÁNDEZ, Angel (1882–1964), a Spanish (Granada) guitarist and composer; first studied violin and played in an orchestra. F. Barrios was among the best guitarists in his country, and he also mastered the flamenco guitar. He taught a few years in the Music Academy of Granada. F.

Barrios is one of the most colorful personalities in guitar music. He played with a metal string guitar and he is told to be the first to record classical guitar music.

Barrios has composed many works which are based on Spanish folk music, and have the form of Spanish folk dances such as sevillana, farruca, jota etc.

Chanterelle has published 44 of F. Barrios's solo guitar compositions: *Complete Works* (Ed. Estrellas).

For a solo guitar: "Aben Humeya, danza árabe"; "Angelita, tango"; "Cantos andaluces"; "Ferruca gitana"; "Guajira"; "Zacateque."

BARRIOS MANGORÉ, Agustín Pio (1885–1944), a Paraguayan guitarist and composer, who is among the most colorful personalities in guitar music. He was born to a family that appreciated music and literature. Barrios was very young when he started to take guitar lessons, and his first teacher, Gustavo Sosa Escalda, made him familiar with the guitar schools of Sor and Aguado and Arcas's and Tolsa's compositions. Barrios amazed people with his skills and already at the age of 13 was granted a scholarship to the Colegio Nacional Asunción, where he, in addition to music, studied mathematics, literature and journalism. He was also a talented graphic artist. As a many sided cultural personality Barrios spoke many languages: Spanish,

Guaran (the national language of Paraguay), English and German and was very interested in philosophy, poetry and theosophy. In 1910, when he had already established his position as a guitar virtuoso, he went for a week's tour to Argentina. Due to the great popularity the tour was prolonged and it lasted for no less than 14 years! He gave concerts in almost all countries in Central and South America. In the early 1910s Barrios was the first in the world to record guitar music. Barrios was an excellent improviser and there were many stories about his spontaneous improvisations in the concerts. From his mother's side he was a member of the Guarani Indian tribe and later he used a nickname *"Nitsuga Mangoré - the Paganini of the guitar from the jungle of Paraguay"* (Nitsuga is Agustín the wrong way round, Mangoré is a noble family name among the Guarani). In 1934–36 Barrios gave concerts in Belgium, Germany, Spain and Portugal. Barrios was at first taught by an Italian musician living in Paraguay, Niccolino Pellegrini, later he completed his studies with the help of the *Musical Lexicon* by Hugo Riemann. Barrios's guitar compositions often contain styles from Baroque, Classisism and Romanticism. In addition to the small pieces (valse, etude, prelude), variations, rondos and potpourris he often uses the forms of folk music (e.g. chôro, estilo, habanera, etc.). His music combines a thorough knowledge of harmony and the use of the possibilities of the guitar. Barrios composed about 300 guitar pieces, of which 92 manuscripts and 43 printed pieces have been preserved and also almost 90 arrangements on European and Latin American music (R. Stover: *Six Silver Moonbeams*: p. 230-36). Some of his compositions have influences from the music of Bach (*"La Catedral"*), some have a more programmatic quality (*"Un sueño en la Floresta"* "A dream on a flower field", *Las Abejas* "Bees")") and some are influenced by the Latin American folk music and the popular music of his time (*"Mazurca Apasionata, Vals op. 8 No. 3,"* "Aire Zamba,"* etc.). Barrios's influence on the guitar music in the Latin America has been great. He was the inspirer of a whole generation including Raúl

Borges, Antonio Lauro, Isaias Savio and Heitor Villa-Lobos. His production contains preludes, etudes, minuets, gavotts, waltzes, mazurkas and romances.

A large number of Barrios's works have been published by Zen-On and Belwin Mills. Richard Stover has published a biography of Barrios, *Six Silver Moonbeams* (1992). Recordings: *Agustín Barrios guitar recordings* 1910–42 parts 1-3, Chanterelle (CHR 011, 012, 013).

For a solo guitar: "Abrí la Puerta Mi China"; "Aconquija" (Aire de Quena); "Aire de Zamba"; "Aire Popular Paraguayo" (Caazapá); "Allegro Sinfónico"; "Altair"; "A Mi Madre"; "Arabescos"; "Armonías de America"; "Canción de Cuna"; "Canción de la Hilandera"; "Capricho Español"; "Chôro de Saudade"; "Confesión" (Confissado de Amor); "Contemplación"; "Córdoba" (Cordobesa); "Cueca" (Danza Chilena); "Danza en Re Menor"; "Danza Guaraní"; "Danza Paraguaya no. 1"; "Dinora"; "Divagación"; "Don Perez Freire"; "El Sueño de la Muñequita"; "Escala y Preludio"; "Estilo Uruguayo"; "Estilo"; "Estudio" (A); "Estudio de Concierto"; "Estudio del Ligado" (A); "Estudio del Ligado" (d); "Estudio en Arpegio"; "Estudio en Si Menor"; "Estudio Inconcluso"; "Estudio No. 3"; "Estudio No. 6"; "Estudio para Ambas Manos"; "Estudio Vals"; "Fabiniana"; "Gavota al Estilo Antiguo"; "Humoresque;" "Ja Che Valle"; "Julia Florida" (barcarola); "Junto a tu Corazón"; "La Catedral"; "La Mabelita"; "La Samaritana"; "Las Abejas"; "Leyenda de España"; "London Carapé"; "Luz Mala"; "Madrecita"; "Madrigal"; "Maxixe"; "Mazurca Apasionada"; "Medallón Antiguo"; "Milonga"; "Minuets A"; "A"; "B"; "C"; "E"; "Oración" (Oración de la Tarde); "Oración por Todos"; "País de Abanico"; "Pepita"; "Pericón"; "Preludio op. 5 no. 1"; "Preludios E"; "a"; "b"; "c"; "e"; "Romanza en Imitación al Violoncello" (Página d' Album, Fuegos Fátutos); "Santa Fe"; "Sargento Cabral"; "Sarita"; "Serenata Morisca"; "Tango no. 2"; "Tarantella" (Recuerdos de Nápoles); "Tua Imagem"; "Una Limosna por el Amor de Dios"; "Un Sueño en la Floresta" (Souvenir d'un Rêve); "Vals de Primavera"; "Vals op. 8 no. 3"; "Vals op. 8 no. 4"; "Variaciónes sobre un Tema de

Tárrega"; "Variaciónes sobre El Punto Guanacasteco"; "Vidalita con Variaciónes"; "Villancico." For a solo guitar (no manuscript): "Adieu"; "Aire Brasilero"; "Aires Andaluces"; "Aires Criollos" (Aires Sudamericanos, Aires Americanos); "Allegro Brillante"; "Arrullo"; "Bicho Feo"; "Barcarola de los Recuerdos"; "Cajita de Música"; "Canzoneta"; "Concerto en Fa"; "Chora Cavaquínho"; "Diana Guaraní"; "Danza Macabra"; "El Arroyo"; "El Carrousell"; "El Hijo Pródigo"; "Estudio" (a); "Fiesta de la Luna Nueva" (Invocación a la Luna); "Flavito" (chôro); "Flores Murchas"; "Gloria e Amor"; "Gran Jota"; "Gran Marcha Heróica"; "Habanera"; "La Bananita"; "La Calesita"; "Lalita"; "Loreley"; "Minuet" (D); "Pantheismo"; "Poema de América"; "Pot-Pourri Lírico"; "Rapsodia Española"; "Rapsodia Latinoamericana"; "Recuerdos del Pacífico"; "Salteñita"; "Saudades do Rio de Janeiro"; "Trémolo Estudio"; "Triste"; "Untitled Romanza in D"; "Vals no. 2"; "Zapateado Caribe." For two guitars: "The voices for the second guitar composed by Barrios: J.S. Bach"; "Allemande"; "Minuet"; "Napoléon Coste: Etyd op. 38 no. 22"; "Moreno Torroba: Danza Castellana"; "Aguado: Estudios"; "Leccións"; "Parras de Moral: Lección no. 3"; "Lección no. 6." For three guitars: "Zapateado Caribe."

BARTOLI, René (born 1941), a French guitarist and composer. The winner of the guitar contest arranged by the French Radio (ORTF) in Paris in 1959. Studied under Presti-Lagoya and Andrés Segovia. Bartoli teaches in the Conservatory of Marseilles and has published records.

For a solo guitar: "Aubade"; "Étude No. 1"; "Vals e-moll"; "Divertissement I, II"; "Préludes."

BARTOLOZZI, Bruno (1911–1980), an Italian composer, theorist and violin player. He graduated with honors from the Conservatory of Florence in violin playing, conducting and composition. Bartolozzi composed using the 12-tone technique and he became famous as a pioneer in using different styles when playing the woodwinds.

for Paula and Eliot

MOUNTAIN SONGS

Edited by Eliot Fisk

Robert Beaser

1. Barbara Allen

©1984 by Helicon Music Corporation
By permission of the Publishers SCHOTT MUSIK INTERNATIONAL, Mainz.

Robert Beaser's Mountain Songs for a flute and guitar consists of eight parts and it is based on American folk music. The duration of the work is ca. 30 minutes.

For a solo guitar: "Adles" (1977); "Ommagio à Gaetano Azzolina" (1972); "3 Pezzi" (1952). For a flute, viola, guitar and percussion: "Repitu." For a violin and guitar: "Serenata." For three guitars and an orchestra: "Memorie per tre chitarre concertanti."

BASHMAKOV, Leonid (born 1927), a Finnish composer. Studied piano playing, conducting and composition in the Sibelius Academy in 1947–54 with Aarre Merikanto. Acted as the principal of Tampere Music Conservatory in 1979–92 and as the conductor of the Tampereen Työväen Teatteri Orchestra in 1960–84. Bashmakov has focused on absolute orchestra works, he has composed six symphonies and seven concertos.

For an accordion and a guitar: "Jomaha" (1992).

BAUMANN, Herbert (born 1925), a German composer and conductor. Studied in the Berlin International Music Institute with Paul Höffer and Boris Blacher. In 1947–53 he was the conductor of the Berlin German Theater. Since 1971 he was the musical leader of the Bayerisches

Staatsschauspiel Theater. Since 1979 he has been a free composer. Baumann has composed theater and chamber music for solo instruments and orchestras.

For a solo guitar: "Toccata, elegia e danza"; "6 Miniaturen." For a mandolin and a guitar: "La Ricordanza." For a female choir and a guitar: "Contrasti" (1961); "Die Moritat vom eigensinnigen Eheweibe" (1968). For a guitar and a string quartet: "Memento." For an oboe, bassoon and guitar: "Sonatine über finnische Volkslieder." For a guitar and an orchestra: "Konzert." For two guitars and an orchestra: "Würzburg Concerto."

BAYER, Johann Gottlieb Eduard (1822–1908), a German guitarist. In 1848–1857 Bayer gave concerts in most West European countries. He published three guitar schools. He used the pseudonym *A. Caroli.*

For a solo guitar: "Raccolta op. 1." For two guitars: "Ländler op. 37"; "Souvenir d'Ems op. 20." For a flute and a guitar: "Duo"; "12 Waltzes op. 8." For a voice and a guitar: "3 Romanze."

BEASER, Robert (born 1954), a composer from the United States. Studied literature, philosophy and music at the University of Yale (doctor's degree in 1986). He studied composition under Toru Takemitsu and Goffredo Petrassi. Beaser also studied conducting and acted as the conductor of Musical Elements and conducted over two hundred premieres of new works in New York. He is the youngest American composer who has won the *"Prix de Rome Prize."*

For a solo guitar: "Canti Notturni"; "Notes on a Southern Sky" (1980). For a flute and a guitar: "Mountain Songs" (1984); "Il est né, le Divan Enfant."

BEDFORD, David (born 1937), an English composer, started to compose at the age of 7. Bedford has studied in London at the Royal Academy of Music with Lennox Berkeley and in Venice with Luigi Nono. After returning from Italy he taught at the Queen's College in London and played the organ in pop groups. Bedford became famous in the 1970s through his chamber music.

For a solo guitar: "You asked for it" (1969). For two guitars: "Verses and choruses" (1986). For two electric guitars: "18 Bricks left on April 21st "(1967). For a flute and a guitar: "Memories of Ullapool" (1987). For a soprano and 10 guitars: "Nurse's Songs with Elephants" (1971). For a guitar, flute, b-clarinet, violin, cello, double bass and a piano: "A Horse, His Name was Hunry Fencerwaver Walkins" (1973). For an electric guitar, bass guitar, percussion and an orchestra: "Star's End" (1974). Bedford also used the electric guitar in his chamber music work "The Ones Who Walk Away from Omelas" (1976).

BEHREND, Siegfried (1933–1990), a German guitarist. Took lessons in piano playing and conducting, became interested in the guitar at the age of 16. He gave guitar concerts around Europe and his records were published by Deutsche Grammophon. Siegfried Behrend was also known as a guitar pedagogue when teaching in the Music Academy of Berlin. He arranged numerous lute pieces and

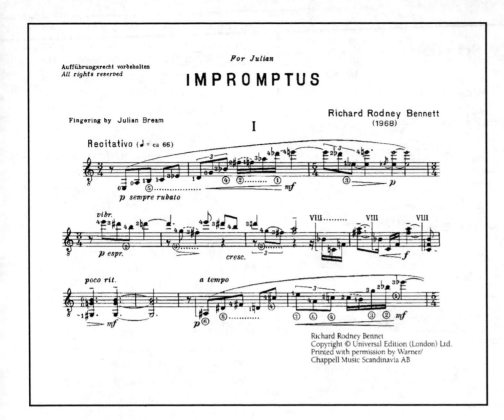

Aufführungsrecht vorbehalten
All rights reserved

For Julian

IMPROMPTUS

Fingering by Julian Bream

Richard Rodney Bennett
(1968)

I

Recitativo (♩ = ca 66)

p sempre rubato

mf

p

vibr.

p espr.

cresc.

VIII   VIII   VIII

f

poco rit.

a tempo

mf

p

mf

Richard Rodney Bennet
Copyright © Universal Edition (London) Ltd.
Printed with permission by Warner/
Chappell Music Scandinavia AB

Bennett uses the 12-note technique in his 5 Impromptus.

classical works and edited the works by the composers of the 20th century.

For a solo guitar: "Chôros Brasileira"; "Danza Africana"; "Danza B"; "Danza Giapponese"; "Danza Greca"; "Danza Inglese"; "Danza Spagnola" (n:ot 1-3); "Danza Tedesca"; "Danza Turca"; "Die Guitarren von Quimet"; "Flamenco Fantasía"; "Greensleeves Fantasía"; "6 Monodien"; "Movimenti"; "Non te Escaparas"; "2 Pezzi per Jim"; "3 Pieces"; "Porque fue sensible" ("Capriccio after Goya"); "Postkarten Suite no. 1 and no. 2"; "Solearilles"; "Solo for Leo Brouwer"; "Sonata on a Japanese Folksong"; "Suite for Isao Takahashi"; "Suite in style of Old Lute Music"; "Tarantella Italiana, Traditional Brunei"; "Trianas"; "Zambrillas"; "Zorongo-danza Mora"; For two guitars: "Arabische Serenade"; "Leipziger Suite"; "Japanese Serenade"; "Jota Aragonesa, Scena Andalusa"; "Serenata española Stiekampfmusik." For five guitars: "Meditation"; "The Mocks in Italy." For a flute and guitar: "Haiku-Suite"; "Legnaniana"; "Spielmusik"; "Triptychon." For a voice and guitar: "Impressionen einer Spanischen Reise"; "Suite espagñola no. 6." For

two guitars and a voice: "Trimorphia." For two mandolines, a mandola, guitar and bass: "Conga für Zuporchester." For a flute, guitar and chamber orchestra: "Konzert Legnaniana."

BELLINATI, Paulo (born 1950), a Brazilian guitarist and composer. Studied guitar playing in the São Paulo Music Academy with Isaias Savio and later with Abel Carlevaro and Oscar Cáceres. Bellinati lived six years in Switzerland, where he continued his studies in the Music Academy of Genoa and taught in the Music Academy of Lausanne. In addition to the classical guitar, Bellinati also plays the cavaquínho (a Brazilian soprano guitar), violão caipira (a 10-string guitar) and violão de seresta (a primitive Brazilian guitar). He has, as a multi-instrumentalist, composer and researcher of music, specialized in Brazilian music. Bellinati's compositions and arrangements are based on the traditional Brazilian rhythms, such as lundu, chôro, bāiao, maxixe etc.

For a solo guitar: "Chôro Sapeca"; "Chôro Sereno"; "Jongo"; "Modinha"; "Suite Contatos"; "Un Amor de Valsa"; "Valsa Brilhante." For two guitars:

"Jongo."

BENGUEREL, Xavier (born 1931), a Spanish composer, mainly auto-didact. His composition style is influenced by Bartók and Schoenberg. Benguerel's success began in the 1960s, when his music was played at several festivals of modern music in Berlin, Zagreb, England, etc.

For a solo guitar: "Cantus" (1982); "Versus" (1974). For two guitars: "Stella Splendens." For four guitars: "Vermelia" (1976). For a guitar and an orchestra: "Concerto"; "Tempo."

BENNETT, Richard Rodney (born 1936), an English composer, also lived in the United States. His father was a famous children's author and his mother a composition pupil of Gustav Holst. R.R. Bennett started to write music when he could barely read. He graduated from the Royal Academy of Music in 1957 studying with Lennox Berkeley and Howard Ferguson, after which he studied two years in Paris with Pierre Boulez. In 1965 he was elected the composer of the year by the English Association of Composers. In 1970–71 he taught composition in Baltimore at the Peabody Institute. Bennett's production includes among other things orchestral, ballett, chamber and vocal music and music for film and the tele-

Richard Rodney Bennett

Photo: Maarit Kytöharju

*Erik Bergman belonged to the pioneers
in Finnish guitar music, he composed a suite
for the guitar already in 1949.*

vision. In the 1960s he composed concert works classified as "fancy jazz", which also influenced his other production. Bennett has been described as a master of many styles and techniques as a composer.

Bennett's solo guitar work dedicated to Julian Bream, *"5 Impromptus"*, has established its position among the central guitar compositions. Also his *"Guitar Sonata" (1983)* – a solo guitar work, which lasts for 18 minutes, is dedicated to Bream, who performed it for the first time for the public in the Scheltenham Festival in 1985 and played the London premiere in Wigmore Hall in 1986. Bennett's "Five Impromptus" and a "Sonata" are composed using the 12-note technique, all the 12 notes are used in the melody in the order the composer gives.

Jim Tosone has done a research on R.R. Bennett's Impromptus and Sonatas, *An Analysis of Richard Rodney Bennett's Guitar Music*, which was published in the American magazine *Guitar Review*, summer issue 1996.

For the solo guitar: "5 Impromptus" (1968); "Sonata" (1983). For a tenor and a guitar: "Lament" (1960). For a guitar and a chamber orchestra (flute, oboe, English horn, bass clarinet, French horn, trumpet, 2 percussionists, celesta, string trio): "Guitar Concerto" (1970), dedicated to Julian Bream.

BERGMAN, Erik (1911-2006), a Finnish composer. Studied composition in Helsinki with Erik Furuhjelm and Bengt Carlson (diploma 1938) and abroad in Berlin, Vienna and Ascona in 1954 with Wladimir Vogel. He also studied musicology and took piano lessons from Ilmari Hannikainen. Bergman was appointed to the Finnish Academy of Arts in 1982. He has been characterized as an expressionist, rhythmist and colorist, who searches his ideas from both chronologically and locally distant cultures. He was enthusiastic experimenter and searcher of new instruments and as an independent pioneer belonged to the leading people of Finnish music life.

Bergman was a pioneer of Finnish guitar music. He composed the first remarkable Finnish solo guitar work, *"Suite pour guitare op. 32"* (1949). This guitar work, which was technically ahead of its time, is dedicated to a Swiss, Hermann Leeb, who taught Bergman the secrets of the guitar. Bergman's second work for the guitar is from 1977, *"Midnight op. 83"* for the solo guitar, which is more avant-garde than *"Suite op. 32"* and written without bars. Mikko Heiniö has described Bergman's

"Midnight" as follows: "The palette of tone colors shines in the Midnight. We can hear tremolos resembling the mandoline, trumming on the strings and the body, glissandos, flageolets, tones damped in different ways etc. The most dramatic effects are the Bartók pizzicati, where the string is splashed onto the fingerboard, a noise resembling that of a iron saw, made by scratching a metal string with a spoon, and an destructive effect resembling the breaking of a coffee service set, which is made by strumming low strings that are lifted on top of each other." The technique described above is called the 'snare drum'. *"The Dialogi"* (Dialogue) for the flute and guitar (1977) belongs to the pearls of the Finnish modern flute-guitar literature. The work is composed without bars. The passionate conversation between the instruments is formed by the fast chords, glissandos, repetitions and free melodies of the guitar and the flute. Also, *"Janus op. 92"* for the violin and guitar (1982) is composed without bars and the composer expresses the tempos of different sections in seconds. In this work Bergman uses the technical possibilities of the guitar in both demanding and creative ways. "Janus", which lasts over 20 minutes, refers to a two-headed mythical creature of the ancient world.

For a solo guitar: "Suite pour guitare op. 32" (1949); "Midnight op. 83" (1977). For a flute and a guitar: "Dialogi

Photo: Clive Barda

Sir Lennox Berkeley

© Bèrben

Sir Lennox Berkeley produced several excellent guitar compositions.

op. 82" (1977). For a violin and a guitar: "Janus op. 92" (1982). For a flute, alto saxophone, guitar and percussion: "Mipejupa op. 96" (1981), dedicated to the Chamber Orchestra, Cluster.

Hector Berlioz

BERIO, Luciano (1925–2003), an Italian composer. He was born into a musical family and at first studied with his organist and composer father. Berio studied serial technique with Luigi Dallapiccola and graduated in 1951 from the Music Academy of Milan. He established a new studio for electronic music to the Radio of Milan, Studio di fonologia, and acted as a musical leader in it. From 1956 onwards he acted as a leader of a concert series Incontri Musicali and as a reporter in a magazine with the same name. In 1962–72 Berio taught composition in the USA in the Juilliard School of Music. Since 1976 Berio acted as the artistic leader of the Rome Academic Philharmony. His music is avant garde and experimental.

For a solo guitar: "Sequenza XI" (1988).

BERKELEY, Sir Lennox (1903–1989), an English composer, half French in origin. Studied linguistics and organ playing in the Merton College in Oxford. Encouraged by Maurice Ravel he completed his studies in Paris in 1927–33 with Nadia Boulanger, who in addition to Stravinsky's neoclassicism has most influenced Berkeley's music. At the same time other music personalities were present in Paris, such as Francis Poulenc, whom Berkeley got to know, and Aaron Copland, Albert Roussel, Arthur Honegger and Darius Milhaud. In Paris, Berkeley converted into Catholism, which also affected his works (e.g. "Missa Brèvis op. 57"). In 1942–45 he worked as a producer of BBC's music programs and composed a great deal of radio and film music. Berkeley has acted 25 years as a professor of composition in England in the Royal Academy of Music. His pupils have been Nicholas Maw and Richard Rodney Bennett, who also has composed several guitar pieces. Berkeley belongs to the most remarkable composers of the 20th century in Great Britain and he was raised to nobility in 1974.

Berkeley's compositions have been described as French fancy and they have shared features with Jacques Ibert's and Francis Poulenc's music. There his natural English characteristics meet with elegance, charm, clearness of structures and avoidance of pomposity. In the late 1950s, Berkeley's style changed from tonality towards a greater complexity. As a guitar composer Berkeley has had connections to Julian Bream and Angelo Gilardino, to whom he has dedicated some of his works.

Berkeley's composition style can be described as instrumental without worn cliches. In *"Sonatina op. 51"* there are three parts, Allegretto, Lento and Rondo, the duration of the work is about 11 minutes. The traditional and the modern way of composing are combined in it. *"Theme and Variations"* (1970) for the solo guitar has, thanks to its natural idiomacy of the guitar, reached a stable position in the repertoires of guitarists. Due to its technical difficulty this excellent concert piece is suitable to be played at an early stage of professional guitar studies.

For a solo guitar: "Sonatina op. 51" (1957), dedicated to Julian Bream; "Theme and Variations op. 77" (1970), dedicated to Angelo Gilardino. For a voice (tenor) and a guitar: *"Songs of*

Gilbert Biberian is a productive guitar composer, who has written both solo and chamber music for pedagogic and concert use.

the Half-Light" op. 65, dedicated to Peter Pears and Julian Bream. For a guitar and an orchestra: *"Concerto" op. 88* (1974), dedicated to Julian Bream.

BERKELEY, Michael (born 1948), an English composer, the eldest son of Sir Lennox Berkeley. Michael was a choir boy at the Westminster Cathedral in his childhood, and it was very crucial for his later development. Later he attended the Royal Academy of Music in London, where he studied composition, song and piano playing. After that he continued his composition studies with Richard Rodney Bennett. In addition to orchestral, opera and chamber music, Michael Berkeley has also composed pieces for the guitar.

For a solo guitar: "Impromptu" (1985); "Sonata in One Movement" (1982); "Lament" (1980); "Worry Beads" (1981). For a recorder and a guitar: "Pas de Deux" (1985). For a violin and a guitar: "A Mosaic for Father Popieluszko" (1985). For two guitars and orchestra: "Double Guitar Concerto" (2004).

BERLIOZ, Hector (1803–1869), a French composer. Berlioz can be regarded a self-learned composer although he was born to a musical family. The guitar and the flute were the only instruments that he played, and he also mentions the guitar in his encyclopedic book about instruments, *Traité d'Instrumentation et d'Orchestration* (1843). In this book Berlioz mentions that it is impossible to write guitar music without knowing the possibilities of the instrument. In his youth Berlioz also acted as a guitar teacher and it can be assumed that the guitar has had an influence on his compositions. For the guitar, Berlioz composed etudes, which Aulagnier published in Paris in the 19th century. Berlioz also used the guitar in his numerous operas, such as *"Béatrice et Bénédicta Benvenuto Cellini"* and in the *Serenade of Mephistopheles* in his work *"Eight Scenes from the Faust."* For a voice and a guitar: *"25 Romances"* (arranged by Berlioz, published by Edit Chantarelle ECH 513).

BETTINELLI, Bruno (1913–2004), an Italian composer. Studied piano playing in the Music Academy of Milan, from which he graduated in 1937. He taught there since 1941 as a teacher in harmonization and since 1957 as a teacher in composition. "Bettinelli started his career as a composer in tonal style but has later moved towards a more modern voice. What is typical of his music, originating from Bartók and Hindemith, is the tendency to give importance to hand work in a constructive manner, a steady command of the bass continuo and a clear handling of the rhythm" (P. Petazzi).

For a solo guitar: "Come una cadenza"; "5 Preludi da concerto"; "Sonata breve, 12 Studi, Improvvisazione"; "Quattro pezzi"; Notturno. For two guitars: "Divertimento à due." For a voice (high) and a guitar: "2 Liriche Autunno-Il Tempo."

BIBERIAN, Gilbert (born 1944), a British composer, guitarist and guitar pedagogue, who was born into a Greek-Armenian family in Istanbul. He has lived in England since 1959. Biberian studied guitar playing in the Trinity College, from which he graduated in 1968. After a successful premiere in Wigmore Hall he got a chance to work in the London Symphonietta and other leading orchestras with Pierre Boulez, Luciano Berio and other famous musicians. Biberian has established and conducted two chamber music ensembles, *Omega Players* (10 guitars, singers and keyboards) and *Omega Guitar Quartet*, to which he has composed music. Biberian has studied composition under James Patten, Elisabeth Lutyens and Hans Keller. Biberian taught guitar playing at the Trinity College in London until 1996, when he became a freelancer artist and teacher in Sheltenham. Biberian has composed a lot of both solo- and chamber music works for the guitar.

For a solo guitar: Songs of the Seasons (1965); "Greek Suite" (1965); "Six Preludes 6 Fugues"; "Sonata no. 1"

Luigi Boccherini, the cellist and chamber composer of the Spanish Prince Don Luis, wrote several quintets for the guitar and string quartet.

(1967); "Sonata no. 2" (1975); "Sonata no. 3" (1977); "Monogram" (1977); "Colombine" (a ballet 1978); "Six Haiku" (1980); "Intro & Dance" (1981); "24 Preludes" (1983, 4 volumes); "Four Waltzes"; "Technical Studies" (6 volumes); "Sonata no 4" (1986); "Intermezzo" (1986); "Anagram" (1989); "Threnody" (1991); "Sonata no. 5" (1994). For two guitars: "Sonata no. 1" (1967); "Sonata no. 2" (1973); "Pierrot" (1978); "Once Upon A Time..." (1985); "Sonata no. 3" (1984); "Gradus Ad..." (1989). For three guitars: "Harlequin" (1982); "Harlequin's Toccata" (1984). For four guitars: "Suite no. 1" (1967); "Quartet in C Sor-Biberian" (1971); "Eight Waltzes" (1971–75); "Quartet no. 1" (1972); "Quartet no. 2"; "Primavera" (1973); "Quartet no. 3" (1977); "Quartet no. 4" (1979); "Greek Serenade" (1973); "Suite no. 2" (1981); "Prims no. 2" (1970). For a flute and a guitar: "1st Sonata" (1976); "2nd Sonata"–(1982); "Folklore II" (1994). For a violin and a guitar: "Otara" (1988). For a viola and a guitar: "Folklore III" (1994). For a cello and a guitar: "Eight Bagatelles" (1974). For a cembalo and a guitar: "Waltzes"

(1980). For a voice and a guitar: "Epigrammes" (a high soprano & a guitar, 1967); "Cantos Nuevos" (for a speaker, tenor and a guitar, to Lorca's poems, 1967); "Upon Julia's Clothes" (for a soprano and a guitar, 1966); "The Sick Rose" (for a soprano and a guitar, 1967). Other chamber music works: For a soprano, a flute, piano, recorder, string trio, string orchestra, 2 brass trios and percussion: "Angelus" (1975). For a flute or an ocarina (1 player), 6- and 10-string guitars (2 players), percussion and voices: "Haiku" (1980). For a French horn (in F) and a guitar: "Capriccio" (1994). For two flutes, percussion and 8 guitars: "Petit Fantasie" (1987). For two guitars, a harp, vibraphone, congo drums (2 players), double bass & sticks & stones: "The Innocent Fox" (1990). For a guitar and an orchestra: "Concerto" (1985). For a cello, guitar and a string orchestra: "Double Concerto" (1989–92).

BLYTON, Carey (1932–2002), an English composer, a close relative of the author Enid Blyton. Studied at the Trinity College of Music in London in

1953–57 and received a bachelor of music degree in 1957. After that he continued his studies in the Music Academy of Copenhagen under Jörgen Jersild. Blyton has, in addition to his composition work, acted as a choir leader, a teacher at the Trinity College of Music and for different publishing companies (Mills and Faber). He has also composed music for films and television. *"In Memoriam John Dowland"*, for a voice and an orchestra, can be considered his main work.

For a solo guitar: "In Memoriam Scott Fitzgerald op. 60b" (1972); "In Memoriam Django Reinhardt op. 64a" (1972); "Saxe Blue op. 65b" (1974); "The Oceans of The Moon, a theme and eight variations op. 75" (1975); "The Bream op. 51" (1967); "Two Japanese Pieces op. 68" (1974); "Yugen op. 80" (1978). For a guitar and an electric guitar: "Bach Chat" (1967).

BOBROWICZ, Jan Nepomucen (1805–1881), a Polish guitarist and composer. Studied in Vienna with Mauro Giuliani in 1816–19. After a short career as a solo player he worked as a secretary in the senate of Cracow and voluntarily joined the Polish army in 1830. Since 1832 he worked in Leipzig as a publisher of Polish books and performed in Gewandhaus together with the violin player Karol Lipinski, the pianist Clara Wieckin etc. Franz Liszt called him *"The Chopin of the guitar."* In addition to his *Guitar School* he has composed ca. 40 compositions for the guitar.

For a solo guitar: "Fantasies on opera themes"; "Variations op: 6, 7, 10, 12, 13, 16, 18, 20, 30"; "Grand Potpourri op. 21"; "Marches op. 19, 25"; "Distraction Rondeau op. 17"; "Rondo Brilliant op. 17"; "Poloneses and Waltzes op. 11 and 24." For a flute and a guitar: "Souvenir de Pologne." For a cello, guitar or a piano: "Grand Potpourri" (composed in co-operation with J.B. Goss).

BOCCHERINI, Luigi (1743–1805), an Italian composer, cellist and guitarist. Boccherini's father played the double bass and Luigi started the career of a cellist and composer and at the age of 13 he succesfully gave concerts in his home town Lucca. Boccherini continued his studies in Rome (1757) and made many concert tours to Venice and performed in the court in Vienna. In 1766 he went for a concert visit to Paris, where the travel continued to Spain in 1768 due to an invitation by the ambassador of the country. In 1770 Boccherini got the vacancy of the cellist and chamber music composer of Crown Prince Don Luis, and later Fredrik Vilhelm II of Prussia appointed him as his chamber composer. He was paid annually for quartets and quintets, but lost the vacancy when Fredrik Vilhelm died.

The birth of the Classicism in the late 18th century can be seen in Boccherini's music. The features of tone color, rhythm and forms make him an original composer. In his music he has used ingredients of the Spanish folk music (e.g. fandango), like Domenico Scarlatti before him. For a long time all that was known about his production was a minuet of a string quintet, which with the numerous arrangements was the musical symbol of the Rococo.

Boccherini used the guitar in his work *Simphonie Concertante in C Major op. 41*", which was composed on the basis of the material of the String Quintet op. 10 no. 4 and dedicated to Marquise Bénavente. Boccherini also composed chamber music for a string quartet and *"Quartetto d'Archi con Chitarra"* for the guitar. He marked them as composed by himself, *"Maestro da Lucca."* Also these works were dedicated to Marquise Bénavente, who was a famous amateur guitarist. The exact number of Boccherini's quintets is unknown, but it is known that in 1904 there was an auction in Berlin, and nine of his guitar quintets were sold there, six of them to the United States Congress Library and three to the Munich Guitar Association. Two of the quintets were identical (the so-called Fandango Quintet's D major material). In these guitar quintets Boccherini used the musical material of his own trios op. 14 no. 3 and piano quintets op. 56, 57, (nos. 2, 4 and 5). The guitar quintets were apparently composed in 1798–99, when he wrote to a publisher (Playel) telling that he had new guitar quintets. It is known that in 1811 the French guitarist and composer François de Fossa, who served as an officer in

Madrid, got Boccherini's quintets to be copied, the quintet *"Variazioni su la Ritirata di Madrid."*

Six of Boccherini's quintets (the Washington Scripts) have been published as reprints by Edizioni Suvini Zerboni: G 445-450 no. 1 d, no. 2 E, no. 3 B, no. 4. D (the so-called Fandango Quintet), no. 5 D, no. 6 g. The guitar quintets owned by the Munich guitar association have been published by Edizion Zimmermann: *"Ersten Quintett"*; *"Fandango-Quintet D"*, *"Zweites Quintett C"* (Ritirata di Madrid), *"Drittes Quintett E."* Julian Bream has arranged the "Fandango Guitar Quintet D" for the guitar and cembalo. The cellist Caspar Cassadó has in co-operation with Andrés Segovia arranged Boccherini's Cello Concerto E major for the guitar.

For a guitar and a string quartet: "6 Quintets: no. 1 d, G 445"; "no. 2 E, G 446"; "no. 3 B, G 447"; "no. 4. D (the so-called Fandango Quintet), G 448"; "no. 5 D, G 449"; "no. 6 g, G 450." "Quintett e, G 451"; "Quintett C (Ritirata di Madrid), G 453." An arrangement for a guitar and a cembalo: "Introduction & Fandango (from a Guitar Quintet no. 4 G 448), arr. Julian Bream." An arrangement for a guitar and an orchestra: "Concerto in E major, arr. Cassádo/Segovia."

BOGDANOVIĆ, Dusan (born 1955), born in Yugoslavia, now an American guitarist and composer, started his musical studies in Yugoslavia and studied composition in the Music Academy of Genoa under P. Wissmer and A. Ginastera and guitar playing under M.L. São Marcos. Bogdanović won the first prize in 1975 in the Genoa contest and made his debut in the Carnegie Hall in New York in 1977. Today he works as a teacher of improvisation, harmonization and composition in the Music Academy of San Francisco. Bogdanović said in an interview for the Italian guitar magazine *Il Fronomo* that in his compositions he is close to improvisation, and that it is a shame that some of the music academies have become museums of music. The most famous works by Bogdanović are Crow (*ballet-poema*), composed for the Pacific Dance Company and *Lyric Quartet*, composed for the Los Angeles Guitar Quartet.

For a solo guitar: "Lento and Toccata" (1978); "Introduction, Passacaglia and Fugue" (1989); "5 Miniatures Printanieres" (1980); "6 Pieces Enfantines" (1977); "Sonata no. 1" (1978); "Blues and 7 Variations" (1982); "Jazz Sonata" (1982); "Sonata no. 2" (1985); "Four Bagatelles" (1985); "Castles of the White City" (1988); "Sharon's Songdance" (1989);

Photo: Per Dybro Sørensen

The Danish guitar composer Axel Borup-Jørgensen has used the 12-note technique in several of his guitar compositions.

"Polyrythmic and Polymetric Studies" (1990); "Raguette no. 1-2" (1991–2); "My Eternal Green Plant" (1991); "Six Balkan Miniatures" (1993); "Jazz Sonatina" (1993); "7 Easier Polymetric Studies" (1993); "Omar's Fancy" (1994); "Little Café Suite" (1995); "Mysterious Habitats" (1995); "A Fairytale with variations for guitar solo" (1995); "7 Little Secrets for guitar solo" (1995); "Unconscious in Brasil"; "Variations on 'Estudio sin Luz'"; "Grashopper Maker's Song"; "Counter-point in 3 voices and Improvisation in the Renaissance Style." For two guitars: "Three Straws" (1987); "Sonata Fantasia" (1990); "No Feathers on this Frog" (1992); "Winter Tale" (1992); "Furioso" (1992). For a guitar and a harp: "Of Toys and Cookies" (1988); "Metamorphoses" (1993). For a solo guitar or a guitar and a harp: "Yano Mori." For a solo guitar and two prepared guitars: "Trio" (1989). For a guitar, percussion and a prepared guitar: "Trio" (1989–91). For three guitars: "Pastorale no. 1" (1991). For four guitars: "Lyric Quarte" (1993). For a cello and a guitar: "Quatre pièces intimes" (1980). For a guitar and a double bass: "Lullaby for Angel Fire" (1992). For a voice and a guitar: "Little Café Suite" (1995); "Mistral Songs" (1991); "6 Native American Songs" (1994). For a mezzo soprano, a flute and a guitar: "Pure Land." For a tenor, flute, double bass and a guitar: "Crow ballet" (1990). For a flute, bassoon, cello and a guitar: "Deep Voices" (1982). For a guitar and strings: "Concerto" (1979).

BOLDYREV, Igor (1912–1980), a Russian composer. Started his musical studies at the age of 14 in the Music School of Sverdlovsk and continued his studies in the Music Conservatory of Leningrad (now St. Petersburg) since 1937 and later in the Music Conservatory of Moscow with Dimitri Shostakovich graduating in 1945. Matanya Ophee has published Boldyrev's music in the collection, *The Russian Collection, Vol. 5: Soviet Guitar Music.*

For a solo guitar: "Long Drawn Out Song"; "2 Musical Moments"; "Sonata"; "Monologue"; "Scherzo"; "Old Romance."

BOLLING, Claude (born 1930), a French composer. He got his musical upbringing in Nice and in Paris. In his composition style he has combined classical and guitar music. Duke Ellington noted Bolling's interest in American jazz music and because of him Bolling made recordings together with Lionel Hampton and Kenny Clark. Bolling has made arrangements for Liza Minelli, Juliet Greco and has composed music for French films. In 1970 he wrote a *Suite for a flute and a jazz trio*, in 1977 a *Suite for the violin and a jazz trio* (piano, double bass and drums). That same year Bolling wrote a concerto for the classical guitar and a jazz trio, which is performed by Angelo Romero and George Shearing's jazz trio.

For a solo guitar: Sonate. For a flute, guitar and a jazz trio: "Picnic Suite" (7 parts). For a guitar, piano, double bass and percussion: "Concertino" (1977).

BOLOCOM, William (born 1938), a composer from the United States. Studied at the University of Washington in 1949–58 starting as a special student at the age of 11. He completed his studies at Mills College in Oakland with Darius Milhaud in 1949–58 and in Paris with Oliver Messiaen in 1959–61 and took part in the Darmstadt courses.

For a solo guitar: "Seasons" (1974).

BONDON, Jacques (born 1927), a French composer. He studied violin and conducting in École César Franck in Paris and composition in the Music Conservatory of Paris with Darius Milhaud and Jean Rivier in 1948–1953. He has worked as the artistic leader of Ensamble Moderne de Paris and in the music administration of the French Radio ORTF and as the conductor of the orchestra of the French Radio and Television.

For a solo guitar: "3 Nocturnes (1971), Swing no. 2" (1972). For two guitars: "Les Folklores Imaginaires." For a soprano and a guitar: "3 Complaintes." For a flute, violin and guitar: "Les Folklores Imaginaires-Suite no 2." For a guitar and an orchestra: "Concerto de Mars" (1966); "Concerto con fuoco."

BORGES, Raúl (1888–1967), a Venezuelan composer, guitarist and pedagogue. Borges taught several world famous guitarists and composers, such as Alirio Diaz, Antonio Lauro and Rodrigo Riéra. Union Musical Española has published several of his compositions.

For a solo guitar: "Canción Antigua, melodia"; "Canción de cuna in D"; "Canción de cuna in G"; "El criollito, vals"; "Estudio"; "Fuente morisca"; "Marisol, valse venezolano"; "Vals sobre motivos franceses"; "6 Venezuelan Pieces."

BORUP-JØRGENSEN, Axel (born 1924), a Danish composer, who was brought up in Linköping in Sweden. He studied piano playing in the Music Academy of Copenhagen since 1946 with Anders Rachlew and harmonization with Jørgen Jersild and Poul Schuerbeck. As a composer he is mainly self-taught. At first Borup-Jørgensen composed in a free tonal style, which had a shade of diatonality and resembled the style of Bartók. In the late 1950s he became interested in the music of the "New school of Vienna," he studied the works of Schoenberg and Webern and took part in the Courses of modern music in Darmstadt in 1959 and 1962. After this his tone voice became pointed and he used an adapted serial technique. His solo guitar composition, *"Morceaux op. 73"* (1974), is composed almost in a strict "Webern" style. Its material is being used in the two larger works, *"Preludier op. 76"* and *"Praembula op. 72."* Many Danish guitarists have recorded Borup-Jørgensen's music.

For a solo guitar: "Morceaux op. 73"; (1974); "Praembula op. 72" (1974–76); "Præludier op. 76" (1976–79); "Für Gitarre op. 86" (1978–79). For two guitars: "Poèsies pour la dame à la licorne" op. 121 (1987); "Paraphrase on a piano piece [op.4] op. 152 No" 1(1995); "Various Movements op. 151 No 2" (1995). For three guitars: "Peripeti" "1st part & an epilogue op. 145 No 1" (1995); "Peripeti" in 2 parts op. 145 No 2 (1995); "Peripeti" with a new, very complex 1 part - to guitar trio "1+2" op. 145 No 3 (1995–96). For 6-24 guitars ad libitum: "Enhjørninger 'unicorns' 12 movm to be combined into suites" (33 combinations suggested, 1992). For an alto, a tenor and a guitar: "Pasticcio on a Goethe text op. 69" (1973). For a soprano and a guitar: "Songs on texts by Sarving op. 104" (1983–85). For a soprano and an alto recorder (or flute/oboe/clarinet) "op. 153" (1976). For a mezzo soprano and a lute (or a guitar): "3 Old Chinese Poems op. 103 No 1" (1983). For an electric guitar and a piano/electric organ and percussion: "Carambolage for 3 op. 79" (1980). For a guitar and a chamber orchesrta: "Concerto"; "Déja-vu" op. 99 (1982–83). For a flute, clarinet, piano, percussion (1), violin, viola, cello and tape: "Sirenernes kyst" (1983–85). An arrangement for two guitars: "Parafrase" (II part from Borup-Jørgensens Sonate for the cello and the piano op. 14) arr. Leif Hesselberg.

BOSCH RENARD, Jaime (1826–1895), a Spanish (Catalonian) guitarist and composer. In 1852 he settled in Paris and gained great popularity and the name *Roy de la Guitarra*, "the King of the Guitar." According to Domingo Prat, Charles Gounod has composed *"Passacaille"* for a solo guitar dedicated to Bosch. In 1877 Bosch's opera, "Roger de Flor," was performed in Teatro Lirico in Paris. Jaime Bosch composed almost 100 pieces for the guitar and published in 1890 a guitar school, *Méthode de guitare.*

For a solo guitar: "Duettino op. 10"; "Brimborion op. 11"; "Etoiles et fleurs op. 12"; "Celia op. 13"; "Fantaisie Dramatique op. 14"; "Souvenir de Barcelone op. 15"; "Retraite espagnole op. 16"; "Allegro de sonate op. 17"; "Meditation op. 18"; "Ballade op. 19"; "Plainte moresque op. 85"; "Pasa Calle op. 86"; "La Rose op. 88"; "Six pièces faciles op. 89"; "Amazone op. 90"; "Au son des cloches op. 91"; "Venise op. 92"; "Les Echos op. 93"; "Cello op. 94"; "Bolero op. 95"; "10 pièces faciles Woo." For a voice and a guitar: "10 Melodies pour guitarre et chant."

BOULEZ, Pierre (born 1925), a French composer, theoretician and conductor. When Boulez studied he had to choose between mathematics and music. He chose music and graduated from the Music Conservatory of Paris after studying with Oliver Messiaen and Arthur Honegger. Boulez has been a pioneer in 20th century music. One of his most famous chamber music pieces is *Le Marteau sans Maître* ("a hammer without a master",

Photo: Faber Music

Benjamin Britten's solo guitar work Nocturnal is one of the most remarkable guitar compositions of the 20th century.

1954), where he uses the guitar. The work is based on the poems by René Char and in it the elegance and sensuality of Balian music can be heard. The premiere of "Le Marteau sans Maître" was in 1955 in Baden-Baden. Boulez also uses the guitar in his work *"Pli selon pli."*

For a mezzo soprano, alto flute, guitar, vibraphone, xylorimba, percussion and viola: "Le Marteau sans Maître", 1954.

BOZZA, Eugène (1905–1991), a French composer and conductor. Studied violin and composition in the Music Conservatory of Paris, where he received the premiers prix, first prize in violin playing in 1924, in conducting in 1930 and in composition in 1934. In 1939–48 he worked as a conductor in the Opéra-Comique in Paris and since 1951 as the leader of École Nationale. Bozza's international reputation is mainly based on his wide production of chamber music for woodwinds.

For a solo guitar: "Deux impressions andalouses;" Trois préludes." For a flute and a guitar: "Trois pièces" (1977); "Polydiaphonie" (1972); "Berceuse et Sérénade." For a guitar and a string quartet: "Concertino da camera" (1970).

BRESGEN, Cesar (1913–1988), a German composer with Italian roots, who studied composition in Munich in 1930–36 and took part in the composition seminars of Paul Hindemith in 1947–50. Since 1939 Bresgen worked as a teacher in the Salzburg Mozarteum. As a composer Bresgen had connections to Webern, Hindemith, Jelinek and Krenek and he also composed using the 12-tone system. He was a skilled improviser and used a lot of folk music in his works.

For a solo guitar: "Malinconia" (1968); "Fioretti." For two guitars: "Fantasia." For a voice and a guitar: "Czechoslovak Suite"; "2 Lieder"; "5 Roumanian Songs." For a speaker and a guitar: "Von Waldern und Zigeunern." For a flute and a guitar: "5 Miniatures." For a choir and a guitar: "Christkindl Kumedi" (1960). For a guitar and an orchestra: "Kammerkonzert" (1965).

BRINDLE... see SMITH BRINDLE, Reginald

BRITTEN, Benjamin (1913–1976), an English composer, who started to study composition at the age of 13 with F. Bridge and also studied piano and viola playing. Since 1930 he studied piano playing and composition with John Ireland at the Royal College of Music. In 1955–56 he made a visit to the Far East and studied Balian and Japanese music. Britten's compositions have a strong tonal tradition in the

Photo: Hannu Annala

Brouwer continues the old guitarist-composer tradition and belongs to the elite of our time's guitar composers.

background. Typical composition forms for him are variations, fugues and dances. In 1963 Britten composed a *"Nocturnal op. 70"* variations for the solo guitar, which is based on a song by a 16th-century lute composer John Dowland, *"Come Heavy Sleep."* Each of the variations is different: I, Musingly; II, Very agitated; III, Restless; IV, Uneasy; V, March-like; VI, Dreaming; and VI, Gently Rocking. Nocturnal is an upside-down variation, where the theme is not reached until the end as the passacaglia based on the work by Dowland leads to it. The work belongs to the greatest guitar compositions of the 20th century and it is dedicated to Julian Bream, who gave the first performance in 1964 at the Aldeburgh Festival. Britten's *Song Suites* with the guitar are dedicated to his life-long company, tenor Peter Pears.

For a solo guitar: "Nocturnal op. 70" (1963). For a high voice and a guitar: "Songs from the Chinese op. 58" (1959); "Folksong Arrangements for High Voice and Guitar Vol. 6" (1961).

BROCÁ, José (1805–1882), a Spanish guitarist and composer. Mainly autodidact, but got some training from Dionisio Aguado. In his own teaching Brocá used Aguado's guitar schools and etudes. One of Brocá's pupils is a Spanish guitarist José Ferrer Esteve. Brocá gave concerts in many Spanish towns, and composed ca. 20 pieces for the guitar.

For a solo guitar: "Fantasiá op. 19"; "El Catalán, vals"; "El Cortesano, shottish"; "El Destino, fantasía"; "El Elegante, vals"; "El Ay, vals"; "El Veloz, vals"; "Fantasía in C"; "Andante sentimentale"; "La Amistad, fantasía"; "Una flor, mazurca"; "Pensamiento español", etc.

BROQUA, Alfonso (1876–1946), a Uruguyan composer. Studied in Schola Cantorum in Paris with Vincent d'Indy, returned to his home country in 1904 and settled in Montevideo. Broqua also composed works for the guitar after being in touch with Emilio Pujol. As a starting point in his compositions, Broqua used the folk music of Uruguay.

For a solo guitar: "Ecos de paisaje"; "7 études créoles"; "7 Evocations"; "Vidala"; "Chacarera"; "Zamba Romántica"; "Milongeos"; "Pampanea"; "Ritmos Camperos." For two guitars: "El Tango" (from Cantos de Uruguay). For a voice, two guitars and a flute: "Chants de l'Uruguay" (El nido, Vidalita, El tango).

BROUWER, Leo (born 1939), a Cuban composer, guitarist and conductor, the professor of composition in the Music Academy of Havanna. Graduated in 1955 from the Music Academy of Peyrellade after studying guitar playing with Isac Nicola, a pupil of Emilio Pujol, being thus a preserver of Tárrega's tradition. Brouwer continued his studies specializing in composition in the Juilliard School and at the University of Hartford with Vincent Persichetti and Stephan Wolpe. After hearing the new music by Stockhausen and Penderecki in Warsaw in 1961 he concentrated more on modern music. In 1961 he became the leader of the music department of the Cuban motion picture institute, ICAIC, and the professor of harmonization and bass continuo in the Music Academy of Havanna. At the same time he also acted as a music expert in the Radio of Havanna. Later he became the professor of composition in the Music Academy of Havanna and a leader of a group of experimental music, GES, in ICAIC. He was also the conductor of the Cuban National Symphony Orchestra and he has conducted different orchestras around the world, such as the Berlin Philharmonics, the Chamber Orchestra of BBC and the National Symphony Orchestra of Mexico. As a guitarist and a composer, Brouwer has visited several music festivals, such as Edinburgh, Toronto, Avignon and Rome. The government of Cuba has granted him scholarships for both composition and giving guitar concerts.

Brouwer's production is usually divided into three groups: the nationalistic, the avantgardistic, and the neoromantic. His early works are folkloristic and they are strongly affected by the socialistic goals of the Cuban revolution. Brouwer's contacts to Luigi Nono and Hans Werner Henze affected his compositions in the 60s and 70s, and they are close to the Central

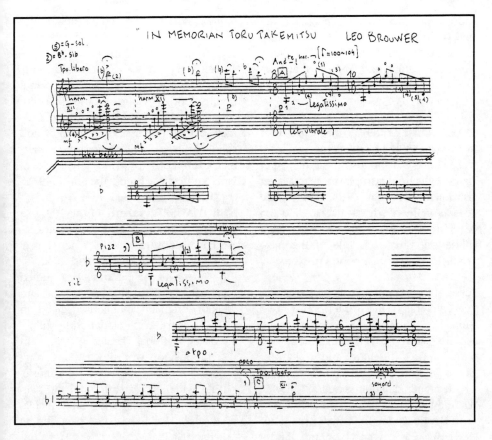

European avantgarde of that time. As his models, Brouwer has mentioned de Falla, Stravinsky, Bartók, Boulez and Stockhausen. Brouwer's *"Sonograma I"* (1963) for a prepared piano, is the first composition by a Cuban with the open form. His production from the late 70s is neoromantic. Brouwer has not based his music on a sonate form or variations or other special existing forms, but differentiates in his work two different ways of handling the basic units of composing: the way where the work develops during the composition process and the way which begins from the fixed, "universal" models. His works are largely influenced by literature, and some compositions are directly based on a literary work, such as *"El Decamerón Negro"* or *"Los Preludios Epigramáticos"*, which is based on poems by Miguel Hernández. Brouwer has continued the old guitar composer tradition, and his works are beautiful combinations of modern ways of expression and the folk music of Cuba. Brouwer's production contains almost 70 pieces for the guitar and compositions for percussion, piano, choir, orchestra and different chamber music ensembles. In addition to that, in almost 70 Cuban motion pic-

tures there is music by Brouwer.

The works composed during the second period, 1964–78, are the most famous. *"Elogio de la Danza,"* composed in 1964, is based on a rhythm, which, according to Brouwer, resembles the rhythmics of the ballets by Stravinsky. *"Canticum"* (1968), is based on a melody, which is surrounded by effects creating color, such as metallico, rasgueado, and tambora. The ideas of "Canticum" are enlarged in *"La Espiral Eterna"* (1971) and it has more room for improvisation. *"Parabola"* (1973–74) is based on African folklore. *"Tarantos"* from 1977, is based on a Spanish flamenco dance with the same name, and Karlheinz Stockhausen's new ideas of the form have been used there. Leo Brouwer's first avantgarde guitar concerto *"Concerto no. 1"* (1972) has used the same ideas as the works mentioned above. It was composed in Berlin, where he was on a visit because of a premiere of *"El Cimarron"*, a work by Hans Werner Henze. This concerto has a lot of room for improvisation, which the conductor and the solo player have to fill. Brouwer's Fifth Guitar Concerto, *"Concerto di Helsinki"* (1991–92) is dedicated to Timo

Korhonen, who gave the first performance in 1992 in a festival in Helsinki. The *20 Études* by Brouwer belong to the most popular modern etudes for the guitar, and Max Eschig has published them in four collections. Études 1-10 were composed during Brouwer's first, the so-called nationalistic period, in 1961–62. These etudes are short and simple, their duration is less than one minute. Études 11-20 were composed in 1980–81, they are longer, technically more demanding and they contain an Afro-Cuban rhythm. The Études are very idiomatic for the guitar and they contain right and left-hand sequences, legato technique and structures of harmony, which include free strings. (Michael Decker). The marks for tempo are not made by the composer but by the publisher Max Eschig. Brouwer has commented on the tempos: "The tempos should be equal to the student's possibilities. Not too slow, so that they can be played cantabile, but not too fast so that they cannot be played clearly."

Paul Century has written a doctoral thesis on Brouwer's music: *Principles of Pitch Organization in Leo Brouwer´s Atonal Music for Guitar* (University of Carolina, 1991).

For a solo guitar: "Suite no. 1 y 2" (1955); "Preludio" (1956); "Danza Característica" (1956); "Fuga no. 1" (1957); "Pieza Sin Título no. 1 & 2" (1957); "Tres Apuntes" (1959); "Estudios Sencillos Cuaderno I (Etudes Simples) 1-5" (1960); "Estudios Sencillos Cuaderno II (Etudes Simples) 6-10" (1963); "Pieza Sin Título 3" (1961); "Pieza para guitarra" (1962); "Tres piezas Latinoamericanas: 1. Danza del altiplano" (1962), "2. Triste Argentino, 3." "Tango"; "Dos aires populares cubanos" (1962); "Estudios sencillos Cuaderno III y IV (Etudes Simples) 11-20" (1980–81); "Un día de Noviembre" (1963); "Elogio de la Danza" (1964); "Canticum" (1968); "La Espiral Eterna" (1970); "Memorias de 'El Cimarrón'" (1970); "Tres Estudios en sonoridades" (1971); "Parábola" (1973–74); "Tarantos" (1973–74); "El Decamerón Negro" (1981); "Preludios Epigramáticos/Hai-Ku" (1981); "Variaciones sobre un thème de Django Reinhardt" (1984); "Paisaje Cubano con

Campañas" (1986); "Sonata" (dedicated to Julian Bream, 1990); "Rito de los Orishas" (1993); "Hoja de Album 'La Gota de Agua'" (1996); "In Memoriam 'Toru Takemitsu'" (1996); "Paisaje Cubano Con Tristeza" (1996). For solo guitar: "Études 21-30"; "Viaje a la Semilla" (2000). For two guitars: "Triptico." For two guitars: "Música Incidental Campesina"; "Micropiezas 1-4, Hommage à Milhaud" (1957–58); "Micropiezas 5" (1958); "Per suonare a due" (1972). An arrangement for two guitars: "The fool on the Hill" (Lennon & McCartney, 1973/74). For four guitars: "Toccata" (1972); "Metafora del Amor" (1974); "Paisaje cubano con rumba" (1984); "Paisaje Cubano Con Lluvia (versión de Castres Serenade) 1984"; "Toccata." For eight guitars: "Acerca del cielo y el aire y la sonrisa"; "Fantasía de los ecos." For a guitar orchestra: "Acerca del Sol y ei aire y la sonrisa" (1979); "Castres Serenade" (1984). For two guitar orchestras: "Exaedros III" (1975). For a voice and guitar: "Dos Canciónes sobre texto de F. García Lorca" (1959). For a voice (soprano), flute, violin, cello, vibraphone, piano and guitar: "Es el Amor Quien ve..."(1973). For the flute, violin and guitar: "Música Incidental" (1962). For the flute, viola and guitar: "Per suonare a tre" (1971). For the flute, oboe, clarinet and guitar: "Homenaje à Falla" (1957). For two violins, a viola, cello and guitar: "Finale." For a flute, oboe, clarinet, cello and guitar: "Finale." For a guitar and a string quartet: "Finale" (1957). For 8 percussions, a celesta, piano, harp, guitar and strings: "Sonograma II" (1964). For a guitar, piano, percussion and a ballerina: "Música para guitarra, piano, percusión y ballerina" (1975). For a guitar and a string orchestra: "Tres Danzas Concertantes" (1958). For a guitar, a string orchestra and percussion: "Música" (1955). Concertos for a guitar and an orchestra: "Concierto no. 1" (1972); "Concierto no. 2 'de Lieja'" (1980); "Concierto no. 3 'Elegíaco'" (1986); "Concierto no. 4 'Toronto'" (1986); "Concierto no. 5 'Helsinki'" (1991–92, dedicated to Timo Korhonen); "Concierto no. 6 'Volos'" (1997). For guitar and orchestra: "Concierto No. 7 de Volos" (1996); "Concierto No. 8 de la Habana"; "Concierto No. 9 Cantata de Perugia" (1999); "Concierto de Benicassim." For two guitars and orchestra: "Double concerto No. 10" (2004). A

double concerto for a violin, guitar and an orchestra: "Double Concierto... 'Omaggio à Paganini'" (1995). Other works for a guitar and an orchestra: "Tres danzas concertantes (1958), Retrats Catalans" (1983).

BRUSTAD, Karsten (born 1959), a Norwegian guitarist and composer, who started to take piano lessons at the age of 7, after which he also played many other instruments. He played the guitar since he was in high school and studied ten years in a music academy with Sven Lundestad. Brustad is one of the most productive guitar composers of Norway.

For a solo guitar: "A Suite" (1987). For two guitars: "Duo Praebo for two Guitars" (1988); "Duo Sacre for two Guitars" (1987); "Nachtstück og Lied ohne Worte"; "Prelude and fugue for Guitar Duo" (1986). For a flute and a guitar: "If night's dawn imposed all" (1987); "Little Suite for Flute and Guitar" (1981); "The Gentle Touch for Guitar and Flute" (1981/87); For a voice (soprano) and a guitar: "Molnkurvor (1986), Swedish text by S.E. Johanson"; "Two Poems for Soprano and Guitar (1987), Norwegian text by K. Hamsund." For a soprano, flute and guitar: "Meditation for Soprano, Flute and Guitar" (1984). For a guitar orchestra: "Vibrations for Guitar Orchestra and Two Soloists" (1991). For a guitar and an orchestra: "Prevratim for Guitar and Orchestra" (1990).

BUCK, Ole (born 1945), a Danish composer. He studied composition from 1963 onwards with Per Nørgård and later with Pelle Gudmundsen-Holmgreen. At first, Buck was influenced by Stravinsky's and Webern's seriality and later he developed a serial technique, where tones are replaced by expressions and natural elements. He developed his technique further, and dominance was given to the repetition of small melodic or rhythmic modules in restricted periods. He has used this technique in his first remarkable and often played work, "Sommertrio" (1968).

For a solo guitar: "Omaggio à Antonio Vivaldi" (1984). For a soprano recorder and a guitar: "Petite suite" (1993). For a flute and a guitar: "14 Preludes" (1972); For a flute, viola and guitar: "Primavera"

(1984). For a flute, guitar and cello: "Sommertrio" (1968), which, like 14 Preludes, is suitable for pedagogic use; "Divertimento" (1994–95). For the flute, clarinet, French horn, trumpet, piano, percussion, violin and cello: "Frühlingsnacht" (1986). For a flute, clarinet, piano, percussion (1), violin and cello: "Aquarels" (1983). For a flute, clarinet, trumpet, harp, piano, guitar, violin, viola and cello: "Landscapes [I]" (1992).

BURGHAUSER, Jarmil (1921–1997), a Czech composer and musicologist. Studied conducting in the Music Academy of Prague and musicology at the University of Karlova. He studied composition with Jaroslav Kricka and Otakar Jeremiás. Burghauser acted in 1946–53 as the choir leader and conductor of the National Theater in Prague. In his composition work he had a starting point in Dvorák's and V. Noviak's music, but he widened his scale with the help of serial technique and experimental methods. He used the pseudonym "Michael Hájku."

For a solo guitar: "Sonata"; "Six Czech Dances"; "Tesknice" (1968). For a flute, viola and guitar: "2 Trios" (1938). For a viola and a guitar: "5 Zamysleni" (5 pensive moods, 1966). For a viola, cello and a guitar: "Surfaces and Lines" (1972).

BURKHARD, Willy (1900–1955), a Swiss composer, studied in the Music Academies of Leipzig, Munich and Paris. He taught composition from 1924 onwards in Bern and from 1942 onwards in the Music Academy of Zürich. Burkhard's music is influenced by the French Renaissance polyphony, J.S. Bach and Bruckner. His music has been described as propagandist, with features of protestant belief and often rough intensity. He thus continued the Swiss tradition created by Frank Martin and Arthur Honegger. Burkhard taught Klaus Huber (born 1924), with whom many modern guitar composers have studied.

For a flute and a guitar: "Serenade op. 71 no. 3" (1945).

BUSSOTTI, Sylvano (born 1931), an Italian composer, artist and director. Started his musical studies at the age of 5 by playing the violin with Margherita

The etudes of the "Bellini of the guitar", Matteo Carcassi, are in a central position in the etude programs of guitarists.

Castellano. In 1940 he started to study in the Music Academy of Florence. Four years later he surprisingly abandoned his studies and concentrated on composition, which he studied by himself in 1949–56. His artistic performances are in the fields of experimental music, painting, graphics, journalism, theater and motion pictures. Bussotti is a representative of avantgarde and he has also arranged concerts of *"anti music."*

For a solo guitar: "Rara" (eco sierologico, 1964–67). For a guitar, strings and a piano: "Sette Fogli - Mobile stabile." For three guitars and a string quartet: "Ultima rara" (1969). For a voice, guitar, cello, woodwinds, piano, harp and percussion: "The Rara Requiem" (1969).

CALATAYUD, Bartolomé (1882–1973), a Spanish guitarist and composer from the island of Palma de Mallorca. Studied guitar playing with the Spanish Antonio Mestro. He was a close friend of Emilio Pujol. Calatayud composed small pieces for the guitar since his childhood, based on the folk music of Mallorca. In the list by Union Musical Española, there are 50 guitar compositions by Calatayud.

For a solo guitar: "Danza Mora"; "Jota aragonesa"; "4 Divertimentos"; "Estudio melódico"; "Moruna"; "Preludio I, II & III"; "3 Piezas fáciles"; "4 Piezas fáciles"; "Sonata típica de Mallorca"; etc. For two guitars: "6 Divertimentos."

CALL, Leonhard de [von] (1767–1815), an Austrian guitarist and composer. In addition to the guitar, de Call also played the mandoline and the flute, which he taught in Vienna since 1801 and worked in the court as a chamber musician. He and an Austrian guitarist Simon Molitor were the pioneers in the guitar music of Vienna. In a list of players published in Vienna in 1807, de Call's skills are praised highly (T. Heck). The same year a publication appeared in Vienna with the use of the capo with the guitar. That work was a quartet by de Call. Later capo and a guitar tuned a third higher were used by Anton Diabelli and Mauro Giuliani. L. de Call was a famous composer, whose compositions were often played since they were not as difficult as those by Mauro Giuliani. de Call also composed a lot of "every day" music for the guitar; often chamber music with a flute, violin, cello or mandolin. During 1802–18, ca. 150 works by de Call were published: sonatas, fantasies, serenades for the solo guitar and chamber music: 50 duets, 40 trios and quartets and quintets.

For a solo guitar: "Sonata in a op. 22." For two guitars: "6 Duets op. 24"; "Sérénade op. 39." For three guitars: "Trio op. 26." For a flute and a guitar: "Duetto"; "Variazioni." For a violin and a guitar: "Duetto" (the same as M. Giuliani's 54b). For a mandoline and a guitar: "Variations op. 25." For a piano and a guitar: "Sonata op. 74"; "Sérénade op. 76"; "Sonate op. 105"; "Sérénade op. 116"; "Sonate op. 143." For two flutes and a guitar: "Variations op. 68"; "Sérénade op. 69." For a flute, viola (or clarinet) and guitar: "Trio op. 134." For a flute, viola and guitar: "Sérénade op: 5; 14; 30; 47; 50; 65; 66; 71; 72; 75; 78; 80-83; 92; 100; 131; 137; 138; 143; 144"; "Nocturne: op: 83; 85-90; 93." For a violin (or flute), guitar,

viola and cello: "5 Quartetti." For a flute, violin, viola, guitar and cello: "2 Quintetti."

CAMILLERI, Charles (born 1931), Maltese/British composer and conductor. In addition to his home country Malta, he studied music at the University of Toronto with John Weinzweig in 1959–63. He worked for the CBS Radio in Toronto in 1959–64, and as the professor of composition in the Music Academy of Toronto. He has worked as a guest lecturer in the United States, the Soviet Union, Scandinavia, and other places in Europe. In his music Camilleri has used the folk music of Malta and he has studied African, Asian and Indian music.

For a solo guitar: "Four African Sketches" (1980); "Fantasia Concertante no. 5"; "Three Pieces from Chemins." For two mandolines, a mandola and guitar: "The Four Elements" (1988).

CANO, Antonio (1811–1897), a Spanish guitarist and guitar composer who began his career as a concert guitarist encouraged by Dionisio Aguado in 1847. Together with his son Federico (1838–1904), he was one of the best guitarists of that time. He gave concerts in France in 1853 and in Portugal in 1855 and he got a very high reputation. In 1859 he got the vacancy as a chamber musician of Sebastian de Borbón and Cano also

Antonio Cano

took care of Borbón's music archive. Since 1874 he worked as a teacher in an institute for deaf-mute people. Cano composed for the guitar fantasies from opera themes, and in 1852 his guitar school, *Método completo*, with 24 pedagogic etudes, was published.

For a solo guitar: "Andante grave"; "Fandango"; "2 Estudios Brillantes de Concierto"; "Seguidillas manchegas." *Complete Works* (Rodriguez).

CARCASSI, Matteo (1792–1853), an Italian guitarist and composer born in Florence, who already at the age of 20 was a well-known guitar virtuoso in Italy. In ca. 1810–15 he moved to Paris (T. Heck), where many famous guitarists of the time lived. These guitarists included Ferdinando Carulli (since 1808), Fernando Sor (since 1813) and Dionisio Aguado (since 1826). In the 1820s, Carcassi made concert visits to London (1822/28) and Germany and he became an internationally known guitarist. He competed for popularity with his fellow countryman Carulli. In 1836 Carcassi made a concert tour to Italy, after which he spent the rest of his life in Paris. A Russian nobleman, Nikolai Makaroff (1810–1890), mentions in his article about guitar art that he has heard many skilled European guitar virtuosos play, also Matteo Carcassi.

Carcassi's playing technique still leans to the lid with the right hand's little finger, which is an old habit used by old guitarists and lutists. This habit was used by Carulli, Meissonnier, Molino and Moretti. The aim was to reduce uncertain plucking, plucking a wrong string, and uneven sound. Sor and Aguado thought that leaning the finger restricted the possibilities to move the hand.

In 1836 Carcassi published a guitar school in three volumes, *Méthode complete op. 59* and *25 Etúdes mélodiques et progressives op. 60*. The school is still in the 20th century being printed in different languages. As an interesting detail, one could mention that this school is the first to tell how to play pizzicato (*étouffer*) with the guitar (Dell' Ara). *Etudes op. 60* has, due to its high quality, retained its central position among the repertoires

of guitar students until today. In Paris, Carcassi became friends with the French guitarist Antoine Meissonnier, who in 1814 started to publish music and also published guitar compositions by Carcassi. His composition style is Italian, i.e. melodic, and he has gotten the nickname *"Il Bellini della Chitarra"* (Dell'Ara). Carcassi's guitar production contains 300 compositions, of which there are 73 opuses. The works contain sonatas, rondos, capriccios, small pieces, fantasies and potpourris from opera themes (Zampa, Wilhelm Tell, etc.).

For a solo guitar: "3 Sonatinen op. 1"; "12 Petites Pièces op. 3"; "6 Valses op. 4"; "Le noveau Papillon... op. 5"; "'Au Clair de Luné', varie op. 7"; "Entrennes aux amateurs (6 Contredanses, 6 Valses et 3 Aria variés) op. 8"; "Amusement, Choix de 12 morceaux faciles op. 10"; "Recueil de 10 petites Pièces op. 11"; "4 Potpourris (Rossini) op. 13"; "8 Divertissements op. 16"; "'Le songe de Rousseau', Air varié op. 17"; "6 Aires variés op. 18"; "Der Freischütz, Fantaisie op. 19"; "Air suisse varié op. 20"; "12 Valses op. 23"; "2me Recucil de 8 Divertissements op. 25"; "6 Caprices op. 26"; "La Muette de Portici, Fantaise op. 33"; "Giullaume Tell (William Tell), Fantaisie op. 36"; "Fra Diavolo, Fantaisie op. 37"; "Le Dieu et la Bayadère, Fantaisie op. 38"; "Zampa, Fantaisie op. 40"; "Rondoletto op. 41"; "3 Air suisse variés op. 44"; "La Campanella de Paganini op. 54/21"; "25 Études mélodiques et progressives op. 60."

CARDOSO, Jorge (born 1949), an Argentinean composer and guitarist. As a member of the Cardoso family he studied medicine, but at the same time he studied music and finally took a degree in both fields. He completed his studies by studying the music of Renaissance and Baroque with Javier Hinojosa. In his home country Argentina he won several music and composition contests in the 1960s, and he has taught in numerous guitar courses. As a composer, Cardoso has faithfully followed the traditions of folk music. Now he lives in Madrid, Spain.

For a solo guitar: "Suite Misionera";

"Suite Sudamericana"; "24 Piezas Sudamericanas." Guitar duets: "Suite Porteña"; "Milonga." For three guitars: "Nueve piezas"; "Tango-set." For four guitars: "Quarteto en Mi mayor 'Yevia'." For a guitar and a string quartet: "Suite Pampeana." For a flute and a guitar: "Suite del litoral." For a violin and a guitar: "Una luz muy lejana" (vidalita). For a piano and a guitar: "Suite Pampeana." For a voice and a guitar: "Canción cuna para un guri, etc." For a guitar and a small orchestra: "Concerto Guaraní." For two guitars and an orchestra: "Suite Indiana." For a guitar and an orchestra: "Cuatro piezas."

CARLEVARO, Abel (1918–2001), a Uruguayan guitarist, composer and pedagogue. He was at first self- taught, but after meeting Andrés Segovia in 1937, Carlevaro became his pupil. Carlevaro gave his debute concert in 1942, and after that he has given concerts and taught in America and Europe. He was one of the first guitarists that have played the Preludes by Villa-Lobos. Carlevaro has taught guitar playing in the Music Academy of Montevideo. Edition Chanterelle has published a series *"Carlevaro Masterclass"*, which contains performance instructions to Villa-Lobos's Preludes and Études. A four-part series by Abel Carlevaro, *Didactic Series for the Guitar*, is widely known. Carlevaro's guitar school, *Escuela de la Guitarra* has been translated into English by Jihad Azkoul and Bartolome Diaz, with the name *School of Guitar, Exposition of Instrumental Theory* (Boosey & Hawkes 1978).

For a solo guitar: "Cronomias 1"; "5 Preludios Americanos" (1953); "5 Estudios" (Homenaje a Villa-Lobos); "Microestudios"; "Milonga Oriental"; "Introducción y Capricho"; "Aires de Vidalita"; "Suite de antiguas danzas Españolas." For a guitar, violin, viola and cello: "Quartet." For a guitar, a string quintet and percussion: "Fantasía Concertante." For a guitar and an orchestra: "Concierto de Plata."

CARTER, Elliott (1908), a composer from the United States. Encouraged by Charles Ives, he went to Harvard to study music with Walter Piston. In

Elliott Carter

1932–35 he continued his studies in Paris with Nadia Boulanger. Unlike his many contemporaries, Carter became directly interested in new music without any Classical-Romantic phases. He has been the leader of the Ballet Caravan since 1940 and taught in the Juilliard School of Music and at many universities, such as Columbia, Yale and Cornell. Carter has composed a work for the solo guitar, *"Changes"* (1983), which is dedicated to the American guitarist David Starobin, who performed it for the first time in New York December 11th, 1983, on the 75th birthday of Carter. According to the composer himself, the work is based on capricios and opposite moods, which are combined with the harmonic and rhythmic structure of the work.

For a solo guitar: "Changes" (1983). For a voice and a guitar: "Tell Me Where is the Fancy Bred" (1938). For a mezzo soprano, speaker and ten instruments (including the guitar): "Syringia."

CARULLI, Ferdinando (1770–1841), an Italian guitarist and guitar composer, born in the same year as Beethoven. Carulli got his first musical education in his home town Naples. He first studied cello and violin playing, later he became interested in the guitar, which was the fashionable instrument of that time, and just gotten its sixth string. The bass register was one fourth wider and the pair strings were taken off. Carulli belonged to the first generation of the great masters of the six-stringed guitar and he became the pioneer in guitarism in Italy. In 1807 Carulli traveled to Vienna, hoping that he would find a publisher for his works and after that, in 1808, to Paris (T. Heck). Carulli soon became the favorite guitarist in the art salons of Paris and he introduced the guitar culture of Naples in France. His popularity lasted until the Spanish Fernando Sor (1813) and a younger competitor from Italy, Matteo Carcassi, came to Paris (Sor in 1813 and Carcassi in ca. 1810-15). In an Italian manner, Carulli's style imitated a small opera orchestra, where a central thought was to imitate the *"bel canto,"* beautiful singing.

In 1810, publisher Carli printed in Paris a guitar school by Carulli, *Méthode Complete de guitarre ou lyre op. 27*, which was published 7 times during Carulli's lifetime, the last with the opus number 241. The *Guitar School*, meant for a 10-string guitar, was published with the op. number 293 and Carulli also published a collection presenting methods of accompaniment, *L'harmonie appliquée à la guitarre*. The school for a six-string guitar contains guitar duos for the teacher and the pupil, *24 Lezioni*. Carulli published 360 opuses of guitar

The production of the Italian favorite guitarist in Parisian salons, Ferdinando Carulli, is very wide, altogether more than 360 opuses.

music: sonatas, rondos, variations, popular music of his time (nocturnos, serenades) and plenty of chamber music for the violin, flute, voice or piano. The best known compositions by Carulli are the duos for two guitars and *Guitar Concertos op. 140 and 207*. His exceptionally wide repertoire of pedagogic music has remained in frequent use by guitar students until today.

An important starting point is the programmaticality of his works, *"La girafe à Paris"* ("the giraf of Paris"), *"The Amours of Venus and Adonis and Les trois jours, Pièce analogue"* ("3 days of revolution in Paris in 1830"). Carulli has also made arrangements of high quality of the works of Haydn, Mozart, Beethoven, Hummel and Rossini. Carulli became friends with the Parisian guitar builder Lacôte and as a result of that cooperation a new 10-string guitar was introduced with 4 additional bass strings.

One of Carulli's most talented pupils was the Italian Filippo Gragnani (1768–1820), who also was an excellent composer of chamber music. Carulli had a son, Gustavo (1801–1876), who studied guitar playing under his father. Gustavo also studied singing and he became a singing teacher (as did Mauro Giuliani's son Michele, who was born the same year).

The Italian Mario Torta has written a doctoral thesis on Carulli's life and compositions: *Profilo biografico - critico e catalogo tematico della opere con numero vol. 1 & 2*. Universita degli studi di Roma (La Sapineza 1989).

For a solo guitar: "Nice e Fileno op. 2" (1807); "3 Sonatine op. 7" (1810); "Grande sonate op. 16"; "Solo op. 20"; "Trois sonates op. 21"; "Trois petites sonates faciles op. 23"; "Grande Sonate op. 25"; "Sonata sentimentale op. 33"; "Sonata op. 42"; "Sonata op. 56 no. 2"; "3 Sonatinas op. 59"; "3 Soli op. 60"; "Potpourri op. 74" (1812); "3 Sonate op. 81" (1815); "Grande sonata op. 83"; "La Paix op. 85" (1816); "6 Valzer op. 101"; "6 Valzer op. 105"; (1816); Solo op. 113" (1817); "24 Preludes op. 114"; "Variazioni, sul margine del un rio op. 142"; "Capriccio op. 186" (1823); "3 Divertimenti op. 209" (1824); "Fantasia op. 228" (1824); "Les Adieux op 229"; "La girafe à Paris, divertissement Africo-Français op. 306." "6 Divertissements op. 317" (1827); "6 Andantes op. 320" (1829); "Fantaisie op. 323"; "La Marseillaise op. 330"; "Les trois jours op. 331" (1830); "Le prise d'Algier op. 327" (1830). For two guitars: "12 Duets op. 27"; "6 Duets op. 34"; "Duets op. 67" (1813); "3 Nocturnes op. 90"; "3 Sérénade op. 96"; "Variations on Carnaval de Venise op. 117"; "Nocturno concertante op. 118" (1817); "3 Nocturne op. 128"; "Bagatelle op. 130"; "Duos: op: 146; 152; 155; 157; 164; 167; 231"; "Nocturne de salon op. 227"; "Duo concertante op. 328"; "Romanzen op. 333." For three guitars: "Petit trio op. 92"; "Grand trio op. 255." For a voice and a guitar: "4 Romances Françaises op. 61"; "12 Ariettes Italiennes Woo." For a flute (or violin) and guitar (more than 30 duets): "6 Sérénade op. 109"; "Nocturno op. 115" (1816); "Nocturne op. 190"; "6 Contradanzas op. 193"; "Fantaisie op 289" (1825); "Fantaisie op. 303" (1826); "Fantaisie op. 337"; "Duos: op. 27; 104-108; 156; 158; 163; 239." For a piano and a guitar: 2 Sonate op. 21"; "3 Duos op. 37" (1811); "Grand duo op. 70"; "Variations (Beethoven) op. 169"; "Nocturno p. 189"; "Duos: op: 32; 70; 86; 127; 131; 134; 150; 151." For a flute, violin and guitar: "3 Trios op. 9"; "Trio op. 12" (1810); "6 Trios op. 24"; "3 Nocturnes op. 119"; "Sinfonia de la 'Gazza ladra' di Rossini." For a violin, viola and guitar: "3 Trios concertantes op. 103." Guitar concertos: "Concerto A", (without a number, published in Vienna, modern print Universal Edition); "Concerto A op. 8(a)", published in Paris in 1809 (Polonaise the same as in the previous concerto); "Petit Concerto de société e op. 140." For a flute, guitar and orchestra: "Concerto in Sol maggiore."

CARY, Tristram (born 1925), a British composer, who has specialized in electronic music. Cary established a studio for electronic music in the Royal College of Music, where he has worked as a professor. He has composed electronic music for television and motion pictures.
For a solo guitar: "Sonata."

CASTELNUOVO-TEDESCO, Mario (1895–1968), an Italian composer and pianist with Spanish roots. Started to play the piano at the age of nine with his mother and continued in the Music Academy of his home town, Florence, with Edgar Samuel Valle de Paz (diploma 1914), and also studied composition with Ildebrando Pizzetti (diploma 1918). Castelnuovo-Tedesco became a famous composer in Europe before he was 20. Before World War II he worked as a pianist and freelance composer in Florence. In 1939, C-T and his family moved to the USA after being persecuted for being Jewish. He settled at first in New York, moved in 1940 to Beverly Hills, California and received USA citizenship in 1946. After the war C-T made summer visits often to Toscana in Italy. From the early 40s until mid 50s, C-T was active in Hollywood's film industry and he composed a lot of film music. Since 1946 he taught composition and orchestration in the Music Academy of Los Angeles.

Castelnuovo-Tedesco was a productive composer, whose production contains operas, oratorios, instrumental concertos, more than 100 piano compositions, over 400 songs and chamber music for different ensembles. As a pianist, C-T often played solos in his own concerts. In 1932 Castelnuovo-Tedesco met Andrés Segovia in Venice, and he gave C-T Fernando Sor's Mozart variations and Manuel Ponce's Folias variations so that he could study them with composing for the guitar in mind. Already the same year, C-T published his first guitar composition *Variazioni attraverso i secoli* ("Variations Through the Century"). The friendship with Segovia led to the composition of a great number of pieces for the guitar and some of the compositions are dedicated to A. Segovia: (op: 71, 77, 85, 87, 95, 124, 133), as well as the *Concerto no. 1 D op. 99* (1939), which was his last work in Italy before he emigrated to the United States. C-T's guitar concerto in D, which was first performed by Segovia in Montevideo, Uruguay in 1939, is the first guitar concerto in the 20th century, and it was followed a couple of months later by Joaquín Rodrigo's, *Aranjuez* and a couple of years later by Manuel Ponce's, *Concierto del sur.* C-T's guitar con-certo has been influenced by Spanish folk music, the second part is a fairwell to Toscana before moving to the USA. In 1961, Castelnuovo-Tedesco met the Guitar Duo Ida Presti - Alexandre Lagoya, to whom he dedicated his works for two guitars: (op. 196 and 199) and a concerto for two guitars and an orchestra, *Duo Concerto in G op. 201.* Castelnuovo-Tedesco was very original and temperamental both as a composer and as a musician. His mastering of forms has been praised in his dramatical and lyrical works. C-T's guitar music is based on a tonal tradition which reflects influences from the Mediterranean countries, mainly Italy and Spain, in a somewhat modern form. As his most important sources of inspiration, C-T has mentioned the living surroundings in Florence and Toscana, the Bible and the texts of Shakespeare.

There are plenty of books and articles about the life of C-T, of which could be mentioned: *N. Rossi: Catalogue of Works* by Mario Castelnuovo-Tedesco (New York, 1977). *G. Saleski: Mario Castelnuovo-Tedesco, Famous Composers of Jewish Origin* (New York 1949). *Corazón Otero: Mario Castelnuovo-Tedesco: su vida y su obra para guitarra.* Articles in guitar magazines: Guitar, February 1978; Guitar Review, No. 37, 1972; Guitar Review, No. 79, 1989.

For a solo guitar: "Variazioni attraverso i secoli op. 71" (1932); "Sonata (omaggio à Boccherini) op. 77" (1934); "Capriccio diabolico op. 85" (1935); "Tarantella, Aranci in fiore op. 87" (1936); "Variations plaisantes sur un petit air populaire op. 95" (1937); "Rondo op. 124" (1946); "Suite op. 133" (1947); "Series 20 Items op. 170" (1954-67); "3 preludi mediterrancé op. 176" (1955); "La guarda cuydadosa, Escarraman op. 177, after Cervantes" (1955); "Passacaglia op. 180" (1956); "3 preludi al Circeo op. 194" (1961); "24 Caprichos de Goya op. 195" (1961); "Appunti op. 210" (1967-68). For two guitars: "Sonatina Canonica op. 196" (1961); "Les guitares bien tempéres (24 Preludes and fugues) op. 199" (1962); "Fuga elegiaca" (1967). For a flute and a guitar: "Sonatina op. 205" (1965). For a piano and a guitar: "Fantasia op. 145"

(1950). For a guitar and a string quartet: "Quintett op. 143" (1950). For a quatro or pentaphonic choir and guitar: "Romancero Gitano op. 152" (for poems by Frederico García Lorca). For a speaker and a guitar: "Platero y yo op 190" (1960, also played as a guitar solo). For a voice and a guitar: "Ballata dell' esilio" (1956); "The divan of Moses-ibn-Ezra op. 207" (1966); "Vogelweide für Baritone und Gitarre op. 186" (1959). For a guitar and an orchestra: "Concerto n:o. 1 D op. 99" (1938-39); "Concerto n:o. 2 C op. 160" (1953); "Capriccio diabolico op. 85b" (1945, arrangement from a solo guitar work). For a guitar and a chamber orchestra: "Serenade in F op. 118." For two guitars and an orchestra: "Duo Concerto in G op. 201."

CHAILLY, Luciano (1920–1999), an Italian composer, graduated in 1945 as a violinist and in 1949 as a composer from the Music Academy of Milan. In 1948 Chailly took part in Hindemith's courses in Salzburg. He worked as the. producer of music programs in Italian Television (1968–71) and as the artistic leader of the La Scala Opera in Milan. Since 1969 Chailly taught composition in the Music Academy of Milan. Chailly's music is influenced by Hindemith and avantgarde music.

For a solo guitar: "Invenzione su quatro note"; "Sonata" (dedicated to Alirio Diaz); "Improvvisazione no. 12." For a guitar, violin, viola and cello: "Recitativo e Fuga."

CHARLTON, Richard (born 1955), an English guitarist and guitar composer, who moved to Australia in 1963. He studied guitar at the Spanish Guitar Center in Brisbane under Stephen Bulmer and James Lloyd and composition for a short period with Mary Egan. As a composer he is auto-didact. Charlton works as a teacher in Edgecliff in the school of Ascham and he is a member of the Sydney Guitar Quartet and Bennelong Players. Charlton's production contains lots of pedagogic compositions for children and youth orchestras.
For a solo guitar: "A Medieval Tapestry"; "Rondo Fantasia." For a clarinet and guitar: "Caprice B." For a flute and a guitar: "Caprice."

CHARPENTIER, Jacques (born 1933), a French composer born in Paris, studied organ playing, conducting and composition with Tony Aubin and philosophy of music with Olivier Messiaen in the Music Conservatory of Paris. In 1953 he made an excursion to Italy and since 1966 he has worked as a music inspector for the French culture department.

For a solo guitar: "Étude no. 1" (1974). For a guitar and a string orchestra: "Concerto no. 2" (1970).

CHAVARRI, López Mario (1871–1970), a Spanish guitarist, composer and conductor. Chavarri studied composition with Felipe Pedrell (1841–1922), a researcher of Spanish folk music and composer. Pedrell saw the possibilities of folk music and he had a great influence on his pupils, to whom also Albéniz, de Falla, Granados, Sarasate, etc., belonged. Chavarri also studied law and esthetics at university. He worked as a teacher in the Music Academy of Heimatstadt and published the musical encyclopedias, *Historia de la Música* (1914) and *Música popular Española* (1927).

For a solo guitar: "Danza lenta"; "Ritmo popular"; "Fiesta lejana en un jardín"; "Nocturno"; "La Mirada de Carmen"; "Lamento y Gitarra"; "Sonata no. 1"; "Sonata no. 2."

CHÁVEZ, Carlos (1899–1978), a Mexican composer and conductor. There were a lot of professional musicians in the Chávez family, and he got his first musical education from his elder brother. Later he studied harmonization with Juan B. Fuentes and piano playing with Manuel Ponce and P.L. Ogazó. In 1922–24 he studied both in Europe and the United States. Chávez worked as the conductor of the Mexican Symphony Orchestra in 1928–49 and as the leader of the National Music Academy in 1928–34. Later, he also acted as the leader of the National Institute for Fine Arts. Chávez did not collect or use folk music in his works, but he brought the Indian roots of Mexican music to his works by using primitive rhythms and folk music instruments. In addition to the "mythi-

cal" Mexican style, his works also reflect neoclassicism.

For a solo guitar: "3 pièces" (1921); "Elegia y Danza"; "Preludio y Yumbo."

CHAYNES, Charles (born 1925), a French composer, studied violin playing in the Music Academy of Tolouse and later composition in the Music Academy of Paris under Darius Milhaud and Jean Rivier. In 1975–90, Chaines worked as the musical leader of the Radio of France.

For a solo guitar: "Fatum" (1979); "Prélude pour Fatum" (1982, didactic music). For two guitars: "Dialogues" (1983). For a flute, oboe, clarinet, bassoon, French horn, piano, harp, guitar, percussion and a string quartet: "Valeurs" (1979). For a guitar and a string orchestra: "Visions concértantes" (1976).

CIMAROSA, Domenico (1749–1801), an Italian composer, known by his late Neapolitan opera buffas, which were the most famous of the kind in the late 18th century. Cimarosa, a son of a bricklayer, was accepted to a Neapolitan Music Academy, Lorento, to study as a non-paying student because of his exceptional talent. There he studied with Sacchini and probably Piccinini. Catherine the Great invited him to the court of St. Petersburg to be the successor of Paisiello in 1787–91 and of Leopold II Salieri as a chamber musician in the court of Vienna in 1791–93. Cimarosa's melodical inventiveness made an impact on Mozart, who composed additional arias to his operas in Vienna. Cimarosa composed nearly 70 operas, 3 oratorios, concertos, and 32 cembalo sonatas in the style of D. Scarlatti, among other things. Cimarosa composed an original work for a voice and guitar, *"Sei canzonette italiane coll' accompagnamento di chitarra."* His cembalo sonatas, the theme of the oboe concerto, etc., are played as arrangements for the guitar. Arrangements have been made by Alice Artz, Julian Bream, Oscar Cáceres, Emilio Pujol and Luise Walker etc.

Domenico Cimarosa

For a voice and a guitar: "Sei canzonette italiane coll' accompagnamento di chitarra."

COMPANY, Alvaro (born 1931), an Italian guitar pedagogue and composer. Alvaro Company is one of the most remarkable guitar pedagogues. He has taken diplomas in conducting in 1955 and in composition in 1956. Company composed his first atonal work for the piano in 1948. He has played the first performances of many famous guitar works, such as Frank Martini's, *"Quatre pièces brèves"* and Darius Milhaud's *"Segoviana."* Alvaro Company has a high reputation as an expert of modern music, and he was given the *"M. Mila Prize"* in 1991, because of his life long didactic work.

For a solo guitar: "Las seis cuerdas" (1963); "Oneiron per Gabriella." For two guitars: "Leos pas de deux" (dedicated to Oscar Ghiglia).

CONSTANT, Franz (1910–1996), a Belgian composer and guitarist. Constant has composed guitar music for different combinations, including a *"concertino"* for the guitar and an orchestra. Constant's composition style has been influenced by the music of Debussy and Ravel. His music has been published by a Belgian publisher, CeBeDeM in Brussels.

For a solo guitar: "Nocturne op. 58"; "Humoresque op. 59"; "Poème op. 60." For four guitars: "Petite suite op. 128" (1989). For a flute and a guitar: "Músique à deux op. 57." For a piano and a guitar: "Sérénité op. 80"; "Estampe op. 81"; "Danse op. 82." For a guitar and an orchestra: "Primavera, Concertino op. 130."

CONSTANT, Marius (1925–2004), a French composer and conductor with Romanian roots. Studied piano playing and composition in the Music Academy of Bucharest. After winning the Enescu Contest in Romania, he continued his studies since 1946 in Paris with Oliver Messiaen, Arthur Honegger, Tony Aubin and Nadia Boulanger, etc. In 1963, he founded a group, Ars Nova, which concentrated on performing new music and on improvisation. M. Constant received several prizes as a composer, such as the *"Italia Prize,"* *"Koussevitsky Prize"* and *"Victoires de la musicue."*

For a solo guitar: "Blues-Variations" (1980); "D'une élégie slave" (1981). For percussion, cembalo, electric guitar, violin, viola, cello and trombone: "14 Stations" (1969–70). For 12 strings and an electric guitar: "Strings" (1972).

CORDERO, Ernesto (born 1946), a Puerto Rican composer and guitarist. Cordero got interested in the guitar at the age of 14 after hearing many guitar artists, such as Andrés Segovia and Rey de la Torre. Ernesto first studied guitar and violin playing by himself, later he studied guitar playing in Spain with Regino Sáinz de la Maza and graduated from the Music Academy of Madrid in 1970. Cordero has also studied composition in Italy and the United States. He has given concerts in Puerto Rico, Europe, and the USA and published several records.

For a solo guitar: "2 Piezas Afro-Antillanas" (Nana para una Negrita, El Cumbancherito); "Album para la juventud, 11 pieces"; "El carbonerito, thème & variations"; "Descarga"; "Mapeyè, canto di Puerto Rico"; "5 Preludes"; "Proteus"; "2 Tiempos de sonata"; "Tres Cantigas Negras." For two guitars: "Dos piezas cortas." For a flute and a guitar: "Fantasía mulata." For a voice and a guitar: "4 Works" (Zenobia, La hija del viejo Pancho-Cadencia, El viaje definitivo); "Mis Primeros Versos" (8 Songs). For a voice, flute and guitar: "Dos canciónes." For a voice, flute, guitar and cello: "Cantata al Valle de Mexico." For a guitar and an orchestra: "Concierto Antillano"; "Concierto Evocativo"; "Concerto de Bayoán."

CORIGLIANO, John (born 1938), a composer from the United States, a son of violinist John Corigliano. Studied composition at the University of Columbia, and graduated in 1959, later he studied in the Music School of Manhattan with Giannini. Corigliano has worked as the music producer for the New York Radio and CBS television. Since 1968, he taught composition in the Lehman College and since 1971 in the Music School of Manhattan.

For a guitar and an orchestra: "Troubadours" (Variations for Guitar and Orchestra, 1993), a recording by Sharon Isbin (1995).

COSTE, Napoléon (1805–1883), a French guitarist, composer and pedagogue. His father was an officer in the Imperial Army, and he hoped that his son would follow his steps and become an engineer officer. His dream was not fulfilled as the boy fell ill. Napoléon started to play the guitar at the age of six with the guidance of his mother, who was an amateur guitarist. Already at the age of 18, Coste taught guitar playing and played as a soloist in the concerts of The Philharmonic Society in Valencienne. In 1830 he

The French Napoléon Coste used guitars with additional bass strings.

moved to Paris and studied harmonization and bass continuo with Fernando Sor. In Paris he also met other guitarists, such as Aguado, Carcassi and Carulli. He published his first guitar compositions in 1840 and won the second prize in a contest for guitar compositions in Brussels in 1856. J.K. Mertz won the first prize. Coste was appreciated as one of the best guitarists in France. His contemporaries have described his playing as clear and powerful. Coste used a guitar with a 7th additional string, D, which widened the scale lower. He also played with a large guitar, which was tuned one fifth lower than normal. Unfortunately, Coste's career as a solo guitarist ended in 1863 due to an accident where he broke his arm. After the accident he continued as a composer. Coste was a Bonapartist and a Freemason.

Coste published more than 50 guitar compositions, such as fantasies, caprices, waltzes and compositions with a program, such as *Le Passage des Alpes* and *Souvenir de Flandres.* The most popular of his works are *25 Études op. 38* and a new edition of Sor's guitar method, to which he composed additional material. Edition

Chanterelle has published Coste's works in nine volumes (ECH 414).

For a solo guitar: "Variations et finale sur un motif favori de la famille Suisse de Weigl op. 2"; "2 Quadrilles de contredanses op. 3"; "Fantaisie sur un motif du ballet d'Armide op. 4"; "Souvenirs de Flandres op. 5"; "Fantaisie de concert op. 6"; "16 Valses favorites de Johann Strauss op. 7"; "Divertissement sur Lucia di Lammermoor op. 9"; "Grand caprice op. 11"; "Rondeau de Concert op. 12"; "Caprice ... sur La Cachucha op. 13"; Polonaise op. 14"; "Le tournoi, fantaisie chevaleresque op. 15"; "Fantaisie sur deux motifs de la Norma op. 16"; "La romanesca op. 19b: Souvenirs, sept morceaux épisodiques nos. 1-7 op. 17-23"; "Grand solo op. 24, Le Passage des Alpes op: 27; 28a; 40"; "Fantaisie symphonique op. 28b"; Divertissement op. 28c, La Chasse des Sylphes op. 29"; "Sérénade op. 30"; "Le départ op. 31"; "Mazurca op. 33a"; "Andante et 25 Études op. 38 Menuet op. 39"; "Feuilles d'automne op. 41"; "La ronde de maiop. 42"; "Marche funèbre et rondeau op. 43"; "Andante et Polonaise op. 44"; "Divagation op. 45"; "Valse favorite op. 46"; "La Source du Lyson op. 47"; "Quatre marches et six préludes op. 48 & 49"; "Adagio et divertissements op. 50"; "Récréation du guitariste op. 51"; "Le livre d' or du guitariste op. 52"; "Six Pieces Originales op. 53"; "Andante et allegro"; "Introducion et variations sur un motif de Rossini"; etc. small pieces, waltzes, catrills. For two guitars: "Scherzo et Pastorale op. 10"; "Duetto" (WoO); The second guitar's part for solo works: "Rondeau de concert op. 12"; "Le Passage des Alpes op. 27"; "Grand Duo" (WoO); "La Source du Lyson op 47." For an oboe (flute or violin) and guitar: "Consolazione, Romance sans Paroles op. 25"; "Les Regrets, Cantilène op. 36"; "Marche et Scherzo op. 33b"; "Le Montagnard, Divertissement Pastoral op 34."

CRUMB, Georg Henry (born 1929), a composer from the United States, who was born into a family of musicians. His father played the clarinet and his mother the cello. Crumb studied viola playing at the University of Illinois and graduated in 1952. He continued composition studies at the University of Michigan in 1953–55. He also took part in Bartók's and Stravinsky's composition seminars and studied in Berlin in 1955–56. Since 1964 Crumb worked as a composition teacher at the University of Colorado.

For a baritone, an electric guitar, electric double bass, electric piano and two percussion: "Songs, Drones and Refrains of Death" (to the text by F. Lorca, 1969). For a guitar, saxophone, harp, double bass and two percussion: "Quest" (1990).

DAMAS, Tomás (born in the early 19th century), a Spanish guitarist, composer and conductor. Gave concerts in Spain in the mid 19th century and conducted the Valladolid Orchestra. Damas published material for learning to play the guitar: *Nuevo Método de Guitarra por cifra compaseda* (1868) and *Método completo y progressivo de guitarra* (1869). Damas composed ca. 100 pieces for the guitar and arranged Spanish folk songs.

For a solo guitar: "Carnaval de Venecia"; "Rondeña"; "Soleá"; "El trémolo, Nocturno característico"; "Un Recuerdo, Vals"; "Variaciones sobre el canto religioso"; "Genio y arte, Gran tanda de valses"; "Fandango"; "La noce, Andante y Polaca"; "Ae viagero artista, un Recuerdo" (a Julian Arcas); "El solitario, tema con variaciones"; "El diplomático"; "Schottich"; "Amor paterno"; "Andante y Scherzo"; "La Azucena, Polka"; "La Marsellesa, Himno Patriótico"; "Fantasía, sobre aires populares Españoles."

D'ANGELO, Nuccio (born 1955), an Italian composer, who first taught himself the guitar. He took part in Alvaro Company's master courses in Florence in 1976 and at the same time he studied composition with Gaetano Giani-Luporini. D'Angelo won the first prize in an Andrés Segovia composition contest in Granada in 1991. At the moment he teaches in the Music Academy of Livorno.

For a solo guitar: "Barcarola" (from 4 Travestimenti); "2 Canzoni Lidie"; "Magie." For a recorder and a guitar: "4 Travestimenti: Alba, Barcarola (guitar solo), Mercato, Sera."

DAVID, Johann Nepomuk (1895–1977), an Austrian composer. Started his musical career as a choir boy in the monastery of Sankt Florian, as also did Anton Bruckner. He studied violin, piano and organ playing and later composition with Joseph Marx. David worked as a professor in Stuttgart in 1948–63 and was known as a bass continuo composer, who has composed 8 symphonies.

For a solo guitar: "Sonata op. 31/5." For four guitars: "Drei folkslieder." For a flute or a recorder and a guitar: "Variations op. 32." For a flute, viola and guitar: "Trio"; "Sonate op. 26."

DAVID, Thomas Christian (1925-2006), an Austrian composer, conductor and music pedagogue. Studied music with his father Johann Nepomuk David and later at the University of Leipzig he studied piano, flute playing and composition. T. David has worked as a flute teacher in the Mozarteum in Salzburg, as a choir leader and conductor in Stuttgart, and as a composition teacher in Vienna. Since 1967 he worked in Teheran pioneering as a music pedagogue and working as the chief conductor in the National Television. In 1973 he returned to Vienna as a composition teacher.

For three guitars: "3 Canzonas." For a cello and a guitar: "Duo-Sonata." For a flute, viola and a guitar: "Trio." For a guitar and an orchestra: "Concerto."

DENISOV, Edison (1929–1996), a Russian composer. Studied mathematics and mechanics and graduated from the University of Tomsk in 1951. In 1951 Denisov was, because of a recommendation by Shostakovich, accepted to the Tchaikovsky Conservatory in Moscow, where he studied piano playing with A. Belov

The Sonata (1977) by the Russian Edison Denisov is an interesting modern composition for a flute and guitar.

and composition with V. Sebalin. He taught himself in that same institution from 1960 onwards. The music composed by Denisov in the 1950s shows the influence of Shostakovich, Stravinsky and Bartók. In the 1960s he shifted to a serial technique and, for example, Schoenberg, Webern and Boulez were among his models. He tried also aleatoric and electronic music. "Denisov was among the first composers who in the 1960s brought new western techniques to the Soviet Union and who could apply them and develop them in an artistically impressing way." (K. Aho).

For a solo guitar: "Sonate" (1981). For a flute and a guitar: "Sonate" (1977). For a violin, guitar and organ: "In Deo speravit con meum" (1984). For a guitar and

an orchestra: "Concerto" (1981).

DIABELLI, Anton (1781–1858), an Austrian music publisher, composer, piano and guitar teacher. Diabelli took his first steps in the field of music with his musician father, Nicolaus Demon, who taught his son the basics of violin and piano playing. Anton started to sing in a choir at the age of seven (1788) in the monastery of Michaelbeurn, which was the preschool for the chapel of Salzburg. He studied in Salzburg in 1790–97. Diabelli, whose parents hoped that their son would become a priest, continued his music studies in 1798 in the monastery of Raitenhaslach. There he got to know Michael Haydn (brother of Joseph Haydn), who became both his teacher in piano and organ playing and a friend for a long time. M. Haydn's influence on Diabelli's development as a composer was remarkable. In 1802 Diabelli left the monastery and moved to Vienna, where he at first worked as a piano and guitar teacher and was also known as an arranger and composer. Where and how Diabelli learned to play the guitar is not known. In the covers of some of his early works published in Vienna (the earliest from 1805) he calls himself "a professor of guitar and piano playing." In Vienna he also worked as a proofreader in the note publishing company of S.A. Steiner, and this is probably what made him interested in publishing. That became, in addition to composing, his central work in his life. In 1818 Diabelli, together with his friend Peter Capp, established his own publishing company, where his job was to choose the works to be published and do the composing and arrangement. This explains the large number of arrangements in his productions. In 1824 Diabelli founded a new company, *Diabelli & Co.* As a publisher he was in touch with the great composers of that time, such as Beethoven, Rossini, Schubert and the guitar composer Mauro Giuliani. The influence of Giuliani, who came to Vienna in 1806, on the popularity of the guitar was considerable. This has probably also affected the width of Diabelli's guitar production, of which most of the works were composed in 1805–20, in other words during the period that Giuliani lived in Vienna (1806–19). Diabelli arranged the orchestral parts of Giuliani's guitar concertos op. 30, 36 and 70 for the piano and the voices for a guitar tuned one third higher.

Diabelli's whole production covers ca. 3000 compositions and arrangements. A third is guitar music, which can be divided into three categories: concert music for the guitar and different ensembles; simple amateur pieces; and arrangements. The ensembles in Diabelli's guitar compositions are exceptionally versatile, only some compositions are for a solo guitar. During his lifetime he was best known for his church music compositions. Diabelli's music has been described as resembling the Biedermier style,

where the melodies are singing, harmonies more courageous than in the Classical style and emotions more controlled than in the Romantic style.

A lecturer of guitar playing in the Sibelius Academy, Jukka Savijoki, has written a doctoral thesis about Diabelli, *Anton Diabelli's Guitar Works: A Thematic Catalogue with an Introduction* (1996). This catalogue contains information about almost 130 original works for the guitar and nearly 500 arrangements.

For a solo guitar: "Märsche, 1 Cantate & Deutsche Tänze op. 5"; "Potpourri op. 14" (no. 1-4); "12 Allemandes op. 25"; "Ouverture op. 26"; "10 pièces favorites op. 28"; "3 Sonates (C, A, F) op. 29"; "6 Eccossaises op. 30"; "30 sehr leichte Übungsstücke op. 39"; "Deux Fugues op. 46"; "Amusements pour les dames op. 89"; "7 Preludes progressives op. 103"; "Grand variazioni (de l' opera Tancredi) op. 104"; "12 leichte Ländler in C op. 121, in D op 127"; "Sonatina WoO"; "2 Rondeaux WoO"; arrangements from the themes by Weber, Rossini etc. For two guitars (1. a guitar tuned one third higher or capo III): "Grande Sérénade op. 51"; "Variazioni sopra un tema favorito op. 57"; "Sérénade op. 63"; "Variationen über ein Thema op. 83"; "Quatrième Sérénade concertante op. 96"; "Vme Grande Sérénade op. 100"; "Millionär Walzer WoO"; "Alpenkönig Walzer WoO"; "Fugue WoO." For three guitars: "Grand Trio op. 62." For a flute and a guitar: "Grande Sérénade op. 67" (b); "Grande Sérénade sentimentale op. 99"; "24 Original Ländler WoO." For a flute (or violin) and a guitar: "12 Allemandes op. 7"; "12 Ungarische Tänze op. 16"; "Potpourri (Aus Beethovens beliebtesten Werken) WoO"; "Rossini-Walzer WoO." For a piano and a guitar: "Theme favori de Rode op. 64"; "Sonatine in A op. 68"; "Sonatine op. 70"; "Sonatine op. 71"; "Variations op. 97"; "Grande Sonate brilliante op. 102"; "12 Valses melodieuses op. 141"; "Differentes pièces très faciles op. 10 (no. 1), op. 31 (no. 2), op. 32 (no. 3), op. 45" (no. 4). For a csakan and a guitar: "Grande Sérénade op. 67" (a); "Themes favories de l'opera Zelmira op. 128"; "24 Original Ländler WoO." For two French horns and a guitar: "Notturno op. 123." For a flute (or vio-

lin) and a guitar: "6 Trio op. 34" (no. 1-6). For a flute, viola and guitar: "Grande Sérénade op. 65, op. 66, op. 95"; "Sérénade op. 36"; "Vme Grande Sérénade Concertante op. 105." For a voice and a guitar: "Witz und Laune, (6 songs) op. 106." For a voice, guitar and flute ad libitum: "6 charakteristishe Gesänge op. 91"; "7 Gesänge für Herz und Gefühl op. 101"; "Lieder der Liebe und Zärtlichkeit (10 songs) op. 98."

DILLON, James (born 1950), a British composer born in Scotland, who at first played in bagpipe and rock bands. Dillon studied acoustics, music and linguistics in Glasgow in 1967–68 and in London in 1972–76. As a composer he is autodidact. Dillon has taken part in the courses of modern music in Darmstadt in the early 80s and has acted as a guest lecturer in several universities in England and the United States (State University New York).

For a solo guitar: Shrouded Mirrors (1988).

DJEMIL, Enyss (1884-1951), real name Francis Paul Demillac, a French composer and music teacher, studied violin playing and conducting in the Music Conservatory of Paris and composition and harmonization under Aubert and Popatz. Djemil worked as a teacher in Baghdad (1947–48) and Paris since 1948.

For a solo guitar: "Caprice, complainte et ronde." For a flute and a guitar: "Petite Suite médiévale" (1917).

DODGSON, Stephen (born 1924), an English composer. Studied composition and French horn in the Royal College of Music, from which he graduated in 1950. After that he continued his studies in Italy. After returning to England he has worked as a composer, a lecturer and a teacher of harmonization and composition in the Royal College of Music until 1982. He has been awarded the Prize of the Royal Philharmonic Society twice. Since the late 1950s, Dodgson has composed music for motion pictures and plays for the BBC. His orchestral productions contain concertos for the cembalo, viola da gamba, viola, piano, cello and bassoon. Stephen Dodgson has increased the number of works available for both solo guitars and chamber music during four decades. A lot of his production is pedagogic works for the guitar and 2 *Concertos for the guitar, the First in 1956 and the Second in 1972* (dedicated to John Williams). *"The 20 Studies"* (1965) and *"Transitional Studies"* (1980), composed by Dodgson and guitar pedagogue Hector Quine in cooperation, give the player a training to modern music. In co-operation with Quine, Dodgson has also composed an etude collection for two guitars, *"Studies in Duo"* (1987). *"Duo Concertante for the Guitar and Cembalo"* was composed because John Williams and Rafael Payana ordered it as they gave concerts in Darlington and London in 1968. The work won the shared first prize in the international composition contest arranged by the French Radio, ORTF, in Paris in 1970. In addition to a large guitar production, Dodgson has also composed for the lute. (See 20th Century Composers for the Lute, Vihuela and Baroque Guitar).

For a solo guitar: "Prelude, Nocturne and Toccata" (1952), the composer has taken the work out of use; "Five Occasional Pieces" (1955); "Partita no. 1" (1963); "Sarabande" (1968); "Fantasy-Divisions" (1969); "Serenade" (1974); "Partita no. 2" (1964); "20 Studies" (1965, composed with H. Quine); "Interlude" ("Summer Daydream", 1977); "Legend" (1977); "Merlin" (1978); "Etude-Caprice" (1978); "Partita no. 3" (1981); "Transitional Studies" (1980, composed with H. Quine); "Twelve Introductory Studies" (1984); "Stemma" (1988); "The Troubled Midnight" (1989); "Partita no. 4" (1990); "Five Attic Dances." For two guitars: (The 3 first works composed with H. Quine): "Take Two, Five simple progressive duets" (1976); "Double Take" (1987); "Studies in Duo" (1987); "Promenade I" (1988). For three guitars: "Follow the Star" (1979). For a guitar, flute and cello: "Pastoral Sonata" (1953/59), the composer has taken the work out of use. For a flute and guitar: "Capriccio" (1980); "In Search of Folly" (1986). For a guitar and cembalo: "Duo Concertante" (1968); "Dialogues" (1976). For a guitar and a string quartet:

"Quintet" (1973). For a cello and a guitar: "Duo for Cello and Guitar" (1974). For a solo violinist, a guitar band (at least 7 players) and a bass: "Divertissement" (1983). For a guitar, flute and viola: "Sonata for Three" (1982). For a voice (tenor) and guitar: "4 Poems of John Clare" (1962); For a high voice and a guitar: "London Lyrics" (1977); For a soprano and guitar quartet (or guitar orchestra): "Hymnus de Sancto Stephano" (1983). For a guitar band: "Personet Hodie (1980), at least 11 guitars"; "Intermezzo" (1987), also suitable for a guitar quartet. For a guitar and an orchestra: "Concerto no. 1" (1956); "Concerto no. 2" (1972).

DOISY, Charles (?–1807), a French guitarist, guitar teacher and instrument salesman. In some sources the name is written Doisy-Lintant, which, according to Philip J. Bone, an English music researcher, is incorrect. Doisy belongs to the most remarkable representatives of the guitar music in the late 18th century. He played both a 5- and a 6-string guitar, and he published a study *Principes Généraux*. Doisy got a high reputation as a guitar teacher in Paris. Later he set up his own music store. Doisy was a productive guitar composer and he composed ca. 200 solo works for the guitar, piano/guitar duos, music for the guitar and strings, and also a rare combination, guitar and brass instruments. Scripts from Doisy's works are accessible in the libraries of Paris and Aam.

For a solo guitar: "Grand concerto"; "Quatre sonates faciles"; "50 variations from theme Folias d'Espagna"; "A collection: Walses, rondeaux, allemandes, airs variés et faciles"; "Fandango" For two guitars: "Trois duos faciles op. 15." For a guitar and a violin: "Sonatine, Trois duos"; "Trois duos, extrèmement faciles"; "Trois duos concertants et faciles." For a guitar and a viola: "Trois duos concertants." For a guitar and a cello: "Grand Duos." For a violin, viola and guitar: "Serenades." For a guitar and a string quartet: "Concertos."

DOMENICONI, Carlo (born 1947), an Italian guitarist and composer. Started his guitar studies in 1960 with Carmen Lenzi Mozzani, whose grandfather was

the famous guitarist Luigi Mozzani (1869–1943). In 1962 and 1964, Domeniconi won the first prize in the International Guitar Festival in Ancona. He took the guitar diploma at the age of 18 in Pesaro and in 1966 he graduated from the College of Western Berlin. He has taught and given concerts in several countries in Europe and has become famous as a guitar composer. Domeniconi has also taught guitar playing in Istanbul, which is why a Turkish influence can be heard in his works, such as the *Koyunbaba Suite."*

For a solo guitar: "Fantasia di luci e tenebre"; "Moon Lights"; "Koyunbaba Suite op. 19"; "Orient express"; "Homage to A. de Saint-Exupéry"; "Suite in modo antico"; "Variations on a Turkish Folk Song"; "Suite Sudamericana"; "Quaderno brasiliano, 7 pieces"; "Variationen über ein anatolishes Volkslied"; "24 Präludien"; "Fantasia di luci tenebre"; "24 Klangbilder"; "Minyo"; "Passacaglia & Fuga"; "Schnee in Istanbul"; "3 Studies for the Spirit"; "Sinbad op. 49"; "Hommage à Jimi Hendrix op. 52"; "Suite caratteristica op. 71." For two guitars: "Naturgeister, suite"; "Sonata in 3 movimenti"; "Watermusic, suite." For four guitars: "4 Stücke"; "Spanish and South American Xmas Carols." For a flute and a guitar: "Sonatina Mexicana"; "Sonata op. 37." For a cello and a guitar: "5 Stücke."

DONATONI, Franco (1927–2000), an Italian composer. Studied composition in the Music Academies of Milan and Bologna and in the Santa Cecilia Academy in Rome with Ildebrando Pizzetti (diploma 1951). He worked as a teacher of composition in the Music Academies of Bologna, Milano and Torino and as a professor of composition in Milan since 1969. The models of Donatoni were Petrassi and Bartók, whose influence can be seen in his early works until the 1960s, when his style became aleatoric and serial. After this he made even more radical, often aleatoric experiments. He won composition prizes and was the composer guest of the Helsinki Biennal in 1985.

For a solo guitar: "Algo – two pieces for the guitar composed in 1977" (dedicated to Ruggero Chiesa and Oscar Ghiglia). For a violin, viola and guitar: "About" (1979). 2 pieces for a soprano and a guitar: "Åse." For a piccolo, bass clarinet, viola, double bass, mandoline, guitar, harp and marimba: "Refrain" (1986).

DONIZETTI, Gaetano (1797–1847), an Italian opera composer, whose success began in 1822 in Rome. Through Naples, Milan and other theater cities, Donizetti soon became known through the whole of Italy. Later he lived in Paris and Vienna. In 1842 he was appointed the chamber conductor and composer in Austria. Donizetti uses the guitar in his opera *Don Pasquale*. A few guitar composers in the Romantic era composed variations and fantasies using themes from the Donizetti's operas. These composers were Mauro Giuliani, Napoléon Coste and Johann Kaspar Mertz.

DOTZAUER, Justus Johann Friedrich (1783–1860), a German cellist, composer and pedagogue. A musician in the chamber orchestras of Meiningen and Dresden in 1801–05 and a solo cellist since 1821. Dotzauer has composed a virtuoso composition for the cello and the guitar, *"Potpourri (La Guitaromanie) op. 21."*

For a cello and a guitar: "Potpourri (La Guitaromanie) op. 21."

DUARTE, John William (1919–2004), an English guitar pedagogue and composer, a central figure in the guitar life of his country. Started his interest at the age of 14 by playing the ukulele and the jazz guitar, six years later (1940) he became more interested in the classical guitar and art music. In addition to guitar music Duarte specialized in musical literature and published several remarkable books and collections about the playing of classical guitar, such as *Bases of Classical Guitar Technique* and *Guitarist's ABC*. He has also arranged a lot of music for the classical guitar. Duarte wrote reviews of concerts and recordings for several magazines. He held master courses for the guitar around the world.

For a solo guitar: "Variations on a Catalan Folk Song op. 25"; "Variations on 'Three blind mice' op. 24"; "Fantasia and fugue on 'Torre bermeja' op. 30"; "English Suite op. 31"; "Sonatinette op. 35"; "Prelude, Canto and Toccata op. 38"; "A flight of Fugues op. 44"; "Suite Piemontese op. 46"; "Suite Ancienne op. 47"; "Sonatina lirica op 48"; "Etude Diabolique op. 49"; "All in a row op. 51"; "Sua cosa op. 52"; "Easy pictures op. 56"; "Tout en Ronde op 57"; "Mutations on the 'Dies irae' op. 58"; "Partita op. 59"; "Petite suite française op. 60"; "Homage to Antonio Lauro, 3 Valses op. 83"; "Danserie No. 2 op. 87" (Tango & Tarantella); "Idylle pour Ida" (Homage to Ida Presti op. 93); "American Universal op. 96"; "Variations sur un thème de Štěpán Rak op. 100"; "Musikones op. 107." For two guitars: "Chanson op. 14"; "Greek Suite op. 39"; "Greek Suite no. 2 op. 89"; "Suite française op. 61"; "Variations on a French nursery song op. 32." "English Suite No. 2 op. 77"; "Guitar duos without tears op. 74." For three guitars: "Trio for three op. 69"; "Little Suite no. 2 op. 79"; "Variations on a Swedish folk song op. 84"; "Little Suite no. 3 op. 81"; "Little Suite no. 4 op. 95"; "Riverboat Suite op. 94." For four guitars: "Going Dutch op. 36"; "English Suite No. 3 op. 78"; "Little Suite op. 68"; "Americana op. 96a." "Ballade op. 53"; "Concerto Democratico op. 108"; "Diptych No. 1 op. 80" (Aria & Toccata). For five guitars and drums: "Bath Water Music op. 114." For six guitars: "Summerset follies op. 109"; "English Suite No. 5 op. 112." For a flute and a guitar: "Sonatina op. 15"; "Danse joyeuse op. 42"; "Memory of a dance op. 64"; "English Suite No. 4 op. 82" (flute/recorder). For a soprano recorder and a guitar: "Un petit jazz op. 92." For a violin and a guitar: "Centone di Sonate I, II, IV op. 67" (Paganini/Duarte). For a guitar and a cembalo: "Insieme op. 72." For a voice and a guitar: "Grown up op. 20"; "Five Quiet Songs op. 37"; "Cradle song op. 16"; "Friends and lovers op. 99"; "Hark, hark, the Ark op. 103." For a guitar and a string quartet: "Guitar Quintet No. 1 op. 85."

DUMOND, Arnaud (born 1952), a French guitarist. Started to study flamenco guitar playing at the age of 11

and shifted later to classical guitar studies in École Normale de Musique in Paris, from which he graduated with honors in 1971. In addition to guitar studies, he studied music with J. -P. Guézec, Nadia Boulanger and Maurice Ohana. After winning the guitar contest of the French Radio, (ORTF) (as the first French guitarist) he has succeeded in several guitar contests around the world (Belgrad, Rotterdam, and Tokyo) and given concerts around the world.

For a solo guitar: "Comme un Hommage à Ravel"; "Comme un Prelude-Comme une Complainte"; "Differences sur Greensleeves"; "Sur un thème Liturgique Orthodoxe"; "20 études de styles: Cinq Haikus Atonaux" (1994); "Lythanie" (1977). For a flute and a guitar: "Medee midi desert" (1980).

DYENS, Roland (born 1955), a French guitarist born in the Republic of Tunisia. Started his guitar studies in Paris with Robert Maison at the age of nine and continued his studies in École Normale de Musique in Paris with Alberto Ponce. In 1979 he won the Palestrina Guitar Contest in Porto Alegre, Brazil and the same year a special prize in the Alessandria Guitar Contest in Italy. As a guitarist he has given concerts in Denmark, Greece, Indonesia and Brazil. Dyens teaches guitar playing in the Music Academy of Chaville. He has also been interested in jazz and improvisation. Dyens has stated that when he plays a concerto, he composes new cadences to replace the original ones. Dyens has also studied composition with Raymond Weber and Désiré Dodene.

For a solo guitar: "Hommage à Villa-Lobos" (1987); "Eloge de Leo Brouwer" (1988); "Libra Sonatine" (1986); "Tango en skaï" (1985); "Vals en skaï"; "Trois Saudades." For two guitars: "Côte Nord." For four guitars: "Costé suol." For a guitar octet: "Côté Sud"; "Rythmaginaires." For a guitar and a guitar orchestra: "Concerto en Si." For a guitar and a chamber orchestra: "Concerto Métis." He has also arranged music for the guitar, e.g. "H. Villa-Lobos's Bachianas Brasileiras no. 5 for the solo guitar and a guitar orchestra."

EASTWOOD, Tom (1922–1999), an English composer. When working for the British Embassy in Ankara, Eastwood privately studied composition with Necil Kâzimakses. Later he studied in Berlin under Blacher and in London with Stein. Eastwood worked for the theater and the radio. The most famous of his works is a chamber opera Christopher Sly.

For a solo guitar: "Blues-Variations" (1980); "D'une élégie slave" (1981). "Capriccio" (1962); "Ballade-Phantasy" (1968); "Amphora" (1971); "Romance et plainte." For an oboe and a guitar: "Uirapuru."

EBEN, Petr (born 1929), a Czech composer and pianist. Studied in the Music Academy of Prague, worked since 1955 as a professor at the University of Prague and since 1990 as the musical director of the Prague Spring Festival. Eben's production focuses on vocal music, where he uses different languages, such as Latin.

For a solo guitar: "Tabulatura Nova" (1979); "Mare nigrum" (1981).

EDLUND, Mikael (born 1950), a Swedish composer who started as a rock musician. Studied musicology at the University of Uppsala in 1970–72, and then composition with Ingvar Lindholm and Arne Mellnäs in the Music Academy of Stockholm in 1972–75. Edlund made excursions abroad in 1977–78 to the United States. Edlund belongs to the remarkable composers of the young generation, and he has achieved success especially with his chamber works. The Swedish Rikskonserter ordered a guitar composition and he composed the *"Små fötter, miniatyr"* (1982), which Magnus Andersson has recorded (Chitarra con forza PS CD 19) and which was published by Bèrben (1986).

For a solo guitar: "Små fötter, miniatyr" (1982).

EESPERE, René (born 1953), an Estonian composer. Studied piano playing in the Music School of Tallinn and graduated as a composer from the

A fascinating guitar work by the Estonian composer René Eespere is Trivium for the flute, violin and guitar. His solo guitar work Evocatio won the first prize in a national composition contest in Estonia in 1996.

Music Conservatory of Tallinn after studying with A. Garsnek in 1977. He continued his composition studies in the Music Conservatory of Moscow in 1977–79 with Aram Khatchaturian and Aleksei Nikolajev. Since 1979 he has taught theory in the Music Conservatory of Tallinn (now Music Academy of Estonia). Eespere's versatile production contains symphony, theater and children's music. Eespere's work for the solo guitar, "Evocatio", won the first prize in the guitar contest in Estonia in 1996. Eespere has also used the guitar in his flute concerto (1995).

René Eespere's *"Trivium"* (1991) is one of the most famous guitar chamber music works in Estonia. Trivium means an intersection of streets. The composer has described "Trivium" as follows: "Three musicians gather to play music, after which they all have to go their own ways."

For a solo guitar: "Evocatio" (1996). For a flute, violin and guitar: "Trivium" (1991).

EINEM, Gottfried von (1918– 1996), an Austrian composer. He was born to a military family in Austria, but was

brought up in Germany and England. Einem worked as a rehearsal pianist in the opera choir in Berlin in 1939–44. At the same time he studied composition with Boris Blacher. In 1948–62, he worked in the executive group of the Salzburg Music Festival and since 1965 as a professor in the Music College of Vienna. Einem has composed several works for the UN. His music shows a motive-rhythmic technique and influences from jazz.

For a solo guitar: "4 Studien op. 34" (1967).

EIRÍKSDÓTTIR, Karólína (born 1957), an Icelandic composer, who studied composition at the University of Michigan with William Albright. In 1983–89 Eríksdóttir worked as the president of the Icelandic Information Center for Music. At the moment she teaches composition in the Music Academy of Reykjavik.

For a soprano, flute, b clarinet, cello, guitar and cembalo: "Some Days" (1991).

The Icelandic composer Karólína Eiríksdóttir.

ESPLÁ, Oscar (1886–1976), a Spanish composer. After studying technique and philosophy Esplá dedicated himself to his composition work. As a composer he is mainly auto didact. He made excursions to France, Belgium and Germany, where he studied a while with Max Reger. Esplá is one of the first composers in Spain who dedicated his life to symphonic music. Esplá's music is tonal and he often uses ingredients from folk music.

For a solo guitar: "Dos Impressiones Levantinas" (dedicated to Andrés Segovia); "Antano"; "Tiempo de sonata."

FALLA, Manuel de (1876–1946), a Spanish composer and pianist, who is considered to be the founder of the Spanish National Art of Music and the most important representative in the 20th century. Albéniz and Granados had paved way for his success. De Falla was especially interested in Spanish folk songs and melodies, on which his impressionistically colored lyrical works often are based. In 1893, at the age of 17, he became familiar with Edward Grieg's music, which gave him an idea to preserve the Spanish national voice. An important model in using national themes in music was his teacher Felipe Pedrell (1841–1922), who studied Spanish folk music. Pedrell recommended music based on Spanish folk music to his pupils. Later models of de Falla were especially French composers Claude Debussy and Maurice Ravel.

De Falla composed only one work for the guitar, "Homenaje." Miguel Llobet had for a long time tried to persuade de Falla to compose something for the guitar. This first modern guitar composition of the 20th century was composed in 14 days in 1920. Also a French magazine, *Revue Musicale*, had a hand in the composing, as they asked de Falla to compose something to honor the memory of Debussy. In "Homenaje", which is a habanera, de Falla quotes a work by Debussy, *"Soirée dans Grenade."* Miguel Llobet gave the first performance of "Homenaje" on February 18, 1921. Andrés Segovia played this composition for the first time in December 1922.

Many works by de Falla have been arranged for the guitar and they have reached a stable position in guitar repertoires. These works are themes from opera, *"La vida breve"* (a short life); ballet, *"El Amor Brujo"* (a possessed love) and *"El sombrero de tres picos"* (a three-corner hat); and a suite for a voice and guitar *"Siete canciónes populares españolas"* (seven Spanish folk songs, originally for a voice and piano). This work was composed in 1914–15. There de Falla directly borrows from Spanish folk tradition. Both the music and the texts express colorful miniature pictures. De Falla spent his last years in Argentina, in the remote town of Cordoba, where he made drafts of his compositions in a small ascetic hut.

For a solo guitar: "Homenaje" (1920). Arrangements for a solo guitar: "2 Dances" (El Amor Brujo); "Danza del molinero" (El sombrero de tres picos). For a voice and guitar: "Siete canciónes populaires españolas" (arr. Miguel Llobet).

FALÚ, Eduardo (1923), the most famous composer of Argentinean folk music, guitarist and singer. Studied composition, arrangement and theory as a private pupil of composer Carlos Guastavino. Falú became interested in the guitar as a young boy and learned very fast to play Argentinean folk songs. As a youngster he played together with César Perdiguero and their duet was very successful both in radio and on stage. Later, Falú continued his career as a solo artist giving concerts around the world. When playing the guitar, Falú used Sor's and Aguado's methods thus reaching a high technical level. As a singer, Falú is a baritone, and he has given concerts as a singer-guitarist and made several radio recordings. He has performed as a duet with his son Juan José Falú and the flamenco guitarist Paco Pena. Falú composes in a Latin American style.

For a solo guitar: "Suite Argentina"; "El Algarrobao"; "La Cuartelera"; also several milonga-, zamba- and chôro compositions.

FARKAS, Ferenc (1905–2002), a Hungarian composer and music pedagogue. After starting his career as a pianist Farkas studied composition with Leó Weiner and Albert Skilós in the Music Academy of Budapest in 1922–27. Later he completed his musical studies in Rome with Ottorino Respighi. In 1933–35 he earned his living as a composer of motion picture music in Vienna and Copenhagen. Farkas taught composition in the Music Academy of Budapest, where he worked as a professor in 1949–75. His pupils included Ligeti and Kurtág. As a composer, Farkas benefited from his experience as a teacher and from his connections to the theater and motion picture music. His musical production varies from operas to operettas. In his music he used several different instruments, and his ideas spring from various sources.

For a solo guitar: "Six pièces brèves" (1971); "Exercitium tonale 24 preludi" (1972); "Sonata" (published in 1980); "Antiche danze ungheresi" (arr. For the guitar by Lázló Szendrey-Karper). For two guitars: "Variazioni ungherese" (1983). For three guitars or a guitar band: "Ugróczi muzsika" (1987); "Citharoedia Strigoniensis" (1972). For a guitar band: "Somogyi emlék" (1977); "Csángó szonatina" (1977). For a voice and a guitar: "Cinque canzoni dei trovatori (1971), in French"; "Török dal Júliához (a Turkish song), for poems by Bálint Balassi"; "Gitár-dalok (Guitar songs, 1983), for poems by Jenö Dsida."

FELD, Jindrich (born 1925), a Czech composer, got first violin lessons from his father and continued his studies in the Conservatory and Music Academy of Prague in 1945–52. Since 1954, he has worked as a free lance composer and in 1968–69 as a teacher of composition in Adelaide, Australia.

For a solo guitar: "Sonata" (1974); "Barbaric Dance" (1974). For two guitars: "Ten Pieces" (1986). For a flute and a guitar: "Two Dances" (1975). For guitar and flute: "Divertimento" (1996). For a violin, guitar and hammond: "Miniatures" (1967–68). For a guitar and a woodwind quintet: "Caprices" (1964).

FENICIO, Edmar (born 1955), a Brazilian guitarist and composer. Studied with Guido Santorsola and Leo Perachi. Fenicio's music is influenced by Brazilian folk music and several composer-guitarists, such as Heitor Villa-Lobos, Ernesto Nasareth, Laurindo Almeida, João Pernambuco, Baden Powell and Luiz Bonfá.

For a solo guitar: "Baiãozinho"; "Frevo"; "Message To Jobim"; "São Sebastião do Rio de Janeiro" (samba); "Suite de Homenagens"; "Velho Tema" (valsa); "4 Romantic Waltzes."

FERANDIÈRE, Fernando (1750–1816) a Spanish violinist, guitarist and composer. Was influenced by Miguel García (father Padre-Basilio). Ferandière worked as a violinist in the cathedral of Málaga and as a music teacher in Madrid. In Madrid he published a remarkable guitar school "*Arte de tocar la Guitarra Española por músic*" ("The Spanish skill to play the guitar with the help of notes") in 1799 (second edition in 1816). It is probably the first school which teaches to play the guitar with modern notes instead of the tablature. Ferandière was a productive composer: he composed more than 200 works for the guitar, which were published in Cádiz and Madrid in 1785–99. In addition to the guitar solos, the pieces include duos (diálogos) for the guitar with a violin or a flute, 40 trios for the violin, guitar and bass, 40 quartets for the violin, viola, guitar and bass, 18 quintets for two guitars, two violins and a bass, 6 concertos for the guitar and an orchestra. Ferandière's production and work prepared ground for e.g. Fernando Sor.

Brian Ferneyhough

FERNEYHOUGH, Brian (born 1943), a British composer. Studied in Amsterdam with Ton de Leeuw and in Basel with Klaus Huber. Ferneyhough has been awarded in several prominent composition contests. He has worked as a composition teacher in Freiburg, Haag, the University of California and e.g. in the Darmstadt courses. Ferneyhough's scores are symbolic and contain lots of instructions. The Swedish guitarist Magnus Andersson, who specializes in modern music, has published an article about performing Ferneyhough's solo guitar work, *Kurze Schatten II Considérations d' un interprète* (Contrechamps nr. 8, Lausanne, 1988).

For a solo guitar: "Kurze Schatten II" (1983–88).

FERRER ESTEVE, José (1835–1916), a Spanish guitarist, pedagogue and composer. Ferrer belongs to the same generation as composer-guitarists Coste, Mertz, Regondi and Zani de Ferranti. At first he studied music with his father, who was a guitarist and music collector. Later he studied with José Broca in Paris, where he himself taught guitar playing and worked as a guitarist in Comédie Françaice for four years since 1878. After this he returned to Spain and taught guitar playing in the Music Academy of Barcelona. There is no complete catalogue of Ferrer's works yet. About 50 works have been published. His compositions contain solos and duets for the guitar, compositions for the flute and guitar and several songs. In addition to being a composer, teacher and performer, Ferrer was an active historian. He published a book about the history of the guitar, *Reseña Historica de la Guitarra,* in Madrid and wrote a manuscript for a guitar school. Ferrer's music contains a wide variety of guitar techniques at different levels.

For a solo guitar: "Recuerdos de Montgri op 1"; "Veladas intimas op. 17"; "2 Tangos op. 19"; "Barcarola op. 54"; "Charme de la Nuit" (11 character pieces); "3 Dances"; "Spanish Favourites." For two guitars: "Minuet & Vals."

FODEN, William (1860–1947), an American guitar virtuoso, composer and arranger with English roots. Foden started his violin lessons at the age of 7, and at the age of 16 he played the violin in orchestras. Foden was also interested in playing the guitar and the mandoline. Since 1877 he worked as a guitarist in the *"St Louis Trio"* (flute, violin and guitar) and founded the same year a mandoline band called *"Beethoven."* In 1904 Foden made his debute in Carnegie Hall and since 1911 he frequently gave concerts in the United States. William Foden was famous for his ability to play tremolos. He was also a remarkable guitar pedagogue, who published a two-volume guitar school, *Grand Method,* in New York. He composed nearly a hundred guitar pieces, whose style can be compared to those of Francisco Tárrega's.

For a solo guitar: "La Favorita Fantasia"; "Spanish Bolero no. 3"; "Gavotte Floral"; "6 Short Preludes." Foden's arrangements for the solo guitar: "Minuet in F"; "Il Grand Gavotte"; "Gondoliera - Bonnie Boat"; "Esperanza - Mexican Danza."

FORTEA, Daniel (1882–1953), a Spanish guitarist and guitar composer. Fortea started to study guitar playing as a young boy according to the methods of Aguado and Tárrega and studied with Tárrega since he was 20 years old. Fortea made excellent progress in his studies, so Tárrega often added guitar duos with Fortea to his concerts. After Tárrega's death in 1909 Fortea moved to Madrid and after successful concert activity he founded the *Academia de Gitarra and Biblioteca Fortea,* a music sheet publishing company, which soon was known around the world. Fortea was a productive composer and he also arranged hundreds of classical and modern works for the guitar and published guitar music composed by F. Sor and M. Giuliani. His Guitar School appeared in 1921 (second edition in 1930). Fortea's compositions are often based on Spanish folk music. Fortea's works are accessible in Ivan Putilin's music collection in the library of the Sibelius Academy in Finland.

For a solo guitar: "Jota Aragonesa"; "Capricho-Estudio op. 13"; "Suite Española op. 22" (1943); "Estudios poéticos op. 25"; "Elegia de Tárrega"; "Cuentos de Madrid, Madrigal"; "Dialogando-Serenata"; "Soleares"; "Mi

Favorita - Mazurca"; "Malagueñas."

FOSS, Lukas (born 1922), a composer from the United States, who was born in Berlin and moved to the United States at the age of 15. Foss studied in Philadelphia in the Curtis Institute of Music and first composed tonal music. In the 1950s, he changed his style to writing experimental music. The three-part guitar concerto *"American Landscapes"* (1989) continues this line. The concerto was ordered by Sharon Isbin, an American guitarist.

For a guitar and an orchestra: "American Landscapes" (1989).

FOSSA, François de (1775–1849), a French guitarist, composer and arranger. De Fossa was a Lt. Colonel in the 23rd regiment of the French army (B. Jeffery: Aguado: *New Guitar Method*, p. xii), who also was an active musician. He started his music studies in the small town of Perpignani. When the revolution started in France, he moved to Spain and served as an officer in the army of Roussillon, which was called *"Legion Pyrénées."* After the war of 1794–95 de Fossa fell ill and stayed in Barcelona. In 1798, de Fossa traveled to America and worked as an officer in Mexico City until 1803 and ten years later he worked for Joseph Bonaparte in France. In 1825 de Fossa got married. He had three children.

As a guitarist he was a close friend of Aguado, with whom he worked in cooperation and Aguado dedicated many of his works to de Fossa and his wife. In a guitar school by Aguado in 1825, there is a description of how de Fossa plays flageolets. As a composer de Fossa was influenced by the most famous composers of his time, e.g. Beethoven, Haydn and Boccherini, whose guitar quintets he wrote out. De Fossa has arranged six quartets for two guitars, composed by Czerny, Haydn Hummel, Mayseder, etc. These arrangements were published in Paris under op. number 17 (Matanya Ophee). "In his compositions de Fossa impressively tried to balance various instruments with each other. Humor is one of his most important musical features, it can be seen in the emphasis, dynamics and imitation in his music.

De Fossa never had to compete or work as a musician. He did not teach, nor did he have to compose amateur level music, instead he composed for fun at the level that he wanted." (Simon Wynberg/Ophee). In addition to original music, de Fossa made several arrangements out of the most popular opera overtures of that time, e.g. fantasies from Rossini's opera themes. (Ed. Orphée).

For a solo guitar: "1e. Fantaisie op. 5"; "Variations on 'La Tyrolienne' op. 1"; "4 Divertimentos after Haydn op. 13"; "3 Rondos"; "5e Fantaisie on Les Folies d' Espagne op. 12"; "Overture to the Opera 'Le Calife de Bagdad' by Boieldieu Woo." Edition Chanterelle has published works about Fossa's chamber music: For a guitar, violin and cello: "3 Trios Concertants op. 18" and for a violin, two guitars and a cello, or alternatively for a violin, guitar, viola and cello: "Quartet op. 19" (first published in 1826). Arrangements: for two guitars: "Six Duos Concertantes... op. 17." For a piano and a guitar: "Ouverture de l'opera Elisabetta de Rossini op. 14."

FRANÇAIX, Jean René Désiré (1912–1997), a French composer and pianist. Studied piano playing with Isidor Philipp and composition with Nadia Boulanger. Françaix's composition style was based on the French tradition, his model was Maurice Ravel. In addition to neoclassicism, Françaix's style also contains bitonality and dodecaphony. Françaix composed operas, symphonies, concertos etc.

For a solo guitar: "2 pieces" (1950); "Priére du soir"; "Divertissement"; "Passacaille"; "Sérénata" (1978). For a voice and a guitar: "Priére du soir-chanson" (1947). For a recorder and a guitar: "Sonata" (1984). For a guitar and an orchestra: "Concerto" (1982–83).

FREIDLIN, Jan (1944), a Russian composer. Graduated from the Music Academy of Odessa in 1971 and worked after that as a composition teacher in a music school in Odessa. Freidlin's music has been published in M. Ophee's series *The Russian Collection* (Vol. 5 Soviet Guitar Music). For a solo guitar: "5 Postludes";

"Strophes of Sappho."

FRICKER, Peter Racine (1920–1990), a British composer and conductor. Was educated in the Royal Music College of London with R.O. Morris and Ernest Bullock. Later he also studied with Mátyás Seiber. Fricker was one of the first well-known English modern composers after WW II. From 1952 onwards he was the head of the Royal Music College of London. When he composed, he could see the whole work in his mind before he wrote anything on paper. His logical style was clearly comprehensive. Fricker's melodic lines were very accurate, yet they were always open for later development.

For a solo guitar: "Paseo op. 31 (1970), dedicated to Julian Bream." For a voice and a guitar: "O Mistress Mine (1961), to texts by William Shakespeare."

FUNK PEARSON, Stephen (born 1950), a guitarist from the United States, from a family where both parents were professional musicians. Funk Pearson studied music in Vassar College and in Hunter College, where he took the master of arts degree as a soloist and composer, after which he studied two years in Europe. He has taken part in the master courses in Siena under Oscar Ghiglia and has also studied guitar playing with J. Tomás, John Mills and David Russell. In addition to classical music, Funk Pearson has been interested in popular music and he has played in pop-jazz, folk and rock bands. In the text leaflet of Funk Pearson's solo CD *Hudson River Debut* (1996) he is described as a real cosmopolitan and life artist, who has traveled to Africa, Cuba, South America, India and Russia. In addition to music he has lived in a hut he built on an island in British Columbia. He has also worked as a breeder of owls and a lifeguard!

For a solo guitar: "Four Skaals"; "Thusslegarth"; "Tsamaloon"; "Brunelle the Dancing Bear"; "Six Mixtures"; "Mummychogs"; "No Just Classical Guitar"; "Ardea Herodias Waltz"; "Box Turtle"; "Sea Peace"; "Pongue"; "Fairgowly"; "Five Bilbarns"; "Jaringhe";

"Six Mixtures"; "Tricoscopie"; "Tusitala." For a flute and a guitar (& cello ad libitum): "K.A.M.I."

FÜRSTENAU, Kaspar (1772–1819), a German flutist and composer. At first he studied oboe playing with his father. After he was orphaned, Anton Romberg took care of him and taught him to play the bassoon, but was more interested in the flute. At the age of 15 he was already a skilled flutist and played in a military band. In 1793–94 Fürstenau made his first concert tour in Germany. In 1794 he became a member of the *"Chamber Orchestra of Oldenburg,"* where he played until the orchestra was abolished in 1811. Fürstenau continued his career as a performing flutist together with his son Anton Fürstenau (1792–1852) in the largest cities of the Europe.

For a solo guitar: "Theme & 6 variations." For a flute and a guitar: "12 Stücke op. 16"; "Variazioni op. 29";. "Suite op. 34"; "12 Stücke op. 35"; "6 Duette op. 37"; "12 Stücke op. 38." For two flutes and a guitar: "12 Stücke op. 10"; "Trio op. 15." For a voice and a guitar: "Canzoni."

FÖRARE, Erik (born 1953), a Swedish composer. Studied at first violin playing in the College of Framnäs and composition privately with Sune Smedsby. In 1975–79 he studied composition in the Music College of Stockholm with Gunnar Bucht and musicology at the University of Stockholm. Förare works as a free-lance composer. He has composed a solo work for the guitar, *"Gran Caprice Vulgaire"* (1982), which has been recorded by a Swedish guitarist Magnus Andersson, who describes it as follows: "In a caprice form the composition comments on the 20th century popular music – the material that music with its opposite whims tries to clean from vulgarity. In the middle of the piece there is a ninth chord to be studied thoroughly. This is followed by 28 motives, which have appeared before, but now in a reversed order."

For a solo guitar: "Gran Caprice Vulgaire" (1982).

GAGNEBIN, Henri (1886–1977), a Swiss composer and the principal of the Conservatory of Genoa in 1925–57. Studied organ playing with Louis Vierne and composition in Lausanne, Genoa and in the Schola Cantorum in Paris in 1908–16 with Vinent d'Indy. Gagnebin worked as the organist in the Rédemption church in Paris in 1910–16 and in the Saint-Jean church in Lausanne in 1916–25, after which he became the principal of the Conservatory of Genoa in 1925. In 1938 Gagnebin founded the Genoa International Music Contest, which he led until 1959.

Gagnebin's production contains 4 symphonies, string quartets, organ and piano compositions etc. Gagnebin composed his guitar solo work, *"Trois pièces"* in March 1953. The work was composed in close cooperation with José de Azpiazu, who got it published with minor changes in the publishing company Symphonia-Verlag with the title, *"Trois pièces pour guitare à Andrés Segovia."* Segovia wrote in his letter to Gagnebin that the work suits well for the guitar. "Trois pièces" was one of the obligatory pieces in the Genoa contest in 1956. Gagnebin's guitar production also contains another piece, *"Elogue"* for the clarinet and the guitar (1965), which is dedicated to M.C. Bauer. A Dutch guitarist living in Switzerland, Han Jonkers, has recorded "Trois pièces" (CD, *A 'Swiss homage to Andrés Segovia'*).

For a solo guitar: "Trois pièces pour guitare à Andrés Segovia" (1953). For a clarinet and a guitar: "Elogue" (1965).

GATAYES, Guillaume- Pierre-Antoine (1774–1846), a French guitarist and composer. Lived when the shift from the five-string to the six-string guitar took place. He dedicated his life to music while in his youth and he played the guitar and harp. Gatayes composed ca. 100 pieces of music and published five editions from his guitar school *Méthode de guitare*, in 1790–1800.

For a guitar and a harp: "Duets." For a violin and a guitar: "9 Duetti." For two guitars: "14 Duetti." For a flute, violin and guitar: "7 Trios."

GEFORS, Hans (born 1952), a Swedish composer, who also lived in Denmark. Gefors first studied composition privately with Maurice Karkoff and from 1972 onwards in the Music Academy of Stockholm with Ingvar Lindholm. After meeting Per Nørgård at the Festival for Young Composers in Copenhagen he continued his composition studies with Nørgård in Århus. After his studies Gefors worked in Denmark as a composer, pedagogue and a reporter for a magazine, *Dansk Musik Tidningen*. In 1988, he was appointed a professor of composition to the University of Lund. With his exceptionally wide production Gefors has managed to create a personal, colorful, energetic and suggestive tone language. Gefors has composed a solo work for the guitar, *"La boîte chinoise"* (1975), which combines the skillful use of rhythmic and melodic ingredients in a virtuoso style typical of the guitar.

For a solo guitar: "La boîte chinoise" (1975).

GERHARD, Roberto (1896–1970), a Spanish composer. Born into a French-Swiss family in Catalonia, later an English citizen. At first he studied with a famous Catalonian musician, Felipe Pedrell, until 1922, after which he continued his studies in Vienna with Arnold Schoenberg (1923–25). Gerhard worked as a professor of composition in Berlin and Barcelona and from 1939 onwards at Cambridge in England until his death. His most important works for orchestra and most of his chamber music were not composed until the 1950s. Gerhard describes his music from this period as athematic. He used the guitar in several chamber music pieces, but has only composed one solo guitar piece, *"Fantasía"* (1957), which is an overture to a vocal suite called *"Cantares"* (1956).

For a solo guitar: "Fantasía" (1957). For a flute, clarinet, mandoline, guitar, hammond, piano, double bass and percussion: "Concert for Eight" (1962). For a flute, piccolo, clarinet, guitar, percussion, piano and violin: "Libra"

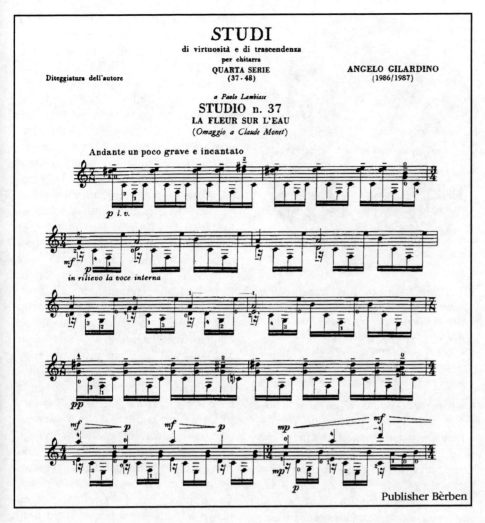

STUDI
di virtuosità e di trascendenza
per chitarra
QUARTA SERIE
(37 - 48)

ANGELO GILARDINO
(1986/1987)

Diteggiatura dell'autore

a Paolo Lambiase
STUDIO n. 37
LA FLEUR SUR L'EAU
(Omaggio a Claude Monet)

Andante un poco grave e incantato

Publisher Bèrben

(1968). For a soprano and a guitar: "Cantares, seven Spanish songs" (1956).

GHEDINI, Giorgio Federico (1892–1965), an Italian composer. Studied piano and cello playing in Turin, where he got a vacancy as a teacher in a conservatory in 1920. Ghedini also taught later in Parma and Milan. He also worked for the Italian Radio and the Teatro alla Scala.

For a solo guitar: "Studio da concerto" (1959).

GILARDINO, Angelo (born 1941), an Italian guitarist, pedagogue and composer. Studied guitar playing and theory in the Viotti Institute, where he taught from 1965 onwards. Since 1981 he has acted as a professor of guitar playing in the Vivaldi State Conservatory. Angelo Gilardino has published literature about guitar playing, e.g. *La tecnica della chitarra* (1980) and *Manuale di storia della chi-*

tarra (1989): *La chitarra antica, classica e romantica* (volume 1) and *La chitarra moderna e contemporare* (volume 2). Gilardino has a high reputation as an expert and a teacher of modern music. Among the most successful of his pupils are the Italians, Marco de Santi and Luigi Biscaldi and the Swede, Magnus Andersson. Asencio, Berkeley, Castelnuovo-Tedesco, Rodrigo, Ruiz-Pipó, etc. have composed music for Gilardino. He works as a music reporter for the publisher Bèrben and his hobbies include visual arts.

For a solo guitar: "Studi di virtuosità e di trascendenza" (60 etudes, composed in 1981-88, published in 5 volumes); "Abreuana" (1971); "Appaloosa" (5 pieces, 1972); Araucaria (1972); "Canzone notturna" (1968); "Estrellas para Estarellas" (1970); "Luceat" (1972); "Musica per l'Angelo della Melancholica"; "Ocram, fantasia" (1973); "Sonata no. 1" (1985); "Sonata no. 2" (1986); "Tenebrae factae sunt" (1973); "Trepidazioni per Thebit" (5 piezas,

1972); "Variazioni sulla Follia." For a solo guitar and a guitar duet: "Poema d'inverno." For a solo guitar and a guitar quartet: "Concerto d'estate"; "Concerto de Córdoba." For a solo guitar and a small guitar orchestra: "Concerto d'autunno." For a guitar and a chamber orchestra: "Concerto 'Leçons de ténèbres'."

GINASTERA, Alberto (1916–1983), an Argentinean composer. Started his musical studies at the age of 12 in the Williams Conservatory, graduated in 1935 and received a gold medal for his composition studies. Since 1941 he worked as a professor of composition in the Buenos Aires National Conservatory. In 1968 he moved to the United States and lived mainly in Switzerland from 1969 until his death. Ginastera's compositions are generally divided into two periods: the works from the first period are emphatically national and their musical models have been e.g. Bartók, Falla and Stravinsky. The works from the second period are based on 12-note technique and they are remarkably more international. The composer himself divided his national style into two parts, the early "objective national" style and the later "subjective national" style.

Ginastera composed one work for the guitar, *Sonata op. 47* (1976), which is dedicated to Carlos Barbosa-

Composer Alberto Ginastera's Sonata op. 47 is inspired by the folk music of Indians and Argentinean Gauchos. It belongs to the most remarkable modern compositions for the guitar.

Lima. The work is one of the most remarkable modern works for the guitar and it is based on the folk music of Native Americans. The first part in the sonata, *Esordio*, is a prelude, which is based on South American Indians' so-called Puna-folklore; the third part, *Canto*, is a rhapsody, which is agagically variable; the second part, *Scherzo*, and the fourth part, *Finale*, are based on Argentina's and Chile's Pampa culture. The work uses a lot of effects typical of the guitar, such as tambora and flageolets. The composer has commented on the composition process: "I had not waited in vain many decades to do this experiment." An arrangement of Ginastera's *"Triste Pampeano"* is also played with the guitar and the *Milonga* with two guitars. Carlos Barbosa-Lima has arranged Ginastera's work, *"Three Argentine Popular Songs"* for two guitars (Triste, Chacarera, Gato).

For a solo guitar: "Sonata op. 47" (1976). Arrangements for a solo guitar: "Triste Pampeano" (arr. de Font); "Milonga" (Mercado); "2 Danzas" (Barbosa-Lima); "Three Argentinean Popular Songs" (Barbosa-Lima). Arrangements for two guitars: "Milonga" (arr. Martinez Zarate); "3 Danzas del Ballet Estancia" (Martinez Zarate).

GIULIANI, Mauro (1781–1829), an Italian composer and guitar virtuoso. Studied cello and bass continuo, but the six-string guitar soon became his major instrument. As a guitarist he probably was auto-didact. It has been said that at the age of 22 Giuliani was a competent cellist, guitarist and guitar composer. He also played the 30-string harp-guitar, which he used in some concerts in addition to the 6-string guitar and the cello (e.g. in Trieste in 1803, performing a concerto for the harp-guitar, composed by himself). Soon after this Giuliani gave up playing the harp-guitar, probably because of difficulties in transporting and tuning (T. Heck). As many Italian musicians at that time, Giuliani went to the northern side of the Alps to make a living, and he also wanted a publisher for his works. Vienna was a center for German-speaking musicians, and they earned good money there. In 1806–19

The Italian Mauro Giuliani was a central figure in the Viennese guitar life in the 19th century. His very wide guitar production consists of solo and chamber music and three guitar concertos. Giuliani's style was influenced by Viennese Classism and Rossini.

Giuliani worked as a guitarist, composer and guitar teacher in Vienna, where he was regarded as one of the most prominent guitarists and guitar composers of that time. In April 1808 Giuliani's *"Guitar Concerto in A op. 30"* was performed for the first time accompanied by a symphony orchestra; the audience praised it. Giuliani's versatile skills as a musician are also demonstrated by the fact that he played the cello in the premiere of Beethoven's 7th symphony in 1813. The appreciation that Giuliani received can be seen in the fact that Napoleon's second wife, Empress Marie-Louise, gave Giuliani several personal presents, such as a ring and a lyre-guitar that Napoleon originally had ordered to her. In addition to these gifts the empress appointed him her chamber musician, *"Virtuoso onorario di camera,"* in ca. 1814. Giuliani also gained the appreciation of other musicians and performed together with the pianists Hummel and Moscheles, the violinist Mayseder, and the cellist Merck, etc. in the garden of the palace of Schönbrunn in the so-called *"Nachtmusiken Concerts,"* which were also called with the name *"Dukaten Concerte."* These six concerts, which were arranged by Count Franz Palffy in 1815, had the elite as the audience: Empress Marie-Louise, Archdukes

Rainer and Rudof, etc. The program consisted of the solos of each artist and finally of chamber music, where virtuosity was combined. In the autumn of 1816 Giuliani made a concert visit to Prague, where he played his Guitar Concerto in A as a soloist, with Carl Maria von Weber as the conductor (T. Heck p. 73-74). In the summer of 1819 Giuliani returned to Italy with considerable debts. As a bohemian artist, his finances had suffered in Vienna. Giuliani first settled down in Rome (ca.1820–23). An interesting document to show that Giuliani had arrived is in one of Beethoven's conversation booklets: "Giuliani ist in Rom." (Konversationsheft XI April 1820. After becoming deaf, Beethoven used conversation booklets). In Rome Giuliani met Paganini and Rossini in 1820–21, and the three were known by the name *"Triumvirato musicale."* Probably they even gave concerts together (T. Heck p. 107). Rossini's influence on Giuliani's guitar production is remarkable, as shown by e.g. the *"6 Rossinianas"* op. 119-124 and numerous variations and arrangements from several themes of Rossini's popular operas. Finally Giuliani settled down in Naples, where he lived until his death and published 29 opuses of guitar music. Giuliani had two musically talented children, who dedicated their lives to music. The son, Michel Barletta (1801–1867), became a notable pedagogue of singing, who worked in the Music Conservatory of Paris (Mauro Giuliani's brother Nicholas also gave lessons in singing working in e.g. St. Petersburg). The daughter Emilia (1813– after 1840) became a famous guitarist and composer.

Mauro Giuliani has had a major influence on the guitar life in Europe. His tremendous popularity can be seen in the fact that still in 1833–35 a magazine called *"Giulianiad"* was published in London. It described Giuliani's style as follows: "he made the guitar sing." Giuliani did not publish an actual guitar school, but many guitarists benefit from not only his etudes, but also from his work *"Studio per la chitarra op. 1"* (1812, Vienna), which contains 120 different arpeggio excercises. The best pupils of Giuliani included the Polish composer-guitarists Jan Nepomucen Bobrowicz and Felix Horetzky.

Mauro Giuliani's guitar production contains 151 opuses and a large number of compositions and arrangements without an opus number. His style was influenced by Viennese Classicism and he composed classical concertos for the guitar and orchestra, sonate form compositions, variations (one third of his production), ländlers, character pieces and etudes. Giuliani's guitar compositions are available in *Edition Tecla*. The production is so wide that it has been published in 39 volumes. Thomas Heck has published a book about Giuliani's life and works, *Mauro Giuliani: Virtuoso Guitarist and Composer* (Editions Orphée 1995).

For a solo guitar: "3 Rondeaux op. 8"; "Sonate C-dur op. 15"; "3 Rondeaux op. 17"; "Variazioni su un tema originale op. 20"; "Divertimenti op. 37"; "Divertimenti op. 40"; "Variazioni sul tema della 'Folies d' Espagne' op. 45"; "Choix de mes fleurs chéries op. 46"; "Studi per chitarra op. 48"; "Le Papillon op. 50" (32 easy pieces, "Butterflies"); "Grand Ouverture op. 61"; "3 Sonatinen op. 71"; "6 Preludi op. 83"; "Variazioni su un tema di Rossini Tancredi op. 87"; "3 Sonatas brillantes op. 96"; "Studi per chitarra op. 100"; "Variazioni su un tema di Händel op. 107"; "Studi per chitarra op. 111"; "Rossinianas op. 119-124 Nos. 1-6"; "6 Arie Nazionale Irlandesi op. 125"; "Studi per chitarra op. 139"; "Sonata Eroica op. 150." For two guitars: "Grandi variazioni concertanti op. 35"; "3 Polonesi concertanti op. 137"; "Variazioni concertanti op. 130." For a voice and a guitar: "6 Cavatine op. 39"; "6 Lieder op. 89"; "6 Ariette op. 95." For a violin and a guitar: "Duo Concertant op. 25." For a flute or a violin and a guitar: "Gran duetto concertante op. 52"; "12 Ländler & Coda, op. 75"; "Duettino facile op. 77"; "Gran Sérénade op. 82"; "Variations op 84"; "Gran Duo Concertant, op. 85"; "Divertimenti Notturni op. 86"; "Serenade op. 127." For a piano and a guitar: "Grand Duo Concertante op. 93" (arr. together with Hummel); "Grand Quintetto op. 65"; "2 Rondeaux op. 68." For a guitar, violin and cello: "Trio, Serenata in La Maggiore op. 19." For a guitar and a string quartet: "Gran Quintetto op. 65." For a guitar and an orchestra: "Concerto per chitarra e archi in La Maggiore op. 30"; "Concerto per chitarra e archi in La Maggiore op. 36"; "Concerto per chitarra e orchestra in Fa Maggiore op. 70."

GNÀTTALI, Radamés (1906–1988), a Brazilian composer, was a virtuoso pianist in his youth and later one of the most productive composers in Brazil. He became famous for his music, in which he combined Brazilian popular music, jazz and classical music of the 1920s. He was very popular among other musicians, and he was regarded as a master. His ideology showed the way for many musicians. For years Gnàttali worked as the conductor of Rio's National Radio Orchestra, as a composer and he also wrote lyrics. His special devotion to modern Brazilian music led to the development of Brazilian popular music and the bossa nova style from the 1930 to the 1950s.

For a solo guitar: "Alma Brasileira"; "Chôro Calido"; "Chôro e Batuque"; "Saudade"; "10 Studies"; "3 Concert Studies"; "Brasiliana No. 13"; "Pequeña Suite." For two guitars: "Corta Jaca." For a piano and a guitar: "Concerto carioca." For a guitar, piano and percussion: "Brasilian Popular Suite." For a cello and a guitar: "Sonata." For a guitar and an orchestra: "Concertino no. 1"; "Concerto de Copacabana"; "Concerto no. 4, a Brasileira."

GRAGNANI, Filippo (1768–1820), an Italian guitarist and composer, who was a member of a family of musicians and lute builders. He studied harmonization and bass continuo in his home town Livorno under Giulio Maria Lucches, who suggested he could have a career as a composer of church music. Gragnani gave concerts e.g. in Italy, Germany and France. As most of his contemporaries, he settled down in Paris (in ca. 1810), where he published his works and became friends with Ferdinando Carulli. Gragnani composed a great deal of chamber music for the guitar, also a few pieces for rare ensembles, such as a quartet for a violin, clarinet and two guitars. He also composed duos for a violin (or flute) and guitar, and trios for a flute, violin and guitar.

For a solo guitar: "Fantaisie op. 5"; "3 Sonatas op. 6"; "Le déluge, Sonate sentimentale op. 15." For two guitars: "3 Duetti dedicate à Carulli op. 4." For three guitars: "Trio op. 12." For a violin and a guitar: "Tre Sonate op. 8." For two violins and a guitar: "Gran Duetto." For a flute, violin and a guitar: "Trio op. 13." For two guitars, a violin and a cello: "Quartetto op. 8." For a flute, violin and two guitars: "Quartetto." For two guitars, a violin, cello, flute and a clarinet: "Sestetto op. 9."

GRAHN, Ulf (born 1942), a Swedish composer. Studied violin, viola and piano playing in the Music Academy of Stockholm in 1966–70. He has lived in the United States since 1972 teaching electronic music and composition at the Georg Washington University. Grahn was a productive composer already as a school boy. His production contains symphonies, concertos, ballets, electro-acoustic works, solo pieces etc.

For a solo guitar: "Four pieces for guitar" (1967); "Two pieces for Erik" (1971); "Fantasia for guitar" (1985). For an alto recorder and a guitar: "Pan" (1968). For a voice and a guitar: "Två dagsedlar" (1971). For a voice, guitar or piano: "Grund" (1966); "Riket" (1966); "Ute Pattavet" (1967). For a voice, flute and a guitar: "Det är någon i närheten" (1971). For a flute, bass clarinet, viola, guitar and percussion: "Rondeau" (1980). For a guitar and an orchestra: "Concerto for guitar and orchestra" (1985).

GRAY, Steve (born 1947), an English jazz musician and composer. He played the piano in the Phil Seamen Quintet. Gray's compositions have been played by e.g. Count Basie, Bob Brookmeyer and orchestras, such as the Danish Radio Orchestra, BBC's Big Band etc. Gray has also composed large-scale works, such as a concerto for a jazz piano and an orchestra. Co-operation with the guitarist John Williams led to the works *Three Pieces for Solo Guitar* (1980) and *Guitar Concerto* (1987).

For a solo guitar: "Three Pieces for Solo Guitar" (1980). For a guitar and an orchestra: "Guitar Concerto" (1987).

GUARNIERI, M. Camargo (1907–1993), a Brazilian composer and conductor with roots in Sicily. Studied music in the Music Academy of São Paulo and since 1938 in Paris. Guarnieri belongs to the musicians who have based their music on Brazilian folk music.

For a solo guitar: "Estudo no. 1"; "Estudios 2-3"; "Valsa chôro"; "Ponteo."

GUASTAVINO, Carlos (1912–2000), an Argentinean composer. Studied in the Music Academy of Buenos Aires and later in London. In addition to vocal music he composed works for the guitar. Most of Guastavino's works are based on Argentinean folk music, but he has also used the sonate form.

For a solo guitar: "Bailecito"; "La Siempre Viva"; "Cantilena no. 1 ja 4"; "Sonatas no. 1-3"; "Tres Cantilenas Argentinas no. 8, 9, 10"; "La Tempranera, zamba." For a voice and a guitar: "Ay, que el alma"; "El Sampedrino"; "Pampa Sola"; "Pueblito, mi pueblo" (Canzone Argentina); "Severa Villafane" (Zamba); "Vidala del Secadal." For a string quartet and a guitar: "Las Presencias no. 6."

GUBAIDULINA, Sofia (born 1931), a composer born in Tatarstan. She studied in the Music Academies of Kazan and Moscow, from which she graduated in 1959 under Vissarion Sebalin. The great models of Gubaidulina are Shostakovich, Webern and Bach. Gubaidulina's music often expresses a religious, mystical-philosophic or literary subject.

For a solo guitar: "Serenade."

HALFFTER, **Cristóbal** (born 1930), a Spanish composer. Studied in the Music Academy of Madrid under Conrado del Campo and got the first prize when graduating. Since 1954 he lived in Paris with his uncle Ernesto Halffter. In 1962–64 Cristóbal Halffter acted as the head of the Music Academy of Madrid and as the professor of composition. His composition style is avantgarde.

For a solo guitar: "Codex I" (1963). For a soprano and a guitar: "Dos canciónes" (1952). For two guitars and an orchestra: "Partita" (1973).

HALFFTER, Ernesto (1905–1989), a Spanish composer and conductor. He was at first taught by his mother and later became a pupil and a friend of Manuel de Falla. With M. de Falla he founded the *"Orquesta Bética de Cámara"* in 1923. Halffter completed the monumentalistic stage oratorio by de Falla, *"Atlantida,"* which made its performance possible in the 1970s. Since 1928 Halffter lived in Paris and London. As a composer he was influenced by Ravel and in his compositions he used a lot of Spanish folk music.

For a solo guitar: "Peacock Pie" (1923); "Danza de la gitarra"; "Danza de la pastora"; "Habanera." For a violin and a guitar: "Madrigal" (1969). For a guitar and an orchestra: "Concierto."

HALLGRÍMSSON, Haflidi (born 1941), an Icelandic cellist and composer, who lives in England and also regularly gives concerts in his home country. Halgrímsson studied cello playing in Italy with Enrico Mainardi and composition in England with Peter Maxwell Davies and Alan Bush. Since the early 1970s Hallgrímsson has played in several British chamber music ensembles, such as *The English Chamber*

Haflidi Hallgrímsson

Orchestra" and "London Symphonietta." He was the leading cellist in The Schottish Chamber Orchestra in 1977–86. Halgrímsson was awarded the music award of the Nordic Council in 1986 for his work *"Poemi" for a violin and a string orchestra* (1984).

For a solo guitar: "Jacob's Ladder" (1984). For a guitar and a cello: "Tristia."

HALLNÄS, Hilding (1903–1984), a Swedish composer. Studied in the Music Academy of Stockholm since 1924 and graduated as an organist, cantor and music teacher. He continued his organ studies in Paris and studied composition in Leipzig with Hermann Grabner. Hallnäs worked in 1933–73 in his home town Gothenburg as the organist of the Johanneberg church and as a theory teacher in the Gothenburg Orchestral School. His compositions are impressionistic and expressionistic and in the 1950s he studied the 12-note technique. Hallnäs has composed 50 works for the guitar.

For a solo guitar: "Partita Amabile"; "Preludier:1-12"; "Serenad"; "Strängaspel: 8 stycken"; "Impromptu"; "Svit no. 2"; "Tre fantasier i svit." For two guitars: "Duo"; "Tre miniatyrer." For a flute and a guitar: "3 dialoger." For a flute, viola and guitar: "Liten svit." For a guitar and a string quartet: "Konsert för gitarr och stråkkvartett."

HAMBRÆUS, Bengt (1928–2000), a Swedish composer and organist. Studied organ playing in 1944-48 with Alf Linder and musicology in

Sofia Gubaidulina

1947–1956 at the University of Uppsala, where he he took the Ph.L. in 1956. He was the first Swedish composer specializing in electronic music. Hambræus worked in electronic studios in Cologne in 1954, Milan in 1959 and Munich in 1963. He worked for the Swedish Radio in 1957–1972 as the director of its chamber music section. Since 1972 Hambræus has worked as a professor at McGill University, Montreal.

For an electric guitar, harp, violin, viola, cello, and a double bass: "Segnali" (1959–60). For a French horn, trombone, electric guitar and a piano: "Transit II" (1963). For a guitar and percussion: "Night-Music" (1988). For a guitar and a cello: "Dos recercadas" (1988).

HAND, Colin (born 1929), an English composer. Graduated from Beckett Park College to be a teacher and studied music in the Trinity College in London. Hand is a professor of both composition and musicology. He has composed orchestral, choir, chamber and instrumental music. In the mid-1970s Hand became interested in composing for the guitar, influenced by Graham Wade, also a contact with John Mills inspired him to compose for the guitar. Because he is keen on teaching, he has composed e.g. *"Fifteen Minutes for Guitar"*, which contains 15 études, which last for a minute each.

For a solo guitar: "Sonatina No. 1 op. 74"; "Sonatina No. 2 'Allotropes'" (1979); "Improvisations on a Medieval Spanish Song op. 104"; "Fifteen Minutes for Guitar." For two guitars: "Sonatella." For a recorder and a guitar: "Aubade"; "A Dancing Dozen"; "Varios."

HARRISON, Lou (1917–2003), a composer from the United States. He studied composition in the San Francisco State College in 1934–36 and privately with Henry Cowell. Harrison studied the music of Schoenberg and the 12-note technique. In 1961/62 he received the Rockefeller scholarship and he traveled in Japan, Korea, Taiwan and Java, which influenced his tone language.

For a solo guitar: "4 Pieces"; "Harp Suite"; "Serenade" (1952). For a flute

Hans Haug from Switzerland has, in addition to his best known guitar work Alba, also composed several other interesting works.

or an ocarino, guitar and percussion: "Canticle No. 3" (1941).

HARTIG, Heinz Friedrich (1907–1969), a German composer. His production was influenced by the *"New School of Vienna."* Hartig's compositions *"Gitarresolo"* and *"Drei Stücke"* reflect a notable familiarity with the techniques of guitar playing and guitar composing. (A. Gilardino).

For a solo guitar: "Gitarresolo" (1951); "Drei Stücke" (Capriccio, Thema mit Variationen, Alla danza). For a choir and a guitar: "Perché op. 28" (1958). For a guitar and a cembalo: "Reflexe op. 52." For a recorder and a guitar: "Fünf Stücke." For a guitar and an orchestra: "Concertante Suite op. 19."

HARVEY, Richard (born 1953), an English composer, conductor and musicologist. His musical interest started at the age of 4 with the recorder and later he played the clarinet in the British Youth Orchestra. Before he was 20, Harvey founded a folk music group, *"Gryphon,"* which was internationally succesful and with which he performed on three continents playing 30 different instruments! Harvey studied composition in the Royal College of Music and has become famous as a

composer for television and drama series. He has worked as a guest conductor in the Royal Philharmonic Orchestra and London Symphony Orchestra, and so he got to know the guitarist John Williams, who was on tour with the orchestra. Together with Williams he has composed a concerto for a guitar and a small orchestra *"Concerto Antico"*, which is based on old dances and songs around Europe.

For a guitar and a small orchestra: "Concerto Antico."

HAUG, Hans (1900–1967), a Swiss composer and conductor. Studied piano and cello playing in the Music Academy of Basel and took part in the master courses of Ferruccio Busoni in Zürich. Later he studied composition and conducting in the Music Academy of Munich. Haug worked as the choir leader and as the conductor of the Symphony Orchestras of the Swiss radio and as a teacher and a guest conductor in several countries. In 1947–60 he taught harmonization and bass continuo in the Music Academy of Lausanne. As a composer Haug is known for his eight operas and various radio operas and operettas. His large production also contains orchestral works, chamber music and motion

Photo: Maarit Kytöharju

picture music.

Haug became interested in the guitar in the late 40s and in 1951 in the guitar composition contest of the Music Academy of Siena, his *Concertino for a guitar and a small orchestra* was awarded, while Alexandre Tansman got a prize for his solo work, *"Cavatina."* Haug's *Concertino* waited to be published until 1970, when Bèrben published it as a facsimile. Inspired by his success, Haug studied the guitar more and in 1953–54 he took regular guitar lessons from José Azpiazu. At these times Haug's first and most frequently played solo guitar work *"Alba"*, was composed, and it has been recorded by e.g. Andrés Segovia and John Mills.

For a solo guitar: "Alba"; "Legende"; "Prelude, tiento et toccata"; "Preludio"; "Rondo Fantastico and Tiento de Compostela." For a flute and a guitar: "Capriccio pour flúte et guitare" (1963, dedicated to duet Werner Tripp & Konrad Ragossnig). For a guitar and a piano: "Fantasia" (1957, dedicated to Luise Walker). For a guitar and a small orchestra: "Concertino" (1951). For a flute, guitar and an orchestra:" Concerto pour flûte, guitare et orchestre" (1966).

HEAD, Brian (born 1964), an American guitarist and composer born in Washington. He studied music and mathematics at the University of Maryland and guitar playing at the

The guitar production of Paavo Heininen consists at the moment of two solo works and a duet for a flute and a guitar. The second solo work, Siniloimi, was published in 1997.

University of Southern California. Brian Head has won international guitar contests and his works are played around the USA.

For a solo guitar: "Sketches for Friends" (33rd Street Ballad, Lobster Tale, November Song, Brookland Boogie).

HEGAARD, Lars (born 1950), a Danish guitarist and composer. Studied guitar playing in the Music Academies of Fyn and Copenhagen with Ingolf Olsen. He took a guitar diploma, which was followed by composition studies with Niels Viggo Benzon and Ib Nørholm. He has studied musicology at the University of Copenhagen.

For a solo guitar: "5 Movements" (1975); "Variations" (1983); "The Conditions of a Solitary Bird, 5 pieces" (1987). For two guitars: "Duo for 2 guitarer" (1974); "Six Studies for Two Guitars" (1989). For three guitars: "Song-lines" (1989, 12 small dances for a guitar trio). For a flute, guitar and double bass: "Trioli" (1978). For four guitars: "Couleurs Croissées" (1986–87). For an alto flute and a guitar: "Configurations" (1987–88).

HEININEN, Paavo (born 1938), a Finnish composer and professor of composition. Studied musicology at the University of Helsinki (B.A. 1959) and piano playing and composition (diploma 1960) with Aarre Merikanto, Einojuhani Rautavaara, Einar Englund and Joonas Kokkonen. He has also studied composition abroad, in Cologne and New York. Since 1993 Heininen has worked as a professor in the Sibelius Academy.

Jukka Savijoki plays a solo guitar work by Heininen *"Touching op. 40"*, on his record, "The Contemporary Finnish Guitar" (BIS LP-207). Savijoki

describes Heininen and his work on the cover of the record as follows: "Heininen has often been labelled an "intelligent" composer, whose music is over-complicated and difficult to follow. It is not so often that one speaks about the firm mood in his music, which covers a wide scale from lyricism to aggressive energety. The work "Touching" is even internationally thought of as exceptional in its notably thorough use of opportunities to express oneself with the guitar." In "Touching" the mainly monotonically and repetitively moving batch makes gentle and sliding glides from one tone field and character to another. As elements of color and tension Heininen uses e.g. glissandos, trills, Bartók pizzicatos, snare drum etc techniques. The solo guitar work composed in 1997, *Siniloimi* is in four parts and more traditional and lyrical in the use of guitar than "Touching." The solo guitar work *"Utazawa no midori e"* is based on the first part's guitar part in a guitar-flute duo *"Utazava no e."*

For a solo guitar: "Touching op. 40" (1978); "Utazawa no midori e" (1991–1996). "Siniloimi op. 67" (1997). For a flute and a guitar: "Utazawa no e" (1991).

HEINIÖ, Mikko (born 1948), a Finnish composer, professor of musicology and pianist. Studied musicology at the University of Helsinki (B.A. 1972, doctorate 1984) and piano playing in the Sibelius Academy in 1971–75 with Liisa Pohjola and composition with Joonas Kokkonen (diploma 1977). Heiniö has acted as a professor of musicology at the University of Turku since 1986. He has held several positions of trust, such as the chairman of Suomen Säveltäjät ry (Society of Finnish Composers) since 1992, the chairman of Teosto (Finnish Composer's Copyright Society), Luovan Säveltaiteen Edistämissäätiö (The Foundation for the Promotion of Finnish Music) and Suomen Sinfoniaorkesterit ry (Association of Finnish Symphony Orchestras) in 1990–93 and member of different executive groups. As a composer Heiniö has as his starting point the fact

Mikko Heiniö, a professor of musicology and a composer, has composed for the guitar pieces like the Champignons à l'herméneutique, for flute and guitar.

Photo: Maarit Kytöharju

that he is a musician himself. He has played the piano as a lied pianist and conducted his own works. "Even though intelligence is a crucial part of Heiniö's thinking as a composer, it is mixed with a great deal of traditional musicianship and emotionality, which pays attention to the listener" (V. Murtomäki). Heiniö has said himself: "The starting point in a composition is phenomenality, which is supposed to reach not only the listener's intellectual interest, but also his emotions."

From a Finnish point of view Heiniö started to compose quite early, in the early 70s. In the "Mushroom Suite" for the flute and guitar, *"Champignons à l'herméneutique"* (1979), Heiniö uses irony and humor, the names of the parts are Pulkkosieni (Paxillus involutus), Suippumyrkkyseitikki (Cortinarius speciosissimus), Myrkkynääpikkä (Galerina marginata), Valkokärpässieni (Amanita virosa) and Sappitatti (Boletus felleus), all Finnish names for different poisonous mushrooms. The name of *"Minimba 1"* (1982) comes from words minimalism and samba, which can be heard in the rhythm, which goes hypnotically through the work repetitively and in

various forms. The Latin American rhythms and the melodies form the Andies are colored with different drummings.

For four (or 3) guitars: "Minimba 1" (1982). For a flute, violin and a guitar: "Trio op. 5" (1971). For a flute and two guitars: "Suite op. 16" (1974). For a child choir, flute, guitar and a string orchestra: "Agnus Dei" (1974). For a flute and a guitar: "Champignons à l'herméneutique" (1979).

HENZE, Bruno (1900–1978), a German guitarist, pedagogue and composer. Studied guitar playing with his father and composition with B. Schreider, a pupil of F. Liszt, and later he continued his studies in the Music College of Berlin-Charlottenburg. B. Henze published a guitar school in 17 volumes and nearly 200 compositions and ca. 1000 arrangements for the guitar, which include the guitar arrangements for the Lute Suites by J.S. Bach.

For a solo guitar: "Fantasia burlesca op. 110." For two guitars: "6 Folk Dances: Goteand Suite"; "Suite in C." For a mandoline and a guitar: Folksongs Around the world.

HENZE, Hans Werner (born 1926), a German composer, who has lived permanently in Italy since 1953. He started to compose already at the age of 12 before any musical education. Henze studied in the Braunschweig National Music School in 1942–44. In 1945 he worked as a rehearsal pianist in the town theater of Bielefeld and in 1946 he continued his studies in the Church Music Institute of Heidelberg and privately with Wolfgang Fortner. Henze soon aroused international interest and he is one of he most productive and versatile post-war composers of dodecaphonic music. In the 1940s and 1950s he composed

many sensational works using freely the 12-note technique with new classical forms. In 1961 Henze was appointed the professor of composition in the Mozarteum in Salzburg (again in 1986) and in 1975 the doctor honoris causa of the English Royal Academy. In the mid-1960s Henze became interested in promoting political goals with the help of music. After turning against middle-class esthetics and engaging himself politically, he thought that music should have a part in the fight for socialism. Henze's production contains symphonies, opera, ballet, motion picture, chamber and instrumental music. Henze has composed several works for the guitar, such as *"El Cimarrón"* (1969–70), which is based on an autobiography of a Cuban slave Esteban Montejo; Leo Brouwer gave Henze ideas to the composition, such as using the cello's bow when playing the guitar, which is used when describing the landscapes of Cuba. Julian Brem asked Henze to compose the sonatas *"Royal Winter Music no. 1 and 2"*, which are based on characters in Shakespeare's plays.

The music of the first sonata is filled with reforms in technique. The

Photo: Regine Koerner

The remarkable German modern composer Hans Werner Henze has composed an exceptional number of both solo and chamber music for the guitar.

guitar is used as an orchestra, and it is played with large nuances in volume and color. The first part, *"Gloucester,"* is based on Shakespeare's drama Richard III, which begins with the monologue of Gloucester Now is winter of our discontent ... The beginning of the first part reminds of the sonata form and there is material of two different themes. The first theme is majestic and based on chords, which follow short apoggituras. The nature of the second theme (tempo giusto) is deceitful and cynical. At the end of the first part the tambora technique is used, and it reflects the plans of the murderer to murder the heirs to the throne of Edward. The second part of the sonata, *"Romeo & Juliet,"* resembles a slow and tender duet, and it uses the 12-note technique. The third part, *"Ariel,"* is a scherzo, fast music, where quick arpeggios take turns with short melodies. The fourth part *"Ophelia"* is a slow bel canto. The music reflects a sad love song with arpeggio waves on the background. The music in the fifth part is humoristic and it tells about a comical company (jester Touchstone, housemaid Anrey and peasant William). The sixth (last) part describes the ruler of the fairies, Oberon, there is magic and metamorphoses in the music. The second sonata continues with the same ideas.

Hans Werner Henze's concerto for the guitar and orchestra *An Eine Aeolsharfe* is based on a poem by Eduard Morike with the same name. One of his ideas while composing was that with an orchestra of 15 instruments the guitar does not need any amplification. The first part, *"On An Aeolian Harp,"* describes the wintery landscape and wind of southern Germany (where Henze comes from). "Aeolian harp" is a sound made by the wind. The name of the second part is *"Question and Answer."* The music resembles an instrumental version of a Renaissance vocal work. The third part is like a scherzo, whose lively music contains lots of humor. The name of the poem is To Philomel and it refers to a person who always guffaws and wants to have fun. Philomel says: "Your sadness is like a musical scale." The fourth part is the most philosoph-

ic. It begins with a guitar solo, which is followed by a long duo with a guitar and a harp and it describes one large plucked instrument. The name of the poem is To Hermann and it tells about a person who has been left by a mistress.

Henze has written about the guitar in a program for the London premiere of Royal Winter Music I in 1977: "The guitar is a 'knowing' or 'knowledgeable' instrument, with many limitations but also many unexplored spaces and depths within these limits. It possesses a richness of sound capable of embracing everything one might find in a gigantic contemporary orchestra; but one has to start from silence in order to notice this: one has to pause, and completely exclude noise."

For a solo guitar: "Royal Winter Music no. 1 (1975–76) and Royal Winter Music no. 2" (1979); "3 Märchenbilder (1980) arr. Reinbert Evers"; "Memorias de El Cimarrón" (L. Brouwer's free arrangement from a vocal music suite by Henze with the same name). "3 Tentoses for a solo guitar from Kammermusik" (1958). For two guitars: "Memorias de El Cimarrón, arr. Jürgen Ruck" (1996). Chamber music: A suite for a baritone, flute, guitar and percussion: "El Cimarrón" (1969–70). For a tenor, and eight solo instruments: guitar or harp, bass clarinet, French horn, bassoon and a string quartet: "Kammermusik" (1958), the work contains 13 parts: 4 for an octet, 3 parts for a tenor and an octet, 3 parts for a tenor and a guitar (II, VIII and X) and 3 Tentoses for a solo guitar (III, V and XI). For a harp, guitar and mandoline: "Carillon, Recitatif and Masque." For a guitar, viola and organ: "Trio Selbst und Zwiegespräche"; "Monologues & Dialogues." For a guitar, harp, cembalo and strings: "Arien des Orpheus" (1979). For a recorder, five percussions, solo guitar and strings: "Deutschlandsberger Mohrentanz no. 1 (1984) and no. 2" (1985). For a guitar and an orchestra (12 instruments): "An eine Aeolsharfe" (1985–86, based on a poem by Eduard Morike), the first guitar concerto by Henze. He has also used the guitar in his works: "Dramatic Scenes from Orpheus no. 1, no. 2"; "3 Mozart's the Orgelsonaten" (1991);

"Spielmusiken" (1979–80); "Symphony no. 6"; "Undine-second Suite" (1958).

HÉTU, Jacques (born 1938), a Canadian composer. Graduated from the Conservatory of Montreal in 1961 under Clermont Pépi. That same year Hétu won composition prizes, such as *"Prix d'Europe"* and *"Canada Council Award."* In 1961–63 he studied in the École de Musique in Paris under Henri Dutilleux. Hétu's composition style has had various phases: tonal, one based on the 12-note technique and since 1963 lyrical-expressionistic.

For a solo guitar: "Suite pour guitare op. 41" (1986). For a guitar and a string orchestra: "Concerto."

HINDEMITH, Paul (1895–1963), a German composer, conductor and theorist. Studied viola playing, bass continuo and composition in the Conservatory of Hoch in Frankfurt. In 1922–29 he played the viola in a Quartet Licco Amar. Paul Hindemith moved to the United States in 1940 and returned in 1953 and settled to Switzerland. In 1955 he was granted the *"Wihuri International Sibelius Award."* Hindemith composed his early works in a free tonal polyphonic style, which was marked by an imaginatory melodics. In the 1930s he shifted to a tonal style based on his own theories, which have been described as neoclassic. His *"Rondo"* for three guitars (1925) is one of the first modern guitar compositions in the early 20th century.

For three guitars: "Rondo" (1925), also an arrangement for two guitars available; "Trisosatz" (composed in 1940, not published).

HINOJOSA, Javier (born 1933), a Mexican vihuela player, lutist, guitarist and composer. Took part in guitar courses in southern Europe and studied with Emilio Pujol in Paris. Hinojosa has published collections for vihuela music and composed modern music for the guitar. He has become famous as a researcher of music and as a teacher of old music.

For a solo guitar: "Te lucis ante terminum" (1972). For two guitars: "4 Pièces Polyphoniques."

HOEK, Jan-Anton van (born 1936), a Dutch guitar pedagogue and composer. Hoek studied theory and composition with Koos Tigges, as a guitarist he is self-learned. In addition to the guitar he also plays the therobo, vihuela and Baroque guitar. Hoek has composed more than a thousand compositions for the solo guitar and for 2-4 guitars. For a solo guitar: "Präludien und Etüden zur Vervolkomnung der Teknik"; "Polyphones Spiel auf der Gitarre"; "Experimentelle Musik"; "Rondo und Polnische Suite"; "Grand fuga"; "Polifonia y Gitarra en la música antiqua" (1977). For three guitars: "Kuckuck."

HOLECEK, Josef (born 1939), a Czech guitarist, guitar pedagogue and composer, who lives in Sweden. Holecek studied in the Music Academy of Prague with professor Sadlik (diploma 1966), continued his studies in Vienna with prof. Karl Scheit and took the diploma in 1967. Holecek worked as a guitar teacher in Prague in 1961–66 and as a guitarist in the National Theatre of Prague in 1961–67. Holecek has been the senior teacher of guitar playing in the Music College of Gothenburg. Holecek gave the first performance of a solo guitar work dedicated to him by Einojuhani Rautavaara, *"Serenades of the Unicorn,"* in Gothenburg. Also Per Henrik Nordgren's *"Butterflies"* have been composed ordered by Holecek. He has published a guitar school *Lär dig spela gitarr I-III* and pedagogic pieces for the guitar.

For a solo guitar: "6 Aquarelles"; "Mini-studies" (1974-75); "Guitar Jokes"; "Guitar Moodes"; "Swedish Romance", etc.

HORETZKY, Felix (1796–1870), a Polish guitarist and composer. He studied guitar playing in Vienna with Mauro Giuliani. Horetzky worked as a guitar teacher in the court of the emperor of Austria and made successful tours to Germany, France and Belgium. In 1820 he moved to England. Horetzky also made tours in England and finally settled down in Edinburgh. In London he took part in publishing a guitar magazine *Giulianiad* in 1835. Hoertzky composed more than 150 works for the guitar, which have been published in Vienna, London, Paris, etc. His production also contains original works for a voice and a guitar and arrangements from the popular music at that time. More information about Horetzky is available in an Italian guitar magazine, *Il Fronimo, no. 12* (1975).

For a solo guitar: "Brilliant Waltzes for guitar op. 2 and op. 9"; "Rondo for guitar op. 11"; "Serenade and Variations for solo guitar op. 12"; "Fantasie-Etude op. 14"; "Grand Variations op. 16"; "Divertmentos op. 17"; "Almenrader op. 30"; "Sixty national hymns for guitar." For two guitars: "Duos for guitar and terz guitar op. 1"; "Six Landler for two guitars op. 10"; "Duos for two guitars op. 13"; "Recollections of Vienna for two guitars." For a voice and a guitar: "Lieder und Romanzen."

HOSOKAWA, Toshio (born 1955), a Japanese composer. After piano playing and composition studies in Tokyo Hosokawa, he continued his composition studies in 1976 in West Berlin with Isang Yun. Hosokawa studied in the Music College of Freiburg with Klaus Huber and Brian Ferneyhough in 1983–86. Hosokawa belongs to the few modern composers who have composed for the lute. He has received several prizes in composition contests, e.g. *The Young Generation in Europe and Energia Music Award."*

For a solo guitar: "Serenade" (2003). For a solo lute: "Intermezzo" (1991). For a soprano and a guitar or harp: "Renka I" (1986), a Japanese text.

HOUGHTON, Philip (born 1954), an Australian guitarist and composer. Houghton, who also has been educated in fine arts (an exam in Fine Arts), has been interested in popular music, such as The Beatles and Jimi Hendrix. He became interested in the classical guitar only in 1973 when he bought his first classical guitar. Philip Houghton studied with Sebastian Jörgensen in Montsalvat, in an Artist Center of Etham, where he later worked as a teacher. Houghton has composed theater and motion picture music, and guitar music has a central position in his production.

For a solo guitar: "Five Exotic Studies"; "Stele, suite."

HUBER, Klaus (born 1924), a composer, born in Switzerland but lives in Germany. Studied at first with Willy Burkhard in Zürich and later under Boris Blacher in Berlin. Huber was noted internationally in the ISCM festival in Rome in 1959. He has worked as a composition teacher in the Music College of Freiburg. Numerous successful modern composers have studied with Klaus Huber. He has used the guitar in the orchestral compositions in his concertos *Concerto for a Double Bass Erinnere dich an G"* (1976–77); *"Concerto for a violin Tempora"* (1969); and in a vocal work "Ausgespannt" (1972).

HUERTA y CATURLA, Trinidad (1804–1875), a Spanish guitarist, singer and guitar composer. Huerta was considered one of the best guitarists in the early 19th century and as an impulsive artist he belongs to the most colorful personalities among the classical guitar. Since he was 14 years old he has studied music in Salamanca, and his

The Spanish guitar composer Don Huerta was a close friend of author Viktor Hugo and opera composer Gioacchino Rossini.

most important teacher was a singer and guitarist Manuel García (father Padre Basilio), who taught Huerta both singing and guitar playing. Later he served in the army of General Riego. After the war he had to escape to Paris, where he worked as a guitarist and teacher. In 1825–26 Huerta gave concerts in the United States (20 years before Zani de Ferranti) and during his eventful journey he gave concerts in Cuba and Martinique, and in the Lesser Antilles in the West Indies, which belong to France. In 1827 he settled down in London and married the daughter of the English guitar builder Luis Panormo, Angiolina, who also composed for the guitar, songs accompanied with the guitar. In London, Huerta successfully gave concerts with the pianist Moscheles and the violinist de Bériot. He moved to Paris in 1830 and got to know the author Victor Hugo and was a close friend of Gioacchino Rossini. Since 1833 Huerta worked as a guitarist in Spain for Queen Isabella II and received several medals. At this time he also gave concerts in Malta, Constantinople, Egypt and Israel. Berlioz mentions in his book *Traite d'Instrumentation et d'Orchestration* (1843), that three of the most famous guitarists of this time are Huerta, Zani de Ferranti and Fernando Sor. Huerta composed pieces based on Spanish folk music and wrote a guitar school (1826), which is mainly based on compositions by other composers. Huerta's scripts are accessible in the Library of the Royal College of Music in London.

For a solo guitar: "6 Valzer op. 2" (Meissonnier, Paris); "Six Waltzes dedicated to the Hon. Miss Fox" (1828, London); "Five Waltzes, second set, dedicated to Miss Howley"; "Three Divertimentos, dedicated to Miss L. Hatton"; "Overture to 'Semiramide', and a Fantasia on 'Semiramide'", (Chappell, London); "Four Divertimentos dedicated to Miss Angiolina Panormo", (published by L. Panormo, London); "Souvenier of Mairena fair, a Mazurca with variations for the guitar"; "Spanish National Cachucha, originally for 8 guitars, from which an arrangement for the solo guitar", (L. Panormo, London); "Variations from Opera Themes."

HUMMEL, Johann Nepomuk (1778–1837), a Bohemian pianist and composer, a pupil of Mozart and Salieri.

Hummel gave concerts as a pianist already at the age of 9 and many contemporaries consider him equal with Mozart and Beethoven. In Vienna Hummel got to know Mauro Giuliani, who showed him the guitar life in Vienna and with whom he performed as a piano-guitar duo. In 1815 a violinist Mayseder, guitarist Giuliani, Hummel and other musicians performed in the garden of the palace of Schönbrunn in the so-called Nachtmusiken concerts, which also were called "Dukaten Concerte." For these concerts Hummel composed for the piano, guitar, violin, flute and cello the works *2 Grande Sérénate* op. 63 and 66 (dedicated to count Palffy, who was the arranger of these concerts), whose guitar parts are composed by Giuliani (T. Heck p. 66). Hummel has written the orchestral parts to three of Giuliani's guitar concertos. Only a few of Hummel's compositions exist in the repertoires today. The remarkable share of the guitar in his production is based on the influence of Giuliani.

For a flute and a guitar (arr. later for two guitars): "6 Valzer e trio op. 91." For a piano and a guitar: "Pot-pourri op. 53, op. 79"; "Hummel and Giuliani have composed in co-operation Giuliani's Grand Pot-pourri National" (Giuliani op. 93). For a guitar, clarinet and cello: "Grande serenata op. 62." For a tenor, piano, guitar, violin and cello: "La Sentinelle" (1816). For a piano, guitar, violin, flute (or clarinet), cello (or bassoon): "2 Grandi serenate op. 63 and 66." For a voice, guitar and other instruments: "Romanze." Nearly all of the guitar parts in Hummel's works are made by Giuliani (Mario Dell' Ara).

HVOSLEF, Ketil (born 1939), a Norwegian composer (used the surname Saeverud until 1980, when he changed it to Hvoslef). Hvoslef studied organ playing in the Music Academy of Bergen. He has studied composition in Stockholm with Karl-Birger Blomdahl and Ingvar Lindholm and in London with Thomas Ranja and Henri Lazarov.

For a solo guitar: "Chitarra solo" (1983); "Suite: Six Pieces for Six Strings" (1966). For a guitar and an organ: "Kirkeduo" (1988). For a soprano,

recorder, guitar and piano: "Kvartoni" (1939). For a flute, clarinet, French horn, piano, guitar and violin: "Sekstett: Post" (1980). For a flute, guitar and strings: "Double Concerto" (1977). An electric guitar is used in "Concerto for Violin and Pop Band" (1979).

HØJSGÅRD, Erik (born 1954), a Danish composer, studied composition with Per Nørgård since 1973 (diploma 1978). Since 1982 he has acted as a teacher in the Music Academy of Copenhagen. Højsgård's solo guitar work, *"C'est la mer melée au soleil"* drew attention in the ISCM world music days in 1983. This work, which is based on large metamorphosis, was composed in cooperation with guitarist Karl Petersen. The composition belongs to the most remarkable Danish modern compositions.

For a solo guitar: "C'est la mer melée au soleil."

IBERT, Jacques (1890–1962), a French composer. Studied composition in the Music Academy of Paris with Paul Vidal. Ibert took part in the First World War and after that he continued his studies. In 1919 he was awarded the *"Prix de Rome,"* and the three years in Rome were very profitable for him as a composer. In 1937–60 Ibert was the director of the Académie de France in Rome and in 1955–56 he was also the administrator of the Réunion des Théâtres Lyriques Nationaux. He traveled extensively in Italy, Spain and Tunisia gaining experience, which affected his work. Ibert's music, which represents several different types, has been described, especially his chamber music, as warm, poetic, strong in rhythm and vivid and perfectly "French" in its colors. His production contains 7 operas, orchestral and vocal music and chamber music.

For a solo guitar: "Française"; "Ariette." For two guitars: "Paraboles I and II." For a flute of a violin and a guitar (harp): "Entr'acte" (1936).

IVANOV-KRAMSKOI, Aleksandr (1912–1973), a Russian guitarist, guitar pedagog and composer. In his child-

Revisione e diteggiatura di
ANGELO GILARDINO e
JUAN JOSÉ SAENZ GALLEGO
(1989/90)

para guitarra
(1933)

© Bèrben

Antonio JOSÉ
(1902-1936)

Allegro moderato

*Antonio José was a talented young composer, whose life ended in the Spanish civil war.
His Guitar Sonata was composed already in 1933, but its premiere was in 1981.*

hood he took violin and piano lessons. In 1931–32 he studied 6-string guitar playing with Piotr Agafoshin, who was taught by Andrés Segovia. He also studied composition with Nikolai Rechmensky and conducting with Konstantin Saradzhev. Ivanov-Kramskoi's career as a guitar pedagog started in 1933. His daughter is also a famous guitar pedagog. Ivanov-Kramskoi was a regular accompanist of tenor Ivan Kozlovsky and violist Leonid Kogan. Ivanov-Kramskoi made recordings and published a guitar school and other material for studying.

For a solo guitar: "Tarantella"; "Prelude in h"; "2 Ekspromti: in E; in A"; "Serenade"; "Improvisazione"; "Scherzo"; "Valse"; "Etyd Humoresk"; "Danza"; "Berceuse"; "Gavotte in E"; "Dreams, study." For a piano and a guitar: "Elegia"; "Valse"; "Tarantella." For a guitar and an orchestra: "Concerto in A minor"; "Concerto in B."

IZNAOLA, Ricardo (born 1949), a guitarist, guitar teacher and composer born in Cuba, but lived in Venezuela since 1970. Ricardo moved from Cuba to Columbia with his parents, and there he started to play the guitar. Later the family moved to Caracas in Venezuela and Iznaola continued to learn the guitar by himself. After this he was accepted to the Éscuela Superior de Música in Caracas as a pupil of Manuel Perez Díaz. Iznaola's development as a guitarist was quick and he won prizes in several guitar contests e.g. the first

prize in the *"Tárrega Contest"* in 1968. That same year he continued his studies in Madrid with Regino Sáinz de la Maza, whose assistant he was in 1973–81. Iznaola has given concerts in the Europe, South and North America, Japan etc. and published several recordings, which contain e.g. a first recording of a Sonata by Antonio José (1933). In addition to his teaching and concerting Iznaola has become famous as a publisher of guitar learning material, e.g. *Kitharologus -The Path to Virtuosity* and *On Practising*. Iznaola has also made arrangements for the guitar, e.g. Maurice Ravel's *Alborada del gracioso* and Manuel de Falla's *"Fire dance."*

For a solo guitar: "Estudio"; "Miniatures No. 1 & 2."

JELINEK, Hanns (1901–1969), an Austrian composer. Jelinek studied piano and violin playing mainly by himself and worked at first in the field of popular music as a restaurant musician and as a motion picture and entertainment composer. Jelinek was also self learned as a composer. In 1918 he took part in a composition course by Schoenberg and in 1920 he studied in the Music Academy of Vienna with Fr. Schmit. Jelinek's music has been influenced by Schoenberg and Mahler, and also jazz music had an impact on his music. In 1952–58 he wrote an introduction to the 12-note technique. Jelinek has used the pseudonym Hanns Elin.

For a flute and a guitar: "Ollapotrida op. 30."

JOLIVET, André (1905–1974), a French composer. His father was an artist in visual arts and mother a pianist. The priest of the Notre Dame, Théodas, took the young André to sing in his choir and taught him organ playing and harmonization. Jolivet's parents encouraged him to study composition. In the early 1930s he continued his studies with Edgar Varèse. Jolivet was one of the establishers of the composer group *La Jeune France* ("The young France"). He made experiments in the fields of shades and rhythms and used arhailic scales.

For a solo guitar: "2 Études de concert" (1963); "Suite, Tombeau de Robert de Visée" (1972). For two guitars: "Sérénade" (1956).

JOSÉ, Antonio [MARTÍNEZ PALA-CIOS, Antonio José] (1902–1936), a Spanish composer. Worked as a music teacher in a Jesuit school in Málaga and as a choir leader in Burgos. He did not use his last name Martínez Palacios, but became famous with his first name Antonio José. His friends included poet Federico García Lorca, painter Salvador Dali and author and composer Adolfo Salazar. Antonio José died dramatically already at the age of 34 when Franco's nationalists imprisoned and shot him in December 1936. His friend F. García Lorca had met the same destiny only a few months earlier. José's four-part sonata, *"Sonata para guitarra"*, which had been forgotten for almost 50 years, was performed entirely for the first time by the Cuban guitarist Ricardo Iznaola in Madrid in January 1981. The sonata, dedicated to Regino Sáinz de la Maza, has been widely known since Ricardo Iznaola and Julian Bream recorded it and after the notes were published. Bèrben first published the music of José's sonata (1990) when Angelo Gilardino and Juan José Sáenz Gallego ordered it. Lately an other, earlier, solo guitar work has been found, Romancillo Infantil, which was published by a Spanish publisher, Opera Tres in 1994. Ricardo Iznaola has written an article about José's guitar compositions, *A Problem in Musical*

Heuristics: The Guitar Works of Antonio José, (Guitar Journal no. 7 1996).

For a solo guitar: "Sonata para guitarra" (1933); "Romancillo Infantil."

KAGEL, Mauricio (born 1931), an Argentinean-German composer. Studied music in his home country and started to compose at the age of 18. He experimented with the use of recorded material in compositions. Kagel, who moved to Cologne in 1957, quickly established his position in the elite of new music in Europe. He has acted e.g. as a professor of composition at the New York State University and as a teacher in the Darmstadt Courses of Modern Music. Since 1974 he has acted as a professor of Modern Musical Theater in the Music College of Cologne. After his debute (1950) he has composed in several experimental styles and become known as a pioneer in instrumental theater. "Kagel is a master in combining motion and sound. His music is a highly developed mixed media, where the accuracy of the motions of the performer, his costume and the shape of the instrument may be as important as the clarity of the melody played, accuracy in the rhythm, articulation or tone color. This kind of music is also called instrumental theater." (J. Tiensuu). The avantgarde group, which had been considered pioneering, got more and more tonalic ingredients since the 1970s. Kagel's exceptionally wide production contains also radiophonic works and motion pictures.

For a guitar, harp, double bass and percussion: "Sonant" (1960). For an electric guitar, bass guitar, amplified double bass, hammond, percussion and tape: "Musik aus Tremens" (1963). For three players (a Spanish guitar, electric guitar, bass guitar, guitar strings, coffee grinder, "walkie-talkies", "electric-fans", etc...): "Unter Storm" (1969). For a clarinet, trumpet, guitar and double bass: "Blue's Blue" (1979). For a voice, b-clarinet, c-trumpet, bass tuba in F/C, violin, piano, two guitars (octave guitars), Spanish guitar, ukulele, mandoline/tenor banjo and percussion: "Kantrimusik" (Pastoral, 1975). For an electric guitar, harp, double bass and a small orchestra: "Sonant" (1961).

KAIPAINEN, Jouni (born 1956), Finland, studied in the Sibelius Academy with Aulis Sallinen in 1975–82. Works as a free composer and is a productive modern composer. "In the late 70s he belonged to a group of new modernists and found his ideals from France with a starting point in an atonality with rich details. He has considered himself as a pluralist, his inspirators have been Zimmermann, Berio and from a distance, Berg and Mahler" (M. Heiniö). Kaipainen's works often have a program heading, such as *"Far from Home"* (composed for the Cluster ensemble: flute, alto saxophone, guitar and percussion) and Tenebrae op. 31 (1991) for a solo guitar, dedicated to Timo Korhonen. *"Tenebrae* (Latin) is darkness, dim, a darkening ritual with Galician origin, which takes place during the three days before Easter Sunday in the combined matinum and laudes prayers. After each psalm a candle is put out, so that the last psalm is canticled in an unlit church. It is a symbol of dimming the light because of the death of Christ." (Weilin & Göös, Suuri tietosanakirja). Tenebrae is an instrumental study of space and time.

For a solo guitar: "Tenebrae op. 31." For a flute, alto saxophone, guitar and percussion: "Far from Home."

KALMÁR, Lázló (1931-1995), a Hungarian composer. Studied composi-

Photo: Maarit Kytöharju

The guitar composition Tenebrae by Jouni Kaipainen is a study about space and time.

tion with Ervin Major and at times privately with Ferenc Farkas. Kalmár has worked for the publisher Editio Música Budapest since 1957 and as a music chief since 1987. He has composed vocal, choir and chamber music and two piano concertos.

For a solo guitar: "Monologo" (1968); "Colour Pieces." For a flute, marimba (vibraphone) and a guitar: "Trio" (1968). For a guitar, conga drums and a double bass: "Combo" (1971–73).

KANGRO, Raimo (1949–2001), an Estonian composer, who studied composition with E. Tamberg and J. Rääts in the Music Academy of Tallinn, form where he graduated in 1973. He taught there (now Music Academy of Estonia) since 1989. In 1972–76 Kangro worked in the Estonian Radio and Television. Since 1977 he worked for the Estonian Composer Union. Kangro received the Estonia State Music Awards in 1978 and 1988. Kangro's music is based on the power of rhythm like in Baroque or rock music. This is also seen in his guitar works, especially in a trio *"Idioms op. 43 a"* and *"Suite for a solo guitar op. 37 a"*, to which he has added elements of improvising and rock.

For a solo guitar: "Seven pieces (Suite) op. 37 a." For a cello and a guitar: "Suite op. 37." For a guitar, cello and chamber orchestra: "Concerto op. 46." These works are published by Editio 49 in Germany. For a flute, violin and a guitar: "Trio 'Idioms' op. 43 a" (1992), which is dedicated to a chamber ensemble Camerata Tallinn. For a violin, vibraphone and guitar: "Kevadnägemused" (Spring imaginations).

KARKOFF, Ingvar (born 1958), a Swedish composer, son of Maurice Karkoff. Studied composition in the Music Academy of Stockholm with Gunnar Bucht in 1978–82 and electronic music with Per Lindgren. He has also studied composition with a guest lecturer, Brian Ferneyhough. Ingvar Karkoff has been active in familiarizing different cultures, such as the African, Latin American and reggae.

For a lute (or alto guitar): "Fyra stycken för luta/altgitarr" (1985); "4 duetter" (1985). For a flute (or alto flute) and guitar: "Suite for flute/alto flute and guitar" (1989/90). For an alto saxophone and a guitar: "Suite for alto saxophone and guitar" (1989/93). For a mezzo soprano, percussion and an electric guitar: "Sömn och tomhet" (1994).

KARKOFF, Maurice (born 1927), a Swedish composer. In addition to composition studies with Erland von Koch, Vagn Holmboe, André Jolivet and Wladimir Vogel, he also studied piano playing and conducting. Karkoff has worked in Stockholm as a teacher of theory and as a music critic. As a composer he has received several awards and he became a member of the Swedish Music Academy in 1977. Karkoff's music, which comprises of tight phrases and strong highlights, has been described as expressive and melodic.

For a solo guitar: "Aspekter för gitarr op. 96" (1968–1970), dedicated to Per-Olof Johnson; "Japansk nocturn" (1969), dedicated to P-O. Johnson; "Svit för sologitarr" (1961/1971). For a violin, viola and guitar: "Trio för violin, viola och gitarr" (1961).

Stephen Kenyon

KENYON, Stephen (born 1962), an English composer and guitarist. He did further studies on guitar playing for four years in London in the Trinity College of Music with Gilbert Biberian. He has also studied with Antonìn Tucapsky, Glen Morgan, Stephen Dodgson and Ricardo Iznaola. He writes for several guitar magazines. Kenyon's composition production contains both concert and pedagogic works for the guitar and also other instruments. In several concert pieces he has combined modern techniques with medieval and Oriental features and Celtic folk music.

For a solo guitar: "Sonatina" (1987); "Elegy" (1989); "Areba - Fantasy on a theme of Bernard Stevens" (1991); "Versa" (1993); "Aquarelle I" (1992); "Aquarelle II" (1993); "Morning Dance" (1993); "Una Pieza Breve" (1993); "Simple Suite" (1993); "Pieces of Eight"; "Scottish Suite" (1997). For two guitars: "Simple Duets" (1993). For three guitars: "Figures of Dawn" (1991). For four guitars: "Four Dances from Hardy's Notebook" (1990). For eight guitars: "Siciliana" (1991). For eleven guitars: "Worlde's Woodsere" (1992). For a flute and a guitar: "Hunting the Wren" (1991). For a solo flute, guitar and a guitar orchestra: "Highgate Wood" (1992). For a bassoon or cello and guitar: "I'll come and go by Carterhaugh." For a guitar, violin, viola, flute, oboe and bassoon: "The Birds of Rhiannon" (1992). For a guitar and an orchestra: "Concerto no. 1 for Guitar solo and orchestra" (1992); For a guitar and a guitar orchestra: "Concerto for Guitar soloist and Guitar orchestra" (1994); For a guitar and a string orchestra: "Concerto no 3 for Guitar solo and String Orchestra" (1997).

KERNIS, Aaron Jay (born 1960), a composer from the United States. Studied in the Music Academy of San Francisco with John Adams in 1977–78, Manhattan School of Music in 1978–81 and Yale school of Music in 1981–83. Since 1984 Kernis has worked as a composer. He has won

Francis Kleynjans

several awards, such as the *"Rome Prize"* 1984–85, the Tippett Award etc. Kernis has worked in cooperation with American guitarists, e.g. David Tanenbaum and Sharon Isbin.

For a solo guitar: "Partita"; "Suite in Three Parts" (1981). For a viola and a guitar: "Morning" (1980). For a guitar and a string quartet: "100 Greatest Dance Hits." For a violin, guitar and an orchestra: "Double Concerto" (1996).

KEURIS, Tristan (1946–1996), a Dutch composer. Studied composition in the Music Academy of Utrecht with Ton de Leeuw in 1962–69. Worked as a teacher in the Music Academies of Hilversum and Utrecht. Keuris gained international fame with his symphony, which won the *"Matthis Vermeulen Prize"* in Amsterdam in 1975. His works have been published by Edition Novello in London.

For a clarinet, mandolin, guitar, marimba, violin and double bass: "Eight Miniatures" (1980).

KIKTA, Valeri (born 1941), a Ukrainian composer, graduated from the Music Academy of Moscow, where he studied composition with Semyon Bogatoryov and Tihon Hrennikov. Kikta has composed theater music and works for symphony orchestras, three piano concertos etc.

For a solo guitar: "Sonata" (1983). Guitar and orchestra: "Concerto"

KLEYNJANS, Francis (born 1951), a French guitarist and composer. Started classical guitar studies at the age of 14 with Alexandre Lagoya and Alirio Diaz. In addition to guitar playing he has studied jazz and arrangement in the music and Art College of Graz. Kleynjans has won the *"Yehudi Menuhin Prize"* and has also received several awards as e.g. the conductor of the Munich Guitar Orchestra. He has given concerts around the Europe and performed in the programs of several French radio stations. Kleynjans is a very productive guitar composer, his production contains more that 300 works for the guitar. He won a guitar composition contest arranged by the Radio France with his work *A l'Aube du Dernier Jour*, performed by Roberto Aussel. At the moment he works as a free artist and lives in Munich.

For a solo guitar: "3 Pièces in A op. 4"; "Hommage à Pachelbel op. 9"; "Ballade No. 3 op. 15"; "7 Études de Concert op. 20"; "Vals No. 12 op. 21"; "5 Nocturnes op. 26"; "8 Études des Concert op. 29"; "A l'Aube du Dernier Jour op. 33"; "Chôro in D op. 36"; "Chôro in Es op. 37"; "Hommage à Satie op. 38"; "7 Éstudines op. 39"; "Cinq Nouvelles Éstudines op. 40"; "Suite in C op. 42"; "6 Petites pièces intimes op. 44"; "3 Valses op. 45"; "2 Pièces op. 47"; "Reverie & 2 Amertunes op. 49"; "Suite Brésilienne op. 51"; "Amertune in b op. 52"; "Vals Venezuelienne op. 55"; "Dernière Éstudine op. 56"; "2 The Dansant op. 57"; "24 Preludes Vol. I op. 58 and Vol. II op. 59"; "2 Barcarolles op. 60"; "2 Valses op. 64"; "Impromptu & Berceuse op. 65"; "16 Vals Sentimentales et Capricieuses op. 66"; "4 Pièces op. 68"; "5 Arias op. 69"; "Chanson in b op. 71"; "Petites Variations op. 86"; "Passacaille sur le mort de Segovia op. 87"; "Vals noble et sentimentale op. 89"; "Feuilles d'Album op. 95"; "Le Coin de l'enface op. 97"; "Arabesque en forme de caprice op. 99"; "3 Miniatures op. 102"; "7 Metamorphoses d'un theme op. 104"; "Bricoles, Babioles et Fabioles Frivoles op. 107"; "Complainte & Elègie op. 108"; "Berceuse d'Aubrac op. 112"; "Introduction, Variations et fugue on a Japanese Theme op. 114"; "Petite suite Aubracoise op. 116"; "Le Coin des Debutantes (30 Prog. pieces) op. 117"; "Hommage à M. de Falla op. 118"; "Capriccio-Hommage à Legnani op.

120"; "Homenaje à Antonio José op. 125"; "Vals créole op. 127"; "Homenaje à Benvenuto Terzi op. 130"; "Le Bal Masqué op. 131"; "Le Lamantin op. 132"; "Variaciones sobre un tema de Martini op. 133"; "Suite Antillaise op. 135"; "En Regardant les Etoiles, fantaisie op. 136"; "Little Suite in G op. 140." For two guitars: "3 Climats op. 50"; "4 Mouvements op. 53"; "Suite Baroque-Aria I op. 72"; "10 Inventions op 76"; "Canons et Arias op. 92a"; "3 Romances op. 100"; "Hommage à Déodat de Séverac op. 105"; "Mirage op. 110"; "Chanson Napolitaine op. 113"; "Pour les Vacances (10 pieces) op. 115"; "2 Pièces op. 122"; "Libellules op. 124"; "Lorsque s'ouvre la petite boîte à Musique." For three guitars: "Suite Baroque op. 72"; "Sonata Oceana Nox op. 111." For four guitars: "2 Melodies op. 48"; "Suite Baroque op. 72"; "The Four season op. 109"; "The Four Elements op. 123." For five guitars: "Suite Baroque - Canon op. 72 No. 1"; "Grand Canon op. 91." For a flute and a guitar: "2 Arias." For a guitar and a string orchestra: "Concerto No. 1 in B op. 62"; "Concertino Baroque (in D) op. 80 no. 2." For two guitars and a string orchestra: "Concerto (in d) op. 101."

KOCH, Erland von (born 1910), a Swedish composer, whose father Sigurd von Koch also was a composer. Studied in the Music College of Stockholm. Von Koch also studied abroad in 1936–38, composition with Paul Höffer, conducting with Clemens Craus and piano playing with Claudio Arrau. Von Koch worked as a teacher in a Music College in Sweden since 1953 and as a professor since 1968. He has been a member of the Swedish Royal Music Academy since 1957. He belongs to the most versatile composers in Sweden: his production contains e.g. 5 symphonies, ballets, motion picture music etc. Von Koch's style has been described as neoclassic; it combines a melodic fluency with a simple harmonization and also often the folk music of Dalecarlia.

For a solo guitar: "Appasionata"; "3

Photo: Maarit Kytöbarju

Olli Kortekangas started to compose for the classical guitar in the 1990s. He has also composed for a guitar orchestra.

Episodes"; "Monolog No. 10." For two guitars: "In Dalecarlian Mood." For a guitar and a string orchestra or a woodwind quintet: "Fantasia Melodica."

KORTEKANGAS, Olli (born 1955), a Finnish composer. Studied composition in the Sibelius Academy with Einojuhani Rautavaara and Eero Hämeenniemi and in West Berlin in 1981–82 with Dieter Schnebel. Kortekangas has worked as a teacher in the Theater College and Sibelius Academy since 1984 and in the Espoo Music Institute since 1985. He has also written on music. He was a founder of a group of new modernists in Finland. "Unlike other members Kortekangas did not have post serialness as his starting point, but had a pluralistic and interartistic direction. Also a certain simplicity has separated Kortekangas from his contemporary postserials." (M. Heiniö).

Kortekangas describes his *Arabesken der Nacht* for a guitar and a chamber orchestra (1995) as follows: "Arabesken der Nacht was partly composed alongside with my opera, Joonan kirja. These two works therefore have an inevitable "shared past", though they do not resemble each other in their musical expressions all the way from the form. My arabesques are surely more than a residue from an exhausting opera work. I think of this as a series of dreams, which mercifully interrupt the continuous esthetic awakeness. Maybe at times there is a shade of a nightmare!"

La banda was commissioned by Jussipekka Rannanmäki for the Guitar Summer Festival in Ikaalinen in 1996. The composer describes the work as follows: "I decided to divide my "band" into three groups, to each of which I wrote both accurate and free parts, and if wanted, the latter may be played with several soloists."

For an alto recorder and a guitar: "Omaggio à M.C. Esher" (1990), dedicated to M. Helasvuo-J. Savijoki, duo. For a guitar orchestra: "La Banda" (1996). For a guitar and a chamber orchestra: "Arabesken der Nacht" (1995), dedicated to Timo Korhonen.

KÕRVITS, Tõnu (born 1969), an Estonian composer. Graduated as a composer from the Estonian Academy of Music in 1994 with Raimo Kangro. Both his father and his grandfather were composers. At the moment Tõnu Kõrvits works in the Estonian Radio in the department of classical music. His composition style has been influenced by minimalism and neoromanticism. Kõrvits received the third prize in the Estonian Guitar Composition contest in 1996 with his solo guitar work *Fantasy*.

For a solo guitar: "2 Études" (1994); "2 Preludes" (1995); "Piece" (1996); "Fantasy" (1996). For two guitars: "Suite" (1991); "Kiss on the Water" (1992); "I.L.Y.B." (1991). For a guitar and a piano: "Long-lasting Farwell" (1993). For an alto flute and a guitar: "To My Spiritual Brother" (1996). For a guitar and a chamber orchestra: "Concerto semplice" (1992). Songs on the Bridge of Encounters (2006).

KOSHKIN, Nikita (born 1956), a Russian composer and guitarist. After receiving a guitar and a record by Andrés Segovia from his grandfather, Koshkin decided to make a career as a musician. He studied guitar playing first with V. Kapayev and G. Emanov and later in the Gnessin Conservatory in Moscow with A. Frauchi and at the same time he studied composition with V. Egorov. Since 1992 Koshkin has taught guitar playing in the Russian National Academy.

Koshkin thinks of himself more as a composer than a guitarist, although his tours as a guitarist have covered the most important concert halls of Europe and even the USA. His music is purposeful and dramatic, but at the same time fun and full of parodies. His music has been influenced by Shostakovich and Prokofiev, who together with Stravinsky were his favorite composes already when he was 4 years old. His rich musical texture contains many surprising elements: references to myths and literary figures, avantgardistic effects and references to popular music. Koshkin's *"Andante quasi Passacaglia e Toccata"* for a solo guitar (1978) composed to Vladimír Mikulka is his first

Chorus Publications © Ole Halén 1991 (Helsinki, Finland)

The solo guitar work by Nikita Koshkin, Three Stops On The Road, has influences from jazz music.

Nikita Koshkin has become known for his work The Prince's Toys, where the toys of a bored prince get alive. His music has been influenced by Shostakovich and Prokofiev.

famous work, but in 1980 he composed his best known guitar work, *"The Prince's Toys"*, also composed to Mikulka. It is based on a story of a bored prince and his toys which he wishes could be alive. As in a miracle, his toys start to live. Koshkin has, in addition to Mikulka, composed to e.g. John Williams and the "Abreu Duo." His work *"Mascarade"* contains 24 pieces, which are suitable for guitar studying all the way from the beginning.

For a solo guitar: "Three Pieces (Drops, Footsteps, Glance) op. 1"; "Variations on a Ukrainian Folksong op. 2"; "Two Pieces (Caravan, Butterflies) op. 3"; "Allemande & Rondo op. 4"; "Ivanov-Kramskoi Memorial op. 5"; "Rain (fantasia for guitar) op. 6"; "Spanish Suite - Dedicated to F. Moreno Torroba op. 7"; "Six Preludes op. 10"; "Two Pieces (Minestrel, Tambourin) op. 13"; "Two Pieces (Ricercar, Branle) op. 15"; "Gagliard, John Dowland Memorial op. 16"; "The Fall of Birds (Passacaglia-Toccata) op. 18"; "Three Railway Stops on the Road op. 19"; "Prince's Toys (suite for guitar) op. 19"; "Northen Lights (piece for guitar) op. 22"; "Piece with Clocks (D.D. Schostakovich Memorial) op. 24"; "Porcelain Tower (Variations on Rak's theme) op. 26"; "Pan (piece for guitar) op. 29"; "Atsuo's Melody (prelude for guitar) op. 30"; "Parade (Jazz-piece for guitar) op. 31"; "Elves-suite for guitar op. 32"; "Usher-valse (piece for guitar) op. 35"; "Tristan playing the lute op. 37"; "Merlin's Dream (tremolo) op. 38"; "Avalon-suite for guitar dedicated to J.W. Duarte op. 39"; "March for guitar op. 41"; "Mascarade - 24 Pieces for beginners in 4 volumes dedicated to Claude Mikulkova op. 42"; "Variations on Duarte's theme op. 44"; "Guitar op. 45"; "Suite Six cordes"; "Six Strings - Suite for Solo Guitar in 6 Movements"; "Oime - Rhapsody for Guitar Solo on Theme by John Duarte"; "Happy Birthday! - 24 Pieces for Guitar Solo"; "Prelude and Waltz (Hommage to Maestro Andrés Segovia) - Guitar Solo"; "Prelude - Guitar Solo"; "Romance - Guitar Solo"; "Three Pieces for Guitar Solo - Marionette, Elegie, Ils Viennent"; "Sonata - in 3 Movements for Guitar Solo"; "The Ballads - Suite in 5 Movements for Guitar Solo." For two guitars: Cambridge Suite; "Concertino op. 21"; "Dawn Faery - Suite for Two Guitars"; "Cambridge Suite - in 5 Movements." For three guitars: "Zapateado - Trio for Three Guitars"; "Lets Play Together"; "Apres Pastorale - in 3 Movements." For four guitars: "Changing the Guard." For a flute and a guitar: "Sonata op. 25"; "Morning Fairy (two dances) op. 27." For a guitar and a cembalo: "Ricercars op. 43."
For a voice and a guitar: "Suite for Voice and Guitar on Poems by Gillaume Apollinaire." For a flute and a guitar: "Sonata op. 25"; "Morning Fairy (two dances) op. 27." For two guitars and a double bass: "The Dealer of Cicadas op. 46." For a guitar orchestra: "Elegy"; "Concerto."

Photo: Maarit Kytöharju
Olli Koskelin.

KOSKELIN, Olli (born 1955), a Finnish composer. Studied clarinet playing in the Conservatory of Helsinki, musicology at the University of Helsinki and composition privately with Jukka Tiensuu and Eero Hämeenniemi. He also studied composition in France with Tristan Murail. Koskelin teaches in the Helsinki Drama College in the Department of Dance Arts. In 1997 Koskelin won a composition contest arranged in connection with a music festival in Turku with his work *Uurre*.

Koskelin has composed a work *Tutte le corde* "All Strings" for a guitar and a tape (1988). Mikko Heiniö has described it as follows: "Koskelin's best known work Tutte le corde goes near to global thinking, of which it is typical that the music forms wide "surfaces" and "waves." Repetition is dominant, even as minimalistic or meditation music. "All Strings", which jingle as large tone fields, do not only refer to the guitar, but also to the tape on the background, which also consists of guitar music."

For a guitar and a tape: "Tutte le corde 'All Strings'" (1988). An arrangement for the solo guitar: "Far and Near" (1989), an arrangement from a piano work Courbures.

KOVÁTS, Barna (born 1920), a Hungarian guitarist, pedagogue and composer. Studied guitar playing and composition with Varga and Szervanski. He was the solo guitarist of the Hungarian Radio since 1938. Kováts founded the first guitar class in Budapest and gave concerts in France and South America. He has lived in Austria and taught guitar playing in Salzburg.

For a solo guitar: "Petit suite"; "Trois mouvements"; "Six fragments"; "Sonata nuova"; "Suite"; "Easy Exercises and Pieces"; "Minutenstücke"; "Nocturne rhapsodique"; "2 Preludes"; "Short Studies Vol. 1 & 2."

KRENEK, Ernst (1900–1991), a composer with origins in Austria, a USA citizen since 1945. Krenek, who had roots in Bohemia, studied in the Music Academy of Vienna with e.g. F. Schreker. In 1938 Krenek moved to the USA because of the political situation, and worked as a professor in different colleges, e.g. in Boston, Minnesota, Los Angeles and Palm Springs. He has given lectures and worked as a conductor around the world. Krenek's wide production can be divided into five main parts: the atonal (1921–23), neoclassic (1924–26), Romantic (1926–31), dodecaphonic (1931–56) and serial (since 1957).

For a solo guitar: "Suite" (1957). For a piano, violin, guitar and recorder: "Hausmusik, 7 Stücke für die 7 Tage der Woche" (1953).

KREUTZER, Joseph (1778–1832), an Austrian composer, who is a typical representative of the German-Austrian Biedermeier (early 19th century) style. Only a few facts are known about his life. In addition to guitar solos, Kreutzer composed chamber music, duos and trios, of which a popular one is a *Trio for a flute, violin and guitar in D op. 9* and a *Trio for a flute, viola or clarinet and a guitar op. 16.*

For a solo guitar: "Variazione op. 7"; "Variazione op. 11-15"; "12 Pièces op. 17." For two guitars: "6 Variazione op. 6." For two flutes and a guitar: "12 Pièces faciles op. 10." For a flute, violin and a guitar: "4 Trios op. 9 A, E, D and C." For a flute, clarinet (or viola) and guitar: "Trio op. 16."

KUČERA, Václav (born 1929), a Czech composer. Studied in the Music Conservatory of Moscow with Vissarion Shebalin. In 1969–1983 he was the president of the Czech Composers' Union and since 1972 he has taught composition and since 1988 acted as a professor in the Music Academy of Prague. Kučera's production is versatile: stage music, symphonies, chamber music and electronic music. His most known solo guitar work, *"Diario" ("Diary") - Ommagio à Che Guevara* (1972) is based on five days in the life of Che Guevara. The work has five parts, Day of Love, Day of Hate, Day of Decison, Day of Battle and Day of Death, the nature of the music is similar to the name of each part. A part of the notation of the work is graphic.

For a solo guitar: "Diario" (1972); "Nouvelles"; "Stilistisches übungen"; "Urgestalten." For a violin and a guitar: "Capricci." For a flute and a guitar: "Aquarelles."

KUMMER, Kaspar [Gaspard] (1795–1870), a German flutist and composer. Was taught in flute playing by Neumeister, and in harmonization and composition by Staps. Since the 1830s he worked as a flutist in the Royal Chapel Orchestra in Coburg and later as a conductor. Kummer was a productive composer, he composed more than 160 pieces, most of them for

woodwind, like the flute, oboe, clarinet and bassoon. Kummer's compositions are entertaining, composed in the German-Austrian Biedermeier style.

For a flute and a guitar: "Op: 5; 18; 34; 38; 40; 55; 56; 63"; "Nocturne op. 40"; "Amusements op. 63" (from the themes of a French composer Auber). For a flute, violin (viola) and guitar: "Sérénade 81"; "Sérénade op. 83"; "Trio op. 92"; For a flute, violin and guitar: "3 Divertissements op. 92." For a flute, violin, viola, guitar and cello: "Quintett op. 75."

KURTÁG, György (born 1926), a composer and pianist born to a Hungarian-Jewish family in Romania. Studied composition in the Ferenc Liszt Academy in Budapest since 1945 with Sándor Veress and since 1949 with Ferenc Farkas (a composition diploma and a piano and chamber music diploma in 1955). Kurtág completed his composition studies in Paris with D. Milhaud, O. Messiaen and M. Stein. His models have been Bartók and Webern. Kurtág belongs to the most remarkable modern composers of Hungary. In 1968 he was appointed the professor of chamber music in the Liszt Academy. A strive for exact polishing of the content is typical of Kurtág and in his music there is a power of expression of extremely tense short moments and flashes. He thus continues the heritage of Anton Webern.

For a solo guitar: "Guitar Pieces op. 15" (1975). For a piccolo, trombone and guitar: "The Little Predicament op. 15b" (1979).

KUTÁVIČIUS, Bronius (born 1932), a Lithuanian composer, pupil of A. Ratsjunase, with whom he graduated from the Music Academy of Lithuania in 1964. Kutávičius has taught in the Pedagogic Institute of Vilna in 1969–74, since 1975 in the Art School of Vilna and since 1985 in the Lithuanian Academy of Music.

For a string quartet and a guitar: "The Clocks of Past" (1977). For two pianos, a soprano, saxophone, guitar and percussion: "Sigute, vargo mergele, as tavo broli" (1993).

KUULBERG, Mati (1947–2001), an Estonian composer. Studied violin playing in the Music School of Tallinn and composition in the Conservatory of Tallinn, from which he graduated in 1971. In 1966–74 he played the violin in the Symphony Orchestra of Estonia (ERSO). He taught composition in the Music School of Tallinn in 1975–80 and since 1986 he acted as a consultant in the Estonian Composers' Union. His music has been described as dynamic and experimental in various styles. In his compositions Kuulberg has combined folk music and classical forms.

For a violin and a guitar: "E point" (1994).

KÜFFNER, Joseph (1776–1856), a German composer and amateur guitarist, who worked as a concert master and conductor in the courts of the German and Austrian episcopes. Küffner worked at first as a chamber musician in Wurzburg, after which he from 1802 onwards worked as a conductor of military music. Küffner composed operas, symphonies and a large part of his compositions are chamber music for the guitar (ca. 50 duos for a flute and a guitar, a violin and a guitar and two guitars, and ca. 30 trios for a flute, violin or viola and guitar). His music was very popular among his contemporaries.

For a solo guitar: "25 leichte Sonatinen op. 80." For two guitars: "12 Duette op. 87"; "60 leichte Übungstücke op. 168." For a flute, violin and guitar: "Sérénade: op: 1; 2; 4; 6"; "Nocturne op. 114." For a flute, viola and guitar: "Sérénade: op: 1; 2; 4; 6; 10; 15; 35; 37; 38; 60; 63; 64; 215"; "10 Pièces op. 12"; "Nocturne op: 75; 110; 114." For a flute, violin, viola and guitar: "Potpourri op. 155." For two flutes, a viola and a guitar: "Quartetti: op: 11; 94; 135."

LAURO, Antonio (1917–1986), a Venezuelan composer and guitarist, born to a family of Italian emigrants. Got his musical education in the Music Academy of Caracas, where he studied guitar playing with Raúl Borges and composition with Vincente Sojo. Lauro studied at first piano playing, but after hearing a concert by Agustín Barrios, he changed to the guitar. He also studied singing and cello and organ playing. Lauro was a leader of a composition class in Collegio Chavez and was a leader of the Coro de Madrigalistas de Venezuela choir. Later Lauro worked in the board of the Venezuelan Composers' Union and as the president of the Asociacion Venezolana de Esperanto. Lauro has composed symphonic, vocal and chamber music. His music was influenced by Venezuelan folk music and the Venezuelan piano composers from the turn of the century. Lauro's guitar music production is tremendous. He is best known by his numerous Venezuelan dances, which the Venezuelan guitarist Alirio Diaz has made famous. An alternation between 3/4 and 6/8 time is typical of Lauro's waltzes. Lauro has also composed pedagogical pieces which are based on Venezuelan folk music. Lauro's guitar music has been studied by a remarkable Venezuelan guitarist, Luis Zea, whose articles about Lauro's music have been published in an English Classical Guitar Magazine.

For a solo guitar: "4 Valses Venezolanos"; "Valses: Maria Luisa"; "Angostura"; "El Marabino"; "Carora"; "El Negrito"; "La Gatica" (Little Cat, a nickname for Lauro's wife) etc. "Etudes: Quatro Estudios en imitaciónes"; "La Catira, estudio"; "Pavana al Estilo los Vihuelistas" (1949); "3 Venezuelan pieces"; "Merengue" (1940); "6 Venezuelan pieces"; "Suite Venezolana" (1964); "Triptico" (three pieces for Andrés Segovia); "Suite homenaje à John Duarte" (1981); "Sonata" (1963, dedicated to Regino Sáinz de la Maza); "Variations on a Venezuelan Children's song"; "7 Chansons traditionelles des enfants de France"; "Aire de Joropo"; "Seis por Derecho." For a guitar and an orchestra: "Concierto para Guitarra y Orquesta" (1956, dedicated to Alirio Diaz).

LEGNANI, Luigi Rinaldo (1790–1877),

an Italian guitarist, composer, pedagogue and guitar builder. Performed in his youth in Ravenna (1807) as a tenor, performing arias by Cimarosa, Donizetti and Rossini. He also studied playing guitar and other

The Sonata (1963) by Antonio Lauro, dedicated to R. Sáinz de la Maza, is rarely heard in concerts.

string instruments. As a guitarist Legnani became famous after performing in La Scala in Milan in 1819 and three months in Vienna in 1822. Legnani also became popular as a singer, he used to add songs to his guitar concerts and he accompanied himself. He gave concerts in Germany and Switzerland in 1825 and in 1835 there was a planned tour, which he had to cancel after an accident, in which a carriage fell down and his arm was broken. In 1836 Legnani became friends with the legendary violinist Niccolò Paganini, and together they planned to give concerts in Torino in August, but they also had to be cancelled because of Paganini's health problems. Researchers have still come to the conclusion that Paganini and Legnani gave concerts together in 1837 and also changed instruments in the concerts playing each other's parts. In 1836 Legnani gave concerts in Munich, in 1838 in Dresden and Berlin, and in the spring of 1842 in Madrid and Barcelona.

Legnani developed a playing technique, of which a good example is his *36 Caprices* in all keys. He worked in cooperation with guitar builders Jakob

Anton Staufer and Nicolaus Ries to make the characteristics of the guitar better. A Legnani-guitar with an adjustable neck was built by several guitar builders in 1830–80. During the last years of his life also he himself built guitars.

Information about Legnani is available in the Italian guitar magazine "Il Fronimo": no. 23 (1978) no. 27 (1979), no. 41 (1982) and no. 49 (1984). Also in a Chanterelle publication no. 429 (Gran studio op. 60) there is a list of 27 sources about Legnani! Legnani composed ca. 250 guitar works, in which there is an influence from Paganini and Rossini. His *Guitar Concerto op. 28* was composed in Cervia in Italy in 1850. He also wrote a guitar school.

For a solo guitar: "Terremoto con variazioni op. 1"; "Variazioni op. 16"; "Fantasia op. 19"; "36 Caprices op. 20"; "Grand studio op. 60"; "Introduzione, Tema, Variazioni e Finale op. 64" (Nel cor piú non mi sento, dalla Mólinaro di Paisiello); "Variazioni: op: 202; 204; 224; 237"; "Potpourri: op. 222; 238"; "6 Capricen op. 250." For a violin (or flute) and guitar: "Duetto concertante op. 23"; "Gran duetto op. 87." For a guitar and

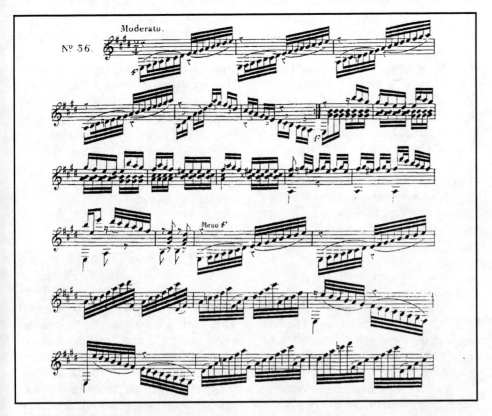

Luigi Legnani may have been influenced by his friend, violin virtuoso Niccolò Paganini, when he composed his 36 Caprices for the solo guitar.

an orchestra: "Concerto op. 28."

LEITE, Antonio da SILVA (1759–1833), a Portuguese composer. After studying theology he became a musician. He probably studied music with Girolamo Sertori. Leite became especially famous when he worked as a teacher and in 1814 he became the conductor of the Oporto Cathedral. He was also a skillful guitarist, who played a third higher tuned Portuguese guitar, for which he published a guitar school in 1796.

For a Portugese solo guitar: "Six Sonatas" (1792); "Estudo de guitarra" (1796); "Menuets"; "Marches"; etc.

LENDLE, Wolfgang (born 1948), a German guitarist, pedagogue and composer. Graduated from the Music College of Saarbrücken with Jiří Jirmal and continued his studies with Andrés Segovia, Alirio Diaz, José Tomás, Alvaro Company and Regino Sáinz de la Maza. He has won several international guitar contests and given concerts in almost all European countries and in both North and South America. Since 1985 he has worked in the Music

Academy of Kassel.

For a solo guitar: "Variations Capricieuses d'Apres Paganini"; "Impulse" (22 excercises from easy to medium level).

L'HOYER, Antoine (1768–ca.1840), a French guitarist, who worked as the guitarist of the Prussian Prince. L'Hoyer is one of the most important guitarists of the 19th century, though too little attention has been paid to him. He never became a professional guitarist, but he made a career in the military forces. Not much is known about L'Hoyer as a composer. Matanya Ophee wrote an article about him in 1990 using the documents of the archives of the library of Paris. In Scandinavia L'Hoyer's life has been researched by a Norwegian guitarist, Erik Stenstadvold, who has also together with Martin Haug published a CD with L'Hoyer's guitar duos. It is assumed that L'Hoyer got his musical education in Paris. His compositions are technically very demanding and they be divided into three groups according to the time and place of publication. Opuses 12–18 were pub-

lished in Hamburg during the last years of the 18th century. The ten next works were published in St. Petersburg in 1804-14. The third period is in 1814-26, when his masterworks were composed. The works before 1814 are mainly composed for the five-string guitar. His compositions have a clear structure and they are original in their melody and rhythm. "The accompanying parts of the skillfully composed duos have been made independent and they contain more details than guitar duos in general." (E. Stenstadvold).

For a solo guitar: "Grosse Sonate op. 12"; "Ouvertüre op. 18"; "Études"; "Fantasies." For two guitars: "Trois duos concertants pour deux guitarres op. 31"; "Fantasie Concertante pour deux guitares, C-major op. 33." For three guitars: "Trio concertant pour trois guitarres op. 29." For a violin and a guitar: "3 sonatas op. 17"; "Grand duo Concertant." For a guitar and a string quartet: "Concerto op. 16."

LINDBERG, Magnus (born 1958), a Finnish composer. Studied piano playing and composition in the Sibelius Academy with Einojuhani Rautavaara and Paavo Heininen (diploma 1981). Lindberg has completed his composition studies with Franco Donatoni, Brian Ferneyhough and Vinko Globokar. Lindberg has worked in the IRCAM studio in Paris and in the studio for electronic music in Stockholm. In his compositions he has made use of the computer, tapes and live electronics. "A liking for theoretic constructions, strict constructivity, tight control over resources and clarity in expression have been the basic qualities of Lindberg from the beginning." (M. Heiniö). Already as a young composer in the 1980s Lindberg achieved international success.

In his work *"Linea d'ombra"* (a line of the shadow) (1981) Lindberg examines tunes by combining different instruments into one "macro instrument." In the work he has aimed at a perfect continuity between the instrumental material and the phonetic elements of speech. The rhythmic models have been derived from the phonetic material, which first thicken into sylla-

Photo: Maarit Kytöbarju

The internationally very successful Finnish composer, Magnus Lindberg, has also used the guitar in a few of his chamber music works.

bles finally ending as a line of an Italian poem "Sorride, sospira, sospenti la morte, giura che un melo si freddo da fiori stasera."

The world of tunes in *"Duo Concertanten"* (1990-1992) is formed by pairs of instruments, which by fulfilling each other have a dialogue. The pairs are flute/oboe, vibraphone/harp, clarinet/cello and viola/double bass.

For solo guitar: Mano a mano (2004). For a flute, alto saxophone, guitar and percussion: "Linea d'ombra" (1981). For a flute, oboe & English horn, mandoline, guitar, vibraphone, harp, solo clarinet, solo cello, viola and double bass: "Duo Concertante" (1992).

LINDE, Hans-Martin (born 1930), a Swiss recordist, flutist and composer born in Germany. Linde studied flute playing with Gustaf Scheck and conducting with Konrad Lechner in the Music College of Freiburg in 1947–51, after which he worked as a solo flutist in the Radio of West Berlin. Since 1957 he has lived in Basel and works in the Schola Cantorum. Linde is an internationally known recorder artist and he has made remarkable recordings of flute concertos by e.g. Leclair, Mozart, Stamiz and Dittersdorf and of recorder concertos by Sammartini, Vivaldi and Naudot. In addition to his composi-

tions he has also published musical literature: *Kleine Anleitung zum Verzieren alter Musik* (1958) and *Handbuch des Blockflötenspiels* (1962).

For an alto recorder and a guitar: "Music for Two" (1983). For alto and bass recorders and a guitar: "Musica da camera" (1972).

LINJAMA, Jyrki (born 1962), a Finnish musicologist and composer, a nephew of Jouko Linjama, and also his father, dir. musices Jaakko Linjama (1909–1983) was a composer. Jyrki Linjama studied composition with Einojuhani Rautavaara in the Sibelius Academy (BA 1989), in Budapest in 1989–91 (Zsolt Durkó) and in Berlin in 1991–92 (Witold Szalonek). He has taught at the University of Helsinki and since 1993 he has been a lecturer of musicology at the University of Turku. "In spite of his post serial starting point, Linjama has from the beginning been closer to an expressionistic late Romantic tone language than other members of his generation." (M. Heiniö).

The Music Institute of Western Helsinki and the Helsinki Guitar Association ordered the *Partita* for a guitar and a string orchestra, and it was performed for the first time in Helsinki in the Auditorium of the Ateneum in November 1996. The guitar part was played by Andrzej Wilkus. The duration of the six part Partita is 27 min. and it is composed in a French Baroque style. The parts are: Introduzione, Intrada, Capricho, Intermezzo,

Sarabande elegiaco and Danza rusticale. In the first part the instruments are equal, but in other parts they take turns in being the center of attention. The fast parts are rhythmically strong and virtuoso. The guitarist's part can be compared to that of a lutist in Baroque, the guitarist also has a central role as the leader of group playing and in the performance he acts as a conductor.

For a guitar and a string quartet: "Partita" (1996).

LLOBET, Miguel (1878–1938), a Spanish (Catalonian) guitarist, arranger and composer. Llobet, who was born in Barcelona, was in his childhood interested in visual arts, he played the violin and the piano, but after hearing a blind guitarist, Antonio Jimenez Manjón, he decided to dedicate himself to guitar playing. Since 1892 Llobet studied with Francisco Tárrega first privately and a couple of years later, at the age of 16, as his pupil in the Music Academy of Barcelona. He gave his debute concert as a guitarist in 1898. Llobet was one of the best guitarists in the early 20th century, together with

Miguel Llobet, the continuator of Tárrega's school, was a remarkable guitarist, composer and arranger.

Agustín Barrios and Andrés Segovia. He gave concerts around Spain and lived in Paris in 1905–10 giving concerts in England, Germany and the British Isles. He gave his first concert in South America in 1910 in Buenos Aires in Argentina, which became his temporary home country. Llobet made tours to the USA (1912) and in the same year to Germany and Paris. When the First World War began, he went back to Buenos Aires and gave concerts in 1925 together with his pupil María Luisa Anido (1907-1996). In the 1930s they made recordings for the Odeon-Parlophone.

As a composer Llobet was influenced by his fellow countryman Manuel de Falla. Llobet's cooperation with de Falla resulted in the only guitar piece by de Falla, *"Homenaje"* (to the memory of Claude Debussy), which Llobet performed for the first time on February 18, 1921. In his works Llobet makes use of the wide tone variation by fingering his works carefully and using the different registers of the guitar. Llobet has been called an "impressionistic guitarist" and he has gotten the name *"the Casals of the guitar."* His composition style has been described as national-Romantic. Llobet was also a remarkable arranger. He arranged e.g. Manuel de Falla's, *"Seven Spanish Folksongs"* and several piano compositions by Albéniz and Granados for one and two guitars. His last years he spent in Barcelona and died of pneumonia in 1938, almost forgotten.

From the ca. 100 publications by Llobet, ca. 25 are original compositions for the guitar. His guitar works are published by Chanterelle (ECH 890).

For a solo guitar: "Mazurca"; "Scherzo-Vals"; "Romanza"; "Preludio en Mi mayor"; "Variaciones sobre un tema de Sor op. 15"; "Estudio en mi mayor" (1899); "Estudio capricho, en re mayor" (1899); "Prelude-original" (ca. 1912); "Preludio en re mayor" (1916); "Respuesta, Impromptu" (1922); "Preludio, en la mayor" (1935). Llobet has also made arrangements for a solo guitar to 16 folk songs, most famous of which are the Catalonian songs: "El testament d'Amelia"; "Canco del Lladre"; "El noy de la mare"; "La pastoreta"; "La filla del marxant", etc.

LUTOSLAWSKI, Witold

(1913–1994), a Polish composer, pianist and conductor. Studied composition in the Music Academy of Warsaw with Witold Maliszewski (diploma 1937). Before that he performed as a solo pianist. In his early works he developed a style, which was influenced by Bartók. Other composers that have affected him are Stravinsky, Ravel and Prokofiev and especially Roussel. In the late 1950s Lutoslawski shifted to a more radical modernism with the so-called aleatoric bass continuo. Typical of his last works were imaginatory subject constructions and a strong sense of form, tune and dynamics. A Spanish guitarist José Azpiazu has arranged Lutoslawski's music for the guitar: *"9 Melodies populaires."*

For a flute, oboe, clarinet, bassoon, French horn, piano, guitar and a string quartet: "Slides" (1988, premiere New York -88)

LUTYENS, Elisabeth (1906–1983), a

British composer, studied in 1922-23 in the Paris École Normale de Musique and in 1926-30 composition with H. Drake and viola playing with E. Tomlinson in the London Royal College of Music. Lutyens is the first composer of dodecaphonic music of her generation. Despite her atonal and serial technique her music is sensuous and lyrical. In her late productions she has tried to avoid all extremes. Lutyens's production contains an especially large number of radio, television and stage music.

For a solo guitar: "The Dying of the Sun op. 73" (1969); "Romanza op. 121" (1977). For a violin, guitar and cello: "Nocturnes op. 30" (1955). For a tenor and a lute: "Dialogo op. 88" (1972). The guitar is included in the following works: "For a soprano and a baritone

Photo: Mayotte Magnus
Elisabeth Lutyens

soloist and an orchestra: Quincunx op. 44" (1959/60). For a female voice and an orchestra: "Concert Aria op. 112" (1976). For a soprano and a string orchestra: "O Saisons. O. Chateaux! op. 13" (1946). For an electric guitar and a string quartet: "Go, Said the Bird op. 105" (1975).

MacCOMBIE, Bruce (born 1943) studied composition at the University of Massachusetts, where he earned a B.A. in 1967 and an M.M. in 1968. He holds a Ph.D. in music from the University of Iowa (1971) and has also studied with Wolfgang Fortner at the Freiburg Conservatory. After four years in Europe, Mr. MacCombie was appointed to the Composition faculty at Yale School of Music. While at Yale he coordinated an annual series of of six concerts of new music and taught various seminars relating to 20th century music literature. The recipient of many prizes and awards, he has been described in the pages of the New York Times as a "deft and evocative craftsman." He is a gifted composer of choral and vocal music, intensely thoughtful and full of passion and color. Recent performances of Mr. McCombie's works have included

"Greeting", in honor of Krzysztof Penderecki's sixtieth birthday, a new version of *"Nightshade Rounds"*, for guitar and string orchestra, commissioned by the Brooklyn Philharmonic for soloist Sharon Isbin and conductor Lukas Foss.

For guitar and orchestra: "Nightshade Rounds" (1988).

MACHADO, Celso (born 1953), a Brazilian guitarist and composer. Machado has used e.g. the folk music of northeastern Brazil and African influences in his compositions.

For a solo guitar: "Chôroso"; "Frevo Bajando" (6 pieces); "3 Toadas Bresiliennes." For two guitars: "Imagenes de Nordeste" (8 pieces); "Modinha Brasiliera" (5 duets); "4 Ponteios Brasiliennes." For four guitars: "Dancas Populares Brasileiras"; "Ponteio" (Agalopado), "Catiga" (Mimar), "Catira" (Bate Sola), "Ciranda" (Roda, Roda), "Frevo" (Esquenta o Pé). "Modinha Brasileira." For a flute and a guitar: "Musiques Populaires Brasiliennes" (6 Pieces).

MADERNA, Bruno (1920–1973), an Italian composer and conductor. Studied composition with G. Malipiero and H. Scherchen. When he graduated from Accademia di Santa Cecilia at the age of 20, he was a skilled musician. Maderna taught in the Conservatory of Venice and in the Darmstadt Courses of modern music. In 1955 he was one of the founders of the studio for electronic music in the Radio of Milan. Since 1967 he taught in the Conservatory of Rotterdam. A typical feature of Maderna's music is a lyrical melody and often a voiced imagination. Maderna's both technically and musically demanding solo guitar work, *"Y después"*, is based on a poem by Federico García Lorca and it is dedicated to Narciso Yepes.

For a solo guitar (10-string): "Y después" (1972). For an English horn and a guitar: "Aulodia per Lothar." For a violin, flute, oboe, clarinet, marimba, mandoline and guitar: "Serenata per un satellite."

MAHLER, Gustav (1860–1911), an Austrian composer and conductor. Mahler was brought up in large family, where he had 13 siblings. His natural gifts led him to the Music Academy of Vienna, where he studied composition and piano playing. Since 1880 Mahler created a career as a brilliant conductor. He used the instruments in a personal way and was very creative. As an indication of this is the use of three guitars in the *"7th symphony (1903) part 4, Lied der Nacht."*

MALIPIERO, Gian Francesco (1882–1973), an Italian composer, uncle of Riccardo Malipiero. Studied composition in Venice in the Liceo Musicale with M.E. Boss, graduated in 1904. His visit to Paris in 1913 became crucial for his development as a composer. There he heard e.g. the premiere of Igor Stravinsky's, "The Rites of Spring." In 1931 Malipiero became the professor of composition in the Music Academy of Parma. Malipiero, together with Casella, Pizzetti and Respighi, belongs to the composers that fought for the earlier Italian musical tradition. His only guitar composition, *"Preludio" (1958)* is an interesting extract of his composition style.

For a solo guitar: "Preludio" (1958).

MALIPIERO, Riccardo (1914–2003), an Italian composer, nephew of Gian Francesco Malipiero. He studied composition in the Music Academies of Milan, Torino and Venice. After giving up his career as a pianist he taught composition in both North and South America, he worked as a critic, for the publisher Suvini Zerboni and also in administrative posts. As a composer he adapted the 12-note system, and was the first to arrange a 12-note system congress to Milan in 1949.

For a solo guitar: "Aria variata su la Follia" (1979). For a voice and a guitar: "2 Ballate." For a flute and a guitar: "Liebesspiel."

MANÉN, Juan (1883–1971), a Spanish violinist and composer. Started his career as a violinist at an early stage, and gave his first concert at the age of 7. He studied with Ibargure and performed around Spain. He made his American debute at the age of 9, conducted an orchestra in Argentina at the age of 10, and composed his first work at the age of 13. He has performed with great success after that around the world. As a composer he is self-learned, but he has gained fame and received several honorary titles, such as that of an honorary professor and other remarkable prizes. Manén has created music out of a national-Romantic base with a strong Catalonian influence.

For a solo guitar: "Fantasia-Sonata op. 22" (1930) dedicated to Andrés Segovia.

MANJÓN, Antonio Jiménez (1866–1919), a Spanish guitarist and composer. Manjón gave concerts at the age of 14 in Portugal, France and England. After this he settled down to live in Paris, where he worked as a guitar teacher. In 1893 he made a visit to South America, where he played in Chile and Argentina and settled down in Buenos Aires. In 1912–19 he lived in Madrid, giving successful concerts, after which he once more returned to Buenos Aires. Manjón played an 11-string guitar.

Robert Spencer had Manjón's compositions in his private collections, and Edition Chanterelle has published 2 collections of Manjón's solo works (ECH 434/435).

For a solo guitar: "La Mariposa, mazurka op. 1"; "Mazurca lírica op. 3"; "Matilde, gavotte op. 4"; "Lola, habanera op. 6"; "Balada op. 7"; "Vorrei morire, melodia de Tosti op. 8"; "Adagio de la sonata XIV (Claro de Luna) de Beethoven op. 9"; "Serenata op. 11"; "La primavera, romaza sin palabras de Mendelssohn op. 12"; "Preludio no. 15 de Chopin op. 13"; "Marcha fúnebre sobre la muerte de un héroe (Beethoven) op. 14"; "Recuerdos de mi patria, mazurka romántica"; "Célebre capricho Andalúz op. 17"; "Cuento de amor, romanza op. 18"; "Aire Vasco op. 19"; "Tres estudios Expresivos op. 25"; "¿Por qué?, vals op. 28"; "Capricho criollo op. 29"; "Primavera andaluza WoO"; "La Aurora, romanza WoO"; "12 Estudios";

"Minueto"; "Rosita"; "Romanza no. 3"; "Quiero y no quiero, habanera"; "Leyenda"; "Del Plata a los Andes"; "Noveletta"; "Canto Andalúz, peteneras"; "Fantasía gitana." For two guitars: "Tú y yo, duetto op. 5." For a voice and a guitar: "Sobre tu Corazon, romanza." For a mandoline or violin and a guitar or piano: "Brisas op. 16."

MANNEKE, Doan (born 1939), a Dutch composer. Studied organ playing in the Music Academy of Brabant (1960–67) and in Brussels with Louis Toe Bosh and composition with Ton de Leeuw in Amsterdam. Since 1972 Manneke has taught improvization and composition in the Music Academy of Sueelinum.

For a solo guitar: "Archipel III" (1987).

MARCO, Tomás (born 1942), a Spanish composer. Studied violin playing, composition and law in Madrid. He completed his studies in France. Since 1967 he has taken part in the Darmstadt courses of modern music. Marco's musical articles have drawn attention both in Spain and abroad. He has won several prizes with his compositions in Spain, the Netherlands (Gaudeamus, 1969) and in the Paris VI Biennale.

For a solo guitar: "Sonata de fuego"; "Albayalde" (1965); "Naturaleza muerta con guitarra" (1975); "Paisaje grana" (1975); "Fantasía sobre fantasía"; "Tarots" (22 concert etudes). For two guitars: "Duo Concertante" (1974). For four guitars: "Arboral" (Concierto armonico no. 2). For a violin and a guitar: "Duo Concertante no. II." For the chimes and a guitar: "Miriada" (1970). For a trumpet, piano, guitar/electric guitar, vibraphone, percussion and cello: "Roulis-Tangage" (1963). For a guitar and an orchestra: "Concerto Eco"; "Concierto Guadiana" (1974); "Concierto del aqua."

MARGOLA, Franco (1908–1992), an Italian composer. Studied violin playing with Roman and composition with e.g. Guerrini, Jachino, Longo and Casello in the Music Academy of Parma in 1926–34. He taught in several conservatories around Italy (e.g. Rome, Milan and Bologna). Margola composed using e.g. the neoclassic style.

For a solo guitar: "6 Bagatelle"; "Ballata da concerto"; "La Brescianella, suite"; "10 composizioni"; "Fantasia"; "Leggenda"; "Notturno"; "8 pezzi facili"; "Preludio da concerto"; "Preludio grandaria scherzo"; "Sonata seconda"; "Sonata terza"; "8 studi da concerto"; "Trittico"; "Ultimo canto"; "2 Preludes." For two guitars: "5 Duetti facili"; "Sonata prima." For three guitars: "Sonata." For a flute and a guitar: "4 Episodi"; "4 Sonate." For a violin and a guitar: "Sonatina." For a piano and a guitar: "Fantasia." For a guitar and an orchestra: "Concerto breve."

MARKUSSEN, Kjell (born 1952), a Norwegian composer and guitarist. He graduated as a guitar teacher from the Music Academy of Adger in 1976. He completed his studies in London in the Guildhall School of Music and Drama taking diplomas in both guitar playing and composition. In addition to his composition he has worked as a guitar pedagogue and a teacher of theory.

For a solo guitar: "Bagatelle" (1983); "Guitar Sonata no. 1" (1985); "Two Lyric Pieces for Guitar" (1976/83); "Two Pieces for Guitar Solo: Fragment, Imitasjon" (1975/85). For two guitars: "Introduction and Allegro" (1989). For a tenor- or soprano recorder: "Mysterium Sanctitatis, The Mystery of the Holiness"

Franco Margola

Miklós Maros, who lives in Sweden, has used the guitar in many of his chamber music works.

(1989). For a flute and a guitar: "Three Pieces for Flute and Guitar: Aquarell, Lullaby, Homage" (1977/79); "Veien framover" (1989). For a guitar, a chamber orchestra (flute/viola, clarinet/bass clarinet, violin, cello, guitar, piano, percussion) and a tape: "Concerto for Guitar, Chamber Ensemble and Tape."

MAROS, Miklós (born 1943), a Hungarian composer, who moved to Sweden in 1968 in order to study with Ingvar Lindholm in the Music Academy of Stockholm in 1968–72. Also the contact with György Ligeti has been very remarkable for his development as a composer. Maros's speciality as a composer is electronic music, which he taught in the studio for electronic music in 1971–80 and in the Music College of Stockholm in 1976–80. He has been the vice president of the Swedish Composers' Union since 1981. Together with his singer wife, he founded the Maros Ensemble, which specializes in electronic music. Maros is also a productive guitar composer, whose production contains remarkable guitar compositions dating back all the way to the late 1970s. Maros often applies the minimalistic style to his compositions.

For a solo guitar: "Drawing" (1983); "Capriccio per Chitarra" (1985); "Darwing" (1983). For two guitars:

"Intonazione per due chitarre" (1984). For an oboe and a guitar: "Goboj" (1987). For a recorder and a guitar: "Epithalam" (1992). For an alto saxophone and guitar: "Sa-Ga" (1992). For a flute, alto saxophone, guitar and percussion: "Clusters for Clusters", dedicated to a Finnish modern music group Cluster. For a soprano, two woodwinds, harmonium, plucked instruments and percussion: "4 sånger ur Gitanjali" (1979). For a soprano, contra-alto, alto flute, viola, guitar and percussion/ 3 players: "Diversion" (1971). For a flute, oboe, bassoon, guitar, harp, cembalo/celesta: "Oolit" (1974).

MARSHNER, Heinrich August (1795–1861), a German composer, a central person in the Romantic period in music, who was a representative of the German opera between Weber's and Wagner's generations. He studied law in Leipzig and moved to Vienna in 1816. Marshner worked since 1822 as the leader of the Dresden Opera and in 1830–59 as a conductor in Hannover. In addition to opera music he also composed for the guitar.

For a solo guitar: "Variazionen op. 2"; "12 Bagatelles op. 4." For a voice and a guitar: "12 Lieder op. 5" (1814).

MARTIN, Frank (1890 –1974), a Swiss composer. Taught improvisation and theory of rhythm in the Jaques-Dalcroze Institute and worked as a professor of composition in the Music Academy of Cologne. Martin's tone language was influenced by e.g. J.S. Bach, Viennese classics and French impressionists and he was exceptionally interested in the problems in rhythm. He studied the 12-note technique developed by Arnold Schoenberg, from which he got impressions for his only guitar composition, *"Quatre pièces brèves"* - "Four short pieces" (1933). The work is based on old French dances. At first it did not get the attention it deserved, which was partly due to Andrés Segovia's negative attitude to the work, and modern music in general. Martin has arranged the work for the piano under the heading "La Guitare - Suite pour le piano" (portrait d'Andrés Segovia, été 1933) and for an orchestra

with the original name. He also wrote two different versions of the work, in 1938 for a Zurichian guitarist Hermann Leeb, who performed the work and in 1951 for José de Azpiazu, who revised it and recorded it in July that same year. A version by Karl Scheit, published by Universal Edition, differs a lot from the earlier versions. Julian Bream was the first to record it and also asked Martin to compose more for the guitar, but that was not possible due to his age. Martin's *Quatre pièces brèves* belongs to the first modern guitar compositions in the 20th century, and has lately reached a permanent position in the repertoires of guitarists. Apparently the work cleared the way for many other modern guitar compositions to come.

For a solo guitar: "Quatre pièces brèves" (1933). For a tenor, guitar and piano four-handed: "Quant n'ont assez fait dodo." For three male voices and three electric guitars: "Poèms de la mort" (1971). For a flute and a guitar : "Drei Minnelieder" (1960), an arrangement by the composer himself from a piece originally composed for a soprano and a piano.

MARTÍNEZ ZÁRATE, Jorge (1923–1993), an Argentinean guitarist and composer. Studied guitar playing in the Music Academy of Buenos Aires under María Luisa Anido. Martínez Zárate married guitarist Graciela Pomponio and they gained international fame as a guitar duo. J. Martínez Zárate taught guitar playing in the Music Academy of Buenos Aires. His production contains his own works and more than 600 arrangements for 1-4 guitars.

For a solo guitar: "Danza"; "Impromptu no. 1"; "Impromptu no. 2"; "Pequena suite"; "Preludio no. 2." For two guitars: "Danza no. 2"; "Introdución & Allegro"; "Preludio."

MATIEGKA [MATÉJKA], Wenzeslaus [Wenzel, Václav] (1773–1830), an Austrian composer and guitarist with Bohemian roots. Got his first musical

The violin (or flute), viola and guitar were very popular in the music of the early 19th century Biedermeier style. In addition to Matiegka, also A. Diabelli, J.K. Mertz, F. Molino, S. Molitor etc. composed for this ensemble.

education as a choir boy in the Kremsier seminarium in Moravia, where he studied bass continuo playing with Erasmus Kärtniss and violin playing with Gert Götz. In the late 1780s he studied law at the University of Prague and piano playing with Jelinek and he became a promising keyboard player. Matiegka arrived in Vienna soon after the year 1800, and started there his career as an organist and choir leader in several churches and taught guitar and piano playing. Vienna was the musical center in the German speaking area, and there the guitar was as popular as the piano. Matiegka became competent in both instruments, but the guitar was still his major instrument, and he is thus an important representative of the Viennese school, together with Anton Diabelli (1781–1858). Matiegka is mentioned in the list of professional musicians in Vienna in 1808 and in a list of guitar composers in 1818 (T. Heck). After getting married Matiegka settled in Leopoldstadt, where he worked as a conductor in the church of St Leopold and composed church music, motets and masses. Since 1808 the Viennese publishers published Matiegka's music for the guitar, and in the covers of the publications he was called *"the Master of the piano and the guitar."*

His guitar production covers more than 30 works of both solo and chamber music, most of which were composed in 1805–17, in a period when also an Italian guitar master, Mauro Giuliani, lived in Vienna (1806–19) and had a great influence on the popularity of the guitar. Matiegka composed e.g. *"Nocturno op. 21"* for a flute, viola and guitar, which Franz Schubert arranged in 1814 and added a cello part in it. The work is known as *"Guitar Quartet in G"* by Schubert. Matiegka's tone language is of the early 19th century Biedermeier, light and joyful.

Matiegka is also known as an arranger. He has arranged e.g. Beethoven's song, *"Adelaide"*, which was performed by a famous singer, Jäger, in Vienna in 1818 and he was probably accompanied by Mauro Giuliani (T. Heck).

For a solo guitar: "12 leichte Ländler op. 1"; "Caprice avec Variations op. 2"; "Sonate op: 2"; "XII Pièces faciles op.

3"; "Fantasie in C-Dur op. 4"; "6 Leihte Variationen op. 5"; "6 Varitionen in A-dur op. 6"; "9 Variationen (Kaiserhymne) op. 7"; "6 Variationen (Molinara) op. 8"; "10 Variations capricieuses op. 10"; "Grande serenade facile C-Dur op. 11"; "12 Menuets brillians op. 15"; "Sonate (facile) C-Dur op. 16" (1807); "Sonate progressives op 17" (1807); "24 Pièces progressives op. 20"; "Sonate in h-moll op. 23" (1811); "15 Variations op. 27"; "8 Variationen D-Dur op. 28"; "6 Sonates progressives op. 31" (1817); For a solo guitar without an opus number: "6 Variations sur un air de Zumsteg"; "6 Variations sur l air de l Opera La Molinara"; "Trauer Marsh auf den Todt des F. Tandler"; "Grande Sonate No. I"; "Grande Sonate No. 2"; "Grande Sonate No. III"; "Grande Sonate No. IV. 10 Variations WoO"; For a violin and a guitar: "Grosse Sonate op. 3"; "Sérénade op. 19"; "3 Sérénata op. 22"; For a clarinet, French horn and a guitar: "Trio op. 18" (1807). For a flute, viola and a guitar: "Nocturno op. 21" (1807); "Grosses Trio op. 24"; "Sérénata op. 26" (1817). For a French horn or a flute, viola and guitar: "Notturno op. 25." (1812). For a violin, viola and guitar: "Grand Trio WoO" (published in 1806); "Trio op. 9"; "Trio op. 24"; "Serenade op. 26." For a cello and a guitar: "Fantasia in forma di sérénata op. 30." Matiegka's arrangements for a voice and a guitar: "W.A. Mozart: Abendempfindung"; "Das Veilchen"; "Vergiss mein nicht. L. van Beethoven: Adelaide von Matthisson." Arrangements for a violin, viola and guitar: "L. van Beethoven: Sérénata op.8."

MAXWELL DAVIES, Sir Peter (born 1934) English composer and conductor. Studied music both in the Royal Manchester College of Music (1952–56) and at the University of Manchester. As a student he was espe-

The English Sir Peter Maxwell Davies is known also as a guitar composer. His guitar production contains e.g. several solo works and chamber music.

cially interested in the music of Boulez, Nono and Stockhausen. His early works, e.g. the Trumpet Sonata (1955) have been influenced by the beforementioned composers. In 1957–59 he studied with Goffredo Petrassi in Rome. His experience as a teacher at the Cirencester Grammar School (1959–62) had a great influence on his development as an artist. In 1967, together with composer and school friend, Harrison Birtwistle, he founded a band, The *"Pierrot Players,"* which in 1970 was called *"The Fires of London"* (with guitarist Timothy Walker), for which Davies composed several musical theater pieces. Davies has composed eight symphonies and eleven concertos. His style has been described as expressive and dramatic. Davies is one of the leading modern composers in Britain, he does not boast about it: in 1970 he escaped the rush of big city life to a lonely island in the Orkneys in northern Scotland. Everyone can decide for himself whether to compare the rugged nature of the island to the neoexpressionistic harsh outlines of his music, which is often softened by a certain mysticism. His music often has a visual starting point, and thus he has succeeded as an opera and ballet composer. Maxwell Davies's *"Guitar Sonata"* is part of a series of three sonatas which are joined by a common theme and form; the two other sonatas are for the organ and piano. He composed the *Guitar Sonata* inspired by the cembalo sonatas of Domenico Scarlatti, whose influence can especially be seen in the first part. The second part explores the darker shades of the guitar. The composer describes the finale as rhythmic but fragile. Timothy Walker gave the first performance of the Guitar Sonata in 1987 in Kirkwall.

Maxwell Davies was raised to the nobility in 1987. His autobiographies have been published by Paul Griffiths: *Peter Maxwell Davies* (Robson Books 1982) and M. Seabrook *MAX The Life and Music of Peter Maxwell Davies* (V. Gollancz 1994).

For a solo guitar: "Lullaby for Ilian Rainbow" (1973); "Hill Runes" (1981); "Sonata" (1984); "Farewell to Stromness." An arrangement for a solo guitar: "Yesterday" (Lennon & McCartney, arr. Davies 1974). Chamber music with a guitar: "From Stone to Thorn" (1971); "Wedding Telegram for Gary Kettel" (1972); "Blind Man's Bluff" (1972). "Fiddlers at the Wedding" (1974); "Tenebrae Super Gesualdo" (1972); "The Light House"; "The Martyrdom of Saint Magnus" (1976); "Points and Dances from Taverner" (1970); "Psalm 124" (1974); "Shakespeare Music"; "All sons of Adam" (1974); "Septet" (1972); "The Blind Fiddler" (1976). For a voice and a guitar: "From Stone to Thorn" (1971); "Dark Angels" (1974). For a flute, clarinet, percussion, guitar, violin and cello: "Renaissance Scottish Dances" (1973).

McCABE, John (born 1939), an English composer and pianist. Due to his bad health he had to spend much time at home in his childhood, and then he listened to music and played the piano. When he started to study in the Liverpool Institute at the age of 11, he had already composed 13 symphonies! He first studied composition with Procter-Gregg in the University of Mancester and in 1964 with Genzmer in the Munich College. McCabe's music is eclectic, and several modern styles and composition techniques are combined there. As a composer he has gotten influences from e.g. Hartmann, Nielsen and Rawsthorne.

For a solo guitar: "Canto" (1968). For a voice, guitar and percussion: "Das letzte Gerichte" (1973).

McGUIRE Edward (born 1948), a Scottish composer. Studied at first flute playing in the youth department of the Royal Scottish Academy of Music with David Nicholson. After studying composition in the London Royal Academy of Music with James Iliff (1966–70), he continued his composition studies in Stockholm with Ingvar Lindholm. McGuire has received awards in several composition contests, e.g. in the *"Carl Flesch Violin Competition"* in Modern Compositions in 1978. His production contains symphony, opera, ballet and other orchestral music. McGuire's works have been performed by the BBC Scottish Symphony Orchestra, Scottish Ballet, Paragon Opera and Glasgow Festival Strings, etc. In 1996 the Bath International Guitar Festival ordered the compulsory piece from McGuire. He plays the flute in a Scottish folk music group *"The Whistlebinkies,"* which has published several records and made a concert tour to China in 1992.

For a solo guitar: "Amazonia (1987) Hommage to Villa-Lobos"; "Music for Guitar(s)" (1973); "Prelude 5" (1981); "Fantasy"; "Great is the Cause of my Sorrow"; "Homage to Joaquín Rodrigo"; "Zalongo Dance Elegy." For a solo guitar or a solo guitar with accompany of one or two guitars: "Music for Guitar(s)." For two guitars: "Autumn Moon"; "Piobaireachd to the Brahmaaputra." For a guitar orchestra: "Dark Cloud." For a flute and a guitar: "Improvisations on Calderon" (1981); "Eastern Echoes", "Fountain of Tears." For a viola and a guitar: "Fast Peace III" (1982). For a cello and a guitar: "Romance." For a double bass and a guitar: "Salama-Shalom." For a flute, guitar and viola: "Cauldron of Improvisations" (1986). For three flutes and a guitar: "Western Light." For a string quartet and a guitar: "The Guest Quintct." For a guitar and an orchestra: "Concerto."

MEISSONNIER, Antoine (1783–?), a French guitarist, composer and music publisher. Got his musical education in Naples, where he studied his favorite instrument, the guitar. From Naples he moved to Paris and worked as a guitar teacher and set up a music publishing company, *Bureau du Journal de Guitarre,* and published e.g. Fernando Sor's opuses 1-34 in 1817–25. Antoine also worked in cooperation as a publisher with his younger brother Joseph (1790–1855), who had a publishing company in Paris. A. Meissonnier also published his guitar school *Nouvelle Méthode ou Leçonsi elementaires pour Lyre ou Guitarre* in Paris. He also composed a comic opera *"La donna carretta"* and guitar music.

For a solo guitar: "3 Rondos op. 2"; "Grande Sonate." For a violin and a guitar: "3 Duos." For a violin, viola and a guitar: "3 Grande trios."

MEISSONNIER, Joseph (1790–1855), a French guitarist and music publisher, younger brother of Antoine M., Joseph studied guitar playing in Paris and dedicated himself to composition and guitar teaching and also set up a music publishing company in Paris. J. Meissonnier published compositions by Lintant, Cassé, Piston and himself. J. Meissonnier's two-part guitar school *Méthode d'Guitarre ou Lyre* contains 100 etudes and small pieces from Castellacci, Küffner, Lami, Carcassi, Rigot, Sor, Molino, Carulli, Giuliani and some of his own.

For a solo guitar: Variations from an aria by Bellini "Nel cor piú ma non sento."

MELLERS, Wilfred (born 1914), an English composer and musician. Studied music in the Leamington College and at the Cambridge University and composition in Oxford with Wellesz and Rubbra, doctor in music in 1963. Mellers has taught at various Universities, e.g. in Birmingham, Pittsburgh and York.

For a solo guitar: "A Blue Epiphany for

Photo: Maarit Kytöharju

Usko Meriläinen has composed a Concerto for the guitar and a chamber music work Simultus for Four.

J.B. Smith" (1973).

MERILÄINEN, Usko (1930–2004), a Finnish composer. Studied in the Sibelius Academy with Leo Funtek and graduated as a conductor in 1953. He also studied composition with Aarre Merikanto (diploma 1955). Meriläinen has conducted several famous Finnish orchestras and choirs and taught musicology at the University of Tampere in 1966–87. He has had several positions of trust, e.g. the vice president of Suomen Säveltäjät ry (Society of Finnish Composers) in 1976–80 and president in 1981–92. Meriläinen was awarded the Wihuri International Fund Sibelius Award in 1965 (together with Bergman and Rautavaara) and he received the government 15-year arts grant starting in 1984. Meriläinen was the adviser of the Tampere Biennale, which has existed since 1986. The wide production of Meriläinen covers stage music, symphonies (5), concertos, music for solo instruments and a chamber orchestra, chamber music (3 string quartets etc.), music for solo instruments and both vocal and electronic music. His works have been described as technically demanding.

Mikko Heiniö describes Meriläinen's chamber music work as follows: "The dialectics of the solid and free rhythm became central dramaturgical means for Meriläinen in the 70s, and the feeling tightens in the *"Simultus for Four"* for the Cluster band (flute, alto saxophone, guitar and percussion)." Meriläinen finished his *"Guitar Concerto"* dedicated to Timo Korhonen in August 1991 and its premiere was in December that same year. Composer Jouni Kaipainen describes the concerto as follows: "The Concerto is two parts and it reflects the policy that Meriläinen now often uses: he combines a vivid first part and a slow, thoughtful second part, which does not contain the virtuoso final that usually exists in concertos. The second part is fantastically colorful and it mostly moves very slowly despite the fact that the soloist has a lot of material written in short notes. The solo player slowly moves towards a stronger expression, which leads to an agitato part and after the eruption of the orchestra to a quasi cadence. Finally the music becomes more and more calm, but not entirely: the bongo drums are still in the previous tempo, and therefore the peak works in two layers. The main impression of that part still is peace, listening and fragile details."

For a flute, alto saxophone, guitar and percussion: "Simultus for Four" (1979). For a guitar and an orchestra: "Guitar Concerto" (1991), dedicated to Timo Korhonen.

MERTZ, Johann Kaspar (1806–1856), a Hungarian guitarist, composer and arranger. Mertz was auto-didact and his career began when he moved to Vienna at the age of 34 and made such a successful debut (1840) that he got the Empress Carolina Augusta as his patron. He also taught guitar playing to the nobles. Mertz played the 8- and 10-string guitars, cello and zither. In 1842 Mertz gave a concert in Dresden together with pianist Josephine Plant, with whom he became friends and whom he married that same year. Mertz gave concerts in e.g. Germany, Poland and Russia, and his wife took part in those visits. In 1846 Mertz almost lost his life, when Josephine accidentally gave him an overdoze of strychnine, which was prescribed for him to an illness. After a long period of recovery he became well and gave a sold-out concert in 1848. After the difficult post-revolution years in Austria-Hungary the couple again gave succesful concerts in the palace of the Count Esterházy and for Louis of Bavaria, who admired Mertz's abilities.

Mertz composed nearly 100 pieces for the guitar and made numerous excellent arrangements, which still belong to the repertoires of guitarists. His composition *"Concertino per la chitarra sola"* won the first prize in 1856 in a guitar composition contest in Brussels, arranged by a Russian amateur guitarist, Nikolai Makaroff, a Frenchman, Napoléon Coste came second. Unfortunately Mertz died during that contest and never received the prize. Mertz also published a short, 29-page *Guitar School*, which contains 15 études. Chanterelle has published his whole production in 10 volumes (ECH 417-426). The German Astrid Stempnik has studied Mertz's guitar compositions: *Caspar Joseph Mertz: Leben und Werk des letzten Gitarristen im Österreichischen Biedermeier.* (Verlag Peter Lang, Frankfurt am Main 1990). The study is in connection to her doctoral thesis at the University of Berlin.

For a solo guitar: "Concertino"; "Capriccio op. 50"; "Fantasie über Webers letzte Gedanken"; "La Rimembranza"; "Pensée Fugitive"; "Harmonie du Soir"; "La Romantique"; "Elégie"; "Les Adieux"; "Pianto dell' Amante"; "Mazurca"; "Le Carneval de Venise op. 6"; "Six Waltzes op. 9"; "Introduzion et Rondo Brillant op. 11"; "Trois Morceaux op. 65" (Fantaisie

CONCERTINO
per la Chitarra sola

J.K.MERTZ

Johann Kaspar Mertz's Concertino won the first prize in a guitar composition contest arranged by the Russian nobleman Nikolai Makaroff in Brussels in 1856.

Hongroise, Fantasie Originale, Le Gondolier); "A suite of Romantic little pieces: Bardenklänge op. 13" (1-15); "Prelude in D major"; "Orgelfuge von Albrechberger"; "5 Walzes"; "3 Nocturnes op. 4." Also arrangments for the solo guitar from 6 of Schubert's songs: "Lob der Tränen"; "Liebesbotschaft"; "Aufenthalt"; "Ständchen"; "Die Post"; "Das Fischermädchen." Also numerous "Fantasies op. 8 from opera themes by Donizetti, Bellini, Rossini, Verdi etc. For a guitar tuned a third higher and a guitar: 3 Trauerlieder"; "Unruhe"; "Vespergang"; "Tarantella"; "Barcarole"; "Impromptu." For a piano and a guitar: "Barcarole"; "Mazurca"; "Divertissement über motive aus Verdi Rigoletto"; "Einsiedlers Waldglöcklein"; "Wasserfahrt am Traunsee." For a flute, viola and guitar: "Trio (from Meyerber's themes) op. 32." For a voice and a guitar: "Songs op. 52."

MIGNONE, Francesco (1897–1986), a Brazilian composer and conductor, son of a musician that moved to Brazil,

and with whom the boy started his flute and piano lessons. He continued his instrumental studies and started his composition studies in the Music Academy of São Paulo, where he graduated in 1917. In 1920 Mignone continued his studies in the Music Academy of Milan, where he studied composition with Ferronte. His Italian background and education can be heard in his works. Mignone returned to Brazil in 1933 to work as a conductor and teacher of conducting in Rio. He was interested in Brazilian nationalistic influences in music, and he studied them and used them as the starting point in his works.

For a solo guitar: "Lenda Sertaneja" (Santos); "12 Etudes" (Barbosa Lima); Nazareth (Sinopoli); "12 Valses" (Barbosa Lima); "Valsa-chôros nos. 1"; 3; 5; 8; 10; 11" (Zoega); "7 Valses de Esquina."

MIGOT, Georges (1891–1976), a French composer, who studied in the

Music Conservatory of Paris with e.g. Nadia Boulanger, Vincent d'Indy and Charles Marie Widor. He won several prizes with the works he had composed in his youth. Migot composed symphonic works for orchestras, chamber music etc. He has also become famous for his essays on music.

For a solo guitar: "Pour un hommage à Claude Debussy" (1924); "Sonate" (1960). For two guitars: "2 Préludes." For a flute and a guitar: "Sonata." For a voice and a guitar: "3 Chants de joije et de soucis."

MILHAUD, Darius (1892–1974), a French composer born to a Jewish family. Started his musical studies at the age of 7. He studied composition in the Music Conservatory of Paris with Leroux and Dukas, and he became one of the most remarkable members of the group *"Les Six."* In the 1920s Milhaud was interested in playing jazz, blues and ragtime. In 1922 he traveled to the USA and played "black jazz" in Harlem. During WW II he lived in Oakland, California. In 1945–62 Milhaud worked as a professor in the Music Conservatory of Paris. The central features of Milhaud's music are polytonality and rhythmic effects often borrowed from jazz and Latin American music.

Milhaud's only guitar composition, *"Segoviana"*, is dedicated to Andrés Segovia. Just as was the case with the "Quatre Pièces Brèves" by Frank Martin (also dedicated to Segovia), Segovia never performed this piece, either. Both works have still got their place among the most important guitar works of the 20th century. Segoviana's tempo mark *"Avec fantaisie"* refers to its fantasy nature. The work is rich in dynamics and it also has an orchestral character.

For a solo guitar: "Segoviana" (1957), dedicated to Andrés Segovia.

MIROGLIO, Francis (1924-2005), a French composer, studied in Marseilles in 1945–47 and in Paris in 1951–52 with Darius Milhaud. In 1959–61 Miroglio worked in the studio for electronic music in the French Radio,

ORTF. In the 1960s he took part in the Darmstadt courses for modern music, where his compositions are often performed. In stead of a strict serialness he has been interested in "artistic movement."

For a solo guitar: "Choréïques" (1958).

MOLINO, Francesco (1768–1847), an Italian guitarist, violinist and composer, son of oboist Giuseppe Ignazio Molino. F. Molino belonged to the first generation of guitarists of the Classical era. In 1783–93 Molino worked as a military musician in the regiment of Piemonte and simultaneously, 1786–89, as a violinist in the Regino Theater. In 1814–18 he worked as the chamber violinist for the King of Sardinia. After leaving the court, Molino still had a permission to use the name *"Professeur de Violin et de Guitare attaché à la Chapelle de S.M le Roi de Sardaigne,"* which he uses on the front page of the guitar school op. 33. According to researchers, during 1793–1814 Molino traveled in Spain and Germany, but there are no documents from these journeys. According to a musicologist Fetis, Molino arrived in Paris in 1820, where he got a high reputation as a guitar virtuoso. Ferdinando Carulli from Naples had already lived in Paris since 1808. The opposite opinions led to conflicts between the supporters of both guitarists. From a modern point of view it could be said that Molino's technique was more advanced: he had given up the old technique where the thumb of the left hand played the bass strings, and he marked the right-hand fingers with p, i, m, a. Similarly to Giuliani, he also played the lyre-guitar.

Molino's guitar and lyre school *Grande Méthode Complète pour Guitare ou Lyre op. 33* appeared in 1824. The second edition appeared with opus number 46 and a Spanish version with op. 49, the latter was meant for publication in Latin America so that he would beat his competitor F. Carulli. Molino was also a productive composer, he composed more than 60 opuses of music, which contain 2 concertos for the violin and a *Concerto for a Guitar and an Orchestra.*

For a solo guitar: "Trois Sonates op. 1"; "Trois Sonates op. 6"; "Douze Thèmes Variés op. 9"; "Divertissements op. 11"; "Trois Sonates op. 15"; "Grande Ouverture op. 17"; "Douze Variations sur l'air...du célèbre Mozart op. 31"; "Grande polonaise et deux rondeaux op. 34"; "Variations brilliants sur l'air favori"; "Nel cor piú non mis sento"; "Grande Sonate op. 51"; "Robin Adair, air ecossais op. 58"; "Grande introducion God save the King varié op. 59." For a flute or violin and a guitar:

The Viennese Simon Molitor belongs to the pioneers in classical guitar playing.

"Trois Duos op. 16"; "Premièr Nocturne op. 37"; "Second Nocturne op. 38"; "Troisieme Nocturne op. 39"; "Trois Duos op. 61." For a violin and a guitar: "Trois Sonates op. 2"; "Trois Duos op. 3"; "Trois Grandes Sonates (avec accompagnement de violon) op. 22"; "Trois Sonates (avec accompagnement de violon) op. 29." For a piano and a guitar: "Premièr Nocturne op. 36"; "Second Nocturne op. 44"; "Troisème Nocturne sur des motifs de Rossini op. 57." For a flute, viola and guitar: "Trois Trios op. 4"; "Trois Trios op. 19"; "Grand Trio Concertant op. 30"; "Second Grand Trio Concertant op. 45." For a voice and a guitar: "Quatre romances op. 53." For a guitar and an orchestra: "Grand Concerto en mi minore op. 56" (published in 1838).

MOLITOR, Simon (1766–1848), an Austrian guitarist and composer, born to the family of a leader in church music. In his youth Molitor studied piano and violin playing. He became famous as a violinist, but in addition to the violin he also played the guitar. Against his parents' wish, he quit his studies at the university and went to Germany, where he played in chamber ensembles and orchestras. In 1788 Molitor moved to Vienna to study composition under Abt Vogler. Since 1796 Molitor worked as a conductor in Venice and in 1798 he moved back to Austria. He got a vacancy as a clerk in the military forces, where he worked until 1831; in addition to that, he also worked as a musician. After retiring in 1831, he dedicated his life to composition and research of the history of the Viennese court opera.

Molitor belonged to the pioneers of the classical guitar playing, and he was among the first guitarists, who settled down in Vienna before Mauro Giuliani. He had an impact on the shift from the pair strings to the modern guitar at the turn of the century, which made the instrument even more popular. In 1811–12 Molitor published a guitar school together with guitarist Wilhelm Klingenbrunner, *Versuch einer vollständigen metodischen Anleitung zum Gitarrspielen*, which became very popular. Molitor was a productive composer, his production contains concertos for the violin and clarinet and both piano and chamber music.

Musicologist Josef Zuth has written a study *Simon Molitor und die Wiener Gitarristik* (1919), which gives a picture of Molitor as a guitarist and contains a catalogue of his works.

For a solo guitar: "Grosse Sonate op. 7" (1806); "Variations sur un Thème original op. 9"; "Marche funébre à la mort de l'éxéllent jouer de Guitarre Mr. François Tendler" (1807); "Recueil de petites Pièces favorites de différents auteurs et un Rondeau original" (1806); "Rondeau avec Adagio op. 10" (1806/7); "Sonate op. 11" (1806/07); "Sonate op. 12" (1807/10); "Sonate op. 15" (1807/10); "6 Ländler." For a violin and a guitar: "Grande Sonate op. 3"; "Sonate op. 5" (1807). For a violin or

The Argentinean guitar virtuoso and composer Jorge Morel was originally an actor.

flute, viola and guitar: "Trio op. 6 "(1805/6); "Trio concertant" (1805/6).

MOMPOU, Federico (1893–1987), a Spanish (Catalonian) composer and pianist. Studied in Paris and was influenced by French Impressionists, the composers of the group *"Les Six"* and Erik Satie. In Spain Mompou is considered the continuer of the tradition of Granados. Mompou composed a six-part suite *"Suite Compostelana"* for the guitar (1962), which is dedicated to Andrés Segovia. The subject is a medieval town, Santiago de Compostela, where Segovia held master courses since 1958. The work is folksy and meditating by nature, only the last part *"Muñeira"* is a little more vivid. Mompou colors his beautiful melodies with small pinches of modern elements.

For a solo guitar: "Suite Compostelana" (1962); "Canción y Danza No. 1"; "Canción" (from Canción y danza No. 6; "Canción y Danza No. 13; La Barca."

MORANÇON, Guy (born 1927), a French organist, conductor and composer. Morançon studied in Paris in the Conservatoire National Supérieur de Musique and has taken part in the courses of Accadémia Chigiana in Siena. Morançon has worked as a church musician in Paris and played in several European countries.

For a solo guitar: "Arabesque"; "Petit livre pour la guitare" (5 pieces); "Suite latine"; "Sirventes."

MOREL, Jorge (born 1931), an Argentinean guitarist and composer with roots in Italy. Learned the basics of guitar playing from his father and studied later composition and guitar playing with Pablo Escobar in the Music College of Buenos Aires. After his graduation he also focused on acting in addition to guitar playing. In 1958 he moved from Buenos Aires to Ecuador and continued there his career as an actor as well as a guitarist. Within a year he moved to Columbia and finally to Cuba, when he decided to give up his career as an actor and concentrate on music. Since 1967 he has lived in New York. Morel's music has features typical of Latin American music, mixed with modern handling of harmony and rhythm. He has made several recordings during his career and held many master courses in guitar playing.

For a solo guitar: "Allegro in Re"; "Canción y danza"; "Chôro"; "Danza para Emiko"; "Guitarreando"; "Little Rhapsody"; "Prelude" (Suite del Sur); "Prelude & Giga"; "Sonatina - to David Russell"; "Virtuoso South American Guitar"; "La Danza" (Tarantella by Rossini); "Latin Impression"; "4 Pieces, Sonatina"; "Variations on a Gershwin theme."

MORENO TORROBA, Federico (1891–1982), a Spanish composer, conductor and critic. Started his musical studies with his father, who was an organist and teacher in the Music Academy of Madrid. He also studied composition with Conrado del Campo. Moreno Torroba worked as a conductor in the Teatro Real in Madrid. Since 1952 he specialized on conducting music for recordings. M. Torroba composed works for the orchestra, church music and two operas among others, but is mainly known as a composer of "zarzuelas" (Spanish operettas). His composition style is national-Romantic and is strongly based on Spanish folk music. M. Torroba still composed in his Spanish national-Romantic style, when the whole Europe was under a strong influence of serialness. He was the first composer to work in cooperation with Andrés Segovia (ca. 50 guitar compositions) and thus greatly influenced the growth of the popularity of the guitar.

M. Torroba's first guitar composition was *"Danza"* (1919), which later became the third part in the *Suite Castellana*. The work has established its position among the most popular guitar compositions. The most famous guitar composition by M. Torroba is the three-part *"Sonatina in A major"* (ca. 1930), from which there also is a version for a guitar and an orchestra. In 1974 M. Torroba composed the *"Dialogos Concerto for the guitar and orchestra"* to Segovia to indicate his friendship. M. Torroba also was close

Federico Moreno Torroba

to the Los Romeros Guitar Quartet, which Celedonio Romero together with his sons formed, and to the Omega Guitar Quartet. He dedicated several of his work to these quartets. M. Torroba has also composed an exceptional concerto, *"Concierto en Flamenco"*, dedicated to the flamenco virtuoso Sabicas.

For a solo guitar: "Aire Vasco"; "Aires de la Mancha"; "Alpujarrena"; "Anoranza"; "Ay, Malagueña!"; "Bolero Meronquin"; "Burgalesa"; "Cancioncilla"; "Capricho"; "Castillos de España"; "Chisperada"; "Contradanza"; "Danza Prima"; "Humorada"; "Improvisación"; "Improvisando"; "Jaranera"; "Jota Levantina"; "Lejania"; "Madrileñas"; "Madroños"; "Marcha del Cojo"; "Mi Farruca"; "Minueto del Majo"; "Molinera"; "Montaraza"; "Nana"; "Nina Merse"; "Nocturno"; "Nocturno no. 2"; "Nostalgia"; "Pieces Caractéristiques"; "Preludes 1, 2, 3"; "Preludio"; "Preludios 1, 2, 3"; "Puertas de Madrid"; "Punteado"; "Punteado y Taconeo Clásico"; "Quien Te Puso Petenera"; "Romance de los Pinos"; "Romancillo"; "Ronda Festiva"; "Ronda Humoristica"; "Rumor de Copla"; "Scherzando"; "Segoviana"; "Serenata Burcalesca"; "Sevillana"; "Sonatina"; "Sonatina y Variación"; "Suite Castellana"; "Suite Miniatura"; "Taconeo Clásico"; "Trianeras"; "Tonada"; "Triptico"; "Verbenera"; "Vieja Leyenda"; "Zapateado." For two guitars: "Madrileñas suite." For four guitars: "Ráfagas, Estampas" (dedicated to the Omega Guitar Quartet). For a piano and a guitar: "Sonatina." For a guitar and a woodwind quintet: "Interludes." For a guitar and an orchestra: "Diálogos" (1974 to A. Segovia); "Concierto de Castilla"; "Hommage à la Seguidilla." For four guitars and an orchestra: "Concierto Iberico" (1976). For a flamenco guitar and an orchestra: "Concierto en Flamenco", dedicated to the flamenco guitarist Sabicas. Arrangements for a guitar and an orchestra: "Two Interluds" (arranged from music for a guitar and a woodwind quintet); "Sonatina" (arranged from a solo guitar work).

MORETTI, Federico (ca.1760–1838), an Italian composer, guitarist and cellist, who lived in Spain. Moretti published several guitar schools, which were very important for the development of the guitar playing: *Prinzipe per la Chitarra*, (Naples 1792), for a five-string guitar in Italian, and *Principos para tocar la guitarra de seis ordenes*, (Madrid 1799), for a six-string guitar, in Spanish, which was also published in Italian in Naples in 1804. Moretti's schools established the technique of playing the classical guitar and they provided a setting for the future development, e.g. Fernando Sor's interest in polyphony. Both Sor and Aguado have in their works expressed their gratitude to Moretti as a pioneer.

For a voice and a guitar: "Doce canciónes spagnole."

MORTENSEN, Jørgen (born 1943), a Danish composer. Studied flute playing in the Music Academy of Århus and musicology at the Universities of Århus and Copenhagen. Mortensen works as a teacher of musical theory and history in the Music Academy of Esbjerg. The composer of the *"Guitar Solo"* (1984) tells that his work was created from the dialogue between the musical forms and the technical and vocal properties of the guitar. The starting point in the composition are the numeral relations that are in connection with the tuning of the guitar, which affect the work's structure. The Guitar Solo is dedicated to Jørgen Bjørslev, who gave the first performance in Karlsruhe in 1984.

For a solo guitar: "Guitar Solo" (1984). For a flute, guitar, cello and percussion: "Presenza" (1985). For a flute, guitar, vibraphone, percussion and double bass: "Seven Sections" (1986).

MOURAT, Jean Maurice (born 1944), a French guitarist, pedagogue and composer. Studied guitar playing with Oscar Ghiglia and later under Oscar Cáceres, Angelo Gilardino and Turibio Santos. Mourat gave duo concerts with a famous flutist, Pierre Lambert. His production covers several guitar compositions and a *Guitar School*. Mourat's music is influenced by E. Satie and the French chanson.

For a solo guitar: "Canción y danza"; "Chôros de invierno"; "14 Miniétudes"; "Interlude"; "Six Couleurs sur la Guitarre"; "Valse triste"; "Suite Vendune"; "Patchwork" (4 études); "Coucher de soleil"; "Mélancolie"; "Les Palmiers"; "La toupie." For a flute and a guitar: "Iberiade" (Hommage à J. Ibert).

MOZZANI, Luigi (1869–1943), an Italian guitarist, pedagogue and composer. Started his guitar studies at the age of 8 and was later a pupil of Miguel Llobet. Mozzani studied oboe playing and composition in the Music Academy of Bologna. In his guitar technique he used the right hand thumb plectrum and developed a new model of the plucked instrument, lyre-guitar. Since 1894 Mozzani worked as a guitarist and pedagog in Paris. His most famous pupil is the Italian Mario Maccaferri. Mozzani explored the guitar and made experiments concerning the structure until his death and he built a great number of guitars during his life.

For a solo guitar: "6 Capricci"; "Coup de vent"; "Mazurca"; "Prière"; "Dolore"; "Serenata"; "Riverenza"; "Romanza"; "Raccoglimento"; "Valse lente"; "Feste lariane, tema con variazioni"; "Melodia notturna"; "Studio 1-3." For two guitars: "Espieglerie"; "Hereuse Rencontre"; "Harpes celestes."

MRÓNSKI, Stanislaw (1926-2005), a Polish composer and pedagogue. Studied theory and composition in Lodzunder Sikorski and graduated from the Department of Musical Pedagogy in 1950, as a theory teacher in 1953 and as a composer in 1957. His guitar compositions have had success in several contests, in 1972 he came second in the composition contest arranged by the French Radio, ORTF. Mrónski's music is influenced by folk music and Witold Lutoslawski.

For a solo guitar: "Vier Stücke" (1975); "Sechs Mazurkas" (1977); "Drei Stücke" (Poem, Passacaglia, Fuge); "3 Etuden"; "3 Preludien"; "Leichte stücke" (1973); "Zwei Zyklen" (1975).

MURAIL, Tristan (born 1947), a French composer, studied composition in the Music Conservatory of Paris with Oliver Messiaen in 1969–72 and in Rome in Villa Medici in 1971–73. Has taken part in the Darmstadt and Avignon courses of modern music. Since 1990 Murail has taught computer composition in the Music Conservatory of Paris. Murail plays e.g. a rare electric instrument, ondes Martenot (ondes musicales), which was invented in the late 1920s, and which works with two high frequency oscillators.

For a solo guitar: "Tellur" (1977). For an electric guitar: "Vampyr!" (from a suite Random Access Memory). For a flute/piccolo, clarinet, harp, electric guitar, viola, percussion and double bass: "Ligne de non-retour" (1971). For two ondes Martenots (an electric instrument), an electric guitar and percussion: "Les Nuages à Magellan" (1973). For electric guitars, percussion, synthesizer and computer: "Random Access Memory" (1984–87).

MURO, Juan Antonio (born 1945), a Spanish guitarist, guitar pedagogue, composer and painter. He studied guitar playing in the Music Academy of Barcelona with José Luis Lopátegui and took the guitar diploma in 1972. Later he studied with Narciso Yepes. He also studied composition for a short time in the Sibelius Academy with Einojuhani Rautavaara in 1972–73. Since 1972 Muro has taught guitar playing in the Conservatory of Helsinki, where he also teaches didactics and chamber music of our time. He is a member of the Finnish Guitar Trio (Kari Äikäs, Ilmari Hytönen and Juan Antonio Muro), which has performed in several famous guitar festivals in Europe and recorded modern Finnish music and the music of M. de Falla and J.S. Bach.

Muro's composition production consists of solo and chamber music, which represents postmodern pluralistic esthetics. He has composed a large number of didactic compositions, where he uses tonality, and which he is best known for. For example *"Basic Pieces for Beginners"* is a popular collection of easy melodic compositions, whose didactic goal is to handle the basics of the right hand. The work is also used as a method in several countries. The composer has recorded his compositions for the German publisher Chanterelle (1997). *"Basic Chamber Music"* is 40 short, tonal and melodic

compositions, which are meant for beginners, but which can also be found in the concert repertoires of advanced guitarists. The music is composed in such a way, that it can be played with two or four guitars. The composer has also arranged the same material for other instruments than the guitar. The JAM Guitar Quartet (the name comes from Muro's initials) has recorded the collection for Chanterelle (1997).

For a solo guitar: "Lettera amorosa" (1988). For two guitars: "Di pensier in pensier" (1989). For three guitars: "Trilogo" (1987). For a guitar orchestra: "The Night" (1988); "The way of the water" (1993). For a flute and a guitar: "Quarrel" (1986). For a soprano and four guitars: "Relato" (1990). For four guitars: "Grand Jeté" (1994). Didactic compositions: "Basic Pieces for Beginners" (Chanterelle); "Basic Chamber music for 2, 3, and 4 Guitars" (Chanterelle). For a guitar, orchestra, piano and cello: "Scivoli" (2000); Basic Guitar Tutor (Canterelle).

MURTULA, Giovanni (1881–1964), an Italian guitarist and composer. Worked as a music teacher and critic in Rovigo. Murtula's production covers more than 100 guitar pieces, his compositions have been published by Bèrben.

For a solo guitar: "Triptychon" (Preludio, meditazione e rondò); "Spanische Serenade"; "Carovana"; "Incontro"; "Preludio"; "Due studi"; "Rondò"; "Rondò fantasioso"; "Piccola suite"; "Tarantella."

MUSGRAVE, Thea (1928), a Scottish composer and pianist. Studied at the University of Edinburgh (1947–50), the Music Conservatory of Paris (1952–54) and as a private pupil of Nadia Boulanger (1950–54). She has taught at the University of London (1959–65) and been a guest lecturer at the University of California, Santa Barbara in the 1970s. Musgrave has worked in cooperation with composer Aaron Copland and also conducted her own operas. Her early works are diatonically lyrical, but later her style developed to be more chromatical, the forms became more abstract and she also used the serial technique. Musgrave's

production also contains electronic music.

For a guitar and a tape: "Soliloquy 1" (1969). For a tenor and a guitar: "Six Patrick Spens" (1961) dedicated to Peter Pears and Julian Bream. For a flute, violin and guitar: "Sonata for Three" (1966). For a guitar and strings: "Soliloquy 2" (1980). For a guitar and nine players: "Soliloquy 3" (a version from Soliloquy 2).

MÄGI, Ester (born 1922), the "Grand Lady" of Estonian composers. Graduated from the Conservatory of Tallinn in 1952 and studied after that in the Music Conservatory of Moscow. In 1954–84 Mägi taught theory in the Conservatory of Tallinn. Ester Mägi's lyrical music is organically bound to the Estonian folk song. She has written symphony and chamber music, "Sinfonia" (1968), "Bukoolika" (1983), the "Old Town Partita", etc. Instrumental music is a central part of Mägi's music. *"Cantus"* (1987) and *"Processus"* (1988) have originally been composed for the cello and guitar, in 1988 Mägi also made a version for the violin and guitar. Mägi's works have been published by German publishers and ed. Antes and Sikorski.

For a solo guitar: "Valse con variazione" (1990); "Three miniatures" (1996). For a cello and guitar or violin and guitar: "Cantus" (1987); "Processus" (1988). For a soprano, flute, violin and guitar: "Põllul laulmine" (1988). For a baritone, flute and guitar: "Haikus" (1993), (arrangement from an original work for a baritone and piano, 1977). For a soprano, flute and guitar: "Maarjasõnajalg" (1990); "Huiked" (1995). For a violin, cello and guitar: "A Tre" (1991).

NAVA, Antonio Maria (ca.1775–1826), an Italian singer, guitarist and composer. Played a role in taking the G key into use in guitar music. Gave concerts in Italy and France and taught singing and guitar playing in London. In 1812 Nava published a guitar school *Nuevo metodo per chitarra* and he composed ca. 70 guitar works, a large part of which are flute-guitar duos. A guitar piece by Nava, *"Stagioni dell' anno* *seasons"* op. 1 was the first work published by a publishing company Ricord in 1808.

For a solo guitar: "Stagioni dell' anno op. 1" (seasons); "Tema con variazioni op. 25"; "Variazioni op. 34"; "Variazioni op. 45"; "2 Divertimenti"; "Potpourri op. 70"; "Introduzione e variazioni su un tema di Mercadante op. 62." For two guitars: "Duetto op. 52." For a flute and a guitar: "Serenata op. 16" (n.1810); "3 Petites duos op. 23"; "Tema con variazioni op. 40." For a violin and a guitar: "Duetto op. 23"; (n. 1812). For a flute, violin and guitar: "Trio op. 67."

NEUMANN, Ulrik (1918–1994), a Danish guitarist and composer, originally a jazz musician. Neumann was a versatile guitarist, who mastered different styles. He worked as an entertainer together with his fellow countryman violinist Sven Asmussen and with his children Ulla and Mikael Neumann. Göran Söllscher gave the first performance of Neumann's last composition, *"Guitar Concerto"* in 1993, and he has also recorded it (Caprice CAP 21514).

For a solo guitar: "Kärleksvals." For a guitar and a small orchestra: "Concerto."

NIEMINEN, Kai (born 1953), a Finnish guitar pedagogue and composer. Studied at the University of Jyväskylä majoring in musicology (BA

Photo: Johanna Mannila
Kai Nieminen

Printed with permission by composer.

In the work Merirunoja (Sea Poems) composed by Kai Nieminen for the poems of Tommi Hautaniemi there is an exciting dialogue between the voice and the guitar.

1977) and in the Jyväskylä Conservatory where he studied the classical guitar and composition with Štěpán Rak in 1976–78. He has studied composition also with Pekka Kostiainen and attended composition master classes with Georg Crumb, Paavo Heininen and Jukka Tiensuu. Kai Nieminen has given composition concerts e.g. in Jyväskylä in 1988, Prague in 1991 and in a Finnish radio, Radio Keski-Suomi in 1992.

Nieminen does not subscribe to any of the schools or 'isms' of the 20th century, claiming that his style contains elements of Impressionism and expressionism in particular, but that the attentive listener will also discern French and South American influences. Basically Nieminen's music is always free-tonal, but he welcomes

20th century inventions as long they are musically justified and serve the substance of the music. In both structure and content the works of Nieminen are frequently in the nature of fantasies, and he readily speaks of dreams and free chains of associations. Nature, the nights, myths, the Lappish landscape and fascination for time are among the primary stimuli for his compositions. The instrumental music of the Spanish and Italian Renaissance and its archaic quality are the genre of early music for which Nieminen feels the greatest affinity. His works are often founded on various synthetic scales and he has a linking for intervals (such as fifths and octaves) that are bare in tone. Meanwhile he tends to avoid soft harmonies in thirds. This gives his music a somewhat bleak, archaic overall quality. Rhythmically it tends to be a dialogue between pulsative and non pulsative motifs, and the rests and silences are almost as important in his often lyrical music as the notes and sounds.

Nieminen composed several works for the guitar already in the 70s and the 80s. During the last few years he has widened his production for several instruments and ensembles, e.g. symphony orchestras: "Vicoli in ombra" (1995) and "Time around Spring" (1997, ordered by Leon Spierer) and for twelve woodwinds and two percussionists "Time around Autumn" (1996). His most famous solo guitar work is *"Yön akvarelleja"* (Water –Colours of the Night 1981); the five parts are Sunset, Rain, Storm, Idyl and Morning dawn. In *"Merirunoja"* (Sea Poems 1979), which is based on texts by Tommi Hautaniemi, there is an exciting dialogue between the voice and the guitar. *"Night Poems in a Clock Shop a Little Before One O'Clock"*, 1989 scored for guitar is based on a legend from the recent past. During the Second World War a certain Jewish clockmaker was able to tell exact time without any clock or watch to help him. He was therefore able to organize the secret escape of Jews abroad even though the Nazis took all the clocks and watches from his shop. Nieminen's composition draws a picture of the old clockmaker, survivor of a concentration camp, as he recalls the atrocities he suffered during the war. Running throughout the work is a motif imitating a ticking clock that is from time to time interrupted by free-rhythm arabesques recalling the Nazis' torture and attempts to destroy the clockmaker's miraculous power. The work is a study in timbre for guitar, an attempt to capture the sounds of various mechanical clock chimes and the tendency of old clocks to produce "little errors in time", as the composer puts it. Real and unreal time are constantly present in the work, as is the relationship between silence and the sounds in the clock shop" (J. Laaksamo).

For a solo guitar: "Temple" (Hommage à Igor Stravinsky, 1976); "Yön akvarelleja" (Water-Colours of the Night, 1981); "Yöpreludeja" (Night Preludes, 1980); "Atmosfera" (1981); "Yömenninkäisiä" (Gnomes of the Night, Hommage à Marc Chagall, 1985); "Yörunoja kellokaupassa vähän ennen yhtä yöllä" (Night Poems, 1989); "Sarcastic Preludes"; "Atmosfera" (1981); "Manaus ja loitsu" (Exorcism and Incantation, 1989); "Hommage à Paul Klee" (Dances of Fear, 1998); Fantasy (1980); "Loitsu" (Charm, 1994); "Hommage à Andrés Segovia" (1993); "Suomalaisesta sävelmästä" (On a Finnish Theme, 1980); "Estampes – Frank Martin in memoriam" (1997). For two guitars: Three Dances for Two Guitars. For a voice and a guitar: "Pohjoisia kuvia" (Northern Images, 1976); "Merirunoja" (Sea Poems, 1979).

NIN CULMEL, Joaquín (1908–2004), a Cuban pianist, conductor and composer. Nin Culmel studied in Paris in Schola Cantorum and in the Music Academy composition with Paul Dukas, and with Manuel de Falla in Granada in 1930–34. He taught composition in the USA at the University of California Berkeley in 1950–74. Nin Culmel composed in the neoclassical style.

For a solo guitar: "6 variaciónes sobre un tema de Milán"; "La Matilde y el Emilio."

NOBRE, Marlos (born 1939), a Brazilian composer, who was the 13th child in a 14-child family, where music was a hobby. His father was an eager amateur guitarist and his mother played the piano. Nobre started to play the piano at the age of 4, taught by his cousin. He was greatly influenced by the carnivals in his home town Recife: his home was located on a street, where different music and folk dance groups performed. At the age of 14 Nobre decided to dedicate his life to music and already at the age of 20 (1959) he won several composition contests in Brazil. In addition to piano playing Nobre also studied cello and guitar playing. He has had the opportunity to study composition with several remarkable composers of today, e.g. A. Ginastera, O. Messiaen, L. Dallapiccola, and A. Copland. Nobre says that as a composer he is influenced by J.S. Bach and W.A. Mozart, and when he composes, he wants to have the facsimiles of Bach's and Mozart's music scores near him. As regards modern composers he says that Bartók and Lutoslawski have had the greatest influence on him. As Nobre knows the guitar very well, his compositions are very idiomatic to the instrument, which can be seen in his numerous guitar compositions.

For a solo guitar: "Momentos I-VII op: 41, 46, 54, 55, 63" (1974–84); "Prologo e Toccata op. 65" (1984); "Entrada e Tango op. 67" (1985); "Serenata op. 83"; "Reminiscencias Hommage à Pernambuco"; "Reminishencias op. 78"; "Homenage à Villa-Lobos op. 46." For two guitars: "Ciclos nordestinos I-II-III op. 5 bis, 13 bis, 22 bis" (1960, 1963, 1966); "Trés dancas brasileiras op. 57" (1983); "Sonatína op. 76" (1989). For four guitars: Fandango op. 69" (1989). For a flute, guitar, piano and percussion: "Sonancias op. 48" (1980). For a guitar and percussion: "Dúo op. 71" (1989). For a voice and a guitar: "Día da Graca." For a flute and a guitar: "Modinha." For a choir and a guitar: "Yanomani." For a guitar and an orchestra: "Concierto para guitarra op. 51" (1980).

NORDGREN, Pehr Henrik (born 1944), a Finnish composer, who has studied composition both in Finland and in Japan, at the Music University of Tokyo with Y. Hasegawa in 1970–73. After getting aqcuainted with the Japanese culture, he has used Japanese influences in many of his works. Nordgren studied musicology at the University of Helsinki (BA 1967) and simultaneously composition privately with professor Joonas Kokkonen. In his compositions Nordgren combines different styles, e.g. 12-note lines, clusters and traditional chords, and he has also used features of folk music in his tone language. Tragic and melancholic shades are typical of Nordgren's style, and they can also be seen in his work for the solo guitar, *Butterflies op. 39"* (1977), which was inspired by the stories about butterflies in Lafcadio Hearn's book Kwaidan. The work was commissioned by a Czech guitarist living in Sweden, Josef Holecek and it is also dedicated to him. In the manuscript of

The Danish composer Per Nørgård has also composed several works for the guitar.

Photo © Morten Juhl

"Butterflies" there are five parts: *Introduction, Souls, Fluttering, Dance and Autumn.* Three parts of "Butterflies" have been published by a Swedish publisher, Gehrmans Musikförlag.

For a solo guitar: "Butterflies op. 39" (1977); Guitar, French horn & cello: "Spellbound Tones op. 132" (2005). For guitar & string quartet: "Quinteto op. 119" (2003). "Come da lontano op. 122" (2003). For a guitar and orchestra: "Concerto op. 126" (2004/2005).

NØRGÅRD, Per (born 1932), a Danish composer. Studied composition in the Music Academy of Copenhagen in 1952–55 with Vagn Holmboen and in Paris in 1956–57 with Nadia Boulanger. In the 1950s Nørgård, as a composer, searched for a "Nordic sound" and studied eagerly the metamorphosis technique of Sibelius. He has been inspired by natural phenomena, and typical of his compositions are unending series. The most famous work by Nørgård is Gilgamesh, which received the Music Award of the Nordic council in 1974. Per Nørgård has taught in Denmark, in the Music Colleges of Odense, Copenhagen and Århus. As a composer Nørgård has been interested in the guitar and he is one of the most productive guitar composers in the Nordic countries.

For a solo guitar: "Returns" (1976); "In memory of" (1978); "Picture Cards"; "In the mood of spades"; "Suite no. 1"

(1985); "Papalagi" (premiere 1.5.1982); "Clubs among jokers" (1989). For three guitars: "Songline" (1992); "Hjerterdame - tur" (1995). For a flute and a guitar: "Mating danse" (1977). For a guitar and a cello: "Variationer søger tema" (1991). For a flute, trumpet, guitar, violin and double bass: "Det er ikke at bære" (1963). For an oboe, electric organ and electric guitar: "Tune In." For an electric guitar, percussion and accordion: "Arcana" (1970). For a flute, clarinet, mandoline, guitar, percussion, violin and double bass: "Prelude and Ant Fugue" (with a Crab Canon,1982). For a tenor, guitar, two choirs, two vibraphones and woodwinds ad libitum: "Libra" (1973).

NØRHOLM, Ib (born 1931), a Danish composer, musicologist, teacher and organist. Nørholm studied composition with one of the most central composers in Denmark, Vagn Holmboe. He has worked as a teacher in the Music Academy of Copenhagen and since 1981 as a professor. In his early works Nørholm used serialness and collage. His later works have been described as epic, pluralistic and eclectic.

For a solo guitar: "Tavole per Orfeo op. 42" (1968), dedicated to guitarist Ingolf Olsen; "Sonata for guitar" (1976); "Sonata no. 2" (1989); "Præludier for guitar" (1995). For a guitar, accordion and vibraphone/marimba: "Dialog" (1975). For six guitars and eight strings: "Orfeusforvandlinger." For a guitar and

an organ: "Kontroverser mellem guitar og orgel" (1975). For a flute, clarinet, percussion, piano, guitar, violin, viola and cello: "Haven med stier der deler sig" (1982). For a flute, guitar, viola and cello: "Medusas Skygge" (1987). For guitar and double bass: "Lynette" (1990).

OBROVSKÁ, Jana (1930–1987), a Czech composer. Became familiar with the guitar through her husband, guitarist Milan Zelenka. Obrovská was a productive modern guitar composer, whose production got an early end by an early death at the age of 57. Her composition *Hommage à Bela Bartók* was the compulsory piece in the 18th Guitar Contest arranged by the French Radio, ORTF.

For a solo guitar: "Due musici"; "Hommage à Choral Gothique"; "Hommage à Bela Bartók"; "Präludien für Gitarre"; "Album für Gitarre"; "Studi di Intervalli"; "Sonata in modo antiquo"; "Four Images of Japan"; "Snadné etudy pro kytaru I & Nové etudy pro kytaru II."

OHANA, Maurice (1914–1992), a French composer and pianist. Was born in the Gibraltar, studied piano playing in Paris with Lazare-Levy and in Barcelona with F. Marshall and philosophy and literature at the University

Maurice Ohana

of Sorbonne. After that he gave concerts in Spain and in England as a solo pianist, until he dedicated himself to composition. He studied composition in Schola Cantorum with D. Lesur and piano playing after WW II in Italy with A. Casella. After returning to Paris, Ohana, together with his three friends, founded a group, *"Groupe Zodiaque"*, whose goal was to defend the freedom of expression against the dictatoric esthetic attitudes that were in fashion. Ohana's wide knowledge of literature and visual arts has affected his music and it is colored by an Andalucian and French tradition, which is in connection with de Falla's and Debussy's music. His music also has references to African folk music. During the period 1965-70 he gave his works names beginning with the letter "s", the reversed Greek sigma symbolizing infinity. Some of Ohana's pieces are meant to be played with either a 6- or a 10-string guitar.

For a solo guitar: "Tiento" (1955–57). For a 10-string guitar: "Si le Jour paraît" (seven pieces, 1963–64); "Cadran lunaire" (four pieces, 1982); "Homage à Luis Milán." For two guitars: "Anonyme XXème siècle" (1988). For a baritone, speaker, 8-12 female voices, a group of instruments including the guitar: "Llanto por Ignacio Sánches Mejias", (for the texts of G. Lorca, 1950). For a guitar and an orchestra: "Concerto Trois Graphiques" (1950–57). For a guitar and strings: "Si le jour paraît."

ORFF, Carl (1895–1982), a German composer. He studied composition with Heinrich Kaminsk, but his style was primarily influenced by his studying the works of old composers, such as Palestrina, Lasso and Schütz and somewhat the music of Stravinsky. Orff's production contains a lot of music drama, like the famous *Carmina Burana* (1937); that was partly due to his work as the conductor of the Theater Münchener Kammerspiele. He was also a remarkable music pedagogue and his work *Orff-Schulwerk* has had a great impact on music teaching.

For a recorder, percussion, guitar and cello: "Einzug und Reigen" (1952).

ORTEGA, Jesús (born 1935), a Cuban guitarist, pedagogue and composer. Became interested in music as a child while listening to his grandfather's flamenco records, but he only started his guitar studies at the age of 17 inspired by his friend Leo Brouwer. He studied in the Music Academy of Havanna with Isaac Nicola. After his graduation he gave concerts around South America, Europe and the Soviet Union, both as a solo guitarist and together with Leo Brouwer. Ortega teaches guitar playing in the Instituto Superior de Arte in Havanna. He has arranged several vihuela works for the guitar.

For a solo guitar: "Tres preludios"; "Recitativo y fuga"; "Puntos."

PADOVETZ, Ivan (ca. 1800–1873), a Yugoslavian (Croatian) guitarist and composer. At the age of 18 he heard Mauro Giuliani play the guitar in Vienna, and he immediately decided to dedicate himself to guitar playing after first playing the violin. Padovetz studied composition with J.K. Wiesner Morgenstein. He lived in Vienna in 1829–1837 and taught guitar playing to the upper class and gave guitar concerts. Padovetz was among the first, who played the 10-string guitar with two necks (a guitar with four additional bass strings: AHCD, which could be raised by a half a tone). The guitar was made by a Viennese guitar builder, Stauffer. The over 200 guitar pieces by Padovetz contain not only pedagogic works, but also variations, fantasies and sonatas. He often used Italian opera themes of his time and folk songs in his works. In his guitar duos he used a guitar tuned a third higher than a normal guitar and the normally tuned guitar. Padovetz published a guitar school called *Teoretisch-praktische Gitarrenschule nebst An wisung zum Spiele einer zehnsaitigen Gitarre* (1842), which is among the first schools for the 10-string guitar.

For a solo guitar: "Variations op. 1, 2, 5, 19, 25, 26"; "Pezzi originali op. 6"; "Bouquet op. 46"; "Fantasien op. 17"; "Rondoletto A op. 53"; "Variations on folk songs Nek se hrusti"; For two guitars: "Concert Variations on 'The

The legendary violinist Niccolò Paganini, who also was a skilled guitarist, has said of the guitar:"I love the guitar because of its harmonies, it follows me all the time on my journeys."

Carnival of Venice' op. 62"; "Polonaisen und duette für 2 Gitarren."

PAGANINI, Niccolò (1782–1840), an Italian violin virtuoso, guitarist and composer, who developed the technique of violin playing to a new level. With his virtuoso style he influenced also other composers in the Romantic era, such as Liszt, Chopin etc. Paganini got his first musical education at the age of five from his father Antonio, who taught him mandoline and later violin playing demanding that he should practise the whole day from morning until evening. The next teacher was the leading violinist in Genoa, Giacomo Costa, and in 1795 Paganini completed his studies with Alessandro Rolla, who also was a skilled guitarist. In 1796 Paganini returned to Genoa and was very interested in the guitar. Apparently Rolla also taught him to play the guitar. In 1801-1809 he worked as a guitarist in Lucca and composed music for the violin and the guitar (the so-called *Lucca-Sonatas*). Since 1809 Paganini concentrated on the life of an artist, and performed in nearly all of the largest cities in Europe.

Publisher Ricordi published the first 5 opuses of Paganini's works in 1820, two series of sonatas for a violin-guitar duo, six sonatas in each, op.2 and 3 and six quartets op 4 and 5, where instead of a second violin there is a guitar. Paganini has used the guitar as an accompanying instrument, and he has also composed nearly 100 pieces for the solo guitar. Chanterelle has published all of Paganini's solo guitar works in three collections: *Part 1: 43 Ghiribizzi; Part 2: 37 Sonate; Part 3 Various Compositions.*

For a solo guitar: "43 Ghiribizzi"; "37 Sonate." For a guitar and a violin: "Sonata concertata" (1804); "Grande Sonata." For a violin accompanied by a guitar: "6 Sonate op. 2" (n.1805); "6 Sonate op. 3" (ca.1805); "Centone di sonate" (18 sonatas, after 1824); "Variazioni di bravura" (caprise 24); "Cantabile"; etc. For a viola and a guitar: "Sonata per la Grand Viola." For a viola, cello and guitar: "Serenata"; "Terzetto concertante" (1833). For a violin, cello and guitar: "Terzetto D-dur." For two violins and a guitar: "Serenata"; "Terzetto." For a violin, viola, guitar and cello: "3 Quartetti op. 4" (1806–16); "3 Quartetti op. 5" (1806–16); "15 Quartetti" (1818–20), from which 1st, and 3rd –6th are lost. For a voice and a guitar: "Canzonetta."

PALAU BOIX, Manuel (1893–1967), a Spanish composer, conductor and music teacher. Palau studied piano playing and composition in Valencia in 1914–19, and after that composition with Koechlin and Bertel and orchestration with Ravel in Paris in 1924–32. Later Palau taught in the Music Academy of Valencia and from 1952 onwards he was the principal there. Palau's music has a spirit of the folk music of Valencia and it has influences from the Mediterranean music.

For a solo guitar: "Allegro"; "Ayer"; "Fantasía"; "Músicas para la corte del magnánimo"; "Paisaje Balear." For a guitar and an orchestra: "Concierto Levantino."

PANIN, Pjotr (born 1939), a Russian guitarist and composer, who studied composition with M. Osokin and guitar playing with Vladimir Slavsky in Moscow. Since the 1960s Panin has played as a soloist for Concert Bureau of Moscowa. He is an Eskimo from his mother's side, and as a composer he

has used their folk music. He has written nearly 250 small pieces and concertos for the guitar. His works have been played by S. Behrend, I. Suzuki and J.P. Jumez, among others.

For a solo guitar: "Capriccio"; "2 Impressiones"; "Sonata-Fantasia"; "Tableaux d´une Exposition": (5me Avenue, Danse Eskimo, Soirée mysterieuse, Humoresque, Impression du Pamir, L'eau vive, Cavalliers de Mongolie, Horizon, Perdu). "Etude-tremolo"; "Fantasy from theme 'El Vito'"; "Allegretto-staccato"; "Östrische Sonatine" (1970). For a guitar and an orchestra: "Concerto no 1" (1980); "Concerto" (1982).

PARGA, Juan (1843–1899), a Spanish guitarist, pedagogue and composer. He studied guitar and piano playing in Madrid. He gave concerts in Italy, France and Portugal. Parga composed solo guitar works in both Romantic and flamenco style.

For a solo guitar: "Polo Gitano y panderos op. 2"; "Guajiras op. 5"; "Polo y Solea op. 4"; "3a Rapsodia de Concierto op. 6"; "Reminiscencias Arabes op. 13"; "Del Ferol a la Habana op. 23"; "Recuerdos de Cádiz op. 24"; "Recuerdos de Sevilla op. 30."

PATACHICH, Iván (1922-1993), a Hungarian composer. Studied composition in the Music Academy of Budapest under Albert Siklós, Janos Viski and Ferenc Szabó. Patachich has worked as a theater conductor and in 1952 he was appointed the leader of the film studio of Budapest. Patachich pioneered electronic music in Hungary; in 1971 he set up the first studio in Budapest, the Exastud (Experimentum auditorii studii). He worked among electronic and computer music in Stuttgart and Utrecht in 1976-77.

For a solo guitar: "Two Etudes I" (1972); "Sedici pezzi" (1966); "Small Studies I" (1972); "Children's Songs I & II" (1976); "Enimi e disegni" (1983). For two guitars: "Duo" (Pomeriggio di villaggio, 1968); "Disegni a penna" (1983); "Pezzetti popolari" (1983). For a clarinet and a guitar: "Tre Abbozzi" (1961). For a violin or flute and a gui-

tar: "Duet" (1961). For a flute and a guitar: "Bagatelli" (1969); "Mosaici" (1978). For a guitar and a double bass: "Invenzioni" (1971). For a flute, viola and guitar: "Modelli" (1975). For a guitar and percussion: "Charaktere" (1976).

PEDRELL, Carlos (1878–1941), a Spanish composer, who lived in Uruguay, nephew of a famous researcher of Spanish folk music, Felipe Pedrell. Carlos Pedrell studied both in Barcelona and in Paris in the Scola Cantorum. In 1906–21 he taught in South America and after that he returned to Paris. His French music also has Spanish influences.

For a solo guitar: "Trois pièces: Página Romántica, Lamento, Guitarreo"; "Danzas de las tres princesas cautivas"; "Zoraida."

PENDERECKI, Krzysztof (born 1933), a Polish composer. Studied composition in Cracow privately with F. Skoyszewski and in 1955–58 in the Music College of Cracow with A. Malawski and S. Wiechowicz, acting there later as a teacher and a principal. He has also worked as an assistant professor in the Folkwang Academy of Music and as a professor at the University of Yale. Penderecki uses modern ways in playing music and he has created a personal orchestral tone using clusters in stead of tone levels and his music is also influenced by Stockhausen, Boulez and Xenakis. Later he has gone towards a traditional tonality and used the conventional composition forms, such as symphony and concerto. He has conducted his own works and won several prizes with his compositions.

For five amplified instruments: cembalo, electric guitar, bass guitar, harp, double bass and orchestra: "Partita" (1971–72).

PERNAMBUCO, João (1883–1947), also known by the surnames Teixeira and Guimarães, a Brazilian guitarist and composer with Indian-Portuguese roots. As a guitarist he was self-taught and played since he was 12 years old. Pernambuco has composed guitar pieces typical of Brazilian folk music:

Nightclub 1960

©Copyright by Editions Henry Lemoine, 24 rue Pigalle 75009 PARIS

The Argentinean Astor Piazzolla reached international success in the 1970s with his new concert tango style, "Tango Nuevo."

chôroses, tangos, waltzes etc. His solo guitar work *"Sons de Carrilhões"* ("sounds of chimes") has, thanks to its folksy nature, gained popularity and spread to the repertoires of guitarists.

For a solo guitar: "Sons de Carrilhões"; "Brasileirinho, chôro"; "Po De Mico, chôro"; "Lágrima, tango"; "Rosa Carioca, foxtrot"; "Interrogando, jongo"; "Seu Countinho Pegue o Boi, canción"; "Grauna, chôro"; "Sentindo, tango"; "Mimoso, chôro"; "Sonho de Magia, valsa"; "Dengoso, chôro"; "Magoado, chôro"; "Estudio no. 1"; "Suspiro Apaixonado, chôro."

PERSICHETTI, Vincent (1915–1987), a composer, pianist and conductor from the United States. Studied composition with Russell King Miller and conducting with Fritz Reiner in the Curtis Institute. In 1942–62 he taught composition in the Music Academy of Philadelphia and since 1947 worked as the leader of the composition department in the Juilliard School of Music and as the publication leader in the music publishing company Elkan-Vogel since 1952. His production varies stylistically from simple diatonicity to free serial and is composition-technically very skilled.

For a solo guitar: "Parable."

PETIT, Pierre (1922-2000), a French composer, music author and member of various music boards. Studied in Paris in École Normale and at the University of Sorbonne with Nadia Boulanger and Henri Busser. Petit worked as the professor of music history in the Music Conservatory of Paris, as the leader of the light music department in the French Radio and as the chief of its music production and the leader of the chamber music department and also as the leader of the École Normale de Musique.

For a solo guitar: "Mouvement perpétuel"; "Thème & variations"; "Sur les Piestes de Flaire." For two guitars: "Tarantelle & Toccata", dedicated to duet Presti-Lagoya. For two guitars and an orchestra: "Concerto" (1964).

PETRASSI, Goffredo (1904–2003), an Italian composer. Studied in the Music Academy of Rome in 1928–33 taking diplomas in both organ playing and composition. He also taught in that institution since 1939 and worked as a professor of composition in the Santa Cecilia Academy since 1958. "Petrassi started his career as a composer in the neoclassical style in the spirits of Hindemith and Stravinsky, was later also influenced by Casella, adapted the 12-note system in the 1950s and directed towards seriality, which he combined with his colorful and rhythmically energetic style" (I. Oramo). Petrassi's solo guitar work *"Nunc,"* shows his interest in the 12-note technique.

For a solo guitar: "Suoni notturni" (1959); "Nunc" (1971). For a guitar and a cembalo: "Alias" (1977). For a harp, guitar and mandoline: "Seconda serenata-trio" (1962).

PIAZZOLLA, Astor (1921–1992), an Argentinean composer and bandoneón artist, the most important personality of the modern tango. Piazzolla studied composition with Alberto Ginastera and Nadia Boulanger. As an eccentric and original artist he still represents one of the most courageous music styles of our time. Based on the traditional Argentinean tango, Piazzolla has created a modern concert tango style, *"Tango nuevo,"* of which polymodalic melody, frequently changing metrics and a tone mastered by bandoneóns are typical features.

Piazzolla was born in the town of Mardel Plata near Buenos Aires. He spent his childhood in New York and proved to be a musical prodigy. When the legendary Carlos Gardel came to the USA to make motion pictures in the mid-1930s, Piazzolla was hired to play; he was barely a teenager. Piazzolla returned to Buenos Aires in 1938, where he got a high reputation as a bandoneónist and arranger in the orchestra of the master of tango that time, Anibal Troilo. Immediately after the WW II he set up an orchestra of his own. Little by little he went further from the traditional patterns and style and started to compose pieces for chamber orchestras and larger combinations. Inspired by American jazz and modern concert music, he gave tango a shake and both broke and widened its traditional form to suit our time. Piazzolla can be said to have saved the endangered tango tradition. Piazzolla saved the Romanticism, but abandoned its tendency towards nostalgy and the pathetic expression of self pity. His tangos have poetry, drama and an intense mood. The music is at the same time crushing and elegant, lyric and passionate. As the new tango was born in the mid-50s, it gave rise to deep passion and Piazzolla was severly criticized. The defenders of the traditional tango attacked him. Tango was partly music, partly religion, and there was no room for dissidents. His music was boycotted. He moved abroad, composed, arranged and achieved success. In the course of years his compositions have won several prizes and most people have already accepted his new tango. Astor Piazzolla has composed hundreds of tangos and dozens of theater and ballet compositions. He has composed and arranged music for different ensembles from solo bandoneóns to symphony orchestras, operas and motion pictures. He often played with large symphony or chamber orchestras adding the inimitable sound of his bandoneón.

Astor Piazzolla composed his first solo guitar work *"Cinco piezas"* - "five pieces" (1980) after hearing William Walton's five Bagatelles played by the Argentinean guitarist Roberto Aussel. Piazzolla's *Cinco piezas's* first part *Campero* is based on the South American milonga, which is a slow and melancholic milonga camera, where arpeggios are repeated on several levels. In the end of the Campera there is a coda, which is formed of chromatic chords and it is followed by a basso ostinato of the free sixth E string. The second part, *Romantico*, is composed in the style of Francisco Caro's 40s' Romantic tango, in the end there are a few raseguados. The third part, *Acentuado*, is remindful of the canyengues tango of the 50s, and it has a lot of strong accents. In the beginning of that part - ritmico, molto accentuado - the syncopes and the imitation of percussion gives is a jazz-

like mood and it resembles the octave playing of jazzguitarist Wes Montgomery. The middle of the third part, cantabile, resembles a milonga rhythm (3+3+2). The fourth part, *Tristón*, is slow and majesthetical. The fifth part, *Compadre*, is typical tango nuevo music in 5/4 time, and it contains chromatics, syncopes, dissonant chords and percussion effects. Piazzolla's Cinco piezas have been recorded by guitarists Wulfin Lieske (Saphir INT 830.877), Jorge Orasion (Etcetera KTC 1023), Baltazar Benitez (Canal Grande CG 9322), David Tanenbaum (New Albion 065 CD), Gerald Garcia (Naxos 8.550273), Ana Maria Rosado (Albany Records TROY 087) and Jukka Savijoki (Ondine 781-2). Another remarkable guitar work by Piazzolla is *"Tango Suite"* for two guitars. Piazzolla composed it in 1983 and dedicated it to the guitar duet Sergio and Odair Assad, which performed it for the first time in Liège. The suite has three parts and it lasts for 15 minutes. One of the most famous works by Piazzolla is *"Histoire du Tango"* (note published 1986 Éd. H. Lemoine) for a flute and a guitar, which is in four parts and describes the history of the Argentinean tango. The first part, *Bordel 1900* reflects the early years of tango in Argentina, Buenos Aires. The second part, *Café 1930* is a romantic ballade. The third part, *Nightclub 1960* is influenced by bossa nova and modern classical music. The fourth part, *Concert d'aujourd'hui* (concert of today), is influenced by Bartók and Stravinsky. The history of tango has been recorded by numerous duets, such as Pierre André Valade & Roberto Aussel (Circé 87103 LD), William Bennett & Simon Wynberg (ASV CD DCH 692), Gro Sandvik & Stein-Erik Olsen (Simax PSC 1083) and Mikael Helasvuo & Jukka Savijoki. In a few recordings the flute part is played with a violin, guitar or bandoneón. Piazzolla's works also include a concerto for the bandoneón and a guitar, *Concerto pour bandoneón et guitare* ("Hommage à Liege"). The concerto has three parts, *Introduction, Milonga* and *Tango*.

In the 1980s and 90s Piazzolla's guitar compositions have established a permanent position in the repertoires of

guitarists and on records. (K. Mattila). In Finland there is the *In Time Quintet*, which is specialized in performing Piazzolla's music in concerts and on records.

For a solo guitar: "Cinco piezas" (5 pieces, 1980). For two guitars: "Tango suite" (1983). For a flute and a guitar: "Histoire du tango." For a bandoneón, guitar and orchestra: "Concerto pour bandoneón et guitare, Hommage à Liége" (1985). "Piazzolla's tangos" arranged for the solo guitar: "Adiós Noniño" (composed 1954, Noniño was the nickname of Piazzolla's father); "Buenos Aires Hora Cero" (comp. 1963); "Río Sena"; "Tanguísimo"; "Milonga del Angel" (comp. 1962); "La Muerte del Angel" (comp. 1962); "Suite Four seasons: Invierno porteño, Primavera porteño, Verano porteño, Otono porteño" (comp. 1965–70, porteño is a harbour); "Maria de Buenos Aires" (1968), theme from an opera tango with the same name; "Bando"; "Chau Paris"; "Rio Sena"; "Triumfal"; "Tanguisimo." Arrangement for two guitars: "Suite Troileana"; "Bandoneón, Zita (his wife), Whiskey, Escolaso (a card game), the suite is dedicated to the memory of tango master Anibal Troilo 1914–1975"; "Lo que vendra"; "Contraba-jeando." Arrangement for three guitars: "L'evacion"; "Le grand tango" (originally for a cello and a guitar). Arrangement for a flute and guitar: "Libertango."

PONCE, Manuel Maria (1882–1948), a Mexican composer and pianist. Manuel was the 12th child in his family, and he learned to read music before he could read books. He composed his first piano piece at the age of five. When he was ten, he joined the church choir and at the age of 13 he worked as an assistant organist and two years later he was given the vacancy in the church of San Diego. Ponce soon moved to the capital city to study piano playing with Vincente Mañas and the Italian Vincente Gabrielli taught him harmonization. After getting bored with the musical atmosphere in the capital, where he did not learn anything new, Ponce started to teach piano playing and ear training in the small town of

The Mexican Manuel Ponce was the "chamber composer" of Andrés Segovia, he has written several guitar masterpieces, e.g. five sonatas and a concerto.

Aguascalientes in order to earn money to be able to buy a grand piano. As he still was drawn to composition, he sold his grand piano and went to an excursion to Europe at the age of 23. Ponce studied composition in Bologna and later piano playing in Berlin. Due to his weak economic situation he moved back to Mexico in 1908. At this stage Ponce became interested in Mexican folk music, which he started to use in his compositions. In 1915–17 he spent some time in Cuba, where he founded a conservatory. In 1917 Ponce was appointed professor of the Conservatorio Nacional in Mexico. That same year he got to know Clementina Maurel, who was of French birth, and whom he married. After this Ponce became interested in the French culture, which can also be seen in his compositions. Ponce spoke several languages as fluently as Spanish, e.g. French, Italian, English and German.

In 1923 the Spanish guitarist Andrés Segovia gave his first concert in Mexico, where he also met Manuel Ponce. Segovia asked him to compose, and that same year Ponce composed his first work for the guitar, *Sonata Mexicana*, where he uses the themes of Mexican folk music. They continued to keep in contact, when Ponce in 1925 traveled to Paris, with the financial aid from the Mexican government. There he studied with Paul Dukas in the École Normal de Musique. In the same school were also Heitor Villa-Lobos and Joaquín Rodrigo, who became close friends with Ponce. In Paris Ponce also studied folk music, how to collect and classify it. In 1927 Ponce started to publish a Spanish music magazine in Paris, *Gaceta Músical*. Segovia helped him to collect material for the magazine. At the same time Segovia kept ordering new compositions from Ponce, who composed most of his guitar production in Paris in 1925–32, e.g. *"Thème varié e Finale"* (1926), *"Sonata III"* (1927) and *"Sonatina Meridional"* (1932). Their cooperation is visible in their letters, where Segovia's enthusiasm towards Ponce's music can be seen. Segovia wrote to Ponce in Geneva in 1928: "I beg on my knees that you would compose a variation from a Spanish folias theme." In 1929 Ponce composed the work *Tema Variaciónes y Fuga sobre las Folias de España*, which is one of the most monumental guitar compositions in the 20th century. "Ponce's impressionistic guitar works often combine a fine fragility and mysticism" (C. Otero). As a composer he was an expert in styles, and he had no difficulties in composing in different styles. Inspired by Segovia, Ponce composed a Classical and a Romantic sonata and a Baroque suite for the guitar. For a long time guitarists performed it as a composition by S.L. Weiss. The suite was composed to Segovia for a concert, where also violinist Fritz Kreisler performed his own compositions under pseudonyms Vivaldi and Corelli. In 1932 Ponce composed the last solo guitar work for Segovia, *"Sonatina Meridional"*, and in 1933 he moved back to Mexico. From that point onwards until 1940 he did not compose for the guitar, because he was not in contact with Segovia. In 1940 Segovia gave concerts in Mexico again performing the Guitar Concerto in D by Mario Castelnuovo-Tedesco. Ponce was inspired by Segovia's performance and continued the work on his own Guitar Concerto, which he had already started in Paris. At the end of 1940 Ponce sent Segovia the music score of his Guitar Concerto, *"Concierto del sur."* The first part is based on Andalucian melodies, the second describes the Arabic surroundings of Granada and the last is about the joyful atmosphere of Seville. Segovia performed it for the first time on October 4th 1941 in Montevideo, Uruguay, Ponce himself as the conductor. In his last years Ponce gave lectures in the South American countries. Miquel Alcázar has written a book "Obra completa para quitarra de Manuel M Ponce, de acuerdo a los manuscritos originales publ. Conaculta Ed. Étoile, Mexico 2000. Corazón Otero has written a biography of Manuel Ponce, *Manuel M. Ponce and the Guitar*, (Ashley Mark Publishing Company).

For a solo guitar: "Sonata Mexicana" (1923); "Sonata Clásica - Homenaje à F. Sor" (1930); "Sonata III" (1927); "Sonata Romántica - Homenaje à Fr.Schubert" (1928); "Sonatina Meridional" (1932); "Suite" (1931); "Thème varié e Finale" (1926); "Sonata de Paganini" (1930); "Tema Variaciónes y Fuga sobre .las Folias de España" (1929); "Variaciónes sobre un tema de Antonio de Cabezón" (1948). "Scherzino Mexicano" (arr. M.L. Ramos); "La Valentina" (arr. M. Ponce); "Estrellita" (arr. M. Ponce); "3 Canciónes populares mexicanas" (arr. M. Ponce); "4 Pieces: Mazurka, Valse, Trópico, Rumba"; "24 Preludes" (1929); "6 Preludios cortos" (1947); "Prelude" (1925); "Estudio en tremolo" (1930); "Homenaje à Tárrega" (1932); "Suite antigua" (1931); "Alborada y Canción" (1927); "Postlude" (1929); "Balletto" (1929); "Vespertina y Matinal" (1946) A part of Ponce's works have appeared with a pseudonyme: "Suite en La" (1929, S.L. Weiss) and "Gavotta" (A. Scarlatti). For a guitar and a cembalo: "Prelude" (1926); "Sonata" (1931). For a voice and a guitar: "La Pajarera" (1925, arr. M. Ponce). For a guitar and a string quartet: "Allegro" (1948, the other parts have not been published). For a guitar and an orchestra: "Concierto del sur" (1941).

PORRO, Pierre Jean (1750–1831), a French guitarist and composer, the reporter of a guitar magazine *"Journal de Guitare"* in Paris. From 1783 onwards he taught guitar playing and worked as a publisher in Paris. The active period of Porro coincides with the shift from the 5-string to the 6-string guitar. He published 37 opuses for the 5- and 6-string guitars and also composed for the lyre-guitar, which was popular in France in the late 18th century. Porro has published a guitar school, *Méthod de guitare à six cordes op. 31.*

For a solo guitar: "Six Menuets et six Allemandes" (1789); "Les folies d'Espagne"; "Nouvelles etrennes op. 4"; "Aire e romanze op: 15; 25." For two guitars: "Duets op: 18, 28, 32." For a guitar and keyboards: "Duets op: 33, 35." For a guitar and a flute or violin: "Duets: op. 11, 17, 19, 20, 30, 36." For a guitar, violin and viola: "Trios op 26, 38." For one or two voices and a guitar: "Arias and Romances." For a guitar and an orchestra: "Two Concertos."

POULENC, Francis (1899–1963), a French composer, one of the members of *"Les Six."* Was called *"the Schubert of France."* In his music Poulenc used French folk songs and multiple third harmonies. He wrote the *Sarabande* for the guitar in 1960 and dedicated it to Ida Presti, though Presti never performed it in a concert. Poulenc also composed the *"L'Embarquement pour Cythère"* for two guitars. Greg Nestor has arranged the *"Sonata"* (1922, originally for the French horn, trumpet and trombone) for the flute and guitar and A. Levering has arranged *"Mouvements Perpétuels."*

For a solo guitar: "Sarabande" (1960). Arrangement for four guitars: "Suite Française, arr. Forrest." Arrangements for a flute and a guitar: "Sonata" (1922), arr. Nestor; For two Guitars: "L'Embarquement pour Cythère."

PRADO, José de Almeida (born 1943), a Brazilian composer. Studied composition in the Music Academy of Santos with Guarnieri. After graduating as a pianist and a composer in 1963, he worked as a piano teacher in the Music Academy of Santos in 1965–69. He has completed his studies in Santiago de Copostela with Clemente Tern (1967) and in Paris with Nadia Boulanger and Olivier Messiaen (1969–73).

For a solo guitar: "Livre pour six cordes" (1974); "Poesiludio no. 1"; "Portrait"; "Sonata no. 1." For a choir and a guitar: "Celebratio amoris et gaudi."

PRAT MARSAL, Domingo (1886–1944), a Spanish guitarist. Studied at first guitar playing in the Music School of Barcelona and later with Miguel Llobet. Prat moved to Buenos Aires, Argentina and he was the first to teach guitar playing according to the methods of Tárrega in South America, and he became a very successful teacher. He eagerly wrote about the methods of guitar playing, composed etudes and made guitar arrangements. His most remarkable work is *Diccionario de Guitarras, Guitarristas y Guitarreros*, which is a thorough Spanish book about guitarists, guitars and guitar builders. It was published in Buenos Aires in 1934 and a reprint was published by Editions Orphée in 1986.

For a solo guitar: "Bajo el Sauce, milonga criolla"; "Danza Española no. 1"; "El Escondido, danza Argentina"; "El Palito, danza Argentina"; "Gran Jota con variaciones"; "Gueya" (1 or 3 guitars); "La Firmeza, danza Argentina"; "10 Studies"; "Recuerdos de Santiago de Estero, triste Recuerdos de Saldungaray"; "Pasionarios"; "Vidalitas"; "El Triunfo."

PRESTI, Ida (1924–1967), a French guitarist, one of the most remarkable of the 20th century. Her father was a piano teacher, who taught his daughter since she was 5 years old. Presti started to play the guitar at the age of 6, and a few years later, in 1932 she had a chance to study with Mario Maccaferri, who then lived in Paris. Presti also continued her music studies with her father studying theory. Her debute as a guitarist took place at the age of 8, and a couple of years later she performed for the first time in Paris. In 1940, a hundred years after Niccolò Paganini's death, she played with his guitar in a memorial concert, achieving sensational success. In 1952 she got married with guitarist Alexandre Lagoya, with whom she formed the legendary Presti-Lagoya Guitar Duo, which gave more than 2000 concerts around the world. Ida Presti's fabulous career got a sudden end, when she died while preparing for her New York concert at the age of 42 in 1967. The Presti-Lagoya Duo made several recordings, which are absolutely among the best of the world.

For solo guitar: "Danse Rhythmique"; "6 Études"; "Étude du matin." For two guitars: "Danse d'Avila"; "Étude"; "Prélude no. 1."

PREVIN, André (born 1929), an American conductor, pianist and composer with German roots. Previn studied in the Music Academies of Berlin and Paris and in 1939 he moved to the USA and studied there e.g. with Mario Castelnuovo-Tedesco. Since 1945 he has worked in Hollywood as a motion picture composer for MGM, and received Academy Awards for his arrangements and compositions. He also played as a jazz pianist in the Benny Goodman Orchestra. After studying conducting with P. Monteux, he occupied posts as the chief conductor of the Houston Symphony Orchestra, the London Symphony Orchestra and the Pittsburgh Symphony Orchestra.

For cello or French horn, guitar and orchestra: "Concerto."

PRIETO, Claudio (born 1934), a Spanish composer. Already as a young boy Prieto showed interest in music and the leader of the local orchestra, Luis Guzmán, was hired to teach him. Later he studied composition in Madrid in the Real Conservatory with Ricardo Dorado and in Italy in the Santa Cecilia Academy with Goffredo Petrassi. During his career Prieto has won several remarkable prizes with his compositions both in his home country and in international contests. In 1969 he was awarded for his flute and guitar duo *"Solo a Solo"* the award for young musicians.

Emilio Pujol was a versatile, influential man in guitar music: a guitar historian, composer, guitarist and pedagogue. He was also a remarkable scholar of vihuela and Baroque guitar music.

For a solo guitar: "Piezas caprichosas" (1980); "Sonata 6 (1988) guitarra de 32 cuerdas"; "Fantasía Balear" (1989); "Sonata 9" (1990) "Canto a Mallorca." For four guitars: "Cuarteto 2" (1974). For a flute and a guitar: "Solo a Solo" (1967–68).

PROSPERI, Carlo (1921–1990), an Italian composer. Studied in Florence with Frazzi and Dallapiccola and took a diploma in French horn playing (1940) and composition (1949). Since 1957 he taught composition in the Music Academy of Florence. He was a member of the Florence Cherubini Academy. Prosperi has composed with a freely applied 12-note technique, in which he was a pioneer in Italy.

For a solo guitar: "Canto del árpeggione" (1974). For three guitars: "Stellae inerrantes" (1970). For a violin and a guitar: "In nocte" (1964). For six violins, guitar and cembalo: "In nocte secunda" (1968). For a voice and a guitar: "3 frammenti di Saffo."

PUJOL, Emilio (1886–1980), a Spanish guitarist, guitar pedagogue, composer and musicologist. He studied guitar playing with Francisco Tárrega in 1902–09, simultaneously with Miguel Llobet and Daniel Fortea. Pujol gave a concert in 1907 in Lerida and his premiere in Barcelona took place in May 1909, a few weeks before Tárrega died. Pujol's international career started in 1912 with a concert in London Wigmore Hall. His friendship with a Spanish court artist, Pablo Antonio de Bejar made a concert in Madrid Ateno Hall possible, and after that Pujol performed for the Spanish Royal Family. In 1912–29 Pujol gave numerous concerts in Europe and in 1918 he made a tour to South America. In 1923 he married a flamenco guitarist, Matilde Cuervas, with whom he later performed as a duo.

Pujol was also a skilled musicologist. He started to study music history with the famous Spanish music researcher Felipe Pedrell. He settled down to live in Paris in the early 1920s and continued his studies of music history in 1926 in the Music Conservatory of Paris with Lionel de la Laurencie. In Paris he started to look for guitar compositions from the 16th and the 17th centuries and started his cooperation with the publishing company Max Eschig. Between 1928 and 1980 Pujol edited 245 guitar pieces, which contained several vihuela and Baroque guitar arrangements for the classical guitar. In the mid-1930s Pujol found a vihuela in a Parisian museum and gave later concerts with a replica of it. In 1926-27 his concert program contained lots of music for both the vihuela and the Baroque guitar. Emilio Pujol stopped giving concerts in the late 40s and started to teach more. In 1947 he was appointed the first professor in the field at the University of Lisboa. Emilio Pujol is also known as a composer of guitar music. He studied harmonization and bass continuo in the Madrid Royal Conservatory with Augustin Campo, who had been a pupil of Dionisio Aguado. Pujol composed over 100 pieces for the guitar and published several transcriptions, especially for two guitars. His historical role in guitar music is forming Tárrega's guitar playing methods into a guitar school. His four-part guitar school *Escuela razonada de la guitarra* (Ricordi Americana, Buenos Aires 1935) contains not only excercises on various techniques, but also 70 etudes for guitar. Pujol's guitar school is in use all the time and thanks to its thoroughness it belongs to the best guitar schools ever. Pujol also made modern versions from Luys de Narváez's (1945) and Alonso de Mudarra's (1949) vihuela books. Together with Miguel Llobet, Pujol can be listed among the most important continuers of Tárrega's school from the 19th to the 20th century.

For a solo guitar: "Aquelarre, etude dynamique"; "Atardecer, crepuscule"; "Bagatela"; "Barcarole"; "Becqueriana, endecha"; "Canción amatoria"; "Canción de cuna, berceuse"; "Canto de Otoño, etude melodique"; "Cap i cúa";

"Cubana"; "El Abejorro, estudio"; "Endecha a la Amada ausente"; "Estudios para quitarra, grado superior"; "Etude No. 1" (a Madeleine Bucher); "No. 2" (a Daniel Fortea); "No. 3" (à Luisa Anido); "Exercices en forme d'Etudes I & II"; "Fantasía breve"; "Festivola, danza catalana"; "Homenaje à Tárrega"; "Impromptu"; "La Libelulla, estudio"; "Tres tambors, melodia catalán"; "Manola del Avapies, tonadilla"; "3 morceaux espagñols" (Tonadilla,Tango espagñol, Guajira); "Ondinas, estudio No. 7"; "Paisaje, tremolo estudio"; "Pequeña Romanza"; "Pizzicato, etude"; "2 Préludes"; "Preludio Romantico"; "Rapsodia Valenciana"; "Romanza"; "Salve"; "Seguidilla"; "Sevilla, evocacion"; "4 Short Pieces"; "Triptyque Campagnard"; "Triquilandia I, II & III"; "Variations sur un Thème Obsédant"; "Veneciana"; "Villanesca, danza campesina." For two guitars: "Canarios"; "Manola del Lavapiés, tonadilla"; "Tyrolienne"; "Ricercare"; "Duet, etude."

PUJOL, Máximo Diego (born 1957), an Argentinean guitarist and composer. Studied guitar playing with Horacio Ceballos and later with Abel Carlevaro and Eduardo Castañera. He studied composition with Leonidas Arnedoa. M. Pujol's starting point as a composer has been the Argentinean tango.

For solo guitar: "5 Preludios"; "Sonatina"; "Elegía por la muerte de un Tanguero"; "Elegía"; "3 Piezas Rioplatenses." For two guitars: "Tiempo del Hombro." For three guitars: "Fin del Siglo." For four guitars: "Grises y Soles." For a flute and a guitar: "Suite Buenos Aires."

PUUMALA, Veli-Matti (born 1965), Finland. Studied composition in the Sibelius Academy with Paavo Heininen in 1984–93 and in Franco Donatoni's composition courses in Siena and with Klaus Huber in Darmstadt, now professor of composition at Sibelius Academy. Puumala belongs to the most talented Finnish composers of his generation, and has achieved success both in his home country and abroad. The actual breakthrough was the premiere of his *Line to Clash* (1991–93) performed by the city orchestra of

Turku in 1993. Puumala's music is by nature fast and virtuoso. About the series of three chamber music works, *"Scorscio", "Verso"* and *"Ghirlande"*, the composer says: "I wanted a form, which could not be divided into clear parts with different tempos, but which would slide from one tempo to another, and where a music which has apparently ended could quickly vividly into new life."

Puumala has also composed the *"Hailin' Drams"* (1991/1992), which belongs to the most interesting and also demanding works of Finnish solo guitar music. Its first version was performed by Jyrki Myllärinen in 1991. After this the composer has edited the composition and the second version was ready in 1992. Hailin' Drams consists of five parts: *Inquieto, Comodo semplice, Fluido, Vivace* and *Sostenuto*. The duration is ca. 13 minutes. It is based on small short stories by a Russian modern writer Daniil Harms, where everything is possible. This does still not mean an uncontrolled stream of actions, but the short stories/fragments/pieces are very carefully built. "Hailin' Drams" is based on a similar regulated series of insane and chaotic happenings. Puumala seems to have a good knowledge of the guitar as an instrument, he has managed to create colorful music idiomatic to it, and he has used its resources without prejudices.

For a solo guitar: "Hailin' Drams" (1991/92). For a violin and a guitar: "Duettino" (1988). For a clarinet, guitar and string trio: "Verso" (1990–91).

QUINE, Hector (born 1936), an English guitarist and pedagogue, teacher of e.g. Julian Bream and David Russell. He worked as a guitarist in the Royal Opera House and was the first professor in the Royal School of Music (1965). He has written a guitar school, *Introduction to the Guitar*, and prepared other material for learning to play the guitar. Quine has worked in co-operation with the English composer, Stephen Dodgson.

For a solo guitar: "Dodgson & Quine: 20 Studies" (1965).

PÄRT, Arvo (born 1935), Estonian composer. Wrote in style influenced by the Russian masters, but later explored the 12-note system. 1973 he discovered the style he calls *"tintinnabuli"* (little bells). His compositions are built around two parts simultaneously composed as one line - one in a stepwise pattern to and from a central pinch, while the others voice the other two notes of the triad around it.

For violin, guitar, vibraplone & chamber orchestra: Fratres.

RAK, Štěpán (born 1945), a Czech guitarist and composer. He was born in a small village in Ukraine when the WW II was almost over. His parents died in a bombardment, after which the Rak family adopted him to the Czech republic. He first studied in the Prague Fine Arts School and later guitar playing in the Music Conservatory of Prague and composition in the arts Academy of Prague. In 1975-80 Rak taught guitar playing in Jyväskylä, Finland and since 1982 he has taught in the Music Academy of Prague.

For a solo guitar: "Variations on a theme of Jaromir Klempir." "Ouverture of Visions"; "Toccata"; "Suite"; "Cry of the Guitar"; "Decem-Partita"; "15 Descriptive Pieces"; "Farewell to Finland"; "Finnish Story"; "Hommage to Tárrega"; "Humours" (26 instructive pieces); "5 Little Fairy tales"; "3 Melodramas" (voc. ad. lib.); "Petite Nocturne"; "3 Pieces"; "Remembering Prague"; "Hiroshima"; "Preludes"; "Voces de Profundis" (1981, based on Hitchcock's motion picture Psycho); "Rhapsodie Slave"; "Romance"; "Russian Waltz"; "5 Studies"; "The Sun"; "Temptation of the Renaissance"; "The Last Disco." For two guitars: "Sonata"; "3 Movements." For three guitars: "4 Moods." For four guitars: "Rumba." For a cello and a guitar: "Romance." For an oboe and a guitar: "4 Pieces." For a guitar and an orchestra: "Concerto" (1975). "Concerto" no 2 (1987).

RASMUSSEN, Karl Aage (born 1947), a Danish composer. Studied composition in the Music Academy of Århus

WAYS **WEGE** **FOR FLUTE AND GUITAR DUET**

DOROGI

CHEMINES

Printed with composers permssion.

In some of his works Herman Rechberger has used a graphical notation, as in the work Ways for a flute and two guitars.

with Per Nørgård and Pelle Gudmundsen-Holmgreen. He has taught in the Music Academies of Århus and Copenhagen. "In the late 1960s, Rasmussen belonged to the young composers that rebelled against the Darmstadt School and were in favor of a montage technique, which is represented by the oldest composers of the century, e.g. G. Mahler, C. Ives, H.W. Henze and J. Cage. After 1970 Rasmussen has gone further from the immediate quotation and collage technique, and aimed at borrowing stylistic elements from earlier eras, varied so that they have lost their stylistic identity." (J. Brincker). In his solo guitar work, *"Lonesome-solo for Guitarist"* (1978), he has used subjects from folk music and music theater; the guitarist sings complainingly: "Don't break my heart", plays the kazoo and beats the floor with his foot... In addition to the classical guitar Rasmussen has also used the electric guitar in his works.

For a solo guitar: "Lonesome-solo for Guitarist" (1978). For a flute and a guitar: "Lullaby" (1976–1987); "Continuo "(1991). For a cello, guitar and percussion: "Melodiske stier" (1994). For an accordion, percussion and electric guitar: "Protokol og Myte" (1971). For a flute, clarinet, guitar, percussion, piano, violin and cello: "Movements on a Moving Line' (1987); "Italiensk koncert" (1981); "Pianissimo furioso" (1982). For a flute, clarinet, electric guitar, percussion, piano, violin and cello: A ballad of game and dream (1971); "Berio-Mask" (1981).

RAUTAVAARA, Einojuhani (born 1928), a Finnish composer. Studied musicology at the University of Helsinki (BA 1952) and composition in the Sibelius Academy with Aarre Merikanto taking a diploma in 1957. He completed his composition studies in 1955 in New York and Tanglewood with Aaron Copland, Vincent Persichetti, Roger Sessions and in 1957–58 in Ascona with Wladimir Vogel and in Cologne with Rudof Pezold. Rautavaara worked as a lecturer in the Sibelius Academy in 1966–76 and as a professor of composition in 1976–91. Rautavaara's composition production is wide: operas, orchestral music, concertos, chamber music and solo instrument works. He belongs to the top of the Finnish composers that create new guitar music. His style consists of a strong personal hold combined with an unending fantasy. With his solo guitar work *"Partita"* (1958) he belongs to the pioneers in Finnish guitar music. As a composer Rautavaara is interested in the mythology of unicorns, a subject that he has used in his two solo guitar works (1977 and 1980) commissioned by Josef Holecek. Of these pieces especially the *"Serenades of the Unicorn"* has established its position as one of the most frequently played modern Finnish guitar compositions. Rautavaara's style of writing is guitaristically amazingly natural, personal and it searches for new dimensions. The "Serenades of the Unicorn" have four parts, and they contain effects forming the mood and color, such as glissandos, micro intervals, and the use of a spoon in creating sound and the "brushing" of the strings with fingertops etc. The composer has described the world of unicorns as follows: "Their world has a fairy-tale atmosphere. In the Serenades the unicorn moves in the Ancient world, not in the Middle Ages, to judge by the names. It still is an ageless creature and in the Monologues it comes to the dreams of very distant masters. So they react in different ways, some are irritated, some fascinated. Apparently, in addition to the language of music, it speaks English." *The Monologues of Unicorn* (1980) contains four parts where the unicorn has a monologue according to the name of the part in the dreams of *J.S.B* (Bach), *Claude-Achille* (Debussy), *Ad Schbeg* (Schoenberg) and *Igor* (Stravinsky). Jukka Savijoki plays both the Monologues of the Unicorn and the Serenades in his LP The Contemporary Finnish Guitar (BIS-LP-176).

Photo: Maarit Kytöharju

In Einojuhani Rautavaara's solo guitar works "Serenades of the Unicorn" and "Monologues of the Unicorn" there is a mythical unicorn that wanders in the world of ancient times.

For a solo guitar: "Partita" (1958); "Serenades of the Unicorn" (1977); "Monologues of the Unicorn" (1980). For a flute/piccolo/alto flute (bass flute) and guitar: "Sonata" op. 83 (1975).

RAWSTHORNE, Alan (1905–1971), an English composer. Studied in the Royal Manchester College of Music composition, cello playing and piano playing with E. Petr. He was one of the most remarkable English composers of his generation, by whom the younger composers were influenced. Rawsthorne was a doctor honoris causa at the Universities of Liverpool, Essex and Belfast. In 1971 Rawsthorne composed the *"Elegy"* for a solo guitar, but it was left unfinished. Julian Bream later completed it and it was published by Oxford University Press in 1975. Bream also recorded this work of the duration of ca. 8 minutes (Julian Bream 70s, RCA SB 6876).

For a solo guitar: "Elegy" (1971).

RECHBERGER, Herman (born 1947), a composer, who has lived in Finland since 1970, but who has his roots in Austria. Rechberger has studied classical guitar playing in Linz, Zürich, Brussels and the Sibelius Academy in Finland. He is also a trained graphic. Rechberger studied composition in the Sibelius Academy under Aulis Sallinen (diploma 1976). He has studied electronic music and worked as a music editor of modern music in the Finnish Radio (YLE) and as an artistic leader of an experimental studio in 1979–84. In addition to the guitar, Rechberger also plays the recorder in e.g. the *"Sonores Antiqui Ensemble."* The recorder is often one of the instruments in his works. Rechberger has in many cases been inspired by the 16th century Renaissance music, whose features he has used as a part of his modern tone language. He has also used a tape recording or live electronics in his works. What is also central in Rechberger's production is the consideration of amateurs. He has composed a large part of modern music that is played by amateurs and children.

Rechberger is a productive guitar composer and thanks to his long and versatile career as a composer he can be regarded as a pioneer in Finnish guitar music. As regards the Finnish composers Rechberger has written the most guitar concertos of them all. *Golpe de corazón* – dedicated to Timo Korhonen – contains minimalistic features. *Concierto floral* (dedicated to the same guitarist) is a large two-part concerto, which lasts for nearly half an hour. The first part is an Elegy filled with romanticism and the second part is El jardin bailando, inspired by a painting by Simberg, the Garden of Death, which also uses several flamenco techniques. *The Concierto Nordico* was written to a pupil. The *El palacio del sonido* (1986) for three guitars is dedicated to the Finnish Guitar Trio (Kari Äikäs, Ilmari Hytönen and Juan Antonio Muro), according to the composer the work can also be played with six guitars or with a tape. The work contains quotes from the compositions of Luys de Narváez. Also the *G4* (1979) for four guitars contains quotes: from Johann Sebastian Bach and Paolo Virchi. In the work there is a page for each of the four guitarists, which consists of symbols, performance instructions and extracts from the notes.

For a solo guitar: "3 Préludes pour guitare" (1990); "Golpe de corazón" (1992). For two guitars: "Prélude 4-Rendez-vous des cordes" (1990); "Hola Miguel" (1993); "Prélude 5" (Le train, 1994). For three guitars: "El Placido del Sonido" (1986) dedicated to the Finnish Guitar Trio, which has also recorded it (Chorus CH 8703). For four guitars: "G4" (1979). For an oboe and a guitar: "Sonatina miniatura" (1971–72). For a baritone and a guitar: "Canciónes" (1972) (also a version for a soprano and a guitar (1984)). For two guitars and a flute: "Ways" (1975). For a recorder, regal and a guitar: "Concort on an Egg" (1986). For a recorder or flute and a guitar: "Eyktime" (1990). For a guitar, harmonica, synthesizer, hurdy-gurdy and children's instruments: "Uuno och Lurifaxen" (1986). For scene machinery, slides and a lute: "Tree-O" (1975). For a piano, voice band, double bass, flute, guitar, banjo and kantele: "Fipolhurugfreitelus" (1993). For a guitar as an orchestra instrument: "Consort music II" (1977); "Venezia" (1985); "Die Nonnen" (opera, 1995); "Zin Kibaru" (multi media work, 1977); "La nave dei pazzi" (also electric guitar, 1996). Concertos for a guitar and an orchestra: "Concierto floral" (1992–93); "Concierto Nordico per chitarra e orchestra" (1993). For four concerting guitars and orchestras: "Goya" (1992).

RECHIN, Igor (born 1941), a Russian composer, studied in Moscow under A. Khatchaturian and in Leningrad under A. Pen Tsernov. The most frequently played works from his production are 24 Preludes & Fugues and Suite Hommenage à Villa-Lobos. He has dedicated his *Guantanamera-Concerto* to the Russian guitarist Alexander Frauchi.

The child prodigy Giulio Regondi achieved great success already at the age of 7 in the largest cities of Europe gaining the name "Child Paganini." In addition to the guitar he also played a small accordeon, concertina.

For a solo guitar: "24 Preludes & Fugues" (1983); "Suite Hommenage à Villa-Lobos" (1979); "Sonata" (1983); "Sonata no. 2"; "Tag für Tag" (24 Small Pieces). For a 7-string guitar: "Sonata" (1984). For two guitars: "Schritt für Schritt" (6 pieces). For a flute and a guitar: "Divertimento, Spring Flowers" (1984). For a guitar and an orchestra: "Guantanamera Concerto" (1983). For a 7-string guitar and an orchestra: "Russian Concerto" (1986).

REGONDI, Giulio (1822–1872), an Italian guitarist and composer, born in Geneva (according to some sources Lyon), who also played the concertina (a small hexagonal accordion) and composed to it, thus not only influencing the development of guitar music but also accordion music. His father was his first teacher and Regondi soon proved to be a prodigy, who got a high reputation on his tours to Europe already at the age of 7. The critics called him the *"Child Paganini."* Regondi settled down with his father in London, where guitar culture flourished in the 1830s. In London he met the publisher of Mauro Giuliani's works, Leonhard Schulz, and Polish guitarist Marek Sokolovski, whose 7-string guitar may have been the model for Regondi's 8-string guitar. In 1830

Giulio Regondi gave concerts in Paris and in 1840–41 he made a tour to Vienna, Prague and Leipzig together with cellist Lidel. After Regondi gave concerts in Paris and met the famous guitarists Matteo Carcassi and Fernando Sor, they both dedicated their works to him. Sor composed his *Fantaisie, Souvenir D'Amitié* op. 46 as a mark of honor to Regondi. As an excellent player of concertina Regondi composed two concertos for it and an orchestra, and numerous chamber music works for a concertina and a piano. His guitar production is short: five works (op. 19-23) and 10 Études for the guitar. Edition Chanterelle has published Regondi's guitar works with a title Complete Concert Works. (ECH 441).

For a solo guitar: "Rêverie, notturno op. 19"; "Fête Villageoise op. 20"; "Les Oiseaux op. 12"; "1er Air Varié op. 21"; "2 éme Air Varié op. 22"; "Introduzione e Capriccio op. 23"; "10 Studies"; "Ouverture to Oberon"; "Wanderstunden."

REICH, Steve (born 1936), a composer from the USA. After first studying philosophy in 1953–57 Reich studied composition in the Juilliard School of Music in 1958–61 with Persichetti and Bergsman and in the Mills College in 1962–63 with Milhaud and Berio. As a composer Reich belongs to the most important representatives of minimalism, as an instrumentalist he plays the keyboard and percussion. He set up in New York a studio and a band for electronic music, which has also performed in Europe. Reich studied African drumming in Ghana in 1970 and Hebrew psalm singing in New York and Jerusalem in 1976–77. As a composer Reich has also been influenced by Balian gamelan music. He composes work from minimalistic material and is especially interested in wide canons and the repetitions of the same melodies of an instrument in different parts. Seppo Siirala describes Steve Reich's work *Electric Counterpoint* (1987), which he has recorded (CD Minima 301) as follows: "Electric Counterpoint is the third work in a series, where the solo instrumentalist plays together with a tape

that he has previously recorded. The first of these is *"Vermont Counterpoint"* (1982) for a flute and the second *"New York Counterpoint"* (1985) for a clarinet. In the work Electric Counterpoint there are at the most 12 guitars and 2 bass parts, on top of which the solo guitarist plays his own part. The composition has three parts: fast, slow, fast, which are in connection with each other without any breaks. The tempo of the slow part is two times slower than the fast parts. The theme in the first part, which grows into a 8 voiced canon, has its origins in the Central African woodwind music."

For a guitar and a tape or 13 guitars: "Electric Counterpoint" (1987). For two guitars or a guitar and a tape: "Nagoya."

REIS, Dilermando (1916–1977), a Brazilian guitarist and composer. Reis, who has mainly lived in Rio de Janeiro, worked for a long time for the Brazil National Radio Company. His recordings are very many-sided, including works by Bach, Barrios and Tárrega as well as Brazilian waltzes and chôroses and ca. 100 solo pieces composed by himself.

For a solo guitar: "Alma Apaixonado"; "Bingo"; "Caboclinho"; "Conversa De Baiana"; "Desengano"; "Divagando"; "Dois Destinos"; "Dr. Sabe Tudo"; "Eterna Saudade"; "Feitico"; "Fim de Festa"; "Flor de Aguape"; "Gente Boa"; "Maguado"; "Noite de lua"; "Promessa"; "Quando chega a Saudade"; "Rosas de Outono"; "Sandrinha"; "Se Ela Perguntar"; "Serenata"; "Sinhazinha"; "Sobradinho"; "Suplica"; "Ternura"; "Uma valsa e Dois Amores"; "Ve se te Agrada"; "Xodo Da Baiana."

REYNOLDS, Roger (born 1934), a composer from the Unites States. Studied at first to be an engineer and later at the University of Michigan with Ross Lee Finney and Roberto Gerhard to be a pianist and composer. Reynolds belongs to the pioneers in electronic and computer music, and he has worked in the studio for electronic music in Cologne, in the Center of Music Experiment, which he set up in the University of California, then in

Tokyo etc. Reynolds is known as an arranger of new music concerts and festivals and he is an appreciated lecturer. As a composer Reynolds is mostly influenced by Varèse and Cage.

For a solo guitar: "The Behaviour of Mirrors" (1985).

RIÉRA, Rodrigo (1923–1999), a Venezuelan guitarist, studied in the music college of Caracas with Raúl Borges, in the Music Academy of Madrid and in the courses of Andrés Segovia in Siena. Riéra composed guitar solos in a Latin American style.

For a solo guitar: "Preludio criolla"; "Valse Venezolano"; "Serenata Ingenua"; "Nana, canción"; "Elorac"; "Danza à Maracaibo"; "Four Venezuelan Pieces" (Melancolia, Monotonia, Nostalgia, Valse).

RILEY, Terry (born 1935), a composer, keyboard player and saxophonist from the USA. Studied composition in 1955–57 in San Francisco State College with Robert Erickson and violin and piano playing and improvization at the University of Berkeley. Since 1962 he studied electronic music in Paris. Riley is especially known as a minimalist, whose music is also improvisational. His music does not represent systematic minimalism. In the 1960s he was a central composer of repetitive music. Riley has been characterized as a solo performer and improvizer. In the 1960s he gave improvizational concerts that lasted for a whole night. His music is also influenced by Indian music, he studied northern Indian song music in India in 1970 and uses the sitar.

For a solo guitar: "Asención"; "Barabas."

ROCHBERG, George (1918–2005), a composer from the USA. Studied in Passaic High School in 1935–39, New York Mannes School in 1939–42 and Courtis Institute of Music in Philadelphia in 1945–48. Rochberg worked at the Universities of Ohio, Pennsylvania and New York. He was awarded the Doctor Honoris Causa degree in several universities and he received awards in numerous composition contests.

For a flute and a guitar: "Muse of Fire" (1980); "Ora pro Nobis - Nach Bach II" (1989). For a flute, harp, guitar, violin, viola and 2nd guitar: "Serenata d'estate" (1955).

ROCH, Pascual (1860–1921), a Spanish guitarist, pupil of Francisco Tárrega. Roch also worked as a guitar and lute builder in Valencia. In the 1910s Roch moved to Havanna, Cuba, where he published his three-part guitar school, *Método Moderno*, which is based on Tárrega's school. Roch's "Modern method" presents in an interesting way e.g. the different effects that can be played with the guitar, and it contains arrangements (mainly made by F. Tárrega) of some of Roch's little pieces, such as 4 Études, Habanera and Valse etc.

For a solo guitar: "4 Études"; "Habanera"; "Valse"; "Sonatina"; "Mormoria de la foresta"; "Balletto"; "Sonatina"; "Soirée madrilene"; "Fuochi fatui."

RODRIGO, Joaquín (1901-1999), a Spanish composer. Rodrigo became blind at the age of three after having had diphtheria. He started to study piano playing and composition in 1917 with Antich in Valencia. Since 1927 Rodrigo continued his composition studies in Paris with Paul Dukas in École Normale de Musique and as a private pupil of Manuel de Falla. In Paris he became friends with other famous composers such as Falla, Honegger, Milhaud, Ponce, Villa-Lobos and Ravel. After finishing his studies in 1932 Rodrigo traveled the following four years, mainly in the central Europe. In 1933 he got married to a Turkish pianist Victoria Kamh, and they returned to Spain. During the civil war in Spain (1936–9) they lived in Paris and Germany. After the war they again returned to Spain and since 1947 Rodrigo acted as a professor of music history at the University of Madrid and was a highly regarded critic. He has been awarded several prizes for his composition work and he was also

Joaquín Rodrigo belongs to the most important Spanish composers. He has composed a remarkably large production of guitar music. His "Concierto de Aranjuez" is the best known guitar concerto and it belongs to the most popular works of classical music.

awarded the Doctor Honoris Causa degree in several universities, such as the University of Salamanca (1963) and San Carlos Academy, Valencia (1969).

Although Rodrigo composed during the 20th century, his music does not represent modern music, but is influenced more by the 16th and 17th century vihuela composers (L. Milán), national-Romantics (E. Granados) and French Impressionists and especially his teacher P. Dukas. Rodrigo's tone language has been described as painting and there are nostalgic ingredients form the Spanish folklore.

During his time in Paris, Rodrigo also met Segovia, who convinced Rodrigo of the possibilities of the guitar as an art music instrument. Rodrigo finally made a decision to compose for the guitar in 1938 after meeting the famous concert guitarist Regino Sáinz de la Maza and a music patron, Marqués de Bolarque, in Madrid. After that and because of being pressured by de la Maza, Rodrigo composed his first guitar concerto, *Concierto de Aranjuez* (1939). Aranjuez in the name of the work refers to a castle built in the 16th century by Carlos V and Philip II, which is considered the symbol of the Spanish freedom. The premiere of the work was on October 9th 1940 in Barcelona. Regino Sáinz de la Maza, to whom the work is dedicated, played the solo guitar. The work was a tremendous success, and because of it, Rodrigo became the most remarkable composer of the post-war Spain. The Aranjuez concerto is absolutely the best known work by Rodrigo, it is the most frequently played guitar concerto, one of the most remarkable guitar compositions and it has established a position among the most popular pieces of classical music.

Rodrigo's production is wide, it covers over ten concertos, orchestral works, stage music, chamber music and solo pieces for e.g. the piano and the guitar. Guitar music has a central position in Rodrigo's music and his co-operation with guitarists produced remarkable solo guitar works, chamber music and in addition to Concierto de Aranjuez, four other guitar concertos: *Fantasía para un Gentilhombre, Concierto para un Fiesta, Concierto Madrigal* (for two guitars and an orchestra) and *Concierto Andaluz* (for four guitars and an orchestra). Fantasía para un Gentilhombre (the Fantasy of a Noble Man) is based on the themes of a Spanish Baroque guitar composer G. Sanz, and it is dedicated to Andrés Segovia. Concierto para un Fiesta was ordered by Texan millionaire parents, the McKays, to their daughter's birthday party. The work was performed for the first time by the Fort Worth Chamber Orchestra lead by J. Giordani in 1983; Pepe Romero, to whom the work is dedicated, played the solo. Concierto Madrigal is dedicated to the famous Presti & Lagoya Guitar Duo. Concierto Andaluz was ordered by a guitarist family, the Romeros, who moved to the United States from Spain, and with whom Rodrigo worked in co-operation. The most popular of Rodrigo's solo guitar works are *Tres piezas españolas* and *Invocatión et Danza* (Hommage à Manuel de Falla), which

won the first prize in the guitar composition contest arranged by Radio Télévison Française, and is one of the most remarkable guitar compositions of the 20th century. Guitarist Jyrki Myllärinen describes the Invocación & Danza in the leaflet of his CD (JCD-22) as follows: *"The Invocación & Danza"*, dedicated to Manuel Falla, is the most profound and successful solo guitar work of the composer… in his time Falla had both directed and encouraged the young Rodrigo in his composition studies, and the deep respect for the master can be sensed in this work. It clearly is a Fallan piece, where the world of El Amor brujo this time lives hidden in the tunes of the guitar. Falla's "gipsy ballet" has clearly been the source of inspiration. Invocación y danza is filled with quotes, both clearly visible and skillfully hidden, and it would not be difficult to fit Martinez Sierra's ballet's texts to be the programmic frame to this composition… The clearest similarities can still be found in the music. Already the deep impressionalistic sound of the opening bars is in its multi-level nature uniquely sensitive and serious Rodrigo. Also the varying 6/8 timed Polo dance is easily associated with Falla, and belongs to the most intensive parts of the composer. As to the organic form structure, Invocación y danza is more remindful of a gipsy camp than the classical symmetry that Rodrigo favored. In the coda, Rodrigo borrows from the master, as did Falla borrow from Debussy in his Tombeau, and the circle is closed. The opening of the piece has the same theme – as it would be the signature of Falla."

Rodrigo's guitar production has been completely recorded by guitarists M. Jean-Bernard (L'Oeuvre Complète pour guitare, Dante LYS DCC 5/6, 1994) and S. Tennant (The Complete Guitar Works, Vol. 1 GHA 126.026,1996). Graham Wade has published a book on Rodrigo's solo guitar works, *Distant Sarabandes* (GRM Publications, 1996). Victoria Kamhi has written a biographical book about Rodrigo, *Hand in hand With Joaquín Rodrigo*, whose English version was published in Pittsburgh in 1992.

For a solo guitar: "Zarabanda lejana" (1926); "Trilogia: Por los Campos de la España (the fields of Spain): En los trigales (1938), Bajando de la meseta (1954), Entre Olivares" (1956); "Elogio de la guitarra" (1971); "Invocación et Danza" (1961); "Junto al Generalife" (1955); "Pastorale" (1965); "Pajaros de primavera" (1972); "Tres piezas españolas" (Fandango, Passacaglia, Zapateado, dedicated to A. Segovia, 1954); "Dos preludios" (1977); "Sonata a la española" (1969); "Sonata Giocosa" (1958); "Tiento antiguo" (1947); "Triptico" (1978); "Un Tiempo fue Itálica famosa" (1980); "Dos pequeñas fantasías" (1987); "Album de Cecilia – 6 piezas fáciles" (arr. Pepe Romero). For two guitars: "Tonadilla" (to Presti-Lagoya, 1960); "Fandango del ventorillo" (arr.). For four guitars: "Dos Piezas caballerescas" (1945, arr. Germer 1986). For a flute and a guitar: "Serenata al Alba del dia"; "Aria antigua." For a voice and a guitar: "Folias Canarias" (1948); "3 Spanish Songs" (1951); "3 Villancicos" (1952); "Coplas del Pastor enamorado" (1935, arr.). For a guitar a pandourrian and a lute: "Estudiantina." For a harp or a guitar and an orchestra: "Sones en la Giralda." For a soprano, piccolo, cornet and vihuela: "Despedida y soledad, Espera de Amado, San Juan y Pascua" (from suite Liricas Castellanas, 1980). For a guitar and an orchestra: "Concierto de Aranjuez" (1939); "Fantasía para un Gentilhombre" (1954, "the Fantasy of a Noble Man" dedicated to A. Segovia); "Concierto para un Fiesta" (1982), dedicated to Pepe Romero. For two guitars and an orchestra: "Concierto Madrigal" (1968). For four guitars and an orchestra: "Concierto Andaluz" (1967), dedicated to Los Romeros Guitar Quartet.

ROGATIS, Teresa de (1893–1979), an Italian guitarist and pedagogue. Got his first guitar lessons from his father and made a debute at the age of 8 as a child prodigy. He studied piano playing and composition in the Music Academy of Naples. Rogatis gave guitar concerts in Italy and Egypt, and worked as a teacher in the Music School of Cairo.

ROJKO, Urôs (1954), a Slovenian composer. Studied piano and clarinet playing in his childhood and started to compose at the age of 15. He continued his studies in the Music Academy of Ljubljana in 1977–81 with Uros Krek and in the Music College of Freiburg in 1983–86. Rojko has taken part in the music courses of Nono, Lachermann etc.

For a solo guitar: "Passing Away on Two Strings."

ROSSINI, Gioacchino (1792–1868), an Italian composer, whose mother was a singer and father a French horn player. Rossini started his music studies in Bologna with padre S. Mattei. Since 1810 Rossini reached success as an opera composer. He used the guitar in his work *The Barber of Seville*, which is his best known work, and in the *Almavivan serenade*, in the *Opera Aureliano*. Influenced by Paganini and Zani de Ferranti, Rossini composed a *Quintet for the guitar and string quartet*. The themes of Rossini's operas *Tancredi, La gazza ladra; Semiramide; La Cenerentola*, have been used by several composers, e.g. Giuliani's *6 Rossinianas* op. 119-124, Diabelli's *Grand variazioni Tancredi* op. 104, Carulli's *Ouverture La gazza ladra* and Mertz's *Oper revue* op. 8 no. 17 *Il Barbiere di Siviglia*.

ROUSSEL, Albert (1869–1937), a French composer. He was a navy officer until 1984, when he resigned from the military forces and started a career as a professional composer, studying first with Gigout and later d'Indy in Paris in Schola Cantorum, where he later taught himself. His music reflects Impressionistic features and influences from Oriental music. Together with Ravel, he is one of the most important representatives of the French music life, after Debussy.

For a solo guitar: "Segovia" (1925), dedicated to Andrés Segovia.

RUIZ-PIPÓ, Antonio (1934–1997), a Spanish composer, pianist and pedagogue, who lived in Paris. Ruiz-Pipó studied Gregorian music, piano and organ playing and chamber music in Barcelona. He studied piano playing with Alfred Cortot and Alicia de Larrocha, whom he greatly admired,

and composition with Blacafori, Bacarisse and Ohana. Spanish guitarist Narciso Yepes made Ruiz-Pipó familiar with the guitar and inspired him to compose for the guitar. The number of his guitar compositions is large.

For a solo guitar: "Canción y Danza nos. 1-4" (4 Chansons et Dances); "Canto libre y Floreo"; "Estancias"; "Hommage à Antonio de Cabezón" (1964); "Tiento por tiento, Hommage à Mudarra"; "Nenia, Hommage à Falla"; "8 Preludios"; "Preludio y Toccata"; "Otoñales" (1993/4); "Tiento por Tiento a A. Mudarra." For two guitars: "Hommage à Villa-Lobos." For four guitars: "Quatro para Quatro." For a voice and a guitar: "Cantos a la noche." For a guitar and an orchestra: "Tablas." For a guitar and strings: "Concertino Tres en raya."

RUNG, Frederik (1854–1914), a Danish guitarist and guitar composer, son of Henrik Rung. Got a vacancy of the guitarist in the Danish Royal Theater already at the age of 12. A few of Frederik Rung's compositions have been collected to the two part collection Albumsblade, 1898. Rung's pieces have been compared to the compositions of Sor and Giuliani, which represent the intermediate level of difficulty.

For a solo guitar: "Idyl"; "Humoreske"; "La Melanconia"; "Etude" (From "Albums-blade").

RUNG, Henrik (1807–1871), a Danish composer and conductor, who played the double bass and the guitar. The most important composer of the Danish *"Golden era."* He studied abroad with the help of a scholarship, e.g. under G. Ricci in Rome, where he felt comfortable among other Scandinavian artists. After returning from Rome to Copenhagen he received the post of a song teacher and in 1842 he was appointed the song master of the Royal Theater. He composed e.g. 8 operas, theater and other stage music. Henrik Rung composed without any special effort melodically beautiful and lively songs, many of which were meant to be accompanied by either piano or guitar. Rung was also a skillful singer, who accompanied himself with the

guitar. He also received the appreciation of his contemporaries as an improviser, in which he could benefit from his excellent guitar playing technique. Danish guitarist Erling Møldrup has recorded Henrik Rung's works on a LP (Philips D.M.A. 058).

For a solo guitar: "Six pièces pour la guitarre op. 1"; "Deux Polonaises pour la guitarre op. 2"; "Kleine Lektionen op. 3"; "Quatre solos composeès pour la guitarre op. 4." For a soprano and a guitar: "Cavatine - Ha, denne tillid søde trøst!" (from opera Stormen på København. Text T. Overskou); "Tre sange med tekst af Johan S. Welhaven: En vårnat, Nøkken, På fjeldet"; "Vintervisite" (Chr. Winther); Solnedgang (A. Munch). For two sopranos and a piano or guitar: "Hafruden." "Ballade af Ingemann componeret for to sopraner med pianoforte eller guitarakkompagnement."

RYPDAL, Terje (born 1947), a Norwegian jazz musician, guitarist and composer, who belongs to the leading jazz guitarists in Europe. Rypdal studied piano playing already since he was 5 years old, and he started to play the guitar at the age of 13, he is a self-learned guitarist. He studied composition in the Music Academy of Oslo with George Russell. In his music he has combined the elements of both jazz and rock, creating new colors of tones by e.g. playing the guitar with a bow. He is also known as a productive composer of art music, he has composed e.g. two operas, five symphonies and concertos (e.g. for an electric guitar) etc.

For an English horn, cello, synthesizer, percussion and guitar: Time: Some Time Ago But Not Yet op. 60. Concertos, see page 163.

RÄÄTS, Jaan (born 1932), an Estonian composer. Graduated as a pianist from the Music School of Tartu and in 1957 as a composer from the Music Conservatory of Tallinn, where he studied under M. Saari and H. Eller. Since 1974 he has worked as the composition teacher in the Music Conservatory of Tallinn (now Music Academy of Estonia), and since that same year he has been the president of the Estonian Composers' Union. Rääts has composed nearly 100 opuses of various music. His most famous work is I Concerto for a chamber orchestra op. 16.

For a violin and a guitar: "Allegro op. 93" (1994). For two guitars: Fragment op. 118. For a guitar, strings and a prepared piano: "Concerto op. 88" (1992). Concertos, see page 163.

SAARIAHO, Kaija (born 1952), belongs to the internationally most successful Finnish composers at the moment. Saariaho studied composition in the Sibelius Academy with Paavo Heininen and in Freiburg with Brian Ferneyhough and Klaus Huber (diploma 1983). Since 1982 Saariaho has lived in Paris, where she has studied electronic music in the IRCAM. Saariaho continues her composition work in Paris. As a composer she is interested in tone colors and surfaces combined to the challenges offered by harmony; usually there are no actual melodies in her compositions. She has actively used the com-

puter and various electronic sound editors (e.g. samplers) in her composition work, and in several works the tape is used.

For a trombone, percussion, piano and guitar: "Aurora" (1979). For a soprano, flute and guitar: "Adjö" (1982/85). For a baritone, clarinet, mandoline, guitar, harp and double bass: "Caliban's Dream" (1992).

SAGRERAS, Julio Salvador (1879– 1942), an Argentinean guitarist, guitar pedagogue and composer, whom his father Gaspar Sagreras (1838–1901) taught to play the guitar. J. Sagreras graduated from the Music Academy of Buenos Aires, and he became the professor of guitar playing in the Buenos Aires Art Academy. Sagreras has written a seven part guitar school (*Las primeras lecciones de gui-*

Photo: Maarit Kytöharju

The internationally successful Finnish composer Kaija Saariaho has used the guitar in three of her chamber music works.

tarra... - Las sextas lecciones de guitarra), which contains realizing études by Sagreras. The 7th part is *Technica superior*, which is based on F. Tárrega's technique exercises.

Chanterelle has published Sagreras's guitar school with the name *The Complete Lecciones* (1-6) and *Téchnica superior* ECH 889 and three collections of guitar works ECH 883-885.

For a solo guitar: "Dulces Cadenzas, Mazurka de Salón op. 1"; "Quejas Amorosas, Vals op. 2"; "Mis Aspiraciones, Gran Fantasía op. 3"; "Espontánea, Gavota op. 5"; "Madrid, Vals Capricho Español op. 6"; "Venecia, Barcarola"; "Capricho op. 7"; "Cadenciosa, Habanera op. 8"; "Zamba y Vidalita Oriental op. 10"; "Estilos criollos op. 11"; "Miradas y Sonrisas, Vals para Guitarra op. 14"; "Melancolía, Sonata op. 15"; "El Inspirado, Vals para Guitarra op. 16"; "La Marcial, Marcha para Guitarra op. 17"; "Pensando en Ella op. 18"; "Tres Piezas Fáciles op. 19" (Marcha; María Luisa; Nostalgia); "Miniatura, Vals op. 20"; "Divagando, Andante Sentimental op. 21"; "Arrullos, Vals op. 22"; "Sonatina, Estudio no. 1 op. 23"; "Delia, Vals Guitarra op. 24"; "Sonatina, Estudio no. 2

© Ricordi Americana

The Guitar School in six parts by Julio Sagreras contains hundreds of excellent etudes.

op. 25"; "Magdalena, Vals op. 26"; "El Pimpollito op. 27"; "Sonatina, Estudio Num. 3 op. 28"; "La Elegante, 2a Gavotta op. 29"; "Rimas, Vals op. 30"; "Sonatina, Estudio IV op. 31"; "Anita, Vals op. 32"; "El Andaluz, Tango Clásico op. 33"; "La Napolitana, Tarantella op. 34"; "Reminiscencias, Nocturno op. 36"; "La Gioconda, Danza de las Horas op. 37"; "La Espiritual, Romanza sin palabras op. 40"; "Elisa, Mazurka op. 41"; "El Melodiso, Vals op. 42"; "Filigrana, Vals op. 44"; "Sonatina, Estudio no. 5 op. 45"; "Sonatina, Estudio no. 6 op. 46"; "Sonatina, Estudio no. 7 op. 47"; "Sonatina, Estudio no. 8 op. 48"; "La Ideal, Romanza sin palabras op. 49"; "La Aristocrática, Gavotta no. 3 op. 50"; "La Bailable, Mazurka op. 51"; "El Rosarino, Vals op. 52"; "Nocturno no. 2 de F. Chopin op. 53"; "Lejos del Bien Amado!, 4a Vals Boston op. 56", "El Porteño, Vals op. 57"; "La Original, Habanera Clásica op. 58"; "Bebita, vals"; "Dedé, estilo"; "El Colíbri, estudio"; "Estudio caprichoso sobre la Güeya"; "Estudio de Ligados"; "Etérea"; "Rapsodia sobre motivos criollos"; "Vals de Godard"; "Pericón"; "Triunfo"; "El zorzal, estilo"; "La cajita de música, scherzo"; "Nelly, zamba"; "Nenufar, vals"; "Violetas, vals fácil."

SÁINZ de la MAZA, Eduardo (1903–1982), a Spanish cellist, guitarist, pedagogue and composer. The younger brother of Regino Sáinz de la Maza, worked as a guitarist in Barcelona. His music is influenced by Spanish folk music and guitar Romanticists, e.g. Tárrega. E. Sáinz de la Maza's most famous work is a tremolo piece *Campañas del Alba* and *Platero y Yo*.

For a solo guitar: "Campañas del Alba, tremolo estudio"; "Añoranza lejana, estudio"; "Bolero"; "Habanera"; "Confidencia, Preludio"; "Evocacion criolla"; "Soñando caminos"; "Homenaje à la guitarra"; "Homenaje à Haydn"; "Homenaje à Toulouse-Lautrec"; "Platero y Yo, suite."

SÁINZ de la MAZA, Regino (1896–1981), a Spanish guitarist, composer and guitar pedagogue, pupil of Daniel Fortea. Older brother of Eduardo Sáinz de la Maza. Worked as the first professor of guitar playing in the Music Academy of Madrid and belonged to the most important Spanish guitarists of

his time. R. Sáinz de la Maza performed for the first time the Concierto de Aranjuez by Joaquín Rodrigo (dedicated to him) in Barcelona November 9. 1940. In Madrid he published a new version of Aguado's Guitar School in 1943, and collections of etudes by the guitar composers of the Classical era, Carcassi, Giuliani. R. Sáinz de la Maza composed in the Spanish national style for the guitar. His music has been published by Union Musical Española.

For a solo guitar: "Zapateado"; "Peteneras"; "Rondeña"; "El Vito"; "Cantilena"; "Soleá"; "Estudio scherzo"; "La frontera de Dios" (Música para película, motion picture music for the guitar); "4 Obras originales" (Baile de muñecas, Meditación, Recuerdo, Minueto).

SANDBERG, Lars (born 1955), a Swedish composer. Studied first composition with Miklós Maros (1971–73) and later in the Music Academy of Stockholm in 1973–76 with I. Lindholm, A. Mellnäs and G. Bucht. He continued his composition studies at the University of Paris in 1977–78 with Iannis Xenakis. In addition to his composition work Sandberg has worked as a theory teacher, reporter in music magazines and producer of radio programs.

For a solo guitar: "Arena" (1982). Guitar & orchestra: "Lonesome" (1982).

SANDSTRÖM, Sven-David (born 1942), a Swedish composer. Studied at first art history and musicology at the University of Stockholm, after which he studied composition in the Music Academy of Stockholm with Ingvar Lindholm and guest lecturers György Ligeti and Per Nørgård.

Since 1986 Sandström has worked as a professor of composition in the Music Academy of Stockholm.

For a solo guitar: "Away From" (1980).

SANTÓRSOLA, Guido (1904–1994), a violinist, composer and conductor with Italian roots, who has lived most of his life in South America. He studied composition in São Paulo with

Photo: Enar Merkel Rydberg
Sven-David Sandström

Agostino Cantu and Lamberto Baldi. Later he worked in Naples and in London in Trinity College of Music and since 1936 in Uruguay. Santórsola also worked as the principal in the Montevideo Éscuela Normal de Música. His composition style was lyrical, but since 1962 he shifted into serial composition technique. Santórsola became interested in the guitar after meeting Segovia in Uruguay during WW II. Santórsola has composed over 20 works for the guitar.

For a solo guitar: "5 Preludios"; "Sonatas 1-5"; "Suite antigua"; "4 Tientos"; "Vals romántico"; "3 Airs of Court"; "2 Brazilian pieces"; "3 Capricci." For two guitars: "Sonata a duo"; "Sonata no. 2"; "Suite All'Antica"; "Triptico, 3 inventiones." For a flute and a guitar: "Sonata a Duo no. 4." For a piano and a guitar: "Sonata a Duo no. 3." For a voice and a guitar: "Cinco canciónes." For a flute, viola, cello and guitar: "Quartetto no. 2." For a guitar and an orchestra: "Concertino" (1942). For two guitars and an orchestra: "Concerto" (1966). For four guitars and an orchestra: "Concerto" (1972); "Concerto no. 2." (1977); "Concerto no. 3" (1983). For a guitar, cembalo and an orchestra: "Double Concerto" (1973).

SAUGUET, Henri [Pierre] (1901–1989) a French composer, who was inspired by the Les Six group, established in Bordeaux a group, *Les Trois.*" Studied composition with J. Canteloube in Montauban and,

recommended by D. Milhaud, with C. Koechlin in Paris. Sauguet gained success above all as a ballet and opera composer; he has also composed symphonies (4), piano concertos (3), sonatas, ca. 150 solo songs and stage and motion picture music. In its color-fullness and with the elegantly light shades his music represents the French music traditions.

For a solo guitar: "Musiques pour Claudel"; "Soliloquy" (dedicated to M. de Falla 1958); "Trois préludes" (1970); "Two pieces" (1973); "Cadence" (1985). For a flute and a guitar: Six pièces faciles.

SAVIO, Isaias (1902–1977), an Uruguayan guitarist, pedagogue and composer. Studied guitar playing with C. Koch and M. Llobet and in the F. Liszt Conservatory in Heimandstadt, where he also studied piano playing and harmonization. Since 1931 he lived in Argentina teaching and giving concerts. In 1940 he moved to Brazil and started to teach in the Music Academy of São Paulo. He taught e.g. A. Rebello, Carlos Barbosa-Lima etc. Savio has composed nearly 100 original pieces for the guitar, most famous of which are the Brazilian dance suites *Cenas Brasileiras I-II*. He has also made several guitar arrangements.

For a solo guitar: "Cenas Brasileiras I-II"; "Cenas Brasileiras-improvisos"; "Evocación del rancho, Rioplatense"; "Hesitacao"; "25 Melodic Studies"; "Nesta Rua, theme and variations"; "Para Nilo tocar - 9 popular children's songs"; "Para Nilo tocar - 9 popular songs"; "2 Pecas - Vidalita, Danca de Boneca"; "3 Pecas originals"; "6 Pecas de meia dificuldade"; "Preludios 3, 4, 5 & 6"; "4 Preludios pitorescos"; "Preludio pitoresco no. 5 - Amanchecendo"; "Preludio pitoresco no. 6 Ternura"; "4 Recreacoes"; "Sarabanda-Giga"; "Serenata campera"; "Suite descritiva"; "Variacoes de gato"; "Cajita de música"; "10 Brazilian Folk Tunes"; "Agogo"; "Batucada"; "Caricia, valsa"; "Celeste y Blanco"; "13 Estudos Elementares op. 4"; "Estudos 1–3" (1945); "Estudo in C. Trémolo"; "Marcha militar"; "Allegretto moderato"; "Mazurca"; "Minuetto" (1928).

Franz Schubert

SCHEIDLER, Christian Gottlieb (1752–1815), a German lutist, guitarist, pedagogue and composer. Scheidler also worked as a cellist and bassoonist in the courts of German Princes. He taught guitar playing in Frankfurt am Main. At an early stage in his career Scheidler played the lute and the theorbo, but as the popularity of these instruments went down in the 18th century, he concentrated on the guitar. Scheidler composed 12 variations for the theorbo from Mozart's theme in Don Giovanni. The work is considered the last lute instrument composition of the 18th century.

For a solo guitar: "2 Sonatas" (ca.1800). For a guitar and violin or flute: "Duo no. 1 D minor." For a violin and guitar: "Duo D major."

SCHUBERT, Franz (1797–1828), an Austrian Classical-Romantic composer. In his childhood he sang in the church choir of Lichtenthal and later in the court choir of the emperor. He learned violin and guitar playing from his father and piano playing from his brother Ignazi. Later he studied composition under Salieri. Schubert used the guitar as an accompanying instrument. Some of the songs (from op. 3, 4, 20, 21, 36, 60) had an alternative

guitar accompaniment published by Anton Diabelli. A modern version of the beforementioned songs is published by Edition Tecla. 1813 Schubert wrote a *Cantata* for three male voices and a guitar for his father's name day, and in 1819 he composed a few waltzes op. 9 a/b for a flute and guitar. The most famous of Schubert's guitar pieces is *Quartet in G* for the flute, viola, guitar and cello (1814), which is his arrangement from a trio by Wenzeslaus Matiegka. This work was only found in 1926.

Austrian guitarist Konrad Ragossnig has arranged guitar accompaniments to a Schubert's song suite *Die Schöne Müllerin* (1823). Also Schubert's *Arpeggione-sonata* (1824) is accompanied with the guitar, although it was originally composed for an arpeggione (a cello with frets) built by a Viennese instrument builder Johann Georg Staufer.

For a flute or violin and guitar: "Original tänze." For three male voices and a guitar: "Kantate Ertöne, Leier zur Festesfeier!'" (1813), modern publication Doblinger 1960. For a flute, viola, guitar and cello: "Quartet in G." Arrangements for the solo guitar: "6 Lieder" (arr. J.K. Mertz).

SCHWANTNER, Joseph (born 1943), a composer from the USA, whose career as a musician started as a classical, jazz and rock guitarist. He studied in the Music Academy of Chicago, Northwestern University (doctoral thesis 1968). Schwantner teaches in the Estman School of Music and Julliard School of Music. Schwantner has composed the first North American concerto for the guitar and an orchestra: *From Afar... a Fantasy for Guitar and Orchestra* (1987). There is also a version of it for the guitar and a chamber orchestra, and it was recorded by Sharon Isbin in 1995.

For a guitar and a chamber orchestra: "From Afar... a Fantasy for Guitar and Orchestra" (1987).

SCHOENBERG, Arnold (1874–1951), an Austrian composer, conductor and artist. Studied in Vienna with Zemlinsky. Schoenberg is the creator

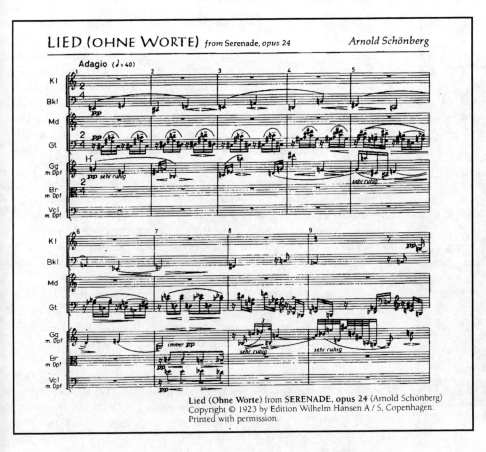

LIED (OHNE WORTE) *from Serenade, opus 24*   *Arnold Schönberg*

Lied (Ohne Worte) from SERENADE, opus 24 (Arnold Schönberg)
Copyright © 1923 by Edition Wilhelm Hansen A / S, Copenhagen.
Printed with permission.

Arnold Schoenberg's Serenade op 24 was the first work
where he used the 12-note technique.

of the atonal style. He taught e.g. Alban Berg, Anton Webern and Hans Apostel etc. In 1933 Schoenberg moved to the USA, where he became a highly regarded pedagogue. In 1923 he composed the *Serenade op. 24 Resplendent night*, for the violin, mandoline, viola, cello, bass clarinet, guitar and a low voice. It was the first work where he used the 12-note technique. Schoenberg also used the guitar in the orchestration examples for the clarinet, bassoon, mandoline, guitar and string quartet, which he prepared for the summer courses in composition in 1921. The examples are based on the music by Luigi Denza, Franz Schubert and Johann Sioly. The German guitarist Siegfried Behrend has arranged Schoenberg's piano pieces *6 Kleine Klavier stücke* op. 19 for the guitar.

For a violin, mandoline, cello, bass clarinet, guitar and low voice: *Serenade* op. 24. Arrangements for the solo guitar: *6 Kleine klavierstücke* op. 19 (arr. Behrend).

SCULTHORPE, Peter (born 1929), an Australian composer, who has studied at the Universities of Melbourne and Oxford. He has worked as a guest lecturer at the Universities of Yale and Sussex and acts as the professor of composition at the University of Sydney. Sculthorpe has been awarded several times for his works and he has been awarded the Doctor Honoris Causa degree at the Universities of Tasmania, Sussex and Melbourne. As a composer he has been influenced by the nature and scenery of Australia. Sculthorpe has worked in co-operation with John Williams, and he has composed music and solo guitar works for Williams's chamber music ensemble Attacca. Williams has recorded these works.

For a solo guitar: "Nocturne" (from a Guitar Concerto, 1980); "From Kakadu" (1993); "Into the Dreaming" (1994). For the guitar, strings and percussion: "Nourlangie" (1989). For a flamenco guitar, classical guitar, jazz guitar and a string quartet: "Cantares" (1980) For a guitar and an orchestra: "Guitar Concerto" (1980).

SEARLE, Humphrey (1915–1982), an English composer and music reporter. After studying at Oxford and in the Royal College of Music in London with Jacob, Morris and Ireland, he continued his studies in the Viennese Neues Konservatorium and as a private pupil of Anton Webern. Being influenced by Webern, he was one of the first British composers to adapt the 12-note system, and he studied the music of Liszt very intensively. He has worked e.g. as a music editor at BBC, as a professor in the Royal College of Music and as a guest professor in the Music College of Karlsruhe.

For a solo guitar: "Five op. 61" (1974).

SEEGNER, Franz G. (early 19th century), an Austrian guitarist and composer, a member of the Imperial Court Chapel in Vienna. According to the small amount of information left about him, he gave concerts in Vienna in 1828 and 1830. Seegner published a guitar school *Praktisch-teoretische Gitarrenschule op. 1*.

For a solo guitar: "Ländler op. 2"; "Capriccio op. 15"; "Capriccios und Variationen"; "Studien für Gitarre" (7 etudes). For two guitars: "Serenata" op. 31. For a violin and a guitar: "Polonaise" op. 29. For a piano and a guitar: "Bravour Sonate." For a string quartet and a guitar: 2 Streichquartett mit Gitarre op. 19; "21." For a guitar and an orchestra: "Konzertvariationen für Gitarre und Orchester" op. 30.

SEGOVIA, Andrés (1893–1987), a Spanish guitarist. He started to perform in Spanish towns already at the age of 14. His international career started in 1920, and since then he gave concerts and made recordings all the way until the 1980s. When WW II broke out, Segovia moved to New York and in 1947 his and chemist Albert Augustine's (1900–1967) co-operation resulted in nylon strings. In the 1950s and 60s Segovia taught in the master courses of both Santiago de Compostela and Siena. He worked in co-operation with several 20th century composers, such as Moreno Torroba, Turina, Castelnuovo-Tedesco, Villa-Lobos, Ponce and Rodrigo etc, and as

Andrés Segovia

Photo: George Clinton

a result a large number of guitar music was composed in the early 20th century. Segovia both composed and arranged lots of music for the guitar. Segovia said about arrangement that it is not only making music compatible for another instrument, and that the goal is always to retain the esthetical nature of the piece. He also stated that he did not want to arrange such piano, violin etc. pieces that are not natural to the guitar, but he chose music that best suited the guitar. As an arranger he continued the tradition of Tárrega and Llobet. Segovia arranged music from different styles and eras, by such composers as Bach, Brahms, Chopin, Frescobaldi, Handel, Purcell, Rameau, Alessandro and Domenico Scarlatti, Schubert, Schumann etc.

In his arrangements Segovia brought out new colors and possibilities for the guitar. As examples of this are his arrangements from Modest Mussorgski's piece "Old Castle" or Isaac Albéniz's Asturias, Zambra Granadina and Oriental. Segovia's arrangements of Bach's solo works, such as Gavotte I-II from Cello Suite nr 6, Sarabande and Bourrée from Violin Partita nr 1, Siciliana from Violin Sonate nr 1 belong to the earliest gui-

tar arrangements of Bach's works. In 1935 Segovia played for the first time J.S. Bach's Chaconne from Violin Partita nr 2 in his concerts in Madrid and Paris. In the arrangement of Chaconne Segovia has widely used the polyphonic and harmonic possibilities of the guitar. His skills in playing raised the appreciation of the guitar. Segovia's own compositions are strongly based on the 19th-century Romantic tradition.

Segovia's compositions for the solo guitar: "Five Anecdotes"; "Macanera"; "Estudio in E"; "Madriguera-Humorada"; "Oración, Remembranza Divertimento"; "Estudio, vals"; "Estudio sin luz"; "Impromptu"; "Tonadilla"; "3 Préludes"; "Prelude in chords." For two guitars: "Divertimento."

Segovia's guitar arrangements: "Isaac Albéniz: Asturias-Leyenda"; "Granada"; "Mallorca"; "Oriental"; "Tango op. 165 no. 2"; "Zambra granadina"; "C. Ph. E. Bach: Siciliana"; "J.S. Bach Gavotte I-II from Cello Suite no. 6"; "Sarabande and Bourrée from Violin Partita no. 1"; "Siciliana from Violin Sonate no. 1"; "Chaconne from Violin Partita no. 2"; "G. Benda: 2 Sonatinen"; "Ludwig van Beethoven: Minuet from Sonata op. 31 no. 3"; "Johannes Brahms: Valse op. 39 no. 8"; "Louis Couperin: Passacaglia"; "Frédéric Chopin: Mazurka op. 63/3"; "Girolamo Frescobaldi: Aria con variazioni"; "G. Fr. Handel: 8 Aylesford cappella"; "Edvard Grieg: Melody"; "Felix Mendelssohn-Bartholdy: Romanza sin palbaras"; "J. Kuhnau 4 Kleine Stücke"; "Henry Purcell: Minuet & Jig"; "Jean Philip Rameau: 2 Menuets"; "Robert Schumann: Bittendes Kind, Fürchtenmachen aus Kinderszenen op. 15, Romance"; "Domenico Scarlatti: Sonata A minor L.187"; "Sonata E minor L.352."

SEIBER, Mátyás (1905–1960), a British

composer born in Hungary. Studied composition in the Music Academy of Budapest in 1919–24 with Zoltán Kodály. Seiber worked as a composition teacher in Frankfurt am Main and taught also jazz, which was his interest for the rest of his life and can also be heard in his music. Seiber also worked as a theater conductor and as a cellist. In 1935 Seiber moved to England, where he wrote an accordion school, taught jazz and composed motion picture music. He taught composition in the Morley College in 1942–57 and was among the best known and most respected composition teachers in Britain.

In his composition style Seiber has combined influences from J.S. Bach and jazz, and in his later works he has elegantly combined influences from Bartók, Schoenberg and folk music with his own tone language. Seiber's career got a sudden end in a car accident on a lecture tour in South Africa. His friend György Ligeti composed the Atmosphères (1961) to honor his memory.

For a solo guitar: "8 Dances" (1956). For a voice and a guitar: "Quatre chansons populaires françaises" (1948); "The owl and pussy-cat."

SIBELIUS, Johan [Jean] Julius Christian (1865-1957). An internationally famous Finnish composer and the creator of the Finnish tone language. Originally Sibelius meant to become a violinist, but soon dedicated himself to composition. The core of his production is formed by seven symphonies, symphonic poetic works e.g. Finlandia (1900) and Tapiola (1926), choir- and vocal music and instrumental compositions, of which the best known is the Violin Concerto in D minor op. 47 (1903, new edit 1905).

The only works where Sibelius has used the guitar are the works composed for Shakespeare's texts from the play "Twelfth- Night", *Kom nu hit, död!* (Saavuthan yö) op. 60 nr 1 and *Hållilå, uti storm och i regn* (Hei ja hoi, miten myrsky se soi) op. 60 nr 2, composed in Helsinki in 1909. The songs were ordered by the Helsinki Swedish Theater and they were also performed for the first time there in a

Jean Sibelius composed in 1909 two songs with a guitar accompaniment to a play by Shakespeare, Twelfth Night.

performance on November 12th 1909. (M. Lüchou p. 116). The guitar parts are very natural for the guitar, which shows that the composer had acquainted himself with the instrument. It is also known that his uncle played the guitar.

For a voice and a guitar: "Kom nu hit, död !"; "Hållilå, uti storm och i regn." "Op. 60 no. 1 & 2" (1909).

SICHRA [SYCHRA] Andrej (1773–1850), a Russian guitarist and pedagogue, born in Vilna with Czech roots. Lived in Moscow since 1801. He first played the harp and later a 7-string guitar (with a G tuning: D, G, H, d, g, h, d1), which was a national instrument in Russia. Sichra composed ca. 75 pieces for the 7-string guitar, fantasies from the opera melodies of his time and variations from the themes of Russian folk songs. Some of his works have been arranged for a 6-string guitar.

SIEGEL, Wayne (born 1953), a composer from the USA. Studied composition in 1971–74 at the Santa Barbara University, where he mainly focused on European avantgarde tradition. He also adapted influences from the American folk music tradition and from Afro-American blues and avant-

garde rock. Siegel completed his composition studies in Denmark in Århus with Per Nørgård (diploma 1977) and in 1986 he was appointed the leader of Danske Institut for Elektroakustisk Musik (DIEM) in Århus. Because of his American background Siegel has a special position in the newer Danish music, as he does not follow the European music traditions similarily to other Danish composers. In his work *Domino Figures* for 10-100 guitars (1979) Siegel uses the canon technique. The work is minimalistic and it is built of ca. 100 "boxes" containing a few notes, and the "boxes" are repeated according to a certain second timing. The first guitar begins, it gives a sign to the next etc. The result has been described as stunning: the sounds of the guitars melt into a tone mass, which moves from one harmony to another. The visual impression reminds falling domino figures, thus the name Domino Figures.

For a solo guitar: "Rosewood Afternoon" (1980). For two pianos or four marimbas or four guitars: "East L.A. Phase" (1975). For two guitars: "Three Canons for Two Guitars" (1985–87). For a voice, guitar and percussion: "Three Songs" (1975–76). For 10–100 guitars: "Domino Figures" (1979).

SIERRA, Roberto (born 1953), a com-

poser from the USA, with Puertorican roots. Especially among the North American guitarists he is best known for his numerous guitar compositions including e.g. *four concertos*. Sierra has worked in cooperation with several guitarists, such as Tanenbaum, Barrueco, Castellani, Andriacchio, Verdery etc.

For a solo guitar: "Pièzas brèves" (1995); "Toccata y lamento." For two violins, a viola, cello and guitar: "Triptico." For a guitar and an orchestra: "Concierto Barocco"; "Concierto" (dedicated to David Tanenbaum). For two guitars and an orchestra: "Concierto." For a violin, guitar and orchestra: "Concierto."

Thorkell Sigurbjörnsson

SIGURBJÖRNSSON, Thorkell (born 1938), an Icelandic composer, pianist and music pedagogue, who has worked in several fields in his country's music life, e.g. as the president of the Association of Icelandic Composers in 1983–88, as a radio reporter, writer and as an administrator. Sigurbjörnsson studied in the Music Academy of Reykjavik and in 1957–61 at the University of Illinois composition with K. Gaburo, electronic music with L. Hiller and piano playing with D. Sanders and took the Master of Music degree. Sigurbjörnsson has also become famous as a pianist abroad, often as

Wayne Siegel

an interpreter of modern Icelandic music. As a composer Sigurbjörnsson has been very productive and his pieces range from children's songs and hymns to chamber music, and very often he has composed music ordered to certain occasions. His style is formed of both entertainment and avantgarde. The subjects often refer to the antique as well as Nordic mythology.

For a flute and a guitar: "Siciliana From Columbine" (1982). For a violin and a guitar: "Vapp" (1993). For a cembalo and a guitar: "Fiori." For a flute, guitar and cello: "Hot Spring Birds" (1984). For a tenor, guitar, flute and viola: "Ballade" (1960).

SINK, Kuldar (1942–1995), an Estonian composer. Studied flute playing in his youth, and after that composition in the Music Conservatory of Leningrad (St. Petersburg) in 1961–66. Typical of Sink's composition style are rich fantasies and a collage technique. Sink has composed several vocal works containing the guitar, a major part of these are dedicated to an Estonian mezzo soprano Leili Tammel.

For a mezzo soprano, flute, viola, guitar and cello: "Sünni ja surma laulud" (Songs of birth and death, to the texts of F.G. Lorca 1985), a 30 minute suite, published by Musiikki Fazer. For a mezzo soprano, flute, guitar, harp and cello: "Aastaajad" (Seasons) for poems by J. Liiv (1987). For a soprano, flute and guitar: "Kodulaul" (Home's song, 1988). For a voice and a guitar: "Ave Maria"; "Pater Noster" (1990). For a soprano, flute, violin and guitar: "Stabat Mater" (1990). For a mezzo soprano, flute and guitar: "Silencio III" 1991. For a soprano, flute, violin and guitar: "Teele teele kurekesed" (Fly, fly stork, 1994).

SMITH BRINDLE, Reginald (1917–2003), an English composer, professor at the University of Surrey. Became interested in the guitar after hearing jazz guitarist Django Reinhardt play. Smith Brindle's interest arose in 1946, when he started his music studies and stopped the almost finished architecture studies. In the 1950s he studied composition in Italy in Accademia di

Reginald Smith Brindle, an Englishman who lived for a long time in Italy, and was one of the pioneers in modern guitar music.

Santa Cecilia with Ildebrando Pizzetti and Luigi Dallapiccola and he also worked in the Italian Radio. Smith Brindle was influenced by both older and younger generation Italian composers. He returned to England in 1967 to teach at the University of Bangor, until he in 1970 was appointed professor at the University of Surrey.

As a composer Smith Brindle has gone through several periods of different composition techniques and styles, from serial to electronic music. What is typical of him as a composer, is frequent changes of style. Smith Brindle has belonged to the pioneers in modern guitar music composers already since mid-1940s. The most famous of his over 70 guitar compositions is *El Polifemo de Oro "Golden Cyclops"* (a Greek mythical giant with one single eye in the middle of its forehead) in 1956. It is a four-part work composed in serial style, and it is based on a poem by Federico García Lorca. It is one of the most remarkable guitar compositions of the 20th century, and it was a pioneer in the development of guitar music.

For a solo guitar: "Fantasia I" (1944); "Serenata I" (1944); "Variations on Three Subjects" (1944); "Fantasia II in D" (1945); "Corrente" (1945); "Chorale and Prelude" (1945); "Chittareo" (1945); "Counterpoint Study" (1945); "Exercise in Arpeggios" (1945); "Fantasia

Passacaglia" (1945); "Serenata II" (1946); "Scherzo" (1946); "Nocturne" (1946); "Berceuse à Diana" (1948); "Fuego Fatuo" (1948); "Sonatina Florentina" (1948); "Danza Pagana" (1948); "Vita Sense" (1948); "Arabesca" (1948); "Serenata III" (1948); "Preludes I-IV" (1948); "Variations No 5" (1948); "Prelude No 5" (1948); "Berceuse II" (1949); "Villanella" (1949); "Omaggio à Manuel de Falla" (1949); "4 Etruscan Preludes" (1949); "Berceuse III" (1950); "Sonata Senese" (1950); "Prelude" (for film Il Serchio, 1950); "Dodecafonic Study" (1952); "Sarabande" (1953, later Memento); "El Polifemo de Oro" (1956); "Memento" (1973, a revision from Sarabande 1953); "Nocturne"; "Do not go gentle" (1974); "November memories" (1974); "Four poems of García Lorca" (1975); "Ten Simple Preludes" (1978); "Sonata No 2 El Verbo" (1976); "Guitar Cosmos" (a pedagogic collection vol. 1&2 1976, vol. 3 1977); "Sonata No 3' "The Valley of Esdralo" (1978); "Sonata No 4 La Brève" (1978); "Sonata No 5" (1979); "Canzona" (1980); "Preludes and Fantasias" (1980); "Variations of two themes of J.S. Bach"; "Vita Senese." For two guitars: "Guitar Duo" (1949); "Chaconne and Interludes" (The Instruments of Peace III, 1978); "Guitarcosmos progressive pieces"; "Las Doce Cuerdas"; "The Pillars of Karnak" (1979, also for four guitars). For three guitars: "Concerto Cum Jubilo" (1974); "Music for Three Guitars" (1970). For a cello and a guitar: "Ten String Music" (1957). For a violin and a guitar: "Five Sketches" (1957). For a recorder and a guitar: "Hathor at Philae." For a voice and a guitar: "2 Poems of Manley Hopkins." For a piano and a guitar: "Three Pieces" (1956). For four guitars: "Concertino" (1949); "Concerto de Angelis" (1973); "The Pillars of Karnak" (1979, also for two guitars). For eight guitars and percussion: "Concerto Brève 'Omnis Terra'" (1971). For a guitar and an orchestra: "Concerto" (1953). "Smith Brindle's arrangements from lute music with a modern notation: da Crema: Intavolatura di liuto (1546) arr. 1954"; "G.B. Terzi: Canzone a 8" (1599 for four lutes) arr. 1973; "Merulo: Canzone a 4 (for two lutes) arr. 1973"; "Casteliona: Intabolatura de leuto" (1535) arr. 1975; "G.B. Terzi: Intavolatura di liuto" (1593) arr. 1975.

SOJO, Vicente Emilio (1887–1974), a Venezuelan composer and conductor. Sojo studied composition with Régulo Rico and since 1910 with Primo Moschin in Caracas. In 1936 he was appointed the principal of Éscuela Nacional de Música in Caracas. Sojo collected and arranged over 400 Venezuelan songs and dances. His Impressionistic music is based on Venezuelan folklore. One of Sojo's composition pupils is well-known Venezuelan guitar composer Antonio Lauro. Sojo has also worked in co-operation with his fellow countryman, guitarist Alirio Diaz, with whom he has arranged Venezuelan folk music.

For a solo guitar: "3 Venezuelan Pieces: El Guitarrero, Dormite mi Niño, Danza Venezolana"; "5 Venezuelan Pieces: "Cántico, Aguinaldo, Canción, Aire Venezolano, Galerón"; "Melodías Venezolanas Vol. 1. (Díaz) - 14 Pieces"; "Vol. 2. - 15 Pieces"; "Quiripa Guatirena."

SOR, [born SORS], Joseph Fernando (born in Barcelona February 1778, baptized on February 14th 1778, died in Paris on July 10th 1839). A Spanish (Catalonian) composer and guitarist. His father, salesman Juan Sor (died 1790) was a skilled amateur guitarist, and therefore Fernando was in touch with guitar playing already as a young boy. It is told that Fernando sang opera arias already at the age of five. At first he also played the strings, violin and cello, but soon he chose the guitar. As a Catalonian Sor was brought up in a Monaster School of Montserrati near Barcelona, where he was accepted as a free student at the age of 12. In Montserrati he studied e.g. harmonization, bass continuo and composition until he was 17. After the Monaster School Sor also studied in a Military College in Barcelona reaching later the rank of a Captain. He became again interested in the guitar after hearing guitar music by Federico Moretti.

In 1797 Sor's opera *Il Telemaco nell'Isola di Calipso* "Telemaccos on the island of Calypso" was performed for the first time in Barcelona, and in 1797–98 it was performed 15 times. This was Sor's debut as a composer and due to this early success Sor traveled to Madrid and settled in the court of Duke Alba together with e.g. painter Goya and composer Boccherini etc. During the Spanish conquest since 1808 he at first fought against the French, but since 1810 he, as many Spanish intellectuels, took care of administrative posts for the French. When Napoleon had to retreat from Spain also Sor had to move to Paris in 1813, and there he became a famous composer and guitarist. After two years in Paris Sor moved to London in 1815, where he gave 7 guitar concerts in 1816–19. In the third London concert in 1817 Sor's *Concertante for guitar and strings* was performed, the famous Spagnoletti played the violin, Challoner played the viola and Lindly the cello. Unfortunately the guitar part of this concerto has not been preserved. In 1819 Sor published in London a collection of Spanish songs accompanied with the guitar (a part also with the piano), *Canciónes Españolas*, which contains seguidillases, which were very popular at the time, and which are related to boleros. Also Sor's best known guitar composition *Variations from Mozart's theme "Oh Cara armonia"* op. 9 had its premiere and was published in London in 1821.

Sor reached great popularity as a ballet, vocal and guitar composer. His best known ballet, *"Cendrillon"* (Cinderella, which also had its premiere in London in 1822), was performed in Paris 104 times and in the opening of the Bolshoi Theater in Moscow in 1823. In London Sor was granted the honorary membership of the Royal Academy in 1822. In 1823 he left, through Paris, Berlin and Warsaw to Moscow together with the charming ballerina Félicité Hullin, who became a prima ballerina in the ballet of Moscow Theater. Apparently she was Sor's wife, as she referred to herself as Hullin-Sors. On his journey to Russia Sor performed in Moscow and for the royal family in St. Petersburg, and attended the funeral of Tsar Alexander and in the coronation of Tsar Nikolai. Around 1826–27 Sor returned to Paris. In Moscow Sor met a famous Russian guitarist Michail Vyssotski, and to remember this, he composed a guitar duo to Vyssotski's theme *Souvenir de Russie* op. 63.

The last 13 years of his life Sor lived in Paris working as a guitar teacher and giving concerts together with his friend Dionisio Aguado (1784–1849), to whom he dedicated his guitar duo *"Les deux Amis"* op. 41 and *Fantasy* op. 30. The last years of Sor's life were filled with sorrow as his daughter Caroline died in summer 1837, after which he himself got cancer. In 1830 Sor published his guitar school *Méthode pour la Guitare* in Paris, and later also German, English and Spanish versions were printed. Sor's French pupil, Napoléon Coste, edited a version of his school (published ca. 1845), to which he added a part on the use of the 7-string guitar. Sor also worked as a singing teacher and sometimes performed as a singer, and he also composed a remarkable number of vocal music; e.g. patriotic Spanish songs, English Theater songs, Italian ariettas, French romances and

The Spanish Fernando Sor lived since 1813 in Paris, where several guitarists competed for fame. He also gained a high reputation in England and Russia.

the beforementioned Spanish seguidillases. His other production contains orchestral works, ballets, operas, symphonies, church music and military brass band pieces.

Sor's guitar production covers 67 works (William G. Sasser, doctoral thesis, University of North Carolina 1960), including sonatas, variations, fantasies, small salon music pieces and excellent études. His composition style is melodic and polyphonic, usually with 3-4 voices. Sor also worked in co-operation with guitar builders, Louis Panormo in London and René Lacote in Paris. Sor's guitar music has remained a central position in the repertoires of guitarists until today.

For a solo guitar: "Six Divertissements, op. 1"; "Six Divertissements, op. 2"; "Thème varié suivi d'un Ménuet, op. 3"; "Deuxième Fantaisie, op 4"; "Six petites pièces, très faciles, op 5"; "Douze Études, op. 6"; "Fantaisie, op. 7"; "Six Divertissements, op. 8"; "Introduction et variations sur un thème de Mozart, op 9"; "Troisième Fantaisie, op. 10"; "Deux thèmes variés et douze ménuets, op. 11"; "Quatrième Fantaisie, op. 12"; "Divertissement, op. 13"; "Grand Solo, op. 14"; "Les Folies d'Espagne avec variations et un ménuet, op. 15a"; "Marche du ballet de 'Cendrillon', op. 15c"; "Cinquième Fantaisie et variations sur 'Nel cor piú non mi sento' de Paisiello, op. 16." "Six Valses" (Cahier I), op. 17; "Six Valses" (Cahier II), op. 18; "Six Airs choisis de l'opera 'La flute Magique' de Mozart, op. 19"; "Introduction et thème varié, op. 20"; "Les Adieux" (La Despidida). op. 21; "Grande Sonate, op. 22"; "Cinquième Divertissement, très facile, op. 23"; "Huit petites pièces, op. 24"; "Deuxième Grande Sonate, op 25"; "Introduction et variations sur l'air 'Que ne suis-je la fougère', op. 26"; "Introduction et variations sur 'Gentil Houssard', op. 27"; "Introduction et variations sur 'Marlborough se´en va-t-en guerre', op. 28"; "Douze Études" (suite de l'oeuvre 6), op. 29; "Fantaisie et variations brillantes, op. 30"; "Vingt-Quatre leçons progressives pour les Commençants, op 31"; "Six petites pièces, op. 32"; "Trois pièces de société, op. 33"; "Trois pièces de société" (seconde collection), op. 34; "Vingt-quatre exercices, op. 35"; "Trois pièces de société, op. 36"; "Sérénade, op. 37"; "Fantaisie et variations sur un air écossais, op. 40"; "Six petites pièces, op. 42"; "Mes ennuis, 6 bagatelles, op. 43"; "Vingt-quatre morceaux pour servir de leçons, op. 44"; "Voyons si c'est ca, six petites pièces faciles, op. 45"; "Souvenir d'amitié, Fantaisie, op. 46"; "Six pièces progressives, op. 47"; "Est-ce bien ça?, op. 48"; "La Calme, Caprice, op. 50"; "A la bonne heure!, op. 51"; "Fantaisie villageoise, op. 52"; "Morceau de concert, op. 54"; "Souvenir d'une soirée a Berlin. Fantaisie, op. 56"; "Six valses et un galop, op. 57"; "Fantaisie pour guitare seule, op. 58"; "Fantaisie elégiaque, op. 59"; "Introduction à l'étude de la guitarre, op. 60"; "Trois duos faciles, op. 61." "Tre danze nazionali spagnole: Bolero, Tirana, Manchegas." For a solo guitar without an opus number: "Air Varié"; "Thème Varié"; "Menuets Composés por la Guitare"; "Marche du ballet de Cendrillon"; "La Candeur Petite rêverie sur la Guitare." For two guitars: "Divertissement pour deux guitares, op. 38"; "Six valses pour deux guitares, op. 39"; "Les deux amis" (Los dos amigos), op. 41; "Divertissement militaire, op. 49"; "Le premier pas vers moi, op. 53"; "Trois duos faciles et progressives, op. 55"; "Divertissement pour deux guitares, op. 62"; "Souvenir de Russie op. 63."

SPOHR, Louis (1784–1859), a German composer, violinist and conductor. Traveled in his youth as a composer virtuoso around Europe and got a vacancy in the court of Gotha. Later he worked as a theater conductor in Vienna and since 1822 as a chamber conductor in Kassel. Spohr also made a contribution as a pedagogue, and he was a remarkable developer of the Romantic opera (Faust 1816, Berggeist 1825).

For a voice and a guitar: "Romance aus Zemire und Azore"; "Sechs Deutsche Lieder op: 37, 41, ja 72."

STAAK, Pieter van der (born 1930), a Dutch guitarist, guitar pedagogue and composer. Studied guitar playing with Andrés Segovia and Alirio Diaz and vihuela playing with Emilio Pujol. Staak has taught in several Swedish *"Liten Gitarrakademi"* courses arranged by the Swedish Guitar and Lute Association (SGLS). Staak is a very productive guitar composer (more than 400 compositions). He has mainly composed for 2-6 guitars or varying chamber music ensembles, often pedagogic works.

For a solo guitar: "Bolero Español"; "8 Easy Pieces"; "5 Exotic Dances"; "3 Moods from the Song of Salomon"; "Prelude No. 1"; "4 Royal Dances"; "5 South American Pieces"; "8 Studies in harmonics." For two guitars: "A bag of sweets" (7 very easy duets); "Easy two" (6 duets); "Easy Two"; "Pocket Music." For three guitars: "3 Comedies" (for three guitars and two other instruments ad.lib.); "A Set of Sketches" (9 easy guitar trios); "Snapshots" (6 pieces); "3 Vignettes." For four guitars: "7 guitar quartets"; "9 easy guitar quartets"; "Quator facile I"; "Quator facile II"; "Six hits." For five guitars: "Concertino III for a solo guitar and a guitar quartet"; "Vals Ecuatorial"; "Xingú." For six guitars: "Scherzo per Sestetto." For a voice and a guitar: "Three Quatrains of Omar Khayyam." For a guitar and an orchestra: "Concertino Romantico" (1961); "Concertino I" (1965); "Concertino II" (1966); "Concertino III" (1970).

STOCKHAUSEN, Karlheinz (born 1928), a German composer, the symbol of the avantgarde. Studied in the Music College and at the University of Cologne e.g. school music, piano playing, conducting, musicology and also composition with Frank Martin. Later he continued his composition studies with Darius Milhaud and Oliver Messiaen and in 1954–57 with Werner Meyer-Eppler. Stockhausen has taught composition in the Darmstadt Courses. In addition to pieces that have detailed music scores, he also uses aleatorics and various improvisation methods and was influenced by Oriental religions and mysticism. Performing his works persupposes meditation, and in his work Ylem (1972) the composer tells the players to close their eyes and get a telepathic connection with each other and the conductor. Stockhausen is also known in the field of electronic music, he set up a studio of electronic music for the Radio of Cologne and has been the leader of it since 1963.

He has also written several articles about musical theory and he has worked as a reporter for the magazine Dei Reihe.

For a solo guitar: "Spiral", dedicated to guitarist K. Böttner.

STRAVINSKY, Igor (1882–1971), a Russian composer. Studied piano playing and composition with Rimski-Korsakov. From 1914 onwards he lived in Paris and Switzerland and in 1939 he moved to the United States. His production is divided into three periods: the Russian, the neoclassical and the 12-note system period. Stravinsky has arranged *Four Russian Folksongs,* from which he made a version for a voice, flute, guitar and harp (1953).

For a voice, flute, guitar and harp: "Four Russian Folksongs" (1953).

SUMERA, Lepo (1950–2000), an Estonian composer. Studied composition in the Music Conservatory of Tallinn with H. Eller and H. Jürisalu and in the Music Conservatory of Moscow with Ledenjov. Since 1981 he taught composition in the Music Academy of Tallinn (now Music Academy of Estonia). Sumera acted as the culture minister in the early 1990s and as the president of the Estonian Composers' Association. His tone language contains minimalism and aleatorics. Sumera's symphonies and chamber music have been performed both in the Nordic countries and other European countries.

For a flute and a guitar: "to BBB and his friends" (1988, BBB is a German guitarist Boris Björn Bagger), there is also a version of it for a viola/mandoline/bassoon/cello and guitar and also flute and two guitars. For a guitar and a piano: "Quasi improvisata" (1988), from which also versions for an electric guitar and a clavere instrument (organ/ synthesizer / cembalo). Lepo

Sumera uses the guitar in the *cadenze of the 4th Symphony* and in theater music *"Lermontov's Masquerade"* (Valse and Galop for a cello and a guitar). For a flute, cello and a guitar: cycle "Odalisques."

SWAYNE, Giles (born 1946), an English composer. Studied at the University of Cambridge, in the Accademia Chigiana in Siena, Royal Academy of Music in London and Conservatoire National Supériéur de Músique in Paris with e.g. Gordon Green, Harrison Birtwistle, Alan Bush, Nicholas Maw and Olivier Messiaen. In

Atli Heimir Sveinsson

1972 Swayne's String Quartet nr 1 was awarded the *"Greater London Arts Association Composer Prize."* Composer Swayne nowadays spends part of his time in London and the rest in his home in Ghana.

Giles Swayne's first solo guitar work *Canto for Guitar* op. 11 was composed in 1972 as comissioned by an English guitarist Timothy Walker. The third solo guitar work *"Solo"* op. 42 (1986) was comissioned by Julian Bream. The modal and partly pentatonic material of the Solo is varied and widened so that it grows into a 12-note line. The composer has said that the idea of that work came so that he felt he had an imaginatory man inside his head, a black old man – an old slave – who lived in America around year

1875. In the evening the man plays an old guitar and tries to remember the melodies that he had heard in Western Africa in his childhood. Along with the melodies he also remembers memories – about a family that he had lost, about a language that he has almost forgotten and about the village life of Africa. He has been torn apart from everything that is important for him and is deeply alone - thus the name – Solo.

For a solo guitar: "Canto for Guitar op. 11" (1972); "Suite for Guitar op. 21" (1976); "Solo op. 42" (1986). For a flute and a guitar: "Songlines op. 50" (1987).

SVEINSSON, Atli Heimir (born 1938), an Icelandic composer. Studied piano playing in the Music Academy of Reykjavik with Rögnvaldur Sigurjónsson. After hearing Stockhausen's *Gesang der Jünglinge,* he decided to start to study composition seriously. At the age of 21 (1959) he traveled to Germany when he lived in a Roman Catholic monastery, and he studied conducting, piano playing and composition in the Music Academy of Cologne and in Kölner Schule für Neue Musik with e.g. K. Stockhausen, G. Raphael, A. Zimmermann etc. He completed his studies in the Netherlands, where he studied electronic music in Bilhoven with G.M. Koegen. The connecting thought of his production, telling stories, dates from this time. "As I was not interested in complicated calculi and systems – they seemed so regular in form – I wanted to tell stories and free fantasy became my central method" (Primus 1/1988 p. 14) After returning to his native country he has been active in Icelandic music life in many ways, in addition to composing he has taught in the Music Academy of Reykjavik, he has worked as a conductor, for the Icelandic Radio and he was the president of the Icelandic Composers' Union in 1972–83. Sveinsson is a very productive composer. He has been described as a provocative experimenter, whose style combines restlessness, absurdity and on the other hand fragile lyricism and epic nature. Sveinsson has composed several concertos, one e.g. for the flute and orchestra (1973), for which he received a composition award given by the Nordic Council (1976).

For a voice, guitar, percussion, piano, viola and bassoon: "Poem of spring" (1968) to a text by Jón Oskar. For a voice, guitar and 2 pianos (four handed): "Dream of the world" (1968). For a coloratura soprano, vibraphone, viola, guitar, cembalo and harp: "Aria" (1977). For a guitar, piccolo, clarinet, cello and piano: "Precious dances" (1983). For a voice, flute, alto saxophone, guitar and percussion: "Karin Mansdotter's Lullaby for King Erik XIV" (1979) to texts by Sakari Topelius. For a contra tenor, guitar, flute, clarinet and cello: "Prayers" (1993), a solo cantata to a text by Sören Kierkegaard. For a guitar, flute, clarinet, cello and piano: "Dansar dyr arinnar" (1983) (11-part suite).

TAKÁCS, Jenö (1902-2005), an Austrian composer, pianist and folk music researcher with Hungarian roots. Takács studied composition in Vienna in 1927–32 and was in touch with the school of Arnold Schoenberg. Since 1934 he taught in the Music Academy of Cairo and made concert tours in the Middle and Far East and the USA. In his music Takács often uses folk music of Hungary and other countries.

For a solo guitar: "Cadenza from Partita op. 55"; "Meditation und Reigen op. 64." For a recorder or flute and guitar: "19 Ganz leichte Stücke op. 105." For a violin and guitar: "Divertimento op. 61a"; "Dialoge op. 77"; "Späte Gedanken" (1969). For a flute, viola or violin and guitar: "Drifting Leaves op. 113." For a flute, cello and guitar: "Spring Music." For a guitar or cembalo and an orchestra: "Partita op. 55" (1949–50).

TAKEMITSU, Toru (1930–1996), a

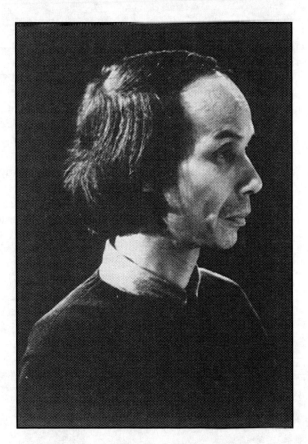

Takemitsu's lyrical and elegic tonal language combines Japanese and western influences in a facinating way.

Japanese composer, mainly self-learned, but studied at times with Kiyse in 1948. The most important models for Takemitsu were at first the chromatic tone language of Berg and Webern and the harmonization of Messiaen, later Debussy, Ravel, Nono and the concretic music of Pierre Schaeffer. The combination of French and Oriental nuances dominate the general picture of Takemitsu's music. He has been most successful in using European influences in music for Japanese instruments, and he has developed a world of tones, which combines Japanese and European influences. Takemitsu started as a motion picture composer at the age of 16 and composed the music for nearly 100 motion pictures. Takemitsu's first wide work *Requiem* (for a string orchestra, 1957) was performed in 1959, conducted by Stravinsky, who thought the work was remarkable.

Toru Takemitsu was also a productive guitar composer, who composed guitar music from the early 1960s until his death. In 1961 he composed for a rare ensemble, a flute, a guitar tuned a third higher than normally and a lute, and the piece is called *Ring*. The name comes from the initials of the parts, "General theme", "Retrograde", "Inversion" and "Noise." The parts can be played in random order and between any two parts comes an Interlude, which is an improvisation based on graphical notation. Takemitsu's first solo guitar work, *"Folios"* (1974), was performed by Kiyoshi Shimura that same year in Tokyo. Flutist, Mikael Helasvuo, has described the Folios as follows: "The voiced richness of the instrument has been maximized with skillful registering, different touches and use of flageolets. One guitar in this Folios suite, which is a sum of three thin Folios, sounds as colorful as a group of various string instruments and small bells. In the coda there is suddenly a message from another world, from the era of folio-shaped note papers: J.S. Bach's choral "Wenn ich einmal soll scheiden" from the St. Matthew Passion about the work *"Toward the Sea"* for alto flute and guitar (1981). Takemitsu has written: "This is a short piece of pastoral (!) music..." After this he composed the piece *"To the Edge of Dream"* for a guitar and an orchestra (1983) and the next year *"Vers, l'arc-en-ciel, Palma"* for a guitar, English horn and an orchestra (1984). Takemitsu's solo guitar work *"All in Twilight"* (1988) is dedicated to Julian Bream. Helasvuo has described the work as follows: "The piece consists of four parts, elegantly rich in atmosphere, contrasting each other lightly and rich in detail. The stylistic variety is many-sided, Romantic, it puts the idea of hazy beauty into the front. Operating with the "entertaining" aspect of guitar idiomacy, the gates of banality are knocked on in a style very typical of Takemitsu, as with a glint of humor, but the gates still remain closed. The general color of the composition is light pastel, according to the painting of Paul Klee, which gave it the inspiration and the name." Takemitsu's devotion to the guitar can be seen in the fact that even when he was seriously ill, only three months before his death, he composed his last wide work *In the Woods* (1995) just for the solo guitar. In this three-part work he has used the guitar's tone qualities very elegantly. The parts of the In the Woods are *Wainscot Pond* after a painting of Cornelia Foss, *Rosedale* and *Muir Woods*, they are scenes from the nature. The music reveals a clear self-inspecting nature of fairwels.

For a solo guitar: "Folios" (1974); "12 songs for solo guitar, based on songs by the Beatles, Gershwin, Arlen and traditional Japanese folk songs"; "All in Twilight" (1988); "Equinox" (1993); "In the Woods" (1995). For two guitars: "Bad Boy" (1961/93). For a flute, a guitar tuned a third higher and lute: "Ring" (1961). The name comes from the initials of the parts, "General theme", "Retrograde", "Inversion" and "Noise." The parts can be played in random order and between two parts belongs an Interlude, which is an improvisation based on graphical notation. For two flutes, two bandoneóns, violin, cello. Also a version for two piccolos, violin, cello, guitar and electric organ: "Valeria" (1965/69). For piano, harp, piano/celesta, vibraphone and female voice: "Stanza I" (1969); For an alto flute and a guitar: "Toward the sea" (1981); For a guitar and an orchestra: "To The Edge of Dream" (1983); For a guitar, oboe d'amore and an orchestra: "Vers, l'arc-en-ciel, Palma" (1984). For 12 female voices, guitar, harp, piano, vibraphone and two orchestras: "Crossing." A double concerto for violin, guitar, and orchestra: "Spectral Canticle" (1995).

TAMBERG, Eino (born 1930), an Estonian composer, studied in the Music Conservatory of Tallinn with A. Kapi, and graduated in 1953. Worked since 1968 in the same music academy and later in the Music Academy of Estonia as a teahcer of composition. The theme in Tamberg's music is often love and eroticism (e.g. Oratorio Amores). His best known works are *"Concerto Grosso"* for an orchestra and *"Trumpet Concerto."*

For a mezzo soprano, flute, violin and guitar: "Night Songs op. 86" (1992).

TAMULIONIS, Jonas (born 1949), a Lithuanian composer. Studied in the Pedagogic Institute of Vilna. Graduated in 1976 from the Music Academy of Vilna with professor E. Balsys. Later he taught composition in the same institute and he also worked as the president of the Lithuanian Composers' Union. Tamulionis's music language is based on neoclassicism and dodecaphony. In his works he has used Lithuanian folk music as a part of his modern style.

For a solo guitar: "Preludia in Albéniz's style" (1973); "Preludia and Dance" (1975); "11 Preludes for the guitar" (1982); "Elogio de la guitarra" (1983); "Preludia-Tokata-Preludia" (1983); "Instrumental Suita" (1986); "Interval's Suita" (1987); "Tokatina" (1989). For two guitars: "Sonata for two guitars" (1978, dedicated to Monica & Jürgen Rost). For a soprano, chamber choir and guitar orchestra: "Lullaby for Dead Children" (1989). For a flute, viola and guitar: "Trio" (1993). For a flute and a guitar: "Sonata" (1993).

TAN, Dun (born 1957) is a graduate of Bejing's Central Conservatory, and holds a doctoral degree in Music Arts from Columbia University in New York. Tan Dun began his composer career with the Peking Opera. He is a winner of the Grawemeyer Award, today's most prestigiouse prize for classical music. Among the many international honors he has received, Tan Dun was cited by The New York Times in 1997 as one of the "Classical Musicians of the Year." He was elected by Toru Takemitsu to get the Glenn Gould Prize in Music and Communication, Seven Desires (2002) Concerto Yi². Dun has composed many successful large scale works as operas, symphonies and concertos, including a *Guitar Concerto*.

TANSMAN, Alexandre (1897–1986), a Polish composer and conductor. After winning the Polish national composition contest he moved to Paris (1919), where he got to know e.g. Ravel, Milhaud and Honegger. In the 1920s he also met Andrés Segovia, who asked him to compose for the guitar. The co-operation between Tansman and Segovia resulted in sev-

eral compositions, such as *Cavatina* (won a prize in the Siena International Composition Contest in 1952), *Danza Pomposa, Suite in Modo Polonico, Mazurca, Segovia and Hommage à Chopin*, which all are dedicated to Segovia. As a composer Tansman was influenced by the music of his fellow countryman, Chopin, and later by Ravel and Stravinsky; he has also written a book about Stravinsky. Musically he was always close to the ideas of Les Six. In his way to use national subjects in his compositions, Tansman can be compared with Milhaud. In 1941–46 he lived in the USA and adopted the principles of neoclassicism.

For a solo guitar: "Cavatina" (1950); "Danza Pomposa"; "Deux Chansons Populaire"; "Hommage à Chopin"; "Hommage à Lech Walesa"; "Invenzione"; "Notturno Romantico"; "Segovia"; "Mazurca" (1926); "6 Miniatyres"; "Pezzo in Modo Antico"; "12 Morceaux trés faciles"; "12 Pièces faciles Vol. 1 & 2"; "Suite in Modo Polonico" (1962); "Three pieces: 1. Canzonetta 2. Alla Polacca 3. Berceuce d'Orient"; "Variations on a Theme of Scriabin." For a guitar and an orchestra: "Concertino" (1946, published in 1991); "Músique de cour" (1960, a suite from Robert de Visée's themes).

TARRAGÓ, Graciano (1892–1973), a Spanish guitarist, violinist and composer, professor in the Liceo Conservatory in Barcelona. Tarragó gave guitar duo concerts together with his daughter Renata (born 1927). Tarragó composed pedagogic programs, études and songs for the classical guitar. As a composer he was interested in Spanish national themes.

For a solo guitar: "25 Estudios melódicos"; "Danza"; "Fandango"; "Garrotín"; "Jota aragonesa"; "Murciana, petenera & Granadina"; "Playera"; "Salmantina"; "Sevillanas"; "Tango & Falsetas para tientos"; "Tango & garrotin gitano"; "El vito-vito, Gallegada & Muñeira." For a voice and a guitar: "Canciónes populares españolas."

TÁRREGA [y EIXEA], Francisco (1852–1909), a Spanish guitarist, composer and pedagogue, who had a

Francisco Tárrega was one of the most remarkable developers of guitar playing technique and he established the use of the so-called apoyando.

major role in the development of guitar playing in the late 19th and early 20th century. He started his guitar studies in Valencia with the famous blind guitar teacher Manuel González *"Cego de la Marina."* After hearing Julián Arcas's guitar concert Tárrega wanted to become his pupil, but that was not possible due to Arcas's constant concert tours (D. Prat). According to Cimadevilla, Tárrega studied with e.g. Tomás Damas. Count Parsenti became Tárrega's patron, and with his help Tárrega studied music in Valencia. In 1869 the young guitarist got a new guitar from guitar builder Antonio Torres. The guitar was louder than before and he thus had a greater opportunity to start a career as a concert guitarist. In 1874 Tárrega continued his studies in Madrid in the Escuela Nacional de Música, supported by Antonio Conesa. There he studied composition, harmonization and according to his father's wishes, piano playing. The young Tárrega soon had to choose between the guitar and the

piano, and after a successful concert in Madrid he chose the guitar. Since 1877 he made a living by teaching and giving concerts. Tárrega got the nickname *"Sarasate of the guitar."* In 1881 he married Maria Josepha Rizo and moved in 1885 to Barcelona. The next years Tárrega worked with a new guitar program, which, in addition to own works, also contained arrangements from piano and chamber music by Mendelssohn, Gottschalk, Thalberg etc. The Spanish composers Albéniz and Granados were his friends, and Tárrega was the first to arrange their music for the guitar, eg. the Granada by Albéniz. It is told, that when Albéniz heard the arrangement played by Tárrega, he thought that it was better than his own original work. During 1885–1903 Tárrega gave concerts around Spain and Europe (1893 London, 1894 Nice, 1900 Naples and Algeria etc.). Tárrega had friends with him on his tours, e.g. English Dr. Walter James Leckie and the wealthy Valencian Mrs. Concepción Jacoby. In Tárrega's home in Barcelona, Valencia street 234, there were often concert evenings, in which his friends and pupils took part.

Tárrega was especially interested in developing the technique of guitar playing: he established the use of a leg support and the use of so-called apoyando plucking, in which he had been influenced by Arcas, as he himself told. F. Tárrega at first played the guitar with his nails, but in the early 20th century he got an arteriosclerosis, because of which his nails did not hold and the guitar virtuoso continued without nails. Tárrega never published a guitar school of his own, although he created a school of guitarists, whose most important continuers were his pupils Emilio Pujol, Miguel Llobet, Daniel Fortea and Pascual Roch. The new method of guitar playing developed by Tárrega was popular in South

America, and e.g. Mario Arenas Rodrigues, Julio S. Sagreras and Isaias Savio based their guitar schools on it. Tárrega's role in developing the guitar culture and conveying it to the 20th century was very remarkable. His ca. 360 manuscripts contain e.g. brilliant concert compositions, intimate little pieces, preludes, études and finger exercises. Tárrega was a remarkable arranger, who with his arrangements from works by e.g. Mozart, Haydn, Beethoven, Chopin, Mendelssohn, Schumann and Bach, widened the repertoire of the guitar. He arranged for the guitar e.g. the Largo from Beethoven's Sonata op. 7 and Adagio from the Moonlight Sonata and a few of Chopin's Piano Preludes.

Tárrega's complete works have been published in 5 volumes by the Spanish publisher Soneto: volume I 30 Estudios Originales (Grado elemental, basic level); volume II Estudios (Grado medio, superior, intermediate and higher level); volume III 35 Preludios originales; volume IV 31 Piezas originales; volume V 175 Transcriptiones. Publisher Chanterelle has published 2 collections of Tárrega's guitar works and arrangements. Vol 1. 48 pieces (ECH 1001) and Vol. 2. 63 pieces (ECH 1002).

For a solo guitar: <u>Mazurkas</u>: "Mazurka sobre un tema anónimo"; "Mazurka en Do «Sueño»"; "¡Adelita!"; "¡Marieta!"; "Mazurca en Sol"; "ym. <u>Polkas</u>: Emilia"; "Pepita"; "Rosita." "El Columpio en Re" (Canción de cuna); "El Columpio en Sol"; "Malagueña"; "Minuetto a la antigua"; "Pavana al estilo antiguo"; "Gavotta María"; "Tango María." <u>Valses</u>: Isabel"; "Gran Vals"; "Paquito"; "Las dos hermanitas"; "Vals en Re." <u>Tremolo études and serenadas</u>: Recuerdos de la Alhambra"; "Sueño"; "Serenata «Capricho Arabe»." <u>Folk dances</u>: "La Alborada"; "Odalisca"; "Danza Mora"; "La Cartagenera." <u>Fantasías</u>: Fantasía sobre un tema de Arrieta, Fantasía sobre un tema de Verdi." <u>Variations</u>: "Variaciónes sobre motivos nacionales"; "Variaciónes sobre un tema de Paganini"; "Variaciónes sobre la jota aragonesa." <u>Études</u>: "Estudio en forma de Minuetto"; "La Mariposa"; "Celebre estudio de Henselt"; "Estudio en la Damas"; "Éstudio de Alard"; "Estudio sobre una giga de Bach"; "Estudio sobre un fragmento de Schumann"; "Estudio de velocidad"; "Estudio de Prudent"; "Estudio de Cramer ym. <u>Preludes:</u> Lágrima"; "Endecha & Oremus; Preludios Nos. 1-7 etc..". For two guitars: "Mazurca"; "Vals a dos guitarras." Tárrega's arrangements: "Largo de Beethoven op. 27"; "Preludios Nos. 6, 7, & 20 de Chopin"; "Menuet de la Fantaisie op.78 de Schubert"; "Menuet de Beethoven"; "Menuet de Haydn"; "Loure de Bach"; "Mazurka de Chopin op. 33 no. 1"; "Minueto de Haendel"; "Scherzo de la sonata op. 2 de Beethoven"; "Largo assai de Haydn"; "Sonata 2a de Bach"; "Fuga de Schumann"; "Andante de Haydn"; "Polka de El Pobre Valbuena"; "Tango de la cadera de El Ratón"; "Feuilles variées de Schumann"; "Fuga de la 1a sonata para violín de Bach"; "Saint-Nicolás de Schumann"; "Sonata op. 13 de Beethoven"; "Preludio 15 de Chopin"; "Minuetto de Mozart"; "Nocturno de Chopin"; "Berceuse de Schumann"; "Au soir de Schubert"; "Minuetto du quatuor à cordes de Mozart"; "Romanza sin palabras número 6 de Mendelssohn"; "Adieu de Weyrauch"; "Romanza de Schumann op. 21"; "Preludio original y fragmento de la 7a Sinfonía de Beethoven"; "Mazurka de Chopin no. 22"; "Dos Preludios sobre fragmentos de Schumann y Bach"; "Marcha fúnebre de Beethoven"; "Marcha de la ópera 'Tannhauser'"; "Rêverie de Schumann"; "Fugueta de Schumann"; "Canzonetta de Mendelssohn"; "Adagio de La Arlesiana de Bizet"; "Marcha fúnebre de Grieg"; "Fragmento de la Sinfonía de Tannhauser"; "Preludio sobre un tema de Mendelssohn"; "Danza de la Sílfides de Berlioz"; "Adagio de la sonata 'Claro de luna' de Beethoven"; "Prelude no. 11 de Chopin"; "Andante de la sonata no. 9 de piano y violin de Beethoven"; "Improvisación de Prudent"; "Vals de Chopin op. 34 no. 2"; "La Arlesiana-Marcha del Rey" (Bizet); "La Africana-Coro del primer acto, La Traviata-Tema"; "El Viajero solitario"; "Andantino Cantabile de Schumann"; "Preludio no. 4 de Chopin"; "Minueto de Haydn"; "Tema de la Séptima de Beethoven"; "Staccato de Grieg"; "La Paloma-habanera"; "Minuet de Bolzoni"; "Mefistófeles de Boito."

TERZI, Benvenuto (1892–1980), an Italian guitarist and pedagogue, also known as a composer. In 1920 he won the first prize in a guitar competition arranged by the magazine "Il Plettro." Terzi published a book *Dizionario dei chitarristi e liutai italiani* (Bologna, 1937) and a guitar magazine, *La chitarra.*

For a solo guitar: "Fantasía di spagna op. 50"; "Serenata notturna"; "Nevicata"; "Carillon"; "Malinconia autunnale"; "Trillo tremolo." For four guitars: "Canzona in Eight Parts."

TESSARECH, Jacques (1862–1929), a French guitarist and composer, by his principal profession he was an engineer in Ajaccio. He gave guitar concerts in France and the USA, and in 1929 he published a work, *La guitare polyphonique*, which contains guitar compositions.

For a solo guitar: "l'Évolution de la guitare"; "Douze pièces e trois études"; "4 Melopees corses."

THEODORAKIS, Mikis (1925–2000), a Greek composer and conductor. Studied composition in the Music Academy of Athens in 1942–49 and in the Music Conservatory of Paris with e.g. Messiaen in 1954–59. At the same time he took part in the resistance movement against the Germans. His music was banned during the 1967 military takeover and due to political reasons he went to exile from Greece. In 1970-74 he made wide tours in Europe. Folk music and the Greek buzuki are central elements in his productions.

For a solo guitar: "Axion Esti" (Architektonidis); "Easy Pieces Vol. 1-3" (each collection contains 15 pieces); "Politia" (15 Pieces). For a guitar, double bass, choir and orchestra: "Lorca."

TIENSUU, Jukka (born 1948), a Finnish composer, cembalist, pianist and conductor, central figure in Finnish new music. Tiensuu studied piano playing in the Sibelius Academy with Merete Söderhjelm and composition with Paavo Heininen (diplomas 1972). He also studied in Freiburg (Staatliche Hochschule für Musik) cembalo playing and composition with Brian Ferneyhough and Klaus Huber. Tiensuu has also studied electronic, computer and Baroque music around Europe and in the USA (The Juilliard School, University of California). He has both as a performing artist and as a composer been interested in Baroque music as well as modern music. As an active musician, Tiensuu has had a part in establishing the Finnish 'Musiikin aika' festival for Modern music and he has acted as the president of the Association for Finnish Modern Music (1979-83) and he has started the Helsinki Biennale, whose artistic leader he was in 1981–87. His works have been awarded several times with notable international prizes, such as the Koussevizky Prize in 1978 and the Sonning Prize in 1978.

Tiensuu has a critical attitude towards composing and he has said: "In our time every piece has to have an own, special reason to be com-

Photo: Maarit Kytöharju

Jukka Tiensuu

posed." The strict attitude has limited the number of compositions, in this way he has constantly found new forms and ingredients for his composition, every one of which has its own, individual character. As a modern composer, Tiensuu has from the very beginning been interested in our time's avantgarde, using in every work new modern techniques of composition, such as rough tone colors and micro intervals.

Tiensuu's solo guitar work, *preLUDI, LUDI, postLUDI* (1974) with a duration of 14 minutes, belongs to the pioneering pieces in wide Finnish guitar compositions together with E. Bergman's Suite (1949) and Ej. Rautavaara's Partita (1958). PreLUDI and postLUDI are by nature expressive and meditating, whereas LUDI is more vivid. The work is composed without bars or indications of time, and Tiensuu colors the composition with e.g. micro intervals, percussion effects and Bartók pizzicatos. The *Sinistro* (1977) for the guitar and accordion is, according to the composer, a "synthesis of · serial, aleatoric, intuitive and stocastic methods." In fact the work is a simultaneous performance of two different pieces, *Dolce amoroso and Auftschwung* (M. Heiniö). The Sinistro contains an independent solo part for the guitar, Dolce amoroso, which has. also established its position as an independent guitar piece. "Sinistro" can be called a 'psychological drama' for an accordion and a guitar. In the introduction the guitarist has to strive to reach the 'same wave length' as the accordion, without success. The accordion soon answers and starts to play a solo piece *Aufschwung*, after which the guitarist gives up. In the end the instruments meet." (N. Nyqvist p. 76). Sinistro has been recorded by Pekka Vesanen and Matti Rantanen (FAILP-1A). The tone language of the Dolce amoroso is strongly dissonant with its wide intervals and a free rhythm. As coloring elements Tiensuu uses e.g. micro intervals, cluster effects and scratching the string with a nail. The work begins slowly and contains an accelerando, which lasts for the whole piece. It includes a crescendo ending in fortissimo, the texture simultaneously growing more complex.

For a solo guitar: "preLUDI, LUDI, postLUDI" (1974); "Dolce amoroso" (1977). "Drang" (1998) for guitar. For an accordion and a guitar: "Sinistro" (1977). For guitar and orchestra: "Aim" (2005).

TIPPETT, Sir Michael [Kemp] (1905–1998), a British composer. Studied

Sir Michael Tippett belongs to the most remarkable English modern composers. His solo guitar work The Blue Guitar has been influenced by a poem with the same name by Wallace Stevens.

composition in the London Royal College of Music with Charles Wood and R.O. Morris, and conducting with A. Boulton and Malcolm Sargent. Tippett, who started to compose relatively late, gained a high reputation in the 1940s. In 1940–51 he worked as the musical leader of the Morley College. After leaving that post he decided to dedicate himself to composition, but he also worked for the radio. Tippett has been awarded several prizes and honorable commendations for his composition work, and he has been especially popular in the USA. In 1991 he published an autobiography, *Those Twentieth Century Blues*.

Tippett has often been described as the most original and personal British composer. As e.g. Vaughan Williams, he was inspired by national sources; the old English polyphonic music, the Elizabethan madrigalists, Purcell and folk music are the typical features that he has combined with his neoclassical style. Typical of Tippett's music is rhythmical inventiveness and an unique polyphonic technique.

Poet Wallace Stevens saw in 1934 in an exhibition a painting by Picasso, "The Old Guitarist." Imposed by it, Stevens wrote a poem The Man with the Blue Guitar, which again Tippett's solo guitar work *The Blue Guitar* (1983) is based on. The Blue Guitar is a three-part sonata, and what is left from Stevens's poem are the moods

that the headings point at. The work contains a bit of blues nuances, rhythmically uneven accents and free variation between major and minor thirds. Tippett composed the work ordered by Julian Bream, and it is dedicated to the memory of conductor Calvin Simmons.

For a solo guitar: "The Blue Guitar" (1983). For a voice (tenor) and a guitar: "Songs for Achilles" (1961).

TRUHLÁR, Jan (1928-2007), a Czech composer. Truhlár studied guitar playing since 1948 in the Music Academy of Prague with Stepán Urban and composition with F. Picha. Truhlár has composed both solo and chamber music for the guitar. His *Guitar Concerto* (1964) reached the 2nd place in the guitar composition contest arranged by the French Radio ORTF.

For a solo guitar: "Impromptu"; "3 Bagately"; "33 Instructive compositions" (pedagogic small pieces for the guitar). For a flute and a guitar: "Sonatina semplice" op. 18; For a guitar and woodwinds: "Divertimento" op. 12; "Quartett op. 14." For a guitar and an accordion: "Kontroverse" (1970). For a guitar and an orchestra: "Concerto" (1964).

TORRENT, Ruiz Jaume (born 1953), a Spanish guitarist and composer. Taught guitar playing in the C.G.M. Liceo Conservatory in Barcelona and worked as a music publisher in Jaume Torrent Editions. Torrent played actively as a soloist, together with flutist Salvador Gratacóse and as a member of the Tarragó Guitar Quartet.

For a solo guitar: "Nits d'estiv"; "Imatges al meu voltant, suite"; "Suite no. 3"; "24 Fantasías Románticas op. 18"; "Fantasía Sonatas: no. 1 in F op. 20"; "no. 2 in f op. 25"; "no. 3 in As op. 26"; "no. in d 4 op. 27"; "no. 5 in Es op. 29"; "1a Collección de Valses" (8 valses) op. 28; "Sonatas: no. 1 op. 30"; "no. 2 op. 31"; "12 Intermezzi - Ciclo de amor op. 33"; "Gradual (24 pieces) op. 34"; "Tres piezas en el espacio op. 48"; "Del mundo de los niños op. 16"; "Referencias op. 47"; "Introducción y capricho"; "Suite no. 1 Nits d'estiu"; "Suite no. 2"; "Imatges al meu voltant";

"Suite no. 3"; "Triptico." For two guitars: "Del mundo de los niños op. 16." For four guitars: "Quarteto no. 1"; "Quarteto no. 2." For a flute and a guitar: "Tres piezas." For a voice and a guitar: "Per una sola veu op. 36."

TURINA, Joaquín (1882–1949), a Spanish composer, pianist and conductor, who studied in Seville, Madrid and in Paris in the Schola Cantorum with d'Indy in 1905–14. After returning to his home country he worked as an opera conductor. Since 1931 he worked as the professor of composition in the Music Academy of Madrid and as a music critic of the daily paper El Debat. In 1941 Turina was appointed the general music leader of the Spanish Culture Ministery. As a composer Turina was mostly a symphonic composer, but also his chamber and piano music is famous (e.g. Seville Suite). His music combines the influence of the French music, e.g. by César Franck, with flamenco music and the Moorish exotic scales. Turina's composition style has been described as Impressionistic. Turina was especially interested in Spanish national music influences, such as the zarzuelas (Spanish operettas). As suggested by Albéniz and Falla, he went into Spanish folk music as the starting point of his compositions.

Almost all of the guitar compositions by Turina were dedicated to Andrés Segovia (opuses: 29, 36, 53, 61, 69). In the *Sonata* op. 61 also jazz influences can be heard, that may have been the reason why Segovia never recorded it. *"La Oración del Torero's"* early version was composed in 1925 for Spanish lutes (laúdes Españoles) and a string quartet, later the composer made a version of it for four guitars.

For a solo guitar: "Sevillana, fantasía op. 29" (1923); "Fandanguillo op. 36" (1926); "Ráfaga op. 53" (1930); "Sonata op. 61" (1931); "Hommage à Tárrega op. 69" (1932); "Sacromonte op. 55." For two guitars: "Garrotín de Ritmos op. 43"; "Cinq danses gitanes op. 55." For four guitars: "La Oración del Torero." Arrangements for a solo guitar: "Ensueño op. 22/2" (arr. Velasco); "Orgía op. 22/3" (Azpiazu); "Miniaturas" (arr. Tokos).

Photo: Anu Tammemagi

Erkki-Sven Tüür is one of the brightest stars in the new generation of Estonian composers. His experiences among rock and cross-over music can also be heard in his art music.

TÜÜR, Erkki-Sven (born 1959), an Estonian composer of the younger generation. Studied flute playing in 1976–80 in Tallinn in the Georg Ots Music School and graduated from the Music Conservatory of Tallinn in 1984 after studying there composition with Jaan Rääts. Later he completed his studies privately with Lepo Sumera. In 1991 Tüür studied in the Karlsruhe Zentrum für Kunst und Medie. In 1989–92 he taught composition in the Music Academy of Tallinn. In the 1990s Tüür has reached international fame; several soloists and festivals have ordered works from him. He received the Estonian State Composition Award in 1991 and 1996, and a second prize from the Unesco Composition Contest. Tüür's tone language has been influenced by serality and minimalism.

For a cello and a guitar: "Spiel" (1991/92). For a flute, violin and guitar: "Draama" (1994), dedicated to Camerata Tallinn. For an electric guitar and a piano: "Architectonics V" (1991). For two electric guitars, bass guitar and an orchestra: "Concerto de facto" (1988).

UHL, Alfred (1909–1992), an Austrian teacher and composer. Studied in the Music College of Vienna, from which he graduated in 1932. He spent the following years in Zürich, Paris, Berlin and Amsterdam. From 1945 onwards Uhl taught in the Music College of Vienna and from 1970 onwards he was the president of the Austrian Association for Composer's Copyrights.

For a solo guitar: "Sonata clássica" (1937); "10 Stücke" (1939); "Französischer Walzer." For a flute and a guitar: "3 Pieces." For a violin, viola and guitar: "Trio" (1928); "Volks- und Kinderlieder."

VÄHI, Peeter (born 1955), an Estonian composer. Studied composition in the Music Conservatory of Tallinn under professor E. Tamberg, and graduated in 1980. Since 1990 he has worked as the manager of the Eesti Konsert and as the artistic leader of the Orient Festival. He has worked in cooperation with an Estonian chamber music ensemble Camerata Tallinn, and it has resulted in his instrumental trios with the guitar. The premiere of the *White Concerto* was on the 100th birthday of A. Segovia in February 1993, the solo guitar was played by H. Mätlik. The German publisher Antes has published Vähi's guitar compositions.

Peeter Vähi's music has impressions from Oriental music and from Baroque, New Age as well as rock

Photo: Even Vähi

The music of Estonian Peeter Vähi has influences from Oriental music. He has composed solo and chamber music for the guitar and the White Concerto for the guitar and an orchestra.

The Brazilian Heitor Villa-Lobos was one of the most productive composers in the 1900s and one of the most colorful personalities in music.

music. The trio *To His Highness Salvador D.* was intuitively composed two weeks before the death of Salvador Dali. It aroused international attention and it has been published by German Edition 49.

For a solo guitar: "Dance of the Moon Goddess" (1996). For a flute, violin and guitar: "To His Highness Salvador D" (to the memory of Salvador Dali, 1988); "Mystical Uniting" (1990). For a guitar and a small symphony orchestra: "White Concerto" (1991).

VASKS, Pēteris (born 1946), a Latvian composer. Studied double bass playing in Lithuania and composition in the Conservatory of the state of Latvia and graduated in 1978. His style is close to expressionism and the *"New Polish School."* He is regarded as one of the most important modern composers of Latvia.

For a solo guitar: "Ventulibas Sonate". ("Sonata of loneliness" 1990).

VERDI, Giuseppe (1813–1901), an Italian composer, grand master of opera. Verdi started his music studies with the organist of his village, and later studied in the Music Academy of Milan. He achieved great success with his opera "Nabucco", after which he composed several operas over a long period of time, which he himself called "the years of galley slavery." He used the guitar in his operas *"Othello" and "Falstaff"*, in a troubadour song in his opera *"Troubadour."* Julian Arcas has arranged a Fantasy from the themes of Verdi's opera *"Traviata"*, and Francisco Tárrega used Verdi's motives in his guitar étude.

VILLA-LOBOS, Heitor (1887–1959), a Brazilian composer and pianist. There is no final biography of Villa-Lobos, although a great deal has been written about him. The information concerning him is often quite contradictory, because he had an eccentric personality and he used to fool interviewers giving inaccurate information about himself. Even his birthday was sometimes a matter of debate, but now it is certain that he was born on March 5th 1887.

Villa-Lobos's father Raoúl, a librarian, was a skilled amateur musician. Raoúl taught his six-year old son to play the cello in his playing nights in their home, where a group of amateur musicians played the arrangements from that time's great operas. As Heitor was also interested in folk music, he also started to play the guitar, saxophone and the clarinet, and at the age of 17 he composed his first composition for the guitar: *"Panquea"* (Pan Cake). In the late 19th century there was a special salon style, the so-called chôros, in use in Rio de Janeiro, and Villa-Lobos played the guitar in a chôros group. Originally the term chôros did not mean any particular style of music, but it was a collective name for all the music (e.g. modinha, tango, polka, schottische) that the chôros groups performed. In 1918 Darius Milhaud and Arthur Rubinstein met Villa-Lobos when he was working as a restaurant musician. Villa-Lobos got thoroughly acquainted with Brazilian folk music and traveled since 1905 around Brazil collecting folk music. There are no proofs of these trips whatsoever, and one should not trust the composer's own narratives.

As a composer Villa-Lobos was self-taught and he hated all dogmaticality. He tried several times to start theory and composition studies in the Instituto Nacional da Musica, but he considered the teaching to be too conventional. When one interviewer asked about his studies, he answered that travelling is his conservatory. Impressionism may have had a strong influence on his composition style, and his idea was to make music based on pure Brazilian style. For Villa-Lobos, Bach represented something overwhelming, and idealization has a central position in his music. On the other hand, also jazz and neoclassicism had a great impact on his music, and based on all this, he created his personal tone language. As a person Villa-Lobos was complex: a genius, but at the same time a natural child with no control. Even his working methods were odd: he invited guests and took part in several conversations simultaneously or he could watch the television as he composed.

Since 1913 Villa-Lobos's production increased remarkably when he settled down and married the pianist Lucilia Guimarães. The wife may have had something to do with the great number of piano works and their technical fluency. As a composer Villa-Lobos made a debute in 1915 in Rio de Janeiro with several composition concerts, and in 1919 he was already a famous composer in Brazil.

A good friend of Villa-Lobos, who frequently visited Brazil, pianist Arthur Rubinstein, encouraged him to study in Paris, which became his home from 1923 until 1930. As Rubinstein thought, his music had excellent opportunities to succeed in Paris. The *"Les Six"* flourished in Paris, and Villa-Lobos's music contained the typical features and esthetics of that group. Also the popularity of jazz in Paris at that time made the reception of his polyrhythmic music easier. In addition to that, Paris was receptive to outside influences, and Villa-Lobos, who came from the distant and exotic Brazil, aroused interest, especially when he made up wild stories about being captured by the Indians. He had apparently read the stories from an anthropological book. Although he later had to take back his words ·in public, his reputation as a mythical composer grew. Villa-Lobos also met Andrés Segovia in Paris in 1924. Afterwards they both wrote about their meeting, though with very different emphasis. After they became friends, Segovia comissioned a guitar étude, but Villa-Lobos composed 12 études. He dedicated his *12 Études* (1924/29) and *Guitar Concerto* (1951) to Segovia.

In 1930 Villa-Lobos returned to Brazil and started to give musical education to the youth and the whole people. In 1932 he was given the responsibility to arrange the music education of his country. In 1942 he founded a conservatory, which worked under the Ministry of Education, to educate music teachers to the schools of the country. His reputation as a music pedagogue spread to the rest of South America, and he was considered the musical representative of the whole of Latin America. Despite his reputation as a pedagogue, Villa-Lobos had hardly any composition pupils at that time. In 1944 the composer started to make visits to the USA, where his works were appreciated, and he gained a high reputation. He continued his travelling life performing mainly his own works. He also gave several concerts in Europe.

Villa-Lobos became a national symbol for the Brazilians. In 1961 a Villa-Lobos Museum was founded in Rio de Janeiro, the first curator was Arminda Neves d'Almeida, pet name "Mindinha", Villa-Lobos's partner after the relationship with Lucilla Guimarães was over, and to whom most of Villa-Lobos's works are dedicated. When Turibio Santos became the curator of the museum, the Guimarães family handed over some manuscripts by Villa-Lobos, e.g. unpublished guitar works that were thought to have disappeared.

Villa-Lobos was a productive composer, whose production covers diverse styles of music and is in amount one of the widest in the history of music, consisting of nearly 2,000 compositions. Villa-Lobos's list of works contains many that have not been found. The reason to this may be that Villa-Lobos considered a piece to be composed when it was ready in his head, i.e. he listed pieces that he had not written down and pieces that he had just only started to compose. His main works are 9 Bachianas Brasileiras and 14 Chôros Suite. In both works the ensembles vary from a solo guitar to huge choirs and orchestras. His production also contains concertos, 12 symphonies, symphonic poems, operas, ballets, cantatas, songs, 17 string quartets, piano and guitar music. As to the quality, Villa-Lobos's production is very uneven.

Heitor Villa-Lobos composed many important works to the guitar literature. In the 14 Chôros Suite, Chôros No. 1 (1921) is a solo guitar work composed to Ernesto Nazareth, and in it the Brazilian folk music spirit can be heard most clearly, compared to the other Chôroses. Later Villa-Lobos also composed an introduction for the suite, Introduction aux Chôros, for an orchestra and a guitar, and it consisted of material borrowed from the early chôroses. The work has been performed very rarely, maybe due to its rare ensemble. The first to record it were Timo Korhonen and the Symphony Orchestra of the Finnish

Radio. Suite Populaire Brésilienne (1908–12) is a five-part Suite with nuances of Brazilian music, but it is based on European salon dances; it is beautiful and entertaining solo guitar music. Villa-Lobos himself arranged for a soprano and a guitar his work "Aria Bachianas Brasileiras no. 5" (1938), originally for a soprano and a cello orchestra. It is perhaps his most famous work, and it has become a classic. He also arranged for a soprano and a guitar the Modinha from a song suite, "Serestas" (1926). In the Impressionistic duet by Villa-Lobos, Distribuçâo de Flôres (1932), "The Distribution of Flowers", for a flute and a guitar, there is a kind of ritual, where he uses the guitar as a drum. The "Mystical Sextet," Sextuor Mystique (1917), is an Impressionistic study of tone colors, composed for a rare ensemble. It is in one part and it has no clear limits. Villa-Lobos's Guitar Concerto (1951) was first composed without a cadence with the name Fantasía Concertante, but on the request of Segovia he added a cadence between the second and the third part. The concerto met with negative criticism at the time, and it was compared to those of Rodrigo's and Castelnuovo-Tedesco's. It was said to lack the "charm and the strong character" that the competitors had, but the criticism can be said to be unfair. The concerto represents the simplified and Impressionistically plain late production, and it has references to his earlier works.

Villa-Lobos's most frequently played work is 5 Preludes for the guitar (1940), and there are also several recordings of it. Each prelude has a title of its own: Prelude no. 1: dedicated to the Brazilian peasant, Prelude no. 2: a North-East Brazilian fight-dance melody, a babbling melody – dedicated to an idler in Rio, Prelude no. 3: dedicated to Bach, Prelude no. 4: dedicated to the Brazilian Indian and Prelude no. 5: dedicated to the boys and girls who go to theater and concerts in Rio. The melodical line of the First Prelude is, according to Villa-Lobos, melancholic description of Brazil, but at the same time it has a malicious mood. The second part, which is in E major, is a scherzo con-

trast to the part in minor, vivid and rhythmical in nature. The Second Prelude has been composed in the spirit of the Brazilian chôro. The Third Prelude has been described as resembling a toccata, in which the subject in the second part is falling and it resembles the Baroque style. The theme of the Fourth Prelude resembles the folk music of the Brazilian Indians. After the fast arpeggios of the middle turn, the music returns to the main theme with flageolets. The Fifth Prelude has been composed in the style of a chôro valse. In the early 20th century the waltz was one of the popular dances in Brazil. Villa-Lobos's 12 Études for a guitar (1924–29) refers to the corresponding collections by e.g. Chopin, Liszt or Debussy. Similar to those, also Villa-Lobos's Études represent high quality concert music, and not only technical excercise pieces. The 12 Études and 5 Preludes are very guitaristic. Villa-Lobos's 12 Études for the guitar were composed during his years in Paris, and they are dedicated to Andrés Segovia. In the preface of the études Segovia writes: "They simultaneously contain astonishing technical solutions and figures for both hands and purely musical values without any pedagogic goals. They are concert pieces with a stable esthetic value." Études 1–6 are real études, and they are based on a technical idea. The First Étude is based on the right-hand arpeggio and the chord possibilities of the guitar are idiomatically taken use of. This results in an interesting harmony, which is ended with flageolets. The idea in The Second Étude is classical and there arpeggios are played along the whole neck. The Third Étude has a subheading "de arpejos" (arpeggios) and the étude uses a combined arpeggio-legato technique and barrée chords. The Fourth Étude has influences from the playing technique of the Brazilian folk guitar, violão, and the composer has used the harmonic possibilities of the guitar very many-sidedly. The dynamic scale varies from piano to forte fortissimo. The Fifth Étude is based on four voice chords, and it has been described as a study about the linear polyphonic possibilities of the guitar in a French spirit. The Sixth Étude has the mood of an

Argentinean tango and it is based on chord sequences. A fast tempo Un peu animé brings a virtuoso character to the music. *Études 7–12* contain versatile techniques of playing the guitar and they are combinations from Brazilian folk music, French Impressionism and American ragtime. The two first études of the second suite (études 7-12) resemble the chôro style with an improvising introduction followed by two or three dance parts. In *études 7-9* Villa-Lobos has used parallelism, which is typical of French Impressionists, Debussy etc. *The Tenth Étude* is based on the repetition of subjects played in a legato technique and polytonality. From the Tenth Étude published by Max Eschig, there are nearly 20 bars missing from bar 21 onwards. These missing bars are accessible in the script that the composer dedicated to his first wife Lucilia Guimarães, and they are held in the Villa-Lobos Museum. The missing part has also been published in the fall issue of 1996 in the American guitar magazine, Guitar Review. Especially the two final bars reveal the nature of Brazilian folk music. *The Eleventh Étude* is the most Brazilian, but it also has French influences. The music contains lots of syncopes and changing tempo. The tone language of the *Twelfth Étude* is the most progressive and it is mainly based on chords that are played in glissandos.

The professor of musicology at the University of Helsinki, Eero Tarasti, has written a very interesting book about the life and production of Villa-Lobos, *Heitor Villa-Lobos ja Brasilian sielu* (Gaudeamus 1987), which has been the source of this text. A good source about Villa-Lobos and his guitar works is also *Heitor Villa-Lobos and the Guitar by Turibio Santos* (original work in Portugese: Museu Villa-Lobos, 1975. English translation Graham Wade, Wise Owl Music, 1985). Jukka Savijoki has made an analytical study of Villa-Lobos's Études, and it has been published in the English magazine, Guitar International; (May, June and July 1987). The Finnish record company Ondine has published the whole production of Villa-Lobos in two CDs recorded by Timo Korhonen (ODE 837-2 and ODE 838-2).

For a solo guitar: "Chôros no. 1" (1920); "Suite Populaire Brésilienne" (1908-12); "Douze Études" (1924-1929); "Preludes" (1940, 5 preludes). For a flute and guitar and a female choir ad libitum: "Distribuçáo de Flôres" (1932). For a soprano and guitar: "Aria from Bachianas Brasileiras no. 5"; "Modinha." For a flute, oboe, alto saxophone, guitar, celesta and harp: "Sextuor Mystique" (1917). For a guitar and an orchestra: "Concerto" (1951); "Introduction aux Chôros."

VIOZZI, Giulio (1912–1984), an Italian composer. Studied in the Music Academy of Trieste with Wührer and Illersberg, and graduated as a pianist in 1931 and as a composer in 1937. In 1939 he returned to Italy and taught composition. His compositions are influenced by late Romanticism and Impressionism.

For a solo guitar: "Fantasia" (1949); "Racconto"; "Sonata" (1984); "Suite Variata" (1978). For a flute and a guitar: "Ninna nanna."

VIÑAS, José (1823–1888), a Spanish guitarist, composer and conductor, studied with Pedro Farreras. Gave concerts in the Western Europe and Russia. Viñas has composed 35 Romantic works for the guitar. His best known works are especially the solo guitar works *"Sueño"* (Dream) and the *"Fantasía-Originale"*, which imitates the piano.

For a solo guitar: "Andante apasionado"; "Andante sentimental"; "Fantasía-Capricco"; "Fantasía-Originale, capricho a imitación del pianoforte"; "Introducción y Andante"; "La Loca, fantasía"; "6 Pequeñas piezas fáciles"; "Recuerdo de la Coata"; "Sueño"; "4 Valses"; "Vals de concierto."

VIVALDI, Antonio, see 'Baroque Lute Composers'.

VUORI, Harri (born 1957), a Finnish composer and lecturer of musicology at the University of Helsinki. Vuori started his composition studies in the Music School of Lahti (now the Conservatory of Lahti) and continued his studies in the Sibelius Academy with Einojuhani Rautavaara and Paavo

Photo: Maarit Kytöharju

Harri Vuori, a teacher in music theory at the University of Helsinki and composer.

Heininen (diploma 1989). In his early works he has been close to neoclassicism and also used the dodekaphonic composition technique. *The Quartetto* has a slow, meditating style of composition, where no melody, figure of rhythm or harmony seems to be present, but it circles in small variations around an imaginatory pulse, which has not been marked in the sheets of music. "The polyphony of the rhythmic fragments is at its most passionate level in the *Mysticae metamorphoses nocturnae* 2 for two sopranos, a violin, cello, guitar, vibraphone and piano" (M. Heiniö).

For a solo guitar: "Mysticae metamorphoses nocturnae" (1994). For two sopranos, a flute, guitar, cello and piano: "Quartetto" (1980). For a violin, cello, guitar, vibraphone and piano: "Mysticae metamorphoses nocturnae 2" (1982/90).

WAGNER, Richard (1813–1883), a German opera composer, conductor and music author. Was born into a cultural family, and studied music in Leipzig. In the 1930s he worked as a conductor in Königsberg and Riga and later he worked as a conductor of a Chamber Orchestra in Dresden. In 1843 Wagner took part in political life and he was considered a state criminal and he had to go into exile to Switzerland.

Wagner's importance in the history of music is based on operas. He used the guitar in *Lucia's and Helden's recitatives* in the melodrama *Enzio,* and in the *Beckmesser's Serenade* in the opera *Die Meistersinger.* The serenade is called *"a Fugue with a coral"* and it is written in a style resembling that of Bach's. Francisco Tárrega has arranged the *"Fragment"* and the *March* from Wagner's opera *"Tannhäuser"* for the guitar.

WALTON, Sir William Turner (1902–1983), belongs to the most remarkable British composers of the 20th century. Started his musical career as a choir singer in the Christ Church Cathedral in Oxford and learnt to play the piano and the violin; he started to compose at the age of 12. Walton, who, as a composer was mainly self-taught, was called the Hindemith of England, although many people regarded him the continuer of Elgar's tradition. In 1946 Walton married a young Argentinean, Susana Gil, who had Spanish roots. Together they lived in Ischia in Italy. It is said that several of Walton's compositions show influence of the Mediterranean area. His production contains opera, ballet, symphony, vocal, chamber and instrumental music. He also worked as a conductor and conducted his works in several concerts around the world, e.g. in Australia, New Zealand (1964) and in the Soviet Union (1971). Walton is a Doctor Honoris Causa in seven universities (e.g. Durham 1937 and Oxford 1942). There are several books about Walton's life and works.

Walton composed a six-part song suite *"Anon in Love"* for a tenor and a guitar (1959), which was performed for the first time in 1960 in the Aldeburgh festival by Peter Pears and Julian Bream. The texts of the songs are based on poems by unknown 16th-and 17th -century writers, collected by Christopher Hassall. Inspired by the success that the suite reached, Bream asked Walton to compose a solo work, which resulted in *Five Bagatelles* (1972) dedicated to Malcolm Arnold on his 50th birthday. Walton was in close contact with composer Arnold, who helped him in the orchestration of a few works. The co-

operation also led to the composition of Walton's only solo guitar work, the beforementioned "Five Bagatelles", which was performed for the first time by Bream in Bath in England in May 1972 and also recorded by him (LP, Julian Bream 70's). The mainly diatonis-tonalic writing style of the Bagatelles is combined to the poetically and rhyth-mically vivid absolute tone language. Walton also arranged the Bagatelles for an orchestra with the name *"Varii Capricci"* (premiere 1976), whose material offers the guitarist an interesting and expanding point of comparison. Walton's long-time interest in the music material of the Bagatelles can be seen in the fact that a few hours before his death (March 8th 1983) he finished a ballet version of the work, Varii Capricci, and it had already been arranged for an orchestra; this was Walton's last musical deed. Studies about Walton's Bagatelles have been published by e.g. Carlos Bonell: *Masterworks - Five Bagatelles* (Guitare June 1983) and Michael Donley: *Walton's Five Bagatelles* (a three-part article, Classical Guitar May/June/July 1990).

For a solo guitar: "Five Bagatelles" (1972). For a voice and a guitar: "Anon. in Love" (1959); "Beatriz's song." For a requinto guitar, bass and two guitars: "2 Pieces" (Henry V Suite).

WATKINS, Michael Blake (born 1948), an English composer, studied composition with Richard Rodney Bennett. Also studied the guitar and lute with M. Jessett.

For solo guitar: "Solus"; "The Spirit of the Earth", both dedicated to Carlos Bonell. For four guitars: "Guitar Quartet."

WEBER, Carl Maria von (1786–1826), a German composer and conductor from the Romantic era. As a son of a theater leader he showed talent in music already at an early age, and he wrote his first opera at the age of 13. Weber was a skilled pianist and he also played the guitar. His production contains operas, symphonies, song plays, concertos, chamber music, lieds and masses. He has used the guitar in

many of his works, especially as an accompanying instrument in his lieds. Weber's *"Divertimento"* op. 38 for a guitar and a piano is an interesting work in the guitar repertoire.

For a voice and a guitar: "Serenata Horch leise, horch"; "Fünf Gesaenge op. 13" (1811); "Sechs Lieder op. 15"; "Maienblümelein op. 23/3." "Fünf Deutsche Lieder op. 25"; "3 Canzonetti mit Gitarre op. 29"; "6 Lieder mit Gitarre op. 42"; "Canti populari op. 54/op. 64"; "6 Lieder op. 71"; For a guitar and a piano: "Divertimento, für Gitarre und Klavier op. 38." "3 works from a song play Donna Diana" (1817): For a flute, viola and guitar: "Menuetti & Trio." For two guitars: "Duetto." For a harp and a guitar: "Romanza."

WEBERN, Anton (1883–1945), an Austrian composer and conductor, a representative of the so-called *"New Viennese school"*, pupil of Arnold Schoenberg. Webern composed in an expressionistic style, based on dode-caphony, and his form structures are tight. In 1925 he composed the *"Drei Lieder op. 18"*, for a voice, an E flat clar-inet and a guitar. The guitar is also pres-ent in Webern's orchestral work *"Fünf Sätze für Streichorchester"* op. 10 (1913).

For a voice, E flat clarinet and a guitar: "Drei Lieder op. 18." For a chamber orchestra (with a guitar): "Fünf Sätze für Streichorchester op. 10."

WESSMAN, Harri (born 1949), a Finnish composer. Studied musicology at the University of Helsinki and com-position in the Sibelius Academy with Joonas Kokkonen in 1973–78 (diploma 1989). Wessman has also taught music theory in the Sibelius Academy, he has worked as a critic and a radio reporter. In his youth Wessman played the cello. He has composed e.g. pieces for chil-dren's choirs, chamber and solo music, some of which are composed for ped-agogic purposes, aiming at making the modern tone language familiar already at an early stage. Wessman's music has been described as elegantly lyrical and non-dramatic in expressions. In an interview in a guitar magazine (Kitaristi 1-1994) he says: ..."music is maybe still above all emotional communication

Harri Wessman started to compose guitar works in the 1970s. Wessman's "Sonata Classique pour guitare seule" received a honorary mention in the composition contest arranged by the French Radio in 1991.

and it should be able to be that, although the trends nowadays blow to other directions. I still defend that idea." He also says "I want to find again simple experiences, to which people have become blind and deaf."

Wessman has been one of the most productive composers of the 1970s. He has described his work *Two Movements for Guitar Quartet* as follows: "My challenge was to create a guitar quartet in the spirit of a string quartet, i.e. so that each player would have an equal music solistic position. In the beginning each of them have to perform a sustained cantabile, and in the second part they play virtuoso tone diction." In his solo guitar work *"Sonata Classicque pour Guitare Seul"* (1991) Wessman uses a relatively rare form in guitar works, the sonata. The work is a three-part free tonalic classical sonata: a sonata-form first part, a slow second part and a vivid final. The performing indications are in French, to create a Gallic spirit. Wessman's sonata received a honorable commendation in the composition contest arranged by the French Radio in 1991. Wessman's compositions are characterized by whole-half scales, seventh- and ninth chord harmonies, fourths, the thinness of the structure and a flexible handling of the rhythm and the tempo.

For a solo guitar: "Four Episodes for a Guitar" (1979); "Three Preludes" (1981); "Sonate Classique pour Guitare Seule" (1991). For two guitars: "A Suite for Four Guitars" (1989). For four guitars: "Two movements for Guitar Quartet" (1978). For a flute and a guitar: "Towards the night" (1978); "Pan and Pitys-nympho" (1979); Duo for a flute and a guitar (1978); "Sonatine" (1993). For two voices, a flute and guitar: "Oksat kasvavat ohitseni." For a flute, alto recorder, guitar and speaker: "Rantalaitumella" (1979). For an accordion, flute and guitar: "Trio" (1981). For two flutes and guitar: "Three Pieces" (1976). For an alto recorder and a guitar: "A Suite for an alto recorder and a guitar" (1979); "Sonatine" (1984). For a choir, a guitar and a speaker: "Matkailun filosofiaa" (1992). For a soprano, flute and guitar: "Min längtan är längre än vinden" (1983). For a flute, two violins, viola, cello, guitar, double bass and drums: "Kanes' bossa."

WESTLAKE, Nigel (born 1958), an Australian composer, who started his musical studies at the age of 12, when his father taught him to play the clarinet. Later Westlake studied bass clarinet playing and composition. Westlake belongs to the most remarkable composers of Australia. In 1992 Westlake won the prize of composers of classical music awarded by the Australian Copyright Association. His production contains chamber, orchestral, television and motion picture music. Westlake's suite for a guitar and an orchestra, *"Antarctica"* (1992), was appointed the best motion picture work in 1993, it has been recorded by John Williams.

For a guitar and an orchestra: "Antarctica" (suite, 1992).

WIDMER, Ernst (1927–1990), a Swiss composer. Studied piano playing and theory in the Music Academy of Zürich and took diplomas in both of them. He also studied composition in the same institute with Willy Burkhard. Later Widmer moved to Brazil, where he developed the Music Academy, which works in connection with the University of Bahia. There he also taught composition and piano playing, and later acted as the principal.

Widmer strongly enbettered the state of modern music in Brazil and Bahia became an important center of new music of Brazil.

For a solo guitar: "Calmo"; "Vivo"; "Ronde"; "Barcarole."

WILLS, Arthur (born 1926), a British organist and composer. Studied music in Canterbury in the College of St. Nicholas and he got his doctor's degree in music in 1957. Wills has worked as an organist and taught organ playing in the Royal Academy of Music since 1964.

For a solo guitar: "Sonata"; "Moods and Diversions"; "Hommage à Ravel"; "Pavane and Galliard."

WILSON, Thomas (1927–2001), a Scottish composer, born in Colorado USA. Studied at the University of Glasgow with Sir Ernest Bullock, Ronald Woodham and Frederik Rimmer (MA 1951, BMus 1954). Since 1957 he worked as a lecturer at the University of Glasgow. In his compositions Wilson used e.g. the 12-note technique. Most of his compositions date from the 1960s. His production contains symphonies, several concertos and choir, chamber and solo instrument music.

For a solo guitar: "Canción"; "3 Pieces" (1961); "Soliloquy" (1969); "Coplas del ruiseñor" (1971); "Dream Music."

WIRÉN, Dag (1905–1986), a Swedish composer and organist. Studied in the Music Conservatory of Stockholm in 1926–31. Wirén represents the same generation in Swedish music as G.de Frumier and L-E. Larsson. Wirén grew in a musical family and he got acquainted with the music of Mozart and Grieg at an early stage. In 1931–33 he studied in Paris with L. Sabanjev, and there he also studied the music of Stravinsky, Prokofiev and the *"Les Six."* Also the music of Nielsen and Sibelius influenced Wirén's development as a symphonic composer (5 symphonies, 1932–64).

For a solo guitar: "Liten Serenad" op. 39 (1939).

WISSMER, Pierre (1915–1992), a French composer born in Switzerland. Studied in Genoa and after that in the Music Conservatory of Paris (1935–38) with Roger-Ducasse. Wissmer also studied bass continuo in the Schola Cantorum with Lesur and conducting in the École Normale with Münch. He was granted French citizenship in 1958. Since 1969 he worked as the leader of the École Nationale de Musique. Wissmer was a member of a composer group called *Jeune France.* He has composed e.g. 6 symphonies and theater music. Wissmer composed duos for the world famous French Ida Presti - Alexandre Lagoya Guitar Duo.

For a solo guitar: "Partita"; "Fantasie." For two guitars: "Barbaresque"; "Prestilagoyana"; "Ritratto del poeta." For a flute and a guitar: "Askok." For a guitar and an orchestra: "Concerto."

YOCOH, Yuquijiro (born 1925), in the town of Hita, Japan. An auto-didact guitarist and composer. Studied at first odontology, but shifted to music. In addition to guitar solos, his production contains chamber music for e.g. voices and the guitar. His best known work is a variation piece for a solo guitar from a folk song theme, *Sakura.*

For a solo guitar: Theme and variations on the Japanese Folk Song "Sakura."

YORK, Andrew (born 1958), an American guitarist and composer born in Atlanta. Graduated from James Madison University in 1980, continued his studies at the University of South California and graduated in 1986. York plays both the jazz and the classical guitar. He has been a member of the *Los Angeles Guitar Quartet.*

For a solo guitar: "Chilean Dance"; "Emergence"; "Faire"; "Green Galliard"; "King Lotvin"; "Lullaby"; "Numen"; "Sunburst"; "Suite" (3 dances); "Sunday Morning Overcast"; "Waiting For Dawn"; "8 Discernments"; "8 Dreamscapes." For two guitars: "Evening Dance"; "Virtu." For three guitars: "Rosetta," "Spieder."

YUASA, Joji (born 1929), a Japanese composer, who together with Toru Takemitsu is one of the most important composers of his country. Yuasa had a leading role in the development of electronic music in Japan in the 1950s. He has won several prizes in composition contests.

For an electric guitar (or several): "Projection VII" (1968).

YUN, Isang (1917–1995), a composer whose roots are in Korea, but was a German citizen since 1971. Studied traditional music of the western countries in Korea and Japan at the Universities of Osaka and Tokyo. Yun also studied in the Music Conservatory of Paris with Revel and Blacher in 1956–57 and in the Music College of Berlin with Rufer and Schwarz-Schilling in 1958–59. He also took part in several Darmstadt Summer Courses. After 1959 he adapted the avantgarde composition technique, which he combined with ingredients from Korean-Chinese music. Since 1964 Yun lived in West Berlin. Due to his political actions, the intelligence service of Korea took him to Seoul, where he was sentenced for imprisonment for life in 1967. In 1969 he was pardoned, and since that he worked in Berlin as a composition teacher in the Music College and since 1974 as a professor. He has composed a chamber music work *"Gagok"* (1972) for a voice (violin), guitar and percussion. The work is dedicated to Siegfried Behrend and there is also a version of it for a voice and a harp (1985) and S. Behrend's arrangement for a voice and a guitar without percussion.

For a voice (violin), guitar and percussion: "Gagok" (1972).

ZANI DE FERRANTI, Marco Aurelio (1800–1878), an Italian guitar virtuoso, composer, poet and linguist, whose roots can be dated back to a Venetian family. His friends were members of the elite of that time, e.g. Berlioz, Paganini, Rossini and pianist Maria Pleyel and author Dumas. In his youth Zani de Ferranti studied languages and literature and music in Lucca and in Bologna. He knew many languages, such as

The Italian guitar virtuoso Zani de Ferranti was a versatile culture personality.

Spanish, English and German. Influenced by Paganini, Zani de Ferranti started to study violin playing with Gerl at the age of 12, after four years he was a skillful violinist. After this he changed to the guitar, which is also thought to have happened at the suggestion of Paganini, who lived in Lucca. In 1820 Zani de Ferranti moved to Paris and then to St. Petersburg, where he for four years took care of the library of Prince Miatleff.

Zani de Ferranti's career as a concert guitarist began in 1824 with concerts in Hamburg and after that in Brussels, Paris and London. In the early 1830s he settled down in Brussels, where he worked as a professor of Italian. In 1834 Zani de Ferranti was appointed the chamber guitarist of the King of Belgium, and besides that he acted as a poet and published several collections. 12 years later he went to a concert tour to the USA together with a pupil of Paganini, violinist Camillo Sivori. When he returned in the early 1850s he once more gave a concert in Paris. In 1859 he moved to Bologna.

Publisher Chanterelle has published 14 collections of Zani de Ferranti's guitar works and his biography (ECH 900).

For a solo guitar: Fantaisie Variée sur l'air Wann I in der Früh auf steh op. 1; Rondo des Fées, Capricietto op. 2;

"Deuxième Fantaisie Variée sur l'air de Cenerentola 'Non piú mesta' op. 2"; "6 Nocturnes Bibliques op. 3"; "Ma dernière Fantaisie op. 4"; "6 Mélodies Nocturnes op. 4(a)"; "Fantaisie Variée sur le Carnevale de Venise op. 5"; "Loin de toi, caprice op. 6"; "La robe légère de Marie, Fantaisie avec variations op. 7"; "Fantaisie Variée sur la Romance d'Otello 'Assisa appie d' un salice op. 7" (same op. 3); "Fantaisie variée sur un thème favori de Weber op. 8"; "Divertissement sur 3 Romances Anglaises Favourites op. 8." "Nocturne sur la Dernière Pensée de Weber op. 9" (same op. 59); "Fantaisie variée sur l'air favori 'O cara memoria' op. 10" (same op. 1); "Introduction et Variations sur l'Air La Hongroise op. 11a"; "8 Caprices op. 11"; "Nouvelles variations sur l'air tyrolien op. 12"; "Fantaisie variée sur un air favori de Tancredi op. 13"; "Fantaisie, variations et finale sur un choeur du Siege de Corinthe op. 14" (same op. 5), "Variations favorites sur la Tyrolienne op. 16"; "Fantaisie variée sur la romance favorite Un castel d'antique structure op. 17"; "Niaiserie musicale sur une Walse suisse op. 19"; "Grandes variations sur la Tyrolienne favorite de Guillaume Tell op. 19" (same op. 6); "Fantaisie variée op. 20"; "God save the King, variation favorite op. 30"; "Fantaisie variée sur l'air anglais 'Oh! no, we never mention her' op. 37"; "6 Walses caracteristiques op. 43"; "La "Sérénade de François Schubert transcrite pour guitare seule" (1846); "Nuit de Walpurgis WoO"; "44 Exercises op. 50"; "8 Pièces faciles

WoO." For two guitars: "Concertante op. 22"; "3 Souvenirs de Moïse", "Divertissement op. 40." For three guitars: "2 Polonaises"; "Concertante pour 3 guitares op. 27." For a piano and a guitar: "Concertino op. 35; "Caprice WoO."

ZEHM, Friedrich (born 1923), a German composer. Started his music studies in Salzburg's Mozarteum and continued in the Music College of Freiburg in 1948–51. Zehm worked as a music teacher, composer and pianist and since 1963 he worked for the music publisher Schott. Typical of Zehm's music is the use of seventh and ninth chords and ostinatos and influences from jazz.

For a solo guitar: "Musica notturna" (four pieces, 1980); "6 Praeludien und Fugen" (1980). For two/three guitars: "11 Stücke für den Anfang" (1980). For a flute and a guitar: "Serenade" (1969). For a mandoline and a guitar: "Sonatina" (1980). For electric organ, electric guitar, bass guitar, drums and an orchestra: "Concerto in Pop" (1972–3). He has also used an electric guitar in his orchestral work "Rhythmophonie" (1970).

ZENAMON, Jaime (born 1953), a Bolivian composer and guitarist. Studied in Israel and Brazil with e.g. Abel Carlevaro, Alvaro Pierri and Turibio Santos. Zenamon has made concert tours to South America, Europe and the Middle East. Today he

lives in Berlin, where he teaches guitar playing and composition. Zenamon has composed pedagogic pieces, which are suitable for different levels.

For a solo guitar: "Demian Suite"; "Introducción y Forreando Caprichoso"; "Reflexoes No. 7"; "Sonando de Alegrias"; "24 Estampas: Vol 1. & 2"; "Un camello da la tierra llamada blues"; "Ventamta de Cristal - Imperrions"; "Motivo de Danza"; "Cinese Blossom"; "Preludio"; "Canción de Cuna"; "Sadmood." For two guitars: "Impressions - 12 Easy Pieces"; "Sonata Andina." For four guitars: "Contrastes." For a flute and a guitar: "3 Retratos."

ZIMMERMANN, Bernd Alois (1918–1970), a German composer. Studied in Cologne and Bonn in 1950–1960. He searched for his personal composition style in atonality and colors of music. He taught in the Music College of Cologne in 1957–70. Zimmermann published a doctoral thesis, *Fugue in Modern Music.*

For a guitar and an orchestra: "Alagona" (Caprichos Brasileiros, 1950–55); "Cabolo" (1950–55); "Un Petit-Rien" (1964). For an electric guitar and an orchestra: "Metamorphose" (1954).

Composers Whose Music Has Been Arranged
for the Guitar

ALBÉNIZ, Isaac Manuel Francisco (1860–1909), a Spanish composer and pianist, belongs to the most remarkable composers of his country. Albéniz studied piano playing in the Music Academy of Madrid already at the age of 8, but ran away from his home to give concerts in several towns in Spain. The music of Albéniz has been influenced by flamenco music. He never composed an original work for the guitar, but arrangements from his very guitaristic works belong to the repertoires of guitarists. According to a story, Albéniz heard F. Tárrega play his piano works on the guitar, and stated that the compositions had found their home in the guitar. The first arrangements of Albéniz's piano works were made by Tárrega. Later his works have been arranged for the guitar by M. Llobet, E. Pujol, A. Segovia, M. Barrueco, K. Ragossnig and R. Balaguer etc. The most famous pieces by Albéniz, which have been arranged for the guitar are: "Suite española op 47": "Granada, Cataluña, Sevilla, Cádiz, Cuba." "Asturias-Leyenda"; "Córdoba"; "Malagueña"; "Tango op. 165 No 2"; "Mallorca"; "Rumores de la Caleta"; "Oriental"; "Torre bermeja"; "Zambra granadina." For two guitars: "Bajo la Palmera"; "Evocación"; "Rumores de la Caleta."

ALBÉNIZ, Mateo (1760–1831), a Catalonian composer, organist, music critic and music researcher. (not related to Isaac Albéniz). Mateo Albéniz has become known among guitarists for his *Piano Sonata*, which Emilio Pujol has arranged for the guitar.

BEETHOVEN, Ludwig van (1770–1827), the most famous composer of the German Classicism. According to Beethoven "the guitar is like a small orchestra!." Although he never wrote for the guitar himself, guitarists have arranged his music. In 1817 Anton Diabelli collected a potpourri from Beethoven's music for the violin or flute and guitar. An arrangement by Ferdinando Carulli, L. van Beethoven's variations for the piano and the guitar are known. Also Beethoven's 4 pieces for the mandoline and cembalo are popular, they are composed in 1795-96. The pieces are: "Adagio in E flat WoO 43 no. 2", "Sonatine in C major 44 no. 1", "Sonatine in C minor 43 no. 1" and "Andante con variazioni WoO 44 no. 2." These four works are arranged for two guitars and they have been published by Ed. "Musica Budapest and G. Henle verlag."

BELLMAN, Carl Michael (1740–1795), a Swedish poet and singer, who used the chittern to accompany his songs. As a musician Bellman was self-learned, and he could not write his pieces down. His art is based on the parody technique that uses familiar melodies as the basis for new poems. Bellman's songs, rich in nuances, were often about wine, the perishing of life and famous people. The best collections are *"Fredmans Epistlar"* (1790) and *"Fredmans Sånger"* (1791). He performed for the elite and the court accompanying his famous songs with the chittern. Most of the melodies probably come from the opéra comique, some from old music books and the rest from Haydn and Händel. There is not one composition that could be proved to be his own. Bellman's music has been also arranged for a voice accompanied with

Carl Michael Bellman

both a solo guitar and an ensemble. Ulf G. Åslund has arranged a wide collection of Bellman's music for two guitars.

BRAHMS, Johannes (1833–1897) a German composer, pianist and conductor. Got his first musical education from his father, who was the double

Johannes Brahms

Ludwig van Beethoven

bass player of the Hamburger Orchestra. Brahms composed a lot already in his youth, but destroyed later a major part of his music. Brahms, who had a good sense of form, developed his Romantic tone language, which was based on Viennese classicism, with Ludwig van Beethoven as an idol. Brahms started to work with the symphony form relatively late, which is a proof of his self-criticism and respect of Classics. "Symphony is no laughing matter in our times", he said. When he at last wrote the first of his four symphonies at the age of 43, he constantly thought that he heard the "steps of the giant [Beethoven] behind him." Johannes Brahm's works have also been arranged for the solo guitar.

Arrangements for the solo guitar: "Vals op. 38/8" (A. Segovia); "Vals op. 39/15" (Ablóniz); "Romanze op. 118 No. 5"; "Intermezzo op. 76 No 7"; "Intermezzo op. 117 No. 2" (H. Käppel). For two guitars: "6 Stücke op. 76" (Krause); "Theme & Variations" (Williams); "Vals op. 39/5."

BUXTEHUDE, Diderik [Dietrich] (1637–1707), a Danish-German organist and composer. Probably lived in ca. 1637–1707. Buxtehude belongs to the most remarkable organ composers of the whole Baroque era. He composed church cantatas and organ works, and worked since 1668 as an organist in the church of Maria in Lübeck, where his church concerts *Abendmusiken"* were very popular. Buxtehude's compositions were published in 1876–78 and a collection of church cantatas in 1904. Most of his works have survived until our days. Buxtehude's works contain more than 100 organ compositions, ca. 120 church cantatas and other religious vocal works and 8 wedding cantatas and chamber music works. His music has been arranged for the guitar by Julian Bream and Erling Möldrup, among others.

CHOPIN, Frédéric (1810–1849), a Polish composer and pianist. His father was born in France, but immigrated to Poland in 1787. Chopin's mother was his first piano teacher, and at the age of 5-6 he played as a child prodigy in charity concerts and in the salons of the nobility. At the same time he composed his first polonaises. Even as a young boy he was in touch with Polish folk songs and dances as he spent his summers with his friends in the countryside of Poland. These influences played a major role when he composed his polonaises and mazurkas based on Polish folk tradition. In 1831 Chopin moved to Paris and soon achieved a high reputation as a composer, piano virtuoso and pedagogue. He gave concerts all over Europe. Chopin belongs to the most remarkable piano composers and artists. His works have also been arranged for the guitar.

Arrangements for a solo guitar: "Mazurca op. 63/3" (Segovia); "Prélude op. 28/4" (Barrios); "Vals op. 70/2" (Nunes); "8 Mazurcas op. 6 & 7" (Bobrowics); "Nocturn"; "Preludie op. 28/4"; "Valse op. 34" (Tárrega).

Claude Debussy

DEBUSSY, Claude (1862–1918), a French composer, the most important representative of Impressionism in the history of music. Studied in the Music Conservatory of Paris starting in 1873. Debussy was in close touch with the authors and painters of his time. His compositions that are based on tone colors and which differ from the traditional tonality, have greatly influenced the development of music in the 20th century. Debussy's many piano compositions were arranged for the guitar and various chamber ensembles in the 1980s and 1990s.

Arranged for a solo guitar: "La Fille aux cheveux de lin" (arranged by e.g. Barbosa-Lima, Kraft, Mills); "La petit negre" (Azpiazu); "Impressions: Clair de lune, Danseuses de Delphes, Dr, Gradus ad Parnassum, Gollivog's Cakewalk, La Fille aux cheveux de lin, Le petit berger, Reverie" (Barbosa-Lima); "4 Dances: Le petit negre, Danse bohemienne, Mazurka, Golliwogs Cakewalk" (Krause); "6 Pièces: Jimbo's Lullaby, The Little Shepherd, danseus de delphes, Dr, Gradus ad Parnassum, La sérénade interromptue" (Vereczkey). For two guitars: "2 Arabesques" (Krause); "Children's Corner, suite" (Krause); "Clair de Lune" (Papas); "Danse Bohemienne" (Bruck/Ross); "Golliwog's Cakewalk" (Roth); "Petite Suite"; "Passepied" (Yamashita). For three guitars: "Clair de lune" (Almeida). For four guitars: "Golliwog's Cakewalk" (Lord). For a clarinet and a guitar: "Arabesque No. 1"; "Danse" (Almeida). For a flute and guitar: "La Fille aux cheveux de lin" (Nesyba); "Le petit berger" (Gangi/Gatti); "Le petit negre" (Gebauer). For a clarinet, flute, oboe, violin and guitar: "Petit suite" (Nestor).

GRANADOS, Enrique (1867–1916), a Spanish composer and pianist, friend of I. Albéniz. Starting in 1877 Granados played as a trio with cellist Pablo Casals and violinist Jacques Thibaut. His music has influences from the tonadillas of Castille and from the early Romantic Spanish music. Granados did not compose originally for the guitar, but guitar arrangements *"Andaluza no. 5"*; *"Valenciana no. 7"*; *"Melancolica no. 10"* from his best known piano suite *"Danzas españolas"* (12 Spanish Dances, 1890) are often played. Spanish guitarist J. Azpiazu has arranged for the guitar all of Granados's Spanish Dances. Also *"7 Valses Poéticos"* and *"Song Suite*

Collectión de 12 Tonadillas" have been arranged for the guitar. M. Llobet's arrangements from the Spanish *Dances for two guitars e.g. no. 5 and 11* are also popular.

GRIEG, Edvard Hagerup (1843–1907), a Norwegian pianist and composer. Grieg was first taught by his pianist mother already at an early age. A desire to compose could be seen in him very early. In 1852–1862 he studied in Leipzig with E.F Wenzel (piano) and M. Hauptmann and C. Reinecke (composition). Grieg developed to be one of the most remarkable representatives of European national-Romanticism. He composed in a personal style and the roots of his works are deep in Norwegian folk music. The emphasis in his works were on piano works and songs, but he also composed orchestral works, chamber music and stage music.

Grieg's piano pieces arranged for the guitar: "3 Lyric Pieces op. 12: Valse"; "Watchman's Song"; "Fairy Dance", (arr. Julian Bream); "Waltz op. 12" (Barbosa-Lima); "Peasants Song op. 65" (Segovia, Barbosa-Lima); "Anitras Dance op. 46/3" (Feybli); "Marcha fúnebre" (Tárrega).

HAYDN, Joseph (1732–1809), an Austrian composer, the first major representative of the Viennese classicism, the developer of the sonata form. Haydn had a major influence on Mozart and Beethoven. Haydn did not compose music for the lute or guitar, but unknown lutists of his time arranged his chamber music for lute ensembles. These works by Haydn are nowadays played as chamber music arrangements for the guitar: "Cassation C", for violin, guitar and cello (originally String Quartet op. 1b Hob III: 6); "Divertimento F" for violin, guitar and cello (originally for trio baryton, which is a 6-string instrument, viola and bass, Hob XI: 44). The most famous guitar chamber music work by

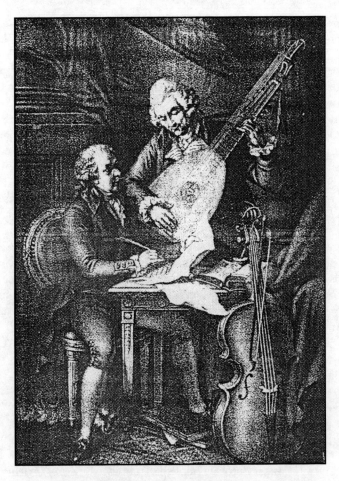

Already when Mozart and Haydn lived, their music was arranged for the lute and the guitar. In the picture Haydn plays the theorbo.

Haydn is *"Lute Quartet D"*, which is an arrangement from a String Quartet op. 2/2 Hob III: 8. Ferdinando Carulli arranged for two guitars the first part of Haydn's *"London Symphony."*

LOCATELLI, Pietro Antonio (1695–1764), an Italian composer and violinist, who studied in Rome under Corelli. Locatelli worked as a chamber musician in Mantova, Kassel and Berlin and settled in 1729 to Amsterdam, where he worked as an appreciated violinist, composer and teacher. His influence on the development of the technique of playing the violin in the 18th century was remarkable. Locatelli's music has been arranged for the violin and guitar by e.g. R. Brojer.

LOEILLET, Jean Babtiste [Loeillet de Gant] (1688–ca.1720), belonged to a Belgian music family that lived in the 17th and the 18th century. Also another composer with the same name, Jean

Baptiste L. (1680-1730) was a member of that family. *"Loeillet de Gant"* probably worked mostly in France, according to Bergmans in the court of the archbishop of Lyon. His sonatas for the alto recorder and bass continuo have been arranged for an alto recorder and guitar by e.g. R. Brojer.

MALATS, Joaquín (1872– 1912), a Spanish composer and pianist, representative of the Spanish national style. Malats's piano composition Serenata española has, as a guitar arrangement, belonged to the favorite pieces of guitar concerts.

MENDELSSOHN-BARTHOLDY, Felix (1809–1847), a German lyrical-romantic composer. Was taught in violin and piano playing and theory. Since 1835 he worked as the conductor of the Leipzig Gewandhaus Concerts and in 1843 he set up the Music Academy of Leipzig, where he invited the leading musicians of that time to teach. Simultaneously he worked in Berlin as the head of music. Mendelsohn-Bartholdy composed e.g. oratories (2), symphonies (5) overtures (e.g. Shakespeare's "Summernight's dream"), two piano concertos and the Violin Concerto in E minor, which became very popular, lyrical piano pieces and chamber music. He was not much in touch with the guitarists of his time, and he did not compose music for the guitar. His music has been very skillfully arranged for the guitar by e.g. Francisco Tárrega and Andrés Segovia.

MOZART, Wolfgang Amadeus (1756–1791), an Austrian composer. As a child prodigy he made wide tours in Europe with his composer father Leopold Mozart in 1762. In 1769 W.A. Mozart was appointed the concert master in the court of archbishop of Salzburg, later he worked as a free artist in Vienna. Mozart's theme *"O cara armonia"* has been used by several guitarist composers in their variations, e.g. Sor, Carcassi, Dobrowizc, Giuliani etc. F. Sor arranged for the solo guitar 6 arias from the opera, *"The Magic Flute,"* "Sor op. 19." Mozart's contemporary Traeg arranged Mozart's *Sonatas KV. 331 and KV. 332* for the flute and the guitar and J.G. Busch arranged 8 themes from the Opera *"The Marriage of Figaro"* for the flute and guitar. Viennese guitarist W. Matiegka has made guitar arrangements to three of Mozart's songs, *"Abendempfiendung"*, *"Das Veilchen"*, *"Vergiss Mein Nicht."* Mozart uses the lute in the fifth aria of G.Fr. Häendel's Cantata, *"Ode auf St Cecilia"* that he has arranged. Also several guitarists of our time have arranged Mozart's works, such as Segovia, Pujol, Scheit, Schwartz-Reiflingen, Fisk, Barrueco, etc.

MUSSORGSKY, Modest (1839–1881), a Russian composer, was taught to play the piano by his mother. Since 1849 he lived in St. Petersburg studying in a Military College. After leaving the military forces in 1858 he became a clerk. At the same time he got to know Dargomyzki and Balakirev, with whom he started the declamation singing. His most famous operas are "Hovanstshina" and "Boris Godunov." In 1874 Mussorgsky wrote for the piano a suite *"Exhibition Pictures,"* which Maurice Ravel orchestrated in 1922. Japanese guitar virtuoso Kazuhito Yamashita arranged it in 1980 for the solo guitar. The part *"Old Castle"* has also been arranged by A. Segovia and M. Ablóniz. There is also an arrangement for two guitars by Wallisch.

PRAETORIUS, Michael (ca. 1571–1621), a German composer, organist and music writer, belongs to the most brilliant composers of the German early Baroque. Worked in Wolfenbüttel as the organist of Prince Heinrich Julius and was appointed conductor in 1604. As a music writer his main work is *Syntagma musicum* (1615–20), which is an important source of information about the music life of that time, especially the instruments and their use. Most of his wide production is arrangements from Protestant chorals and liturgical texts. In 1612 Praetorius

published a collection *"Terpsichore,"* which contains 312 arrangements from 4-6-voiced dance melodies of French dance masters. The dances *"Courant"*, *"Ballet"* and *"Volta"* have been taken into use from this collection as guitar arrangements, and so have several other dances arranged for 3-5 guitars.

SCARLATTI, Domenico (1685–1757), an Italian composer and cembalist, son and pupil of composer Alessandro Scarlatti. Domenico Scarlatti worked in 1715–19 as the conductor of the Roman St. Peter's church and later as a cembalist in the courts of London, Lisbon and Madrid. D. Scarlatti's reputation as a composer is mainly based on his *Cembalo Sonatas*, of which there are more than 550. Scarlatti's Sonatas have been arranged for the guitar by e.g. A. Segovia, M. Ablóniz, C. Barbosa-Lima, M. Barrueco, J. Duarte, E. Fisk, L. Brouwer, etc.

SCHUMANN, Robert (1810–1856), a German composer and music critic, born into a publisher family. Since 1828 he studied law at the University of Leipzig. Schumann started to play the piano at the age of 13, but got later a stress injury in his arm, and he could not continue. In 1840 Schumann married a famous pianist, Clara Wieck. Robert Schumann is one of the most important representatives of the German Romanticism. A few of his works have been arranged for the guitar by F. Tárrega *"Berceuse"*, *"Fuga"*, A. Segovia *"Fürchtenmachen aus Kinderszenen* op. 15", *"Romanze"*, *"Canción del norte* op. 68", M. Ablóniz *3 Pezzi* op. 68 and W. Götze "14 Stücke for Two Guitars".

SEIXAS, (José António) Carlos (1704–1742), a Portuguese composer, organist and cembalist, the most remarkable representative of the 18th century Portuguese music. He has marked most of his original manuscripts with his first names only, *"José António Carlos."* Already at the age of 14, in 1718, he became the successor of his organist father in the cathedral of Coimbra, and he held this vacancy until his death. Seixas's role as a composer is mainly based on his *Cembalo*

Sonatas, which represent the gallant style between the Baroque and the Classic era. His Cembalo Sonatas have been arranged for the guitar by e.g. Javier Hinojosa.

SOLER, Padre Antonio (1729–1783), a Spanish organist and composer. Worked as a conductor in the cathedral of Lérida, and since 1752 as an organist and choir leader in the monastery of El Escorial. He studied under Domenico Scarlatti and also taught the royal family. Soler was a representative of the gallant style. His music reflects a spirit of dance and musicality and a liking of the Spanish folk music. Soler composed e.g. *"Sonatas for the Cembalo."*

TELEMANN, Georg Philipp (1681– 1767), a central German Baroque composer, who in the 18th century was even more famous than J.S. Bach. In the library of Warsaw there is a lute tablature by an unknown lutist, which contains two suites by Telemann, *Partie G-dur* and *Partie Polonaise B-dur* (a Polish Partita), which Telemann composed for a clavere instrument while in Silesia in Poland for six months. The suite contains dances that were famous in Poland at that time. The composer of these partitas is Melante, which was his pseudonym. Also his sonatas for solo instruments (recorder, violin) and bass continuo have been arranged for the beforementioned instruments and the guitar.

See also 'Composers of Other Plucked Instruments'.

YUPANQUI, Atahualpa (1908–1992), an Argentinean guitarist, composer and poet with Indian roots, originally Héctor Roberto Chavero. Studied classical guitar with Bautista Almiróni. Already as a young boy he was interested in music, especially folk music and dances, which originated in the countryside and the Argentinean pampa, far away from Buenos Aires. In the 1930s he traveled around Argentina, Peru and Bolivia, mostly riding a horse. He was proud of being a South American and as time passed he got his name Atahualpa Yupanqui as a mark of respect for the

Inkas. He collected folk music and composed more than 1,100 songs, of which ca. 700 have been recorded, and theater and motion picture music. His works, both music and poems, show his respect for and close contact with the earth. It was only in the late 1940s that his music became known around South America. Later he also made tours in Europe and Japan; he has performed in over 50 countries and published ca. 50 LPs. He has lived in Paris for a long time, where he gave a concert with Edith Piaf in 1949. His best known songs arranged for the guitar are: *"Camino del indio"*; *"Nostalgia Tucumana"*; *"Zamba del adios"*; *"El payador perseguido"*; *"Piedra y camino"*; *"Guajira."*

Abril, Anton García (born 1933) Spain
Concierto Mudéjar (1985)
Concierto Aguediano (1979)

Absil, Jean (1893-1974) France
Concerto op. 155 (1971) Pour guitar & petit orchestra

Adaskin, Murray (1906-2002) Canada
Divertimenti no. 5, 2 guitars

Alchourrón, Rodolfo (1934-1999) Argentina
Quatre pièzas

Alfonso, Javier (1904-1988) Spain
Suite en style ancien (1953)

Almeida, Laurindo (1917-1995) Brazil
Concerto no. 1, small orchestra
Amazonia
Lobiana
Almeida, Laurindo-Varela, Dan: Latiniana

Ambrosius, Hermann (1897-1983) Germany
Konzert no. 1
Konzert no. 2

Angulo, Eduardo (born 1954) Mexico
Concierto

Angulo, Héctor (born 1932) Cuba
A los estudiantes del 71

Apivor, Denis (1916-2004) England
Concertino op. 26 (1954)
The Tremulous Silence (El silencio ondulado) op. 51 (1972)

Ardévol, José (1911-1978) Cuba
Música para guitarra y orquesta

Arnold, Malcolm (1921-2006) England
Serenade op. 50 (1955), chamber orchestra
Concerto op. 67 (1958/59)

Arran, John (born 1954) England
Concerto

Asafjev, Boris (1884-1949) Russia
Concerto (1939)

de Azpiazu, José (1912-1986) Spain
Concerto Baroque

Bacarisse, Salvador (1898-1963) Spain
Guitar Concerto

Baervoets, Raymond (born 1930) Belgium
Concerto (1958)

Ballou, Esther Williamson (1915-1973) USA
Concerto for Guitar & Chamber Orchestra

Barati, George (1913-1996) USA
Concerto (1976)

Barbi, Matteo (19th century) Italy
Concerto
Duo Concerto, 2 guitars

Barbier, René Auguste (1890-1981) Belgium
Concerto op. 98 (1960)

Bartolozzi, Bruno (1911-1980) Italy
Memorie, 3 guitars (1975)

Baston, John (fl. 1708-1739) England
Concerto, chamber orchestra

Baumann, Herbert (born 1925) Germany
Konzert, chamber orchestra (1958)
Würzburg Concerto, 2 guitars
Würzburger Konzert (1992)
Memento (1962)

Becerra-Schmit, Gustavo (born 1925) Chile
Concierto, 2 guitars
Concierto no. 1 (1964)
Concierto no. 2, guitar and jazz orchestra (1968)

Bedford, David (born 1937) England
A Horse, His Name Was Hunry Fencewawer Walkins
(1972/73)
Star's End (1974), electric guitar, bass guitar, percussion

Behrend, Sigfried (1933-1990) Germany
Legnaniana, flute, guitar and chamber orchestra (1960)
Altdeutsche Tanzmusik, chamber orchestra (1971)
Campionana, 2 guitars, chamber orchestra
Conserere, chamber orchestra
Konzert (1983)
Spanische Impressionen (1981)
Spanische Impressionen (1981), chamber orchestra
Spanisches Konzert (1981)
Spanisches Konzert (1981), chamber orchestra
Stierkampfmusik
Stierkampfmusik, chamber orchestra

Belaubre, Noël Louis (born 1932) France
2 me Symphonie Concertante, chamber orchestra (1972)

Belluci, Giacomo (born 1928) Italy
Chordasei (1979)
Geometries, guitar & cello

Beltrami, Roberto (born 1958) Italy
Concerto, chamber orchestra (1996)

Benguerel, Xavier (born 1931) Spain
Concerto (1971)
Tempo (1983)

Bennett, Richard Rodney (born 1936) England
Guitar Concerto (1970), chamber orchestra

Berkeley Sir, Lennox (1903-1989) England
Guitar Concerto op. 88 (1974)

Berkeley, Michael (born 1948) England
Double Concerto (2004) two guitars and orchestra

Betancur-Gonzalez, Valentin (born 1952) Spain
Concierto no. 2, chamber orchestra (1980-81)

Bettinelli, Bruno (1913-2004) Italy
Concerto (1981) chamber orchestra

Biberian, Gilbert (born 1944) England
Concerto (1985)
Double Concerto (1989-92), cello, guitar and string
orchestra

Biondi, Juan Carlos (20th century) Argentina
Concierto

Blanquer, Amando (born 1935) Spain
Concerto, Homenaje a Juan Ramón Jiménez (1974)

Boccherini, Luigi (1743-1805) Italy
Concerto in E (arr. Cassádo/Segovia, originally for cello)

Bodorová, Sylvia (1930-1999), Slovakia
Canzone da sonar (1980)

Bogdanoviç, Dušan (born 1955) USA
Concerto (1979)

Bolling, Claude (born 1930) France
Concerto (1977), guitar and jazz trio

Bondon, Jacques (born 1927) France
Concerto de Mars (1966)
Concerto con Fuoco, chamber orchestra (1981)

Boogaard, Bernard van den (born 1952)) Netherlands
Concertino (1977) guitar, harp and chamber orchestra

Borup-Jørgensen, Axel (born 1924) Denmark
Concerto, Déjà-vu, chamber orchestra op. 99 (1982-83)

Bottje, Will Gav (20th century) USA
Commentaries
Dances real & imagined

Bozza, Eugene (1905-1991) France
Concertino da camera, guitar and string quartet (1970)

Bresgen, Cesar (1913-1988) Germany
Kammerkonzert (1965)

Brouwer, Leo (born 1939) Cuba
Tres danzas concertantes (1958), chamber orchestra
Concerto no. 1 (1972)
Concerto de Liege no. 2 (Quasi una fantasía) (1980)
Retrats Catalans (1983)
Concerto no. 3 Elegíaco (1986)
Concerto no. 4 Toronto (1987)
Concerto no. 5 di Helsinki (1991-92)
Concerto no. 7 de Volos (1996) for guitar and orchestra
Concerto no. 8 de la Habana
Concerto no. 9 Cantata de Perugia (1999)
Concerto de Benicassim
Double concerto, omaggio à Paganini (1955) violin, guitar
Double concerto no. 10 (2004) for two guitars and orchestra

Brumby, Colin (born 1933) Australia
Guitar Concerto (1985)

Brustad, Karsten (born 1959) Norway
Prevratim (1990)

Burgess, Anthony (1917-1993) England
Concerto Grosso, 4 guitars

Cano, Francisco (born 1940) Spain
Concierto Oriental

Cardi, Mauro (born 1955) Italy
Silete Venti per chitarra e ensemble (1986)

Cardoso, Jorge (born 1949) Argentina
Concierto Guarani
Suite Indiana, 2 guitars and orchestra
Quattro piezas

Carlevaro, Abel (1918-2001) Uruguay
Concierto del Plata
Fantasía Concertante, guitar, percussion, string quartet

Carulli, Ferdinando (1770-1841) Italy
Concerto in A op. 8a, chamber orchestra
Petit Concerto de société in e op. 140, chamber orchestra
Duo Concerto in G, flute, guitar and chamber orchestra

Casanova, André (born 1919) France
Concerto da camera (1974)

Castelnuovo-Tedesco, Mario (1895-1968) Italy
Concerto no. 1 in D op. 99 (1939)
Serenade in F op. 118 (1943) chamber orchestra
Capriccio diabolico op. 85b (1945) (comp. arr.)
Concerto no. 2 in C op. 160 (1953)
Concerto op. 201, 2 guitars (1962)

Casterede, Jacques (born 1926) France
Concerto (1973)
Concerto no. 2 (1986)
Rapsodie pour un jour de fête

Cerf, Jacques (born 1932) Switzerland
Concerto capriccioso

Chappel, Herbert (born 1934) England
Caribbean Concerto

Charpentier, Jacques (born 1933) France
Concerto no. 2 (1970), chamber orchestra

Chaynes, Charles (born 1925) France
Visions Concértantes (1976), chamber orchestra

Chiereghin, Sergio (born 1933) Italy
Duo Concerto (1984), 2 guitars

Chobanian, Loris O. (born 1933) Iraq/USA
Concerto

Constant, Franz (1910-1996) Belgium
Primavera, concertino op. 130

Constant, Marius (1925-2004) Romania/France
Strings, electric guitar, cembalo and chamber orchestra

Cordero, Ernesto (born 1946) Puerto Rico
Concierto Evocativo (1977)
Concierto Antillano (1983)
Concierto de Bayoan
Concierto Criollo, guitar and string quartet
Fantasía sobre tres cuadros de José Campeche (1974)

Corigliano, John (born 1938) USA
Troubadours (1993)

Corregia, Enrico (born 1933) Italy
Ephemeral, chamber orchestra

Croucher, Terence (born 1944) England
Concerto

Curtis-Smith, Curtis (born 1941) USA
Songs and Cantillations (1983)

Dagosto, Sylvain (born 1927) France
Échos du soir, chamber orchestra

Damase, Jean-Michel (born 1928) France
Ballade (1975)

David, Thomas Christian (1925-2006) Austria
Konzert

Degadillo, Luis Abraham (1887-1961) Nicaragua
Concertino in G

Delanoff, Robert (born 1942) Germany
Konzert für Gitarre (1973/74)
Konzert, 4 guitars (1988)

Denisov, Edison (1929-1996) Russia
Concerto (1981)

Dodgson, Stephen (born 1924) England
Concerto no. 1 (1956)
Concerto no. 2 (1972)

Domeniconi, Carlo (born 1947) Italy
Concertino in Fa (1978)
El Mato (1979)
Concerto per chitarra e archi (1986), chamber orchestra
Concerto (1987)
Concerto no. 5 (1988)

Domingos Brandão, José (born 1904)
Lusitano

Duarte, John W. (1919-2004) England
A Tudor Fancy

Dyens, Roland (born 1955) France
Concerto Métis, chamber orchestra

Falckenhagen, Adam (1697-1761) Germany
Concerto in F, lute & chamber orchestra

Fash, Johann Friedrich (1688-1758) Germany
Concerto in D, lute & chamber orchestra

Feldmann, Klaus (born 1951) Germany
Doppel konzert (1982), 2 guitars

Fernández, José Manuel (born 1956) Spain
Concierto no. 1

Fetler, Paul (born 1920) USA
3 Impressions

Flosman, Oldrich (1925-1998) Czech Republic
Concertino (1978)

Fongaard, Björn (1919-1980) Norway
Concerto op. 143 no. 2 (1977)

Foss, Lukas (born 1922) USA
Orpheus, guitar, violin, viola, cello (1974)
American Landscapes (1989)

Françaix, Jean-René Désiré (1912-1977) France
Concerto (1982-83)

Francis, Mark (born 1936) France
Guitar concerto

Franco, John (1908-1988) USA
Concerto lirico no. 5 (1971)

Frost, Donald (born 1951) USA
Concerto no. 1 (ed. 1983)

Fulkerson, James (born 1945) USA
Guitar Concerto (1972)

Fürstenau, Wolfram (1928-1992) Germany
Renaissance pour le Presence, guitar and piano

Galán, Natalio (1917-1985) Cuba
Concierto (1957)

Galindo (Dimas), Blas (1910-1993) Mexico
Concerto for Guitar and Symphonic Band (1988)

Gentile, Ada (born 1947) Italy
Shading

Gervasio, Raffaele (1910-1994) Italy
Duo Concerto, violin and guitar, chamber orchestra

Giacometti, Antonio (1957) Italy
Zone di confine, guitar and string band and three percussions

Gilardino, Angelo (born 1941) Italy
Concerto "Leçones de ténèbres", chamber orchestra

Giuliani, Mauro (1781-1829) Italy
Concerto in A major op. 30, chamber orchestra
Concerto in A major op. 36, chamber orchestra
Variations op. 38, chamber orchestra (arr. Tortona)
Concerto in F major op. 70, chamber orchestra
Variations & Polonaise op. 65 guitar and string quartet, arr. for an orchestra

Glise, Anthony (born 1956) USA
Concerto no. 1 "The Glohe Rooms" op. 11

Gnàttali, Radamés (1906-1988) Brazil
Concertino no. 1
Concerto de Copacabana
Concerto no 4, à Brasileira, chamber orchestra
Concerto Carioca no. 1, electric guitar

Gould, Morton (1913-1996) USA
Troubadour Music, 4 guitars (1968)

Grahn, Ulf (born 1942) Sweden
Concerto (1985)

Gramatges, Harold (born 1918) Cuba
Para la dama duende
Concerto

Gray, Steve (born 1947) England
Guitar Concerto (1987)

Green, Ole-Carsten (1922-2003) Denmark
Concertino (1985)

Grisoni, Renato (born 1922) Italy
Cantico di sora luna (Fantasia) op. 82

Guedes, Rafael (born 1956) Cuba
Concierto Latinoamericano

Hájku, Michael (pseudonym of Burghauser, Jarmil) (1921-1997) Czechoslovakia
Concerto (Ommagie a F. X. Brixi) (1978)

Halffter, Cristóbal (born 1930) Spain
Partita (1973)

Halffter, Ernesto (1905-1989) Spain
Concierto

Hallnäs, Hilding (1903-1984) Sweden
Konsert för gitarr och stråkkvartett, quitar & string quartet

Hartig, Heinz Friedrich (1907-1969) Germany
Concertante Suite op. 19 (1954)

Harvey, Richard (born 1953) England
Concerto Antico

Haufrecht, Herbert (1909-1998) USA
Divertimento (1982)

Haug, Hans (1900-1967) Switzerland
Concertino, chamber orchestra (1950)
Duo Concerto, flute and guitar (1966)

Hauswirth, Hans (1901-1979) Germany
Konzert, 2 guitars

Haydn, Joseph (1732-1809) Austria
Concerto in Sol no. 2 (1786) (arr. Azpiazu original 2 lire musicali)

de Heer, Hans (1927-2002) Netherlands
Concerto, chamber orchestra (1968)

Hekster, Walter (born 1937) Netherlands
Concerto (1981)

Henze, Hans Werner (born 1926) Germany
An eine Äeolsharfe) (1985-86)

Hétu, Jacques (born 1938) Canada
Concerto, chamber orchestra

Hewitt, Harry (born 1921) USA
Concerto op. 463

Heydecker, Thomas (20th century) England
Concerto Serenissime, 2 guitars

Hlouschek, Thedor (1911-2000) Germany
9 Volktänze für Gitarre und Ensemble (1972/74)
Kleines Konzert, chamber orchestra (1975)
Concerto Barocco, chamber orchestra (1979)
Konzert für Gitarre und Kammerorchester (1988/89)

Hovhaness, Alan (1911-2000) USA
Guitar Concerto op. 325 (1979)
Guitar Concerto op. 331 (1979)

Hultberg, Sven (1912-1991) Sweden
Sequenze seriosi, guitar and bass guitar (1979)
Zdenko (Precious Rock), guitar and bass guitar (1980)

Hundsnes, Svein (born 1951) Norway
Concerto, chamber orchestra (1983)

Hunt, Oliver (1934 2000) England
Concerto

Hvidtfelt Nielsen, Svend (born 1958) Denmark
Lovesong, guitar and cello (1987-88)

Hvoslef, Ketil (born 1939) Norway
Double Concerto (1977), flute, guitar and chamber orchestra

Hyldgaard, Søren (born 1962) Denmark
Concertino

Hämeenniemi, Eero (born 1951) Finland
Concerto (1980) electric guitar

Handel, Georg Friedrich (1685-1750) Germany
Concerto in B op. 4 no. 6 (arr. Azpiazu, original for organ)
Concerto in A, chamber orchestra (arr. Barbosa-Lima)

Ibarrondo, Félix (born 1943) Spain
Amairuk (1979) chamber orchestra
Abyssal, 2 guitars (1982)

Ivanov-Kramskoi, Aleksander (1912-1975) Russia
Concerto in a
Concerto no. 2 in B

Jalkanen, Pekka (born 1945) Finland
Concerto for Guitar and Small Orchestra (1988)

Johanson, Bengt (1914-1989) Finland
Concerto, electric guitar and chamber orchestra

Johanson, Bryan (born 1951) USA
Toccata Festiva op. 46

Josephs, Wilfred (1927-1997) England
Encore op. 82b (1972) guitar, harp, cembalo and orchestra
Sartoga Concerto op 82a (1972) guitar, harp, cembalo and orchestra

Jouvin, Pierre (20th century) France
Concerto

Kagel, Mauricio (born 1931) Argentina
Sonant (1961), electric guitar, harp, double bass and orchestra

Kangro, Raimo (1949-2001) Estonia
Konzert op. 46, guitar and cello

Kaschlajew, Murad (born 1931) Russia
Scherzo

Kelkel, Manfred (born 1929) Germany
Zagreber Konzert op. 19

Kelly, Bryan (born 1934) England
Guitar Concerto (1978)

Kenyon, Stephen (born 1962) England
Concerto no 1 (1992) guitar & guitar orchestra
Concerto no 3 (1997) chamber orchestra

Kernis, Aaron Jay (born 1960) USA
Double Concerto (1996) violin, guitar and orchestra

Kikta, Valeri (born 1941) Russia
Concerto

Kirchtein, Harold (20th century) Germany
Serenata-dolorosa

Kleynjans, Francis (born 1951) France
Concerto no. 1 in B flat op. 62, chamber orchestra
Concertino Baroque no. 2 in D op. 80, chamber orchestra
Concerto op. 101 in D, 2 guitars and chamber orchestra

von Koch, Erland (born 1910) Sweden
Fantasia Melodica, chamber orchestra or woodwind quintet

Kohaut, Karl (1726-1784) Austria
Concerto in A, lute & chamber orchestra
Concerto in B flat, lute & chamber orchestra
Concerto in D, lute & chamber orchestra
Concerto in F no. 1, lute & chamber orchestra
Concerto in F no. 2, lute & chamber orchestra

Kõrvits, Tõnu (born 1969) Estonia
Concerto Semplice (1992), guitar & chamber orchestra
Songs on the Bridge of Encounters

Koshkin, Nikita (born 1956) Russia
Concerto

Kotoński, Wlodzimierz (born 1925) Poland
Concerto per quattro, harp, guitar, cembalo, piano and chamber orchestra

Kox, Hans (born 1930) Netherlands
Concertino chitarristico, 3 guitars (1981)

Krebs, Johann Ludwig (1713-1780) Germany
Concerto in C, lute & chamber orchestra
Concerto in F, lute & chamber orchestra
Concerto in G (arr. in F, Chiesa), lute & chamber orchestra

Labrouve, Jorge (born 1948) Spain
Concerto (1980)

van den Langenberg, Jan (born 1954) Netherlands
Concerto

Lauro, Antonio (1917-1986) Venezuela
Concierto (1956)

Lazaro, José (born 1941) Spain
Concierto no. 2

Le Bordays, Christiane (born 1937) France
Concerto de Azul (1970)

de Leeuw, Ton (1926-1996) Netherlands
Concerto (1987-88), 2 guitars and a chamber orchestra

Legnani, Luigi (1790-1877) Italy
Concerto op. 28

Letelier, Alfonso (1912-1994) Chile
Concierto op. 29 (1960/61)

L'Hoyer, Antoine (1768-ca. 1840) France
Concerto op. 16, string quartet

Linjama, Jyrki (born 1962) Finland
Partita (1996), guitar & string quartet

Llanas, Albert (born 1957) Spain
Concierto, chamber orchestra

Machover, Tod (born 1953) USA
Concerto (1978)

Maiztegui, Iaidoro (20th century) Spain
Homenaje a cuatro vihuelistas Españoles del siglo XVII

Marcello, Benedetto (1686-1739) Italy
Concerto in c (b) (original for oboe)

Marco, Thomas (born 1942) Spain
Concierto Eco
Concierto Guadiana (1974)
Concierto def agua

Margola, Franco (1908-1992) Italy
Concerto breve

Mari, Pierrette (born 1929) Ranska
Concerto (1971)

McGuire, Edward (1948) Scotland
Concerto for guitar & strings (1988)

Meijering, Chiel (born 1954) Netherlands
De geur blijft hangen (1982), 3 guitars

Méranger, Paul (born 1936) France
Concerto op. 25 (1981)

Meriläinen, Usko (1930-2004) Finland
Guitar Concerto (1991)

Miletic, Miroslav (born 1925) Yugoslavia
Concerto (1977)

Molino, Francesco (1768-1847) Italy
Grand Concerto en mi minore op. 56, chamber orchestra

Montes, Alfonso (born 1955) Venezuela
Fantasía Venezolana, 2 guitars

Montsalvatge, Xavier (1912-2002) Spain
Metamorfosis de concerto (1982)

Morel, Jorge (born 1931) Argentina
Suite de Sur

Moreno Torroba, Federico (1891-1982) Spain
Dialogos (1974)
Sonatina (composer's arr. for guitar and chamber orchestra)
Concierto de Castilla

Homenaje a la seguidilla
Concierto Ibérico, 4 guitars (1976)
Concierto en Flamenco, flamenco guitar
(12) Interludios (original for a woodwind quintet) arr. for guitar and orchestra
Romancillos

Morricone, Ennio (born 1928) Italy
Terzo Concerto

Mortari, Virgilio (1902-1993) Italy
Piccolo Concerto, chamber orchestra

Musgrave, Thea (born 1928) Scotland
Soliloquy II (1980) chamber orchestra
Soliloquy III (1980) (version of Soliloquy II, guitar and 9 instruments)

Neuman, Ulrik (1918-1994) Denmark
Guitar Concerto (1993)

Nicolau, Dimitri (born 1946) Greece
Concerto no. 1 op. 69

Noble, Ramón (1920-1999) Mexico
Concertino Mexicano

Nobre, Marlos (born 1939) Brazil
Concierto para guitarra op. 51 (1980)

Noda, Teryuki (born 1940) Japan
Concerto (1986)

Nogueira, Theodoro A. (born 1913) Brazil
Concertino (1969)

Nordgren, Pehr Henrik (born 1944) Finland
Concerto op. 126 (2004/2005)

Novák, Jan (1921-1984) Czech Republic
Concerto per Euridice

Ohana, Maurice (1914-1992) France
Concerto, Trois Graphigues (1950-57)
Si le jour paraît..., guitar and chamber orchestra

Otero, Francisco (born 1941) Spain
Canción Desesperada (1977)
Endecha para una encordatura, 2 guitars (1974)

Palau, Manuel (1893-1967) Spain
Concierto Levantino (1947)

Panin, Pjotr (born 1939) Russia
Concerto no. 1 (1980)
Concerto (1982)

Parrot, Ian (born 1916) England
Concertino (1973), 2 guitars and a chamber orchestra

Patachich, Iván (1922-1993) Hungary
Concerto (1961)

Perez Puetes, José Angel (1951) Cuba
Etcétera, 2 guitars
Para una hada con hilos de oro
Estimulaciones

Peruzzi, Aurelio (born 1921) Italy
Concerto, 4 guitars(1973)

Petit, Pierre (1922-2000) France
Concerto (1964), 2 guitars

Pezzati, Romano (born 1939) Italy
Aura, recorder and guitar and chamber orchestra (1984)

Piazzolla, Astor (1921-1992) Argentina
Concerto, Hommage à Liége (1985), bandoneón, guitar and chamber orchestra

Picchi, Silvano (born 1922) Argentina
Divertimento, 2 guitars (1951)

Pizzini, Carlo Alberto (1905-1981) Italy
Concerto para tres hermanas

Ponce, Manuel Maria (1882-1948) Mexico
Concierto del Sur (1941), dedicated to A. Segovia

Porrino, Ennio (1910-1959) Italy
Concerto dell' Argentarola (1953)

Previn, André George (born 1929) Germany/USA
Concerto, cello or French horn and guitar

Prodigo, Sergio (born 1949) Italy
Concerto no 3 op. 69 – Provenzale

Prošev, Toma (1931-1996) Macedonia
Gitarrenkonzert op. 38 (1968)

Quelle, Ernst August (born 1931)
Variationen über ein Irishes Volkslied, chamber orchestra

Rak, Štěpán (born 1945) Czech Republic
Concerto in C (1975)
Vodni Znameni (Water Mark)
Concerto no 2 "Hiroshima" (1987)

Ravinale, Irma (born 1942) Italy
Sinfonia concertante

Rechberger, Herman (born 1947) Finland
Concerto Floral (1992-93)
Concerto Nordico (1993)
Goya (1992) 4 guitars & orchestra

Rechin, Igor (born 1941) Russia
Guantamera Concerto (1983)
Russian Concerto (1986), 7-string guitar

Remacha, Fernando (1898-1984) Spain
Concierto (1955)

Rodrigo, Joaquín (1901-1999) Spain
Concierto de Aranjuez (1939) (dedicated to R. Sáinz de la Maza)
Fantasía para un Gentilhombre (1954) (dedicated to A. Segovia)
Concierto Andaluz (1967), 4 guitars
Concierto Madrigal (1968), 2 guitars
Concierto para un Fiesta (1982)
Rincones de España (arr. Romero)
Sones en la Giralda (arr. Romero)

Ruders, Poul (born 1949) Denmark
Psalmodies (1989)

Ruiz, **Lopez** Valentin (born 1939) Spain
Concierto de Bellver
Suite del amor de amores

Ruiz-Pipó, Antonio (1934-1997) Spain
Tablas, guitar and strings (1968)
Concertino, Tres en raya, chamber orchestra (1978)
Concerto no. 3 (1993)

Rypdal, Terje (born 1947) Norway
Ineo, electric guitar, choir and orchestra op 29 (1983)
The Vanguardian op. 46 (1989), jazz guitar
In Autumn, electric guitar, trumpet and orchestra (1979)
Déjà-vu op. 54 (1991), soprano saxophone, bass clarinet, baritone saxophone, electric guitar and orchestra
Largo op. 55 (1991), electric guitar, strings and percussion
Double concerto op. 58 (1992), 2 electric guitars and orchestra

Rääts, Jaan (born 1932) Estonia
Concerto op. 88 (1992) chamber orchestra
Concerto for violin, guitar & orchestra op.106 (1998)
Concerto for two guitar & orchestra op.111 (1999)
Concerto for flute, guitar & orchestra op.117 (2001)

Sandström, Sven-David (born 1942) Denmark
Lonesome (1982/83)

Santórsola, Guido (1904-1994) Italy/Uruguay
Concertino (1942)
Concerto no. 2 (1977)
Concerto no. 3 (1983), chamber orchestra
Concerto, 3 guitars
Concerto (1966), 2 guitars
Concerto (1972), 4 guitars
Double Concerto (1973), guitar and cembalo
Concerto no. 5, guitar and double string quartet
Concertino, 3 guitars and cembalo or piano
Recitativo, Fantasia e Finale, strings, guitar and celesta

Schafer, R. Murray (born 1933) Canada
Guitar Concerto (1989)

Schmidt, Ole (born 1928) Denmark
Koncert (1976)

Schneider, Heinrich (1890-1978) Canada
Scherzo Capriccioso

Scholz, Bernd (1911-1969) Germany
Japanisches Konzert

Schwantner, Joseph (born 1943) USA
From Afar… a Fantasy (1987), also a version for chamber orchestra

Schwertsik, Kurt (born 1935) Austria
Guitar Concerto (1979) op. 35

Schulthorpe, Peter (born 1929) Australia
Guitar Concerto (1980)
Nourlangie for Guitar, Strings & Percussion (1989)

Seegner, Franz (fl. early 19th century) Austria
Konzertvariationen op. 30

Selby, Philip (born 1948) England
Concerto
From the Fountain of Youth

Sierra, Roberto (born 1953) USA
Concierto Barocco
Concierto (for D. Tanenbaum)
Concierto, 2 guitars
Concierto, violin and guitar

Smit Sibinga, Theo (1899-1958) Netherlands
Concert (1958)

Smith Brindle, Reginald (1917-2003) England
Concertino (1951), chamber orchestra
Concerto (1953)
Guitar Concerto (1977)

Sprongl, Norbert (1892-1983) Austria
Konzert, flute and guitar

van der Staak, Pieter (born 1931) Netherlands
Concertino Romantico (1961)
Concertino I (1965)
Concertino II (1966)
Concertino III (1970)

Stradella, Alessandro (1644-1682) Italy
Concerto grosso, 2 violins, guitar (originally lute) and chamber orchestra

Strandsjö, Göte (1916-2001) Sweden
Concertino (1955)

Taira, Yoshihisa (born 1938) Japan
Pénombrest (1981), 2 guitars

Takács, Jenö (1902-2005) Hungary
Partita op. 55a (1949-50), guitar or cembalo and orchestra

Takemitsu, Toru (1930-1996) Japan
To the Edge of Dream (1983)
Vers, l'arc-en-ciel, Palma (1984), oboe d'amore, guitar and orchestra
Spectral Canticle (1995), guitar, violin and orchestra
Grossing, 12 female voices, guitar, harp, piano, vibraphone and orchestra

Tan, Dun (born 1957) China
Concerto Yi² (1996)

Tanenbaum, Elias (born 1924) USA
Concerto (Waves 1983)

Tansman, Alexandre (1897-1986) Poland/France
Concertino (1946, published in 1991)
Músique de cour (1960)

Theodorakis, Mikis (1925-2000) Greece
Lorca, guitar, double bass, harp and orchestra

Tomasi, Henri (1901-1971) France
Concerto
Pastorales provençales, 2 guitars, flute, piccolo and chamber orchestra

Torok, Alan (born 1947) Austria/Canada
Guitar Concerto (1980)

Truhlár, Jan (1928-2007) Czech Republic
Concerto (1964)

Tulev, Toivo (born 1958) Estonia
Moradas, 3 electric guitars

Twigg, Geoffrey (born 1951) England
Concerto

Tüür, Erkki-Sven (born 1959) Estonia
Concerto de facto (1988), 2 electric guitars, bass guitar and orchestra

Ugoletti, Paolo (born 1956) Italy
Serenata

Walker, Timothy (born 1943) South Africa/England
Concerto for a Rainbow

Valla, Manuel (1920-1984) Spain
Concerto

Walter, Fried (1907-1996) Germany
Reflexe
Suite

Vargas-Wallis, Darwin Horacio (born 1925) Brazil
Rapsodia para dias de duelo y Esperanza (1961/62)

Watkins-Blake, Michael (born 1948) England
Clouds and Eclipses (1973)
Psallein (1971), guitar, cembalo and percussion

Weiss, Harald (born 1949) Germany
Nachtmusik, guitar, guitar orchestra, strings and percussion

Weiss, Johann Sigismund (1690-1737) Germany
Concerto in D, lute & chamber orchestra

Werdin, Eberhard (1911-1991) Germany
Concertino, flute, guitar and chamber orchestra

Verhagen, Marc (born 1943) Belgium
Concerto (1986)

Westlake, Nigel (born 1958) Australia
Antarctica, Suite for Guitar & Orchestra

Wiener, Jean (1896-1982) France
Duo Concerto, 2 guitars (1966)

Villa-Lobos, Heitor (1887-1959) Brazil
Concerto (1951)

Wissmer, Pierre (1915-1992) Switzerland
Concerto

Vivaldi, Antonio (1678-1741) Italy
Concerto in A RV82 (originally lute trio in C), chamber orchestra
Concerto in D RV93 (originally lute quartet), chamber orchestra
Concerto in C RV425 (originally mandolin concerto), chamber orchestra
Concerto in d RV540, viola and guitar, chamber orchestra (originally viola d'amore and mandolin)
Concerto in G RV532, 2 guitars (originally 2 mandolins), chamber orchestra

Vlad, Roman (born 1919) Romania, Italy
Ode super "chrysea phormix", chamber orchestra (1962/64)

Wüsthoff, Klaus (born 1922) Germany
Collagen
Concierto de Samba, 3 guitars (also chamber orchestra)

Vähi, Peeter (born 1955) Estonia
White Concerto (1991)

Yoshimatsu, Takahashi (born 1953) Japan
Pegasus Effect op. 21, Concerto

Zehm, Friedrich (born 1923) Germany
Concerto in Pop (1972-73), electric guitar, organ, bass, percussion and orchestra

Zimmermann, Bernd Alois (1918-1970) Germany
Alagona (Caprichos Brasileiros) (1950-55)
Cabolo (1950-55)
Un "Petit-Rien" (1964)
Metamorphose (1954), electric guitar

Complementary List of Composers
who have Composed Music for the Guitar

Aguirre, Julian (1868-1924) Argentina

Alais, Juan (1844-1914) Argentina

Alcazar, Miguel (born 1942) Mexico

Alemann, Eduardo A. (born 1922) Argentina

Alfonso, Nicolas (1913-2001) Spain

Amador, Efrain (born 1947) Cuba

Ameller, André (1912-1990) France

Amy, Gilbert (born 1936) France

Anderson, Beth (born 1950) USA

Andriopouios, Ilias (born 1950) Greece

Angulo, Eduardo (born 1954) Mexico

Angulo, Hector (born 1932) Cuba

Anido, María Luisa (1907-1996) Argentina

Applebaum, Edward (born 1937) USA

Araujo, Francisco (born 1949) Brazil

Arca, Paulo (born 1953) Italy

Ardévol, Jose (1911-1981) Cuba

Argento, Dominick (born 1927) USA

Arolas, Eduardo (1892-1924) Argentina

Arran, Jon (born 1945) England

Assad, Sergio (born 1952) Brazil

Ayala, Hector (1914-1989) Argentina

Azevedo, Waidyr (1923-1980) Brazil

Baden Powell, Roberto (1937-2001) Brazil

Baksa, Robert (born 1938) USA

Balada, Leonardo (born 1933) Spain,USA

Barlow, Fred (1881-1951) France

Basevi, Abramo (1818-1885) Italy

Bauer, Jerzy (born 1936) Poland

Bauld, Alison (born 1944) Australia

Beat, Janet (born 1937) England

Becker, Günther (1924-2007) Germany

Behr, Franz (1837-1898) Germany

Bellow, Alexander (1912-1976) Russia, USA

Benedetti, Fred M. (born 1957) USA

Benham, Patrick (born 1940) England

Bensa, Olivier (born 1951) France

Beraldo, Primo (born 1924) Italy

Berg, Gunnar (1909-1989) Denmark

Bialas, Günther (1907-1995) Germany

Blanquer, Amando (born 1935) Spain

Boda, John (1922-2002) USA

Bonell, Carlos (born 1949) England

Bonfá, Luiz (1922-2001) Brazil

Boudounis, Evangelos (born 1950) Greece

Bowers, Timothy (born 1954) England

Boydell, Brian (1917-2000) Ireland

Bracali, Gianpaulo (born 1941) Italy

Branca, Glenn (born 1948) USA

Braun, Peter Michael (born 1936) Germany

Bravo, Enrique (born 1962) Venezuela

Bridges, Ben (born 1953) USA

Brotons, Salvador (born 1959) Spain

Brown, Ken (born 1948) USA

Brubeck, Dave (born 1920) USA

Brule, Pierre Marcel (born 1950) Canada

Brumby, Colin (born 1933) Australia

Bryars, Gavin (1925-1999) England

Buchrainer, Michael (born 1950) Austria

Burgess, Anthony (1917-1993) England

Burkhart, Franz (1902-1978) Austria

Byrd, Charlie (1925-1999) USA

Calbi, Otello (1917-1995) Italy

Calleja, Francisco (1891-1950) Spain, Uruguay

de Camargo Fernandez, Marcelo (born 1956) Brazil

Cammarota, Carlo (1905-1990) Italy

Campaña, José Luis (born 1949) Argentina

Camps, Pompeyo (1924-1947) Argentina

Campoianu, Dumitru (born 1929) Romania

Cardew, Cornelius (1936-1981) England

Carfagna, Carlo (born 1940) Italy

Carillo, Julian (1875-1965) Mexico

Carr, Edwin (born 1920) New Zealand

Carre, Albert (1852-1938) France

Carreño, Inocente (born 1919) Venezuela

Carroli, David (born 1947) England

Castaldi, Paolo (born 1930) Italy

Castellanos, Evencio (1915-1984) Venezuela

Castérède, Jacques (born 1926) France

Castillo, Manuel (born 1930) Spain

Catullo, (da Paixao Cearense) (1866-1946) Brazil

Cavalcanti, Nestor de Hollanda (born 1949) Brazil

Cavallone, Franco (born 1957) Italy

Cavazzoli, Germano (born 1940) Italy

Cecconi, Raffaele (born 1947) Italy

Cerha, Friedrich (born 1926) Austria

Cerf, Jacques (born 1932) Switzerland

Chadwick, Roland (born 1957) Australia

Charlton, Andrew (1928-1997) USA

Charnofsky, Jordan (born 1967) USA

Chassain, Olivier (born 1957) France

Chaviano, Flores (born 1946) Cuba

Chazarreta, Andres (1876-1960) Argentina

Cherubito, Miguel (born 1941) Argentina

Chiereghin, Sergio (born 1933) Italy

Chobanian, Loris (born 1933) Iraq, USA

Cimma, Pier Luigi (born 1941) Italy

Cisneros, José R. (born 1915) Venezuela

Clementi, Muzio (1752-1832) Italy

Coco, Julian B. (born 1924) The Dutch Antilles

Coinel, Robert (born 1959) France

Compton, John (born 1950) England

Condin, Wolfgang (born 1959) Germany

Cooperman, Larry (born 1951) USA

Corcoran, Frank (born 1944) Ireland

Cordero, Roque (born 1941) Panama

Correggia, Enrico (born 1933) Italy

Côté, Rolland (born 1951) Canada

Cottam, David (born 1951) England

Coulanges, Amos (born 1954) Haiti

Cowie, Edward (born 1943) Australia

Criswick, Mary (born 1945) England

Croucher, Terence (born 1944) England

Cruz de Castro, Carlos (born 1941) Spain

Curtis-Smith, Curtis (born 1941) USA

D'Arros, Yves (born 1954) France

Dagosto, Sylvain (born 1927) France

Dams, Norbert (born 1951) Germany

Darias, Javier (born 1946) Spain

De Voe, Donald (born 1972) USA

Defaye, Jean Michel (born 1932) France

Degni, Vicenzo (1911-1992) Italy

Delerue, Georges (1925-1992) France

Dellacasa, Giancario (born 1952) Italy

Denhoff, Michael (born 1955) Germany

Desderi, Ettore (1892-1974) Italy

Desportes, Yvonne (Berthe) (1907-1994) France

Diederichs, Yann (born 1952) Germany

Diemer, Emma Lou (born 1927) USA

Digmeloff, Germain (1883-1981) France

Dihescu, Violeta (born 1953) Romania, Germany

DiPalma, Mark (born 1959) USA

Doërr, Charles-Kiko (born 1911) France

Dohl, Friedhelm (born 1936) Germany

Dojcinovic, Uroš (born 1959) Serbia

Dorward, David (born 1933) England

Drabble, Lawrence (born 1929) England

Drdla, Franz (1868-1944) Romania

Dreyfus, George (born 1928) Australia

Drigo, Riccardo (1846-1939) Italy

Drogoz, Philippe (born 1937) France

Dubois, Pierre Max (born 1930) France

Dufourt, Hugues (born 1943) France

Dunsser, Richard (born 1959) Austria

Durand, Marie-Auguste (1830-1909) France

Durko, Zsolt (1934-1997) Hungary

Döhl, Friedhehlm (born 1936) Germany

Echecopar, Javier (born 1955) Peru

Esinar, José Ramon (born 1954) Spain

Enriquez, Claudio 'Pino' (born 1961) Argentina

Eötvös, Jozsef (born 1962) Hungary

Erb, Donald (born 1927) USA

Erbse, Heimo (1924-2005) Germany

Erdmann, Dietrich (born 1917) Germany

Eriksson, Jan-Olof (born 1949) Sweden

Erni, Michael (born 1956) Germany

Eynard, Camille (1882-1977) France

Ezaki, Kejiro (born 1926) Japan

Fabini, (Felix) Eduardo (1882-1950) Uruguay

Falú, Juan José (born 1948) Argentina

Fampas, Dimitri (1921-1996) Greece

Farinas, Carlos (born 1934) Cuba

Farquhar, David (born 1928) New Zealand

Fauré, Gabriel (1845-1924) France

Feldbusch, Eric (born 1922) Belgium

Feldmann, Klaus (born 1951) Germany

Fellagara, Vittorio (born 1927) Italy

Fernández Alvez, Gabriel (born 1943) Spain

Fernández, Eduardo (born 1952) Uruguay

Fernández, Oscar Lorenzo (1897-1948) Brazil

Ferrari-Trecate, Luigi (1884-1964) Italy

Ferrer, Edgar R. (born 1964) Argentina

Feuerstein, Robert (born 1949) Canada

Fink, Michael (born 1939) USA

Fonseca, Carlos Alberto (born 1933) Brazil

Fontana, Fabio (born 1961) Italy

Fraiolo, Vincent (born 1953) USA

Françeries, Marc (born 1936) France

Freidlin, Jan (born 1944) Russia

Friedel, Kurt Joachim (born 1921) Germany

Friessnegg, Karl (1900-1981) Austria

Frost, Donald (born 1951) USA

Fujii, Keigo (born 1956) Japan

Fulkerson, James (Orville) (born 1945) USA

Gabus, Monique (born 1924) France

Gagnebin, Henri (1886-1977) Switzerland

Gagnon, Claude (born 1950) Canada

Galan, Natalio (1917-1985) Cuba

Galindo, Blas (1910-1994) Mexico

Galindo, José Antonio (born 1946) Spain

Gammie, Ian (born 1943) England

Gangi, Mario (born 1923) Italy

García de Leon, Ernesto (1852-1952) Mexico

García Laborda, José Maria (born 1946) Spain

García, Gerald (born 1949) Hong Kong, England

Gardner, John (born 1917) England

Gargiulo, Terenzio (1905-1972) Italy

Gartenlaube, Odette (born 1922) France

Gasparini, Luigi (born 1955) Italy

Gasser, Luis (born 1951) Spain

Gast, Wolfgang (born 1955) Germany

Gaudibert, Eric (born 1936) France

Gavarone, Gerard (born 1943) France

Geddes, John Maxwell (born 1941) England

Generaux, Roger (1941-1978) France

Genzmer, Harald (born 1909) Germany

Gerber, Heinz (born 1953) Germany

Giacometti, Antonio (born 1957) Italy

Gianfreda, Massimo (born 1954) Italy

Gilardi, Gilardo (1889-1963) Argentina

Gilbert, Anthony (born 1934) England

Giorginakis, Kiriakos (1950-1989) Greece

Gismonti, Egberto (born 1947) Brazil

Giuranna, Barabara (1902-1998) Italy

Gomez Crespo, Jorge (1900-1971) Argentina

Gomez, Calleja (1874-1938) Spain

Gonzaga, Chiquinha (1847-1935) Brazil

Gonzaga, Luis (1912-1989) Brazil

Gonzáles, Luis Jorge (born 1936)

Gore, Dennis (born 1947) England

Gorecki, Henryk (born 1933) Poland

Gottschalk, Louis Moreau (1829-1869) USA

Götze, Walter (1885-1965) Germany

Gramatges, Harold (born 1918) Cuba

de Grandis, Renato (born 1927) Italy

Grau, Eduardo (born 1919) Spain

Gregory, Paul (born 1956) England

Grimm, Friedrich Karl (born 1902) Germany

Gross, Eric (born 1926) England, Australia

Grossnick, Horst (born 1957) Germany

Grünhagen, Norbert (born 1942) Germany

Guimarães, João Pernaumbuco (1883-1947) Brazil

Guinjoán, Joan (born 1931) Spain

Gutierrez, Miguel Angel (born 1958) Spain

Guyun (V.Gonzalez Rubicra) (1908-1987) Cuba

Hába, Alois (1893-1973) Czech Republic

Hadjidakis, Manos (born 1925-1994) Greece

Halffter, Rodolfo (1900-1987) Spain

Hand, Frederick (born 1947) USA

Hara, Hiroshi (born 1933) Japan

Harris, Albert (born 1916) USA

Haubensak, Edu (born 1954) Switzerland

de Heer, Hans· (born 1927) Netherlands

Heider, Werner (born 1930) Germany

Heinze, Walter (born 1943) Argentina

Hekster, Walter (born 1937) Netherlands

Helguera, Juan (born 1932) Mexico

Heller, Stephen (1813-1888) Hungary

Hellerman, William (born 1939) USA

Henke, Matthias (born 1953) Germany

Henriquez, Josep (born 1951) Spain

Hess, Ernst (1912-1968) Switzerland

Hirayoshi, Takekuni (born 1936) Japan

Hoch, Peter (born 1937) Germany

Hoddinott, Alun (born 1929) England

Hollos, Mate (born 1954) Hungary

Horns, Joaquín (born 1906) Spain

Hovhaness, Alan (Vaness Scott) (1911-2000) USA

Hubler, Klaus Karl (born 1956) Germany

Hubner, Tilman (born 1960) Germany

Humble, Keith (born 1927-1995) Australia

Humel, Gerald (born 1931) USA

Hummel, Bertold (1925-2002) Germany

Hunt, Oliver (1934-2000) England

Ifukube, Akira (1914-2006) Japan

Iiriti, Mauro (born 1952) Italy

Ishii, Maki (born 1936) Japan

Jakola, Arto (born 1947) Finland

Jalkanen, Peklea (born 1945) Finland

Joachim, Otto (born 1910) Germany, Canada

Johanson, Bryan (born 1951) USA

Johnson, Timothy Ernest (born 1968) USA

Jolas, Betsy (born 1923) France, USA
Juliá, Bernardo (born 1922) Spain
Jung, Helge (born 1943) Germany
Jurkowski, Edmund (1935-1989) Ukraine, Poland
Jämbäck, Kari (born 1960) Finland
Kadosa, Pal (1903-1983) Ukraine
Kalabis, Viktor (1923-2006) Czech Republic
Kang, Sukhi (born 1934) Korea
Kangas, Juho (born 1976) Finland
Kaplan, José Alberto (born 1935) Argentina, Brazil
Kaufmann, Armin (1902-1980) Austria
Kelly, Bryan (born 1934) England
Kelterborn, Rudolf (born 1931) Switzerland
Kern, Jerome (1885-1945) USA
Kerr, Harrison (1897-1978) USA
Kilvington, Chris (born 1944) England
Kindle, Jürg (born 1960) Germany
Kinsey, Avril (born 1955) England, South Africa
Kirschbaum, Cristoph (born 1958) Germany
Klebe, Gieselher (Wolfgang) (born 1925) Germany
Koch, Gareth (born 1962) Australia
Kocsar, Miklós (born 1933) Hungary
Kohn, Karl (Georg) (born 1926) Austria, USA
Komter, Jan Marten (1905-1984) Netherlands
Kondo, Jo (born 1947) Japan
Konietzny, Heinrich (1910-1983) Germany
Kont, Paul (1920-2000) Austria
Košťál, Arnošt (born 1920) Czech Republic
Kotoński, Wodzimierz (born 1925) Poland
Kounadis, Arghyris P. (born 1924) Greece
Kropfreiter, Augustus Franz (born 1936) Austria
Kubizek, Augustin (born 1918) Austria
Kvech, Otomar (born 1950) Czech Republic
Labrouve, Jorge (born 1948) Argentina, France
Lagoya, Alexandre (1929-1999) Egypt, France
Lajarrige, Marc (born 1945) France
Lambert, Richard (born 1951) England
Lambro, Philip (born 1935) USA
Lancen, Serge (Jean Mathieu) (born 1922) France
Langer, Michael (born 1959) Austria
Lasala, Angel (1914-2000) Argentina
Lawall, George (born 1952) Germany
Lazaro, José (born 1941) Spain
Le Gars, Marc (born 1954) France
Lechthaler, Josef (1891-1948) Austria
Leclercq, Norbert (born 1944) Belgium
Lecuona, Ernesto (1896-1963) Cuba

Leduc, Jacques (born 1932) Belgium
Lejet, Edith (born 1941) France
Lemaigre, Philippe (born 1950) Belgium
Lemeland, Aubert (born 1932) France
Lennon, John Anthony (born 1950) USA
Lerich, Pierre (born 1937) France
Lind, Ekard (born 1945) Germany
Lindsay, George C. (1855-1943) USA
Linke, Norbert (born 1933) Germany
Linneman, Marie (born 1948) Netherlands, England
Linsky, Jeff (born in 1952) USA
Lombardi, Luca (born 1945) Italy
Lopez-Graca, Fernando (1906-1994) Portugal
Lotz, Hans Georg (born 1943) Germany
Lovelady, William (born 1945) England
Lumsdaine, David (born 1931) Australia
Lund, Gudrun (born 1930) Denmark
Lutzemberger, Cesare (born 1918) Italy
Löfvenius, Stefan (born 1950) Sweden
MacCombie, Bruce (born 1943) USA, Iceland
Maceda, José (1917-2004) Philippines
Madureira, Antonio (born 1949) Brazil
Maes, Jef (1905-1996) Belgium
Magen, Eli (born 1935) Israel
Maghini, Ruggero (1913-1977) Italy
Mairants, Ivor (1908-1998) Poland, England
Maldonado, Raúl (born 1937) Argentina
Mamangakis, Nikos (born 1927) Greece
Mamlok, Ursula (born 1928) USA
Mannino, Franco (1924-2005) Italy
Manzoni, Giacomo (born 1932) Italy
Maravilla, Luis (born 1914) Spain
Marcus, Bunita (born 1952) USA
Marsh, Steve (born 1949) England
Marshall, Nicholas (born 1942) England
Martin Llado, Miguel (born 1950) Spain
Mas, Jean Luc (born 1956) France
Masala, Roberto (born 1954) Italy
Matos Rodriguez, G. H. (1900-1948) Uruguay
Matsudaira, Yoriaki (born 1931) Japan
Medek, Tilo (born 1940) Germany
de Meester, Louis (1904-1987) Belgium
Meier, Jost (born 1939) Germany
Meranger, Paul (born 1936) France
Mersson, Boris (born 1921) Switzerland
Mestres Quadreny, Josep (Maria) (born 1929) Spain
Middleton, Owen (born 1941) USA

Migot, Georges (1891-1976) France

Miliaressis, Gerassimos (born 1918) Greece

Mills, John (born 1947) England

Mindlin, Adolfo (born 1922) France

Miteran, Alain (born 1941) France

Mittergradnegger, Günther (1923-1992) Austria

Miyoshi, Akira (born 1933) Japan

Mojžíš, Vojtěch (born 1949) Czech Republic

Molina, Luis Manuel (born 1959) Cuba

Montes, Alfonso (born 1955) Venezuela

Montsalvatge, Xavier (1912-2002) Spain

Monti, Alessio (born 1947) Italy

Montreuil, Gerald (1927-1991) Canada

Moreno, Juan Antonio (born 1953) Spain

Mortari, Virgillo (1902-1993) Italy

Mosso, Carlo (1931-1995) Italy

Moyano, Ricardo (born 1961) Argentina

Muñoz Molleda, José (1905-1988) Spain

Mustonen, Olli (born 1967) Finland

Muthspiel, Wolfgang (born 1965) Austria

Nardelli, Mario (born 1927) Croatia

Narváez, José-Luis (born 1953) France

Nazareth, Ernesto (1863-1934) Brazil

Neumann, Ulrik (1918-1994) Denmark

Nieman, Alfred (born 1913) England

Nockalls, Martin (born 1954) England

Noda, Teruyuki (born 1940) Japan

Nogatz, Hubertus (born 1956) Germany

Northcott, Bayan (born 1940) England

Norton, Christopher (born 1953) New Zealand

Novák, Jan (1921-1984) Czech Republic

Nunn, Ruth (born 1954) England

Nuttall, Peter (born 1949) England

Oehring, Helmut (born 1961) Germany

Oliver, Stephen (born 1950) England

Olshanskij, Anatoli (born 1956) Russia

Orbon (de Soto), Julian (1925-1991) Spain, USA

Orrega-Salas, Juan (born 1919) Chile

Orsolino, Federico (1918-1993) Italy

Otero, Francisco (born 1940) Spain

Ourkouzounov, Atanas (born 1970) Bulgaria

Paamino, Cristobal (born 1958) Ecuador

Pagan, Juan (born 1955) Spain

Paik, Byung-dong (born 1936) Korea

Palola, Erkki (born 1957) Finland

Pairman, David (born 1947) England

Parnott, Jan (born 1916) England

Pastor, Segundo (1916-1992) Spain

Paubon, Pierre (1910-1995) France

Paulus, Stephen (born 1949) USA

Pearson, Robin J. (1941-1983) England

Peixinho, Jorge (born 1940) Portugal

Penicaud, Eric (born 1952) France

Peraldo Bert, Nilo (1915-2002) Italy

Persch, Ralf (born 1960) Germany

Peruzzi, Aurelio (1921-1995) Italy

Pessina, Carlo (born 1960) Italy

Petric, Ivo (born 1931) Slovenia

Pettoletti, Pietro (1825-1840) Italy

Pfister, Hugo (1914-1969) Switzerland

Philba, Nicole (born 1937) France

Philippi, Raimund (born 1963) Germany

Pilsl, Fritz (born 1933) Germany

Pinkham, Daniel (1923-2006) USA

Piris, Bernard (born 1951) France

Pitfield, Thomas (Baron) (1903-1999) England

Pittaluga, Gustavo (1906-1975) Spain

Pizzini, Carlo Alberto (1905-1981) Italy

Platts, Kenneth (born 1946) England

Platz, Robert H. P. (born 1951) Germany

Plaza, Juan B. (1898-1965) Spain

Porrino, Ennio (1910-1959) Italy

Porter, Cole (1891-1964) USA

Pousseur, Henri (born 1929) Belgium

Powell, Ihel (born 1923) USA

Pratesi, Mira (born 1923) Italy

Prodigo, Sergio (Born 1949) Italy

Purser, John (born 1942) England

Pütz, Eduard (1911-2000) Germany

Pütz, Friedrich (born 1950) Germany

Queiroz, José Oliveira (1897-1968) Brazil

Rainier, Priaulx (1903-1986) South Africa

Ramírez, Ariel (born 1921) Argentina

Ramovs, Primoz (1921-1999) Slovenia

Ratkowski, Torsten (born 1954) Germany

Ravinale, Irma (born 1942) Italy

Rebours, Gerard (born 1950) France

Regan, Michael (born 1947) England

Regner, Hermann (1928-1982) Austria

Reinbothe, Helmut (1929-1991) Germany

Renault, Jean Marc (born 1954) France

Reutter, Hermann (1900-1985) Germany

Reverdy, Michèle (born 1943) France

Richer, Jeannine (born 1924) France

Riley, Dennis (born 1943) USA

Ritchie, Anthony (born 1960) New Zealand

Ritchie, John (born 1921) New Zealand

Rivier, Jean (1896-1987) France

Robinson, Andrea (born 1956) New Zealand

Robles, Daniel (1871-1942) Peru

Rodriguez Albert, Rafael (1902-1979) Spain

Roe, Betty (born 1930) England

Roland, Claude-Robert (born 1935) Belgium

Roldan, Amadeo (1900-1939) Cuba

Roman, Johan Helmich (1694-1758) Sweden

Romero, Celedonio (1918-1996) Spain, USA

Rorem, Ned (born 1923) USA

Rosetta, Giuseppe (1901-1985) Italy

Rougier, Thierry (born 1957) France

Roux, Patrick (born 1962) France, Canada

Rovenstrunck, Bernhard (born 1920) Germany

Royal, Timothy (born 1947) England

Rózsa, Miklós (1907-1995) Hungary, USA

Ruoff, Axel D. (born 1957) Germany

Ryterband, Roman (1914-1979) Poland, USA

Sacchetti, Arturo (born 1941) Italy

Saenz, Pedro (1915-1995) Spain, Argentina

Sagreras, Gaspar (1838-1901) Argentina

Salonen, Esa-Pekka (born 1958) Finland

Salvador, Matilde (born 1918) Spain

Samama, Leo (born 1951) Netherlands

Samazeuilh, Gustave (1877-1967) France

Sander, Peter (born 1933) Hungary, England

Sandi, Luis (1905-1996) Mexico

di Sandro, Raimondo (born 1937) Italy

Santoro, Claudio (1919-1989) Brazil

Santos, Enrique (born 1930) Mexico

Santos, Ramon (born 1941) Philippines

Sardinha, Annibal Garoto (1915-1955) Brazil

Sari, Josef (born 1935) Hungary

Saumell, Manuel (1810-1870) Cuba

Saxton, Robert (born 1953) England

Shaller, Erwin (1904-1984) Austria

Schat, Peter (born 1935) Netherlands

Scheld, Gerhard (born 1957) Austria

Schibler, Armin (1920-1986) Switzerland

Schiffman, Harold (born 1957) USA

Schlee, Thomas Daniel (born 1957) Austria

Schlosberg, Benoit (born 1954) France

Schlutz, Leonhard (1814-1860) Austria

Schlutz, Wolfgang (born 1948) Germany

Schneider, Gary M. (born 1957) USA

Schneider, Gunther (born 1954) Austria

Schuller, Gunther (born 1925) USA

Schumann, Gerhard (1914-1976) Germany

Schwartz, Francis (born 1940) USA, Puerto Rico

Schwertsik, Kurt (born 1935) Austria

Schytte, Ludvig (1848-1909) Denmark, Germany

Scisi, Giacinto (1905-1988) Italy

Scott, Cyril (1878-1970) England

Searle, Leslie (born 1937) USA

Selby, Philip (born 1948) England

Sergidis, Andreas (born 1911) Greece

Sfogli, Corrando (born 1961) Italy

Shand, Ernest (1868-1924) England

Shekov, Ivan (born 1942) Bulgaria

Shevchenko, Anatoly (born 1938) Ukraine

Shiels, Andrew (born 1957) Ireland

Sidney, Anthony (born 1952) Italy

Siegl, Otto (1896-1978) Austria

Sierra-Fortuny, José Maria (born 1925) Spain

Sinesi, Quique (born 1960) Argentina

Sitsky, Larry (born 1934) Australia

Skempton, Howard (born 1947) England

Snijders, Herman (born 1953) The Dutch Antilles

Soares de Souza, Francisco (1905-1986) Brazil

Solares, Enrique (born 1910) Guatemala

Somers, Harry (1925-1999) Canada

Sommerfeldt, Oistein (1919-1994) Norway

Spahlinger, Mathias (born 1944) Germany

Sprongl, Norbert (1892-1983) Austria

Srebonjak, Aljoz (born 1931) Yugoslavia

Stadlmair, Hans (born 1924) Austria

Starer, Robert (1924-2001) Austria, USA

Steffens, Walter (born 1934) Germany

Steptoe, Roger (Guy) (born 1953) England

Stevens, Bernard (1916-1983) England

Stiles, Frank (born 1924) England

Stimpson, Michael (born 1948) England

Sting Sumner, Gordon (born 1951) England

Stoker, Richard (born 1938) England

Stover, Richard (born 1948) USA

Strasfogel, Ignace (1909-1994) Poland

Strategier, Herman (1912-1988) Netherlands

Stroe, Aurel (born 1932) France

Styng, Jorma (born 1958) Finland

Sugar, Reszo (1919-1988) Hungary

Sulpizi, Fernando (born 1936) Italy

Summaria, Davide (born 1943) Italy

Surinach, Carlos (1915-1997) Spain, USA

Suslin, Viktor (born 1942) Russia

Suter, Robert (born 1919) Switzerland

Takahashi, Yuji (born 1938) Japan

Tamez, Gerardo (born 1948) Mexico

Taranu, Cornel (born 1938) Romania

Tchaikovsky, Boris (born 1925) Russia

Teixeira, Nicanor (born 1928) Brazil

Tenzi, Massimo (1922-1993) Italy

Tesar, Milan (born 1938) Czech Republic

Thome, Françis (1850-1909) France

Thompson, Virgil (Garnett) (1896-1989) USA

Tisné, Antoine (born 1932) France

Togni, Camillo (1922-1993) Italy

Tomasi, Henri (Fredien) (1901-1971) France

Ton-That, Tiêt (born 1933) Vietnam, France

Torok, Alan (born 1948) Austria, Canada

Tosi, Daniel (born 1953) France

Tower, Joan (Peabody) (born 1938) USA

Towner, Ralph (born 1940) USA

Trojahn, Manfred (born 1949) Germany

Tsilicas, Jorge (born 1930) Argentina

Tsukatani, Akihiro (1919-1995) Japan

Tucapsky, Antonin (born 1928) Czech Republic, England

Turina, José Luis (born 1952) Spain

Turok, Paul (born 1929) USA

Ugoletti, Paolo (born 1956) Italy

Ulian, Alberto (1920-1996) Uruguay

Ung, Chinary (born 1942) USA

Vandermaesbrugge, Max (born 1933) Belgium

Vanhall, Johann Baptist (1739-1813) Czech Republic

Vasquéz, Edmundo (born 1938) Chile, France

Vecchia, Wolfgango dalla (born 1923) Italy

de la Vega, Aurelio (born 1925) Cuba, USA

Velazquéz, Leonardo (born 1935) Mexico

Ventura, José (1817-1875) Argentina

Vercken, François (born 1928) France

Verdery, Benjamin (born 1955) USA

Vianna, Alfredo Pixinguinha (1898-1973) Brazil

Victory, Gerard (1921-1995) Scotland

Villa Roja, Jésus (born 1940) Spain

Villar, Rogelio (1875-1937) Spain

Vinay, Vittorio (born 1942) Italy

Visser, Dick (born 1928) Netherlands

Vitiello, Frédéric (born 1960) France

Vivier, Claude (1948-1983) Canada

Vogel, Wladimir (1896-1984) Russia, Switzerland

Vogelin, Fritz (born 1943) Germany

Vojtíšek, Martin (born 1950) Czech Republic

Wagner-Regeny, Rudolf (1903-1969) Russia, Germany

Walker, Luise (1910-1998) Austria

Walter, Fried (1907-1996) Germany

Walters, Gareth (born 1928) England

Wanders, Bob (born 1955) Netherlands

Wanek, Friedrich (1929-1991) Germany

Weiner, Leo (1885-1960) Hungary

Weiner, Stanley (1925-1994) USA

Weinzweig, John (Jacob) (1913-2006) Canada

Weiss, Harald (Born 1949) Germany

Wellesz, Egon (Joseph) (1885-1974) Austria, England

Werdin, Eberhard (1911-1991) Germany

Wettstein, Peter (born 1939) Germany

Whettam, Graham (born 1927) England

White, Michael (born 1931) USA

Whitworth, John (born 1951) USA

Widmer, Ernst (1927-1990) Switzerland, Brasil

Wikmanson, Johan (1753-1800) Sweden

Wildberger, Jacques (1922-2006) Switzerland

Wilson, James (born 1951) USA

Winters, Geoffrey (born 1928) England

Wolff, Christian (born 1934) USA

Worschech, Romain (born 1909) France

Wüsthoff, Klaus (born 1922) Germany

Yoghourtjian, James (born 1934) USA

Young, Kenneth (born 1955) New Zealand

Zagwijn, Henri (1878-1954) Netherlands

Zappa, Frank (1940-1993) USA

Zaradin, John (born 1944) England

Zbinden, Julien-Fraçois (born 1917) Switzerland

Ziffrin, Marilyn (born 1926) USA

Zuccheri, Luciano (1911-1981) Italy

Zukewar, Haim D. (born 1956) Uruguay